MW01027148

DOMINION THEOLOGY: BLESSING OR CURSE?

DOMINION THEOLOGY: BLESSING OR CURSE?

H. Wayne House / Thomas Ice

MULTNOMAH

Portland, Oregon 97266

Cover design by Judy Quinn

Dominion Theology, Blessing or Curse?
© 1988 by H. Wayne House and Thomas D. Ice
Published by Multnomah Press
Portland, Oregon 97266

Multnomah Press is a ministry of Multnomah School of the Bible,
8435 Northeast Glisan Street, Portland, Oregon 97220.

Printed in the United States of America

Library of Congress Cataloging-in-Publication Data

House, H. Wayne.
    Dominion theology, blessing or curse? : an analysis of Christian reconstruction / H. Wayne House, Thomas D. Ice.
        p.   cm.
    Includes index.
    ISBN 0-88070-261-3
    1. Millennialism—History of doctrines—20th century.
2. Theonomy—History of doctrines—20th century. I. Ice, Thomas D.
II. Title.
BT891.H6 1988
236'.3—dc19   88-29111
                                                                    CIP

88 89 90 91 92 93 94 95 – 10 9 8 7 6 5 4 3 2 1

Contents

Preface

From 1974 until 1986 I was a Christian Reconstructionist. I was attracted to the movement because it boasted of a consistent biblical worldview. Since I was and still am a premillennialist, I tried for many years to create a blend of Reconstructionism with premillennialism. In fact, a booklet written by a former member of a church I pastored reflects much of my thought and struggle to produce such a synthesis. (David Schnittger, *Christian Reconstruction from a Pretribulational Perspective*, Southwest Radio Church, 1986.) However, I finally realized that one cannot be a Reconstructionist and a premillennialist.

In many ways it was great being a Reconstructionist, yet also frustrating. It was great to know we had the answers to the problems of modern society. It was frustrating that we never really made true progress. Yes, on certain days we were able to rationalize that progress was being made, but it was only that—a rationalization. I now know that God has not been pleased to give the necessary graces to his church for the kind of victory dominionists decree.

At one point I decided that I wanted to become a postmillennialist, thereby becoming a true and consistent Reconstructionist. However, I could not find a scriptural basis for postmillennialism. So I went to Tyler, Texas, to meet with some Reconstructionist leaders, thinking they would be able to give me the scriptural basis I had yet to discover for myself. I was ready and wanted to be convinced from the Bible that postmillennialism was the eschatology of Holy Writ. I had already thought through the consequences of such a shift and was willing to make the needed changes.

Yet on the drive home, as I thought through what I had discussed with those leaders and compared it with Scripture, I was greatly disappointed. They had not come close to offering anything convincing. All they offered was an anti-premillennial position, not a pro-postmillennial viewpoint.

Because I kept insisting on exegetical proof, not just theological explanations of how postmillennialism would work if it were true, Gary North later accused me of being a nuisance to them in Tyler. In a 23 June 1986 letter, North said to me:

> Your longstanding attempt to hold to dominion-reconstruction and also maintain Darbyism [dispensationalism] is a form of intellectual schizophrenia. This is why you keep bugging us in Tyler with your nitpicking criticisms (e.g., "you postmils have never produced any detailed exegesis," a 1983 statement to Ray Sutton).

I was amazed that North would consider someone who was seeking exegetical answers for postmillennialism guilty of "nitpicking criticisms."

After exchanging a few letters, North, in a short, handwritten note on the first page of one of my letters, which he apparently did not read, issued the following challenge: "Put this stuff in a book and I will read it. No time for private letters *this* long! Again, if you've got the answers, publish them. Your movement needs answers!"

Well, here it is, and as far as we know, it is the first book-length reply to the Christian Reconstruction movement. Other works are currently in the mill, but someone had to be the first to return their volley.

As I mentioned earlier, in order to be a Reconstructionist, one has to adopt some form of postmillennialism. "The point of Christian reconstructionism that is a main bone of contention in the wider debate today, is not that it teaches the victory of God's kingdom on earth . . . but that it teaches the victory of God's kingdom on earth *during and continuous with our present era*."[1] A premillennialist believes that Christ's intervening judgment will destroy current society and then Christ will institute millennial conditions. Once I realized the antithesis of the two positions, I had to side with Scripture and leave behind Reconstructionism. These conflicting views impact the *way* believers are involved in this present society. Both viewpoints believe in present involvement, but the question is "How and in what ways are we commissioned to be involved in this world?"

David Chilton once offered me the following exegetical support for postmillennialism:

> That's why my book started in Genesis. I wanted to demonstrate that the Paradise Restored theme (i.e., postmillennialism) is not dependent on any one passage, but is taught throughout Scripture. . . . The fact is, postmillennialism is on every page of the Bible.[2]

My challenge is simply this: Since postmillennialism is on every page of the Bible, show me *one* passage that requires a postmillennial interpretation and should not be taken in a premillennial sense. After fourteen years of study it is my belief that there is not one passage anywhere in Scripture that would lead to the postmillennial system. The best postmillennialism can come up with is a position built upon an inference.

I believe many are attracted to the dominion position because they have an agenda, such as politics or social reform, for which they believe Reconstructionism provides the vision to lead them to success. While the Bible promises a certain kind of success within the framework of God's current purpose for the church, I believe that like all other postmillennial movements in history, Reconstructionism will leave behind a group of disillusioned people. Most are attracted to dominion theology through the back door, rather than through the front door of biblical study. They are arriving at these views not from the study of Scripture but by the romantic attraction of changing the world. We must let Scripture set the agenda.

The days ahead should prove interesting as premillennialists and Reconstructionists engage in a debate which is sure to produce heat and by God's grace light as well.

My blessed hope, however, continues to be that Christ will soon rapture his Bride, the church, and that we will return with him in victory to rule and exercise dominion with him for a thousand years upon the earth. Even so, come Lord Jesus!

Thomas D. Ice

1. Kenneth L. Gentry, Jr., "The Reduction of Christianity: A Review Article," *The Counsel of Chalcedon* (vol. 10, nos. 2 and 3; April-May 1988), p. 31.

2. Personal letter from David Chilton to Thomas Ice, December 2, 1986, p. 5.

Acknowledgments

We wish to express appreciation to Rob Schwarzwalder, Joe O'Day, Chris Corbett, Robert Dean, Randy Gleason, and Russell Bowers for their assistance at various stages in the project. We are grateful to Charles Colson, Norman Geisler, Charles Ryrie, John MacArthur, Jr., Hal Lindsey, and Dave Hunt for their willingness to read, endorse, and promote this book. We also wish to express our appreciation to our wives who have been patient during the production of this work. May this book stimulate debate about the important topics included herein and be for the glory of Christ.

PART 1

THE ORIGIN AND BASIS OF CHRISTIAN RECONSTRUCTIONISM

Chapter 1

What Is Christian Reconstructionism?

S ome Americans may identify the word *Puritan* with a colonial-era pilgrim trudging through the snow, blunderbuss in hand, hunting turkey for Thanksgiving. The Salem witch-trials may also come to mind, and with them the image of a gaunt, austere man in a floor-length frock and a menacing look in his eye, ready to erupt in Pharisaic anger at anyone having fun. This idea of Puritanism, perpetuated by such writers as H. L. Mencken and not sufficiently corrected in history classrooms, in large part is a myth.[1] What usually is not taught about the Puritans was their enjoyment of bright clothing, their vivid intellectual lives, and their commitment to establishing a Christian society in America. The Puritans wanted a government that would adhere rigidly to the civil code of the Old Testament, thereby creating a model of the kingdom of God on earth for all the world to see.

They failed in their attempt. The reasons for the Puritans' failure are not relevant here, but their effort to build a Christian society is. It is being imitated today by a small and increasingly influential group of persons who believe that only through the establishment and enforcement of Old Testament civil law can America—and the world—be saved from destruction. Calling

themselves Christian Reconstructionists, they propose to institute a theocratic government in America, and they are gaining
support in some elements of the evangelical community.

WHY THIS BOOK?

The need for a book about the Reconstruction movement
becomes obvious when the movement itself is considered. The
Reconstructionists offer nothing less than a radical shift on
some of the basic beliefs and practices which embody contemporary evangelical understanding. Christian Reconstructionism
argues for a way of thinking about God's law, his plan for the
future, and the role of the church fundamentally different from
that commonly accepted among mainstream evangelicals.

The Reconstructionists cannot be dismissed as a passing,
and therefore irrelevant, side-current on the course of evangelical thought. As will be discussed later, the Reconstructionists have garnered support from such disparate groups as
old-time fundamentalists, charismatics, and some members of
the evangelical intelligentsia.

Their radical proposals—including the stoning of rebellious adolescents, capital punishment for homosexuals, and the
elimination of political pluralism—combined with their growing influence evoke one conclusion: Christian Reconstructionism must be carefully scrutinized by Christians concerned
about the church's, and America's, future.

This book is offered as an examination of the history,
goals, and beliefs of the Christian Reconstruction movement.
Its intent is to offer a balanced critique of the movement (citing
positive and negative features), to explain its views, and to
determine their implications for the church and for society.

BASIC BELIEFS

Various lists have been made of the key beliefs of the
Reconstructionists, but those beliefs most central to Reconstructionism are:

1. A belief in the sovereignty of God. Reconstructionist understanding of this belief leads to controversial conclusions, as will be seen;
2. Postmillennialism;
3. The application of the judicial laws of Moses in modern society;
4. Presuppositional apologetics;
5. The "covenant" concept as the key to understanding the Bible and history and the basis of Christian living.[2]

We shall describe the two major areas that are in primary deviance from contemporary evangelicalism and Protestant Christianity in general—theonomy and postmillennialism—in the next two chapters. In the second portion of the book we will carefully and fully analyze these ideas.

THE LEADERS OF THE MOVEMENT

According to one of Reconstructionism's leaders, Gary North, the movement "did not exist 20 years ago."[3] Its rise can be attributed in large part to the efforts of three men, Rousas J. Rushdoony, Greg Bahnsen, and North.

Rousas J. Rushdoony

Born in New York City in 1916,[4] Rousas Rushdoony is the son of Armenian immigrants. He traces his ancestry through an unbroken family chain of pastors to the fourth century A.D. Rushdoony was educated at the University of California (B.S., M.A.), the Pacific School of Religion, and Valley Christian University (Ph.D.). After working in a Chinese youth ministry in San Francisco, he was a missionary to the Paiute and Shoshone Indians and pastor of several Presbyterian churches. His first book, *By What Standard?*, was published in 1959. It has been followed by twenty-nine other volumes, a remarkable output for one author. His first books were not overtly Reconstructionist and earned him a reputation as a thoughtful observer of the American scene.

Rushdoony established the Chalcedon Foundation in 1965 in Vallecito, California. Staffed by twelve persons, its publications include *Chalcedon Report* (a monthly newsletter) and the more scholarly *Journal of Christian Reconstruction*. Chalcedon also has its own book publishing division, Ross House Books. Among Chalcedon's staff and board of affiliates are educational historian Samuel J. Blumenfeld, *Washington Times* columnist and television commentator John Lofton, and investment counselor R. E. McMaster, Jr. Otto Scott, one of Rushdoony's closest associates, is a senior editor of *Conservative Digest*; Rushdoony and Lofton are contributing editors to the same publication.

Rushdoony's most significant publication to date is his two-volume work, *Institutes of Biblical Law*. A massive (1600-page) study of the relationship of the Ten Commandments and modern society, the publication of volume 1 in 1973 marked a turning point in the Reconstructionist movement. As a systematized attempt to apply the Ten Commandments to American society, it arrested the attention of the evangelical scholarly community and gave new impetus to Rushdoony's philosophy.

Rushdoony continues to live in Vallecito, reading (he owns a personal library of about thirty thousand volumes), writing, and speaking at Christian Reconstruction conferences. In recent years he has been involved in a number of "church-state education trials."

Gary North

Perhaps the most controversial of the leading Reconstructionists is Gary North.[5] Known for gleefully attacking ideological foes, North has gained attention for his stinging literary assaults as much as for his views. Armed with a Ph.D. in economics from the University of California-Riverside, North was for several years editor of *The Journal of Christian Reconstruction*. Though married to Rushdoony's daughter, North is reportedly no longer on speaking terms with Rushdoony. Said to have been preceded by several years of friction, the break came in 1981 over an article North wanted to publish in *The*

Journal of Christian Reconstruction. North approved the article's argument that Passover blood on the doorpost bore symbolic overtones of virginity; Rushdoony said such thinking reeked of a fertility cult.

North now lives in Tyler, Texas, where his Institute for Christian Economics works closely with Geneva Ministries. It has been suggested that North chose the somewhat isolated location of Tyler because of his belief in the eventual downfall of the American economy. *The Journal of Christian Reconstruction* has printed several "survivalist" articles, including a "theology" of survivalism based on the model of Noah preparing the ark to escape the flood. North believes in a feudal-type economy:

> the best place for 'the remnant' to be is in a rural setting, in an estate where one can be self-supporting, from which to rebuild our apostate civilization into the kingdom of God. . . . [North] holds that this approach rebuilt European civilization (after the fall of Rome) with biblical law which the modern church has squandered, resulting in judgment, which is paving the way for the coming millennium.[6]

Another North distinctive is the personal invective for which much of his writing has become known. North's take-no-prisoners rhetoric often draws as much, if not more, attention to itself than his arguments do.

North's literary hit-and-run tactics should not blind his critics to the seriousness of his theological, economic, and political views. They evidence a profundity of thought which merits consideration in its own right.

Greg Bahnsen

Greg Bahnsen[7] is regarded by some to be the most thoughtful of the Reconstructionists. Bahnsen is reported to have read some of Rushdoony's works as a boy and was the first student at Westminster Seminary to simultaneously obtain Master of Divinity and Master of Theology degrees. With a Ph.D. in philosophy from the University of Southern California, he taught for some time at Reformed Seminary in Jackson, Mississippi. His major work, *Theonomy in Christian Ethics*, was a bombshell in the evangelical theological community. The book's central thesis is that all of God's law (i.e., the law of Moses not abrogated by the New Testament)—even the last "jot and tittle" (Bahnsen's phrase)—should be applied directly to American life. While acknowledging the invalidity of the ceremonial laws for Christian practice, Bahnsen charges that all the strictures of the Mosaic penal code should be applied directly to American civil law. The book evoked widespread criticism and the controversy surrounding it led ultimately to Bahnsen's dismissal from Reformed Seminary. Bahnsen has so modified some of his views that one observer, after hearing Bahnsen lecture, remarked that "theonomy is dying the death of a thousand qualifications." Perhaps an overstatement, this comment suggests that Bahnsen is willing to interact with his critics.

Bahnsen currently pastors a small Orthodox Presbyterian church in California and is dean of the graduate school of a local teacher's college. Bahnsen's views, although shocking to some and questioned by most of the evangelical theological community, are presented in a scholarly manner. His research and thoroughness have elevated his theological credibility and given him an attentive, if unpersuaded, audience.

Other Leaders

The field of Christian Reconstructionist leadership grows with the movement.[8] David Chilton, a former colleague of Gary North, is perhaps best known for his book *Productive Christians in an Age of Guilt Manipulators*. This book is a response to Ronald J. Sider's *Rich Christians in an Age of Hunger,* regarded by Reconstructionists as a socialist tract which misinterprets Scripture to justify its arguments. Chilton, now a pastor in Placerville, California, is considered the leading spokesman for Reconstructionists in the field of eschatology. *Paradise Restored: An Eschatology of Dominion* is the major statement of Reconstructionist postmillennialism. He has also written several other works, including *Days of Vengeance*, a postmillennial commentary on the Book of Revelation.

Joe Kickasola is a professor of international affairs at CBN University and teaches from a theonomist viewpoint. Joseph C. Morecraft III pastors Chalcedon Presbyterian Church in Atlanta and was an unsuccessful Republican Congressional candidate in 1986. Gary DeMar heads the Institute of Christian Government in Atlanta and has become a visible player with his book *The Reduction of Christianity*. James Jordan is scholar and pastor at the Reconstructionist church in Tyler, Texas. He also does some work for Gary North and is a prolific and, among the Reconstructionists, an influential writer and thinker. Ray Sutton, a Dallas Seminary graduate, also lends his pen to the Reconstructionist movement and pastors Good Shepherd Episcopal Church in Tyler, which recently changed from Westminster Presbyterian Church. Sutton's book, *That You May Prosper*, is viewed by some Reconstructionists as a foundational work on covenants.

THE RISE OF CHRISTIAN RECONSTRUCTIONISM

The challenging and prolific writers who constitute the leadership of the Christian Reconstruction movement have been aided in their efforts by the political climate of the 1980s. Disillusionment with big government, concern over America's moral decay, and the failure of the Great Society programs combined to activate the conservative movement in America in the 70s and 80s. Conservative evangelicals have been increasingly active in voicing their concerns about the social crises plaguing the United States. The Reconstructionists not only share these concerns, but offer what to some are convincing solutions for them. According to one observer, Reconstructionism "provides an immediate alternative 'for religious and political conservatives' who aren't going to take it anymore."[9]

With their belief that ultimate victory is assured (the church will set up a theocratic government, will evangelize the world, and will usher in the earthly reign of Christ), the Christian Reconstructionists extend an appealing, upbeat, and aggressive agenda to evangelicals tired of the one-step-forward, two-steps-back world of American politics. They publish material relating to many disciplines, including law, economics, and social and educational policy. Their many books and articles provide an arsenal of ideas for proponents of the Reconstructionist philosophy.

As Rodney Clapp points out in his *Christianity Today* article, few in the Christian Right accept the whole Reconstructionist menu of ideas. Points of agreement between Reconstructionists and other evangelicals generally relate to economics, the moral bankruptcy of society, and the subsequent need for Christians to become involved in America's political life. Among those influenced by Reconstructionist thought are Pat Robertson,[10] John Whitehead, Herbert Schlossberg, and the late Francis Schaeffer and his son, Franky.[11] Gary J. Moes, editor of Rushdoony's *Chalcedon Report,* gave the following account concerning a worldwide Christian gathering.

> One of the most noteworthy and heartening observations emerging from the Lord of the Nations conference was the repeated report that throughout the world key Christian pastors, scholars and change agents are coming to a realization of reconstructionist, theonomic and dominion principles. Many attributed their insights to the work of Chalcedon and its founder, Dr. R. J. Rushdoony.[12]

In addition to influencing some mainline evangelical leaders, the Reconstructionists have developed a significant following in the charismatic movement.[13] The link between the two groups (Rushdoony claims that twenty million charismatics worldwide are Reconstructionists) is their mutually "optimistic" view of the future. Moes goes on to point out some other characteristics of those who are accepting Reconstructionist beliefs:

In the vast majority of such instances, these theological insights have been accompanied by a renewal of charismatic spiritual gifts and forms of worship and a fervent commitment to social action, ranging from feeding the hungry to protection of human rights.[14]

Believing in the eventual earthly triumph of the church, the Reconstructionists have found a natural ally in the "positive confession" wing of the charismatic movement. Sometimes derisively called "name it and claim it" by critics, "positive confession" teachers urge their adherents to use their "authority" in Christ to overcome all impediments to materially successful lives. This philosophy is particularly attractive to those in the lower-middle class hoping to escape the economic restrictions of their life styles.

Gary North defends positive confession leaders for their belief (which North shares) that "God does not want His people to be poor and sick." While denouncing the New Age implications of some aspects of the "positive confession" movement, North applauds the movement for having an "optimistic" view of life and notes that "positive confession" leaders "have become operational postmillennialists."[15]

Christian Reconstructionists emphasize that believers should exercise "dominion" authority, or their power in Christ, to advance his lordship of all things. In other words, since Christ's dominion extends to all of life, the Reconstructionist agenda should be advanced boldly. The promised land belonged to Israel, but first Joshua and company had to claim it by annihilating its occupants.[16] A similar situation exists in America today. Those forces mitigating against God's kingdom must be challenged and destroyed by a church militant and confident of triumph.

Gary North summarizes the dominion philosophy in his article, "Jesus' Legacy to His People: The World":

Adam forfeited his lawful inheritance when he rebelled against God. Satan appropriated this inheritance as an illegal squatter. He conquered the world in one day by Adam's default.

Jesus' ministry restored the inheritance to His people. He announced a worldwide ministry of conquest, based on the preaching of the gospel of peace. Christians are required to pursue the same program of world dominion which God originally assigned to Adam, and reassigned to Noah (Gen. 9:1-17).[17]

What the charismatics and Reconstructionists have in common, then, is a belief that Christ's power can be drawn upon to vanquish worldly adversaries—not only social and political evils (which Reconstructionists emphasize), but personal and material ones as well (which positive confession groups emphasize).[18]

SUMMARY

The prominence of the Reconstructionist movement is attributable to dynamic leaders, a bold and seemingly integrated world view, an extensive and comprehensive publishing ministry, the political climate of our era (especially among evangelicals), and the simultaneous rise of the charismatic movement. The Christian Reconstruction movement deserves analysis because of its thoughtful, startling, and thorough challenge to contemporary evangelicalism and American life generally. Its views must be considered with care by what Thomas Jefferson called "a candid world."

Chapter 1, Notes

1. Leland Ryken has provided a helpful corrective to our understanding of the Puritans in *Worldly Saints: The Puritans as They Really Were* (Grand Rapids, Mich.: Academie Books, Zondervan Publishing House, 1986) and *Work and Leisure in Christian Perspective* (Portland, Ore.: Multnomah Press, 1988).

2. See Rodney Clapp, "Democracy as Heresy," *Christianity Today*, 20 February 1987, 18-19; Gary North, "Apologetics and Strategy," in *Tactics of Christian Resistance*, ed. Gary North (Tyler, Tex.: Geneva Divinity School Press, 1983), 107.

3. Gary North, "Cutting Edge or Lunatic Fringe?" *Christian Reconstruction,* January-February 1978, 1, quoted in Thomas Ice, "An Evaluation of Theonomic Neopostmillennialism," *Bibliotheca Sacra* 145 (July-September 1988):282.

4. R. J. Rushdoony, "The Vision of Chalcedon," *The Journal of Christian Reconstruction* 9 (special double issue, 1982-83):128. See also Ice, "Theonomic Neopostmillennialism," 282-3, and Clapp, "Democracy," 18, 22.

5. See Ice, "Theonomic Neopostmillennialism," 283, n. 11.

6. See ibid., 283; Clapp, "Democracy," 17-22.

7. See Ice, "Theonomic Neopostmillennialism," 284; Clapp, "Democracy," 17ff.

8. Clapp, "Democracy," 21.

9. Ibid., 17ff.

10. Pat Robertson recently disavowed on the 700 Club (24 May 1988) any connection with Christian Reconstructionism.

11. Clapp, "Democracy," 21.

12. Garry J. Moes, "The Lord of the Nations," *Chalcedon Report*, July 1988, 9.

13. This union is unusual in view of the strong Reformed bias against basic charismatic and Pentecostal theology on the gifts, Wesleyanism, and Arminianism.

14. Moes, "Lord of the Nations," 9.

15. Gary North, "The Attack on the 'New' Pentecostals," *Christian Reconstruction* 10 (January-February 1986):2.

16. An example of this kind of language can be seen from the hand of Gary North in *Unconditional Surrender* (Tyler, Tex.: Geneva Press, 1981), 210.

17. Gary North, "Jesus' Legacy to His People: The World," *Biblical Economics Today* 9 (April-May 1986):4.

18. Clapp, "Democracy," 21.

Chapter 2

What Do Christian Reconstructionists Mean by Theonomy?

Theonomy derives from two Greek words meaning "God" and "Law." The Reconstructionists believe that the Law of God, or Biblical Law, as codified in the Old Testament should be instituted as the law of the United States and every nation on earth before the return of Christ. This is a striking position: If Reconstructionists succeed, and are consistent with their theory, blasphemy would be a criminal offense, homosexuality a capital crime, and slavery (in some form) reinstituted.

The two most significant books to defend this position are Rushdoony's *Institutes of Biblical Law* and Bahnsen's *Theonomy in Christian Ethics*. These books are expositions of the nature of Old Testament law and its applicability to modern life. Each is long, thorough, and expresses a remarkable breadth of thought and scholarship. They remain, within the movement, the uncontested foundation for more recent works on social policy by authors such as North, Chilton, Sutton, and DeMar.

The views of the theonomists have generated heated controversy. Bahnsen was forced to resign from Reformed Seminary's faculty because of his book. Meredith Kline, a respected professor at Westminster Seminary, calls Bahnsen's *Theonomy* "a delusive and grotesque perversion of the teachings of Scripture."[1] This word of intense criticism is evidence of the impact the Reconstructionists have had in the publication of their views.

As mentioned earlier, Bahnsen, Rushdoony, and their theonomist colleagues cannot be dismissed as crackpots. Their movement is growing, and their arguments are too forceful to be lightly disregarded. However controversial, Reconstructionist theonomy must be considered.

THE MEANING OF THEONOMY

Greg Bahnsen states his understanding of theonomy as follows: "The Christian is obligated to keep the whole law of God as a pattern for sanctification and that this law is to be enforced by the civil magistrate where and how the stipulations of God so designate."[2] The "whole law of God" is here defined to include "the civil precepts of the Old Testament" which are a universal blueprint of perfect social justice.[3] Bahnsen has argued that to reject his view is to embrace autonomy or antinomianism, a life and world without law.[4]

Rousas Rushdoony maintains a position similar to Bahnsen's regarding the enforcement of the Mosaic law in civil government today. As John Frame notes, Rushdoony contends that "almost all of the Old Testament civil law is literally normative for civil government today . . . apart from biblical law, there is no standard for our behavior in this world."[5]

THE PERCEIVED THEONOMIC NECESSITY

Theonomists present law-keeping to be imperative in two widely encompassing areas. These are Christian living and civil government. Recalling Bahnsen's description, for the Christian the law is "a pattern for sanctification," and for the public official it is a ruling grid from which he dare not depart without forfeiting peace and prosperity.

In the area of Christian living, all Christians agree that God's directive to believers is to be holy as he is holy, which cannot be achieved apart from obedience to God's commands. But theonomists center God's commands for today on Old Testament law. Thus, Rushdoony flatly states that "man grows in grace as he grows in law-keeping, for the law is the way of sanctification."[6] Indeed, for Rushdoony the believer is "dead to the law" (Galatians 2:19; Romans 7:4) only on the level of justification, but "alive to the law" as a requisite for practical living. He states that "the purpose for Christ's atoning work was to restore man to a position of covenant-keeping instead of covenant-breaking, to enable man to keep the law. . . ."[7]

Further, Reconstructionists appropriate for the church (seen as the new Israel) the material blessings for obedience— and curses for disobedience—originally promised by God to defunct national Israel.[8] Hence the urgent tone of their appeal to the rest of the church: To ignore the Reconstructionist system of ethics is to fall miserably short in the area of sanctification. This quenches the Holy Spirit and blunts the intended blessings of God upon his church.

But the curses and blessings are not only for the church, but for all of society as well. Sanctification therefore requires not only private obedience to the law, but dictates one's relationship to neighbors and the rest of society. This includes active stances on cultural norms, and social, economic, and political issues. The theonomic goal for the Christian cannot stop at a godly personal life, but must insist on pursuit of a godly society where the government is made an obedient minister of God's Old Testament justice. According to Reconstructionists, this deliberate pursuit is the only way in which a believer can fully love his neighbors and truly obey the Great Commission. Every area of the Christian's personal life, and every area of life in the Christian's society, must become conformed to the whole law of God.[9]

Theonomists see such conformity as demanded by God's sovereign commission of civil magistrates to restrain and punish municipal evil (law-breaking), while upholding public good. They argue that God appoints rulers to be his ministers of justice in society. When performing their tasks faithfully in deference to his law, civil officials are to be obeyed without exception. They are, in many cases, God's ministers of temporal wrath (North even suggests they are secondary ministers of God's eternal wrath when sending those guilty of capital crimes to their greater judgment). Since theonomists define standards of good and evil in terms of the Old Testament law, they view this divine appointment of magistrates as a specific assignment to enforce that very code on a worldwide basis. Bahnsen cites what he terms "religious titles" given to civil rulers—Hebrew and pagan—as proof of their inherent theocratic purpose. He also contends that pagan nations surrounding Israel were commanded in the Old Testament to obey the Mosaic law.[10]

The final imperative for the Reconstructionists' drive to institute the Mosaic civil code is grounded in their interpretation of man's original purpose. They see the command to subdue the earth, given in Genesis 1 to Adam and Eve, as an eternally binding covenant which finds its paramount expression in the Mosaic law. The covenant is not merely with God's designated people, whether Israel or the church; it extends to all men.[11] Only when every magistrate institutes the entirety of God's law, including the most strict Mosaic penal codes, will man be fully restored as God's viceregent over the earth, exercising the dominion mandate lost by Adam in the Garden of Eden. God's law is "a plan for dominion" under him,[12] "God's program for conquest."[13]

THE BASIS OF THE MODERN THEONOMIC THOUGHT

The Reconstructionists assert that the church and state must conform to the Old Testament law based on five lines of argument. These are:

1. Hermeneutical: Interpreting the New Testament strictly in light of the older revelation.

2. Developmental: Seeing the Mosaic law as the historical pinnacle for civil government.
3. A logical deduction drawn from the character of God.
4. Specific Scripture texts, particularly Matthew 5:17-19.
5. Precedent in church history.

Hermeneutical

One of the main distinctives of the theonomic position is that unless an Old Testament law is specifically *negated* in the New Testament, it is still in force. Bahnsen states that "The Old Testament laws are taken to be binding unless the New Testament particularly/specifically abrogates a given law. This is in opposition to dispensationalism which contends that only those laws affirmed by the New Testament are binding today."[14] Rushdoony states, "In the New Testament, only apostolically received revelation was any ground for any alteration of the law. The authority of the law remained unchanged."[15] One looks in vain, however, through his *Institutes* to find any admission of a significant apostolic revision in other than "ceremonial" laws. (Even ceremonial codes are usually considered by theonomists to remain in force in a mode which is more appropriate to our current understanding of the redemptive work of the Messiah.)[16] In light of this, the concept of abrogation has been defined by one writer as "the declaring invalid of the natural meaning of a commandment for the Christian dispensation"[17]—in other words, the whole Old Testament law is binding today.

Developmental

A driving Reconstructionist impulse, as touched upon earlier, is the fulfillment of the perceived dominion mandate. This is said to be an eternal covenant given to Adam to establish the kingdom of God on earth. Adam failed to keep the covenant, yet it is binding upon his ancestors. Regarding the original covenant, theonomists assert, "There is not one word of Scripture to indicate or imply that this mandate was ever revoked. There is every word of Scripture to declare that this mandate must and shall be be fulfilled."[18] The means which theonomists advocate for exercising dominion and fulfilling the covenant is to institute the civil laws given to Moses.

But why choose the Old Testament Hebrew social order? The Mosaic civil ("judicial") laws are seen by theonomists as the pinnacle of social development as revealed by God, with minor New Testament adjustments. In their interpretation of history, man is to subdue the earth for God. God's means to equip man for this task has always been revelation—his "law-word." The revelation was originally to Adam, renewed with Noah, and developed further in the call to Abraham. *But the basic contention of theonomy is that God's covenant has been expressed as a full social program only in the revelation to Moses.* This program was echoed and emphasized in the histories, proverbs, psalms, and prophets. It was then "re-established" by Christ to "a new elect people . . . the people of the law," the church.[19]

Armed then with "the civil precepts of the Old Testament," which Bahnsen says "are a model of perfect social justice for all cultures, even in the punishment of criminals," the Reconstructionists' role for the contemporary church (the universal church is meant rather than the institutional church) is clear: "As the new chosen people of God, the Christians are commanded to do that which Adam in Eden, and Israel in Canaan, failed to do. One and the same covenant, under differing administrations, still prevails. Man is summoned to create the society God requires."[20]

The Character of God
Bahnsen and his colleagues argue that theonomy is logically deduced from the character of God. Their position is this:

1. God is changeless (immutable).
2. God's law is a reflection of his perfect character.

3. God's laws are, therefore, changeless and binding on all human endeavor from the time the
   laws were given to the present.[21]

Bahnsen states: "God's revealed standing laws are a reflection of His immutable character and, as such, are absolute in
the sense of being non-arbitrary, objective, universal and established in advance of particular circumstances."[22]

The Re-establishment of the Law
in Matthew 5:17-19

This passage is viewed as the definitive affirmation of
the theonomic philosophy:

> "Do not think that I came to abolish the Law or the
> Prophets; I did not come to abolish, but to fulfill.
> For truly I say to you, until heaven and earth pass
> away, not the smallest letter or stroke shall pass
> away from the Law, until all is accomplished. Who-
> ever then annuls one of the least of these command-
> ments, and so teaches others, shall be called least
> in the kingdom of heaven; but whoever keeps and
> teaches them, he shall be called great in the kingdom
> of heaven."

Bahnsen writes that "fulfill" "is the most crucial word
for understanding this passage."[23] After an extensive consideration of possible meanings of the word, Bahnsen concludes
that the best translation is "to confirm."[24] The obvious implication is that the laws of the Old Testament, rather than being
put aside, are confirmed by Jesus to be in full effect. Jesus
"confirmed and restored (the law) to full measure."[25]

The History of the Church

A fifth argument of the Reconstructionists is that
theonomy has precedent throughout the history of the church.
Rushdoony and North are fascinated with medieval feudalism,
which they view as a valid pattern of theonomic life.[26]

Feudalism, which was erected on the rubble of the Roman Empire, is seen as an effective means of articulating a theonomic way of life. The expected desire of the American republic and its attendant social disintegration are viewed as giving feudalism a modern rebirth.

The Reconstructionists also believe there is a historical line between themselves and the Reformers. Geneva Ministries in Tyler, Texas, is so named because Geneva was the base of John Calvin's work. Geneva Ministries published Calvin's sermons on the law in Deuteronomy for a number of years in a monthly newsletter called *Calvin Speaks*.

Most notably, the Puritan movement and its effort to theocratize early New England are viewed with particular enthusiasm. Gary North has labeled himself as a "neo-puritan." Bahnsen quotes "An Abstract of the Laws of New England" (1641) in *Theonomy in Christian Ethics*. A recent article states:

> In the Puritans, theonomists see a movement that used biblical law as a tool of dominion, an attempt to make the Old Testament case laws the basis of their systematic reconstruction of all areas of life—indeed, to build a Christian (i.e., Puritan) society. The theonomist views any failure of the Puritans (such as the Salem witchcraft trials) as a violation of otherwise sound biblical principles.[27]

As another author notes, most theonomists cling to the Puritans with tenacity. They evidently find comfort that something like a theonomic system was once tried in America.[28]

THE CONTENT OF THEONOMIC TERMINOLOGY: WHAT IS THE LAW AND HOW MUCH OF IT MUST WE FOLLOW?

Reconstructionists call upon all Christians to follow what is variously phrased as "the whole law of God," "biblical law," or simply "the law." Yet there is room for at least initial confusion about what they mean by these terms. On the one hand, any revelation by God is said to constitute his "law-word." On the other, we have seen how theonomists regard the "civil," or "judicial," or "standing" laws given to Moses to be the paragon for all societies in all ages. But what of the Hebrew laws of animal sacrifice, food offerings, and dietary and clothing restrictions—are these also for today in their literal form?

The issue of definition is critical because the Reconstructionist agenda is so extensive and radical. Furthermore, dispensationalists—whom many Reconstructionists accuse of antinomian heresy—also say that we should follow "God's law," yet with a very different content poured into the terminology. Three steps will be helpful in sorting out the problem:

1. The law we are to follow is seen by theonomists as broader than the Mosaic code, and includes consideration of all biblical revelation. Yet,

2. The Old Testament "Hebrew social order" is seen as the historical zenith and divine model for the future. However,

3. Modifications do exist, mainly in what Reconstructionists call "ceremonial" and "case" divisions of the law. Almost all ceremonial laws are considered to have been fulfilled and superseded in Christ. Some case laws are changed, for reasons not always clear in theonomist writings.

First, Reconstructionists are not hesitant to say that God's instructions cannot be limited to the Mosaic law. Rushdoony states that "the Biblical concept of law is broader than the legal codes of the Mosaic formulation. It applies to the divine word and instruction in its totality."[29] We have also seen how the theonomist principle of abrogation allows for apostolic changes based upon later revelation.

Second, however, it should hardly be necessary to further demonstrate that Reconstructionism holds the Old Testament law, specifically the Mosaic law, to be the social model deliberately given by God for all time. Nevertheless, it is absolutely critical to eliminate any margin for misunderstanding. Bahnsen speaks of a single set of rules which he calls "the whole law of God," the "Old Testament standing laws," "the civil precepts of the Old Testament (standing 'judicial' laws)," "every jot and tittle of the Older Testamental law," "the *law* known in the *Old* Covenant (in Jeremiah's day)," and the "revealed standards of social justice found in the Old Testament law."[30] His evaluation of this set of rules is that they "are a model of perfect social justice for all cultures, even in the punishment of criminals" and "a paragon for all nations at all times in history."[31] He writes: "Christ, you see, directs us to obey Moses as well!"[32]

Looking into the first two pages of the *Institutes of Biblical Law*, one finds Rushdoony praising "the Hebrew social order," then citing the Puritan New Haven Colony's adoption of "the law of God, without any sense of innovation." What was this law? According to his excerpt of their records, they attempted to institute " 'the judiciall lawes of God, as they were delivered by Moses' " to " 'be a rule to all the courts in this jurisdiction.' " This was not some "Puritan aberration," but "a truly Biblical practice and aspect of the persisting life of Christendom." The Mosaic code they tried to establish was "that law which must govern society, and which shall govern society under God."

Third, the theonomists bring together these potentially contradictory positions by severely limiting the apostolic revisions to the law. They grant that such revisions were legitimate, but seem to admit the existence of few. This should not be surprising in light of their presuppositions, outlined above, that Old Testament revelation stands until explicitly abrogated by new, and that the Mosaic law was the model order for all human history.

More specifically, theonomists explain how improvements could occur in the "perfect social order" by dividing the law into three parts: ceremonial, moral, and case. *Ceremonial laws* are defined by Bahnsen as those which involved Hebrew activities such as sacrifices, offerings, feast days, ritual places, and the priesthood. The purpose of the ceremonial law was to emphasize the merciful character and redemptive plan of God. In short, it symbolically foreshadowed the coming atonement.

Moral laws were designed to reflect the absolute righteousness and judgment of God by showing the way to live a holy life, and by defining, punishing, and restraining sin through rigid penal sanctions. While moral laws were broad principles, such as the Ten Commandments, the *case laws* enforced and illustrated the moral laws by application to particular situations. For example, Rushdoony sees the Leviticus 19:13 prohibition against defrauding one's neighbor as a case law application of the general commandment, "You shall not steal" (Exodus 20:15; Deuteronomy 5:19).[33] Theonomists also call case law "civil law" and "standing judicial law."[34]

The crucial Reconstructionist argument is that the Mosaic ceremonial laws are not to be literally performed by Christians in this age, while all of the moral laws, and all or most of the case laws, are indeed so mandated. How do they come to this conclusion?

They assert that the performance of the atonement in history by the Messiah did not contradict the meaning or validity of the ceremonial laws, but did fulfill and "supersede" their "stop-gap and anticipatory" external observances.[35] Bahnsen states that the ceremonial law *is still a requirement of every person*, being no different in this respect than the rest of the law. Christians are still "required to observe the Old Testament ritual."[36] But "with Christ's obedient life, sacrificial death, and the accomplishment of salvation under the New Covenant, the ceremonies have been finally observed for all God's people . . . all Christians have had the ceremonial laws observed for them finally and completely *in Christ*."[37] Rushdoony offers the additional contention that some aspects of the ceremonial system have merely been altered into a form that is more appropriate to our New Covenant understanding of the atonement. Communion, for instance, can be called "the Christian Passover." Circumcision and baptism contain similar Old Covenant connections.[38] While "the law of the covenant remains, the covenant rites and signs have been changed."[39]

But the moral and case laws can never be changed, according to Reconstructionist theory. These reflect God's immutable, righteous character. They are the given means of implementing the dominion covenant and subduing the earth. They are never viewed by Reconstructionists to be abrogated in the New Testament as a practical requirement, as are the ceremonial laws. In the Sermon on the Mount, for example, Rushdoony sees "the full implication of the law, their personal as well as civil implications, their requirements of the heart as well as of the hand."[40] Of the epistles, they "repeatedly restate the Law."[41] (A random survey of citations from the epistles in Rushdoony and Bahnsen finds that most passages are viewed either as restatements of Mosaic moral laws or merely as new case laws.) Passages commonly used by non-Reconstructionists to indicate that the whole law ended as a requirement with the death of Christ are said to refer to justification or to "the death-dealing nature of sin in relation to the holy law" or merely to the ceremonial law.[42]

Nevertheless, vague areas exist. One is the question of how to positively differentiate ceremonial laws and the other two kinds. Bahnsen says the New Covenant supersedes all Old Covenant ceremonial "shadows." This changes the "applicability of sacrificial, purity, and 'separation' principles." It also redefines the people of God, and alters "the significance of the promised land."[43] But are each of these areas substantially unconnected with moral and case laws? Do "purity" and "separation" have more to do with the atonement (ceremonial law) than with the righteous character of God (moral law)? Is "the significance of the promised land" somehow ceremonial and altered because of fulfillment in the work of Christ? "First-fruit offerings" are said to be ceremonial and no longer required, while nonceremonial tithes—to which they are admitted to be closely connected—are still considered to be in force. Why?[44] These are difficult but important questions for which theonomists have no clear-cut answers.

Bahnsen himself admits the presence of typological (ceremonial) elements in such "moral" laws as those involving marriage, but then appeals to the distinction between "first order functions" of such commands, which he says determine their final classification as either moral or ceremonial.[45] Yet he declines to offer even a partial list to demonstrate the practical classification of Mosaic commands. He suggests it is up to every Christian to do so for himself.[46] Rushdoony is eager to compile such a listing, yet is somewhat ambiguous on the role of Mosaic dietary laws, even coming into disagreement with Bahnsen.

A second vague area is the distinction between moral and case laws, including how literally case laws should be brought into our New Covenant era. Reconstructionists state that the entire "civil" (i.e., case) law is to be instituted as a social blueprint. Yet Bahnsen concedes that case laws should be applied relative to specific circumstances of a given culture, as long as the principle underlying the particular regulation is kept intact. For instance, he suggests that the law requiring a protective fence around the typical Hebrew rooftop porch (to prevent a person from falling off) would imply a modern law directing that all swimming pools have protective fences.[47] But this is an easy example. Modern extrapolations to the hundreds of case laws would multiply and become more complex, with each updated application carrying the full weight of divine law and demanding exact enforcement.

This raises questions of subjectivity and the danger of, in effect, adding to God's Word, leading perhaps to both the ancient Pharisaism and contemporary bureaucratization decried by the Reconstructionists themselves. Many other unanswered questions arise in the theonomists' attempts to distinguish moral law from case laws and decide which case laws are open to progressive recodification. Is the law by which disobedient children are put to death a broad moral law or a specific case law applying the commandment to obey parents? Certain Old Testament capital crimes are admittedly abrogated in the New; but on what grounds? (Bahnsen and Rushdoony apparently disagree on this point.)[48] Must the witnesses against a person take the initiative in the actual execution, as required by the law? And what of the apparent divergence of opinion on the question of the sabbath? Should the sabbath be kept? If so, with what stipulations? Should sabbath-breakers be executed? What constitutes breaking the sabbath? Surveying three major Reconstructionist writers, Bahnsen parts with North and Rushdoony on this potentially explosive matter. North and Rushdoony favor wholesale modification based upon individual conscience in the New Covenant era, while Bahnsen makes no mention of any such exception.[49] These are some of the socially and theologically significant issues which remain uncertain.

The Reconstructionists are firm about most positions, however. These include:

- General decentralization of government and other social structures within a theocentric, Christian framework.
- Strong private property rights with limited state or institutional church interference.
- Restitution as an important element of the criminal justice system.
- Voluntary slavery.
- A strong national defense until the entire world is "reconstructed."
- Application of the death penalty for virtually all of the capital crimes listed in the Old Testament law, including adultery, homosexuality, fornication, apostasy, incorrigibility in children, blasphemy, and perhaps sabbath-breaking, along with murder and kidnaping.
- A cash, gold-based economy with limited or no debt.

Many of these will be addressed in chapter 4, in which a possible "reconstructed society" is envisioned.

In conclusion, one matter is certain—the social implications of Reconstructionism proceed rigorously from the foundation of the Mosaic law. And those implications, like the law, are both wide and deep. As Greg Bahnsen puts it:

> [God] did not deliver to us merely some broad and general moral principles, but He revealed very extensive, specific and all encompassing commands. Theonomy is crucial to Christian ethics, and all the details of God's law are intrinsic to theonomy. Here is the heart of the present thesis.[50]

Chapter 2, Notes

1. Meredith G. Kline, "Comments on an Old-New Error," *The Westminster Theological Journal* 41 (Fall 1978): 172.

2. Greg L. Bahnsen, *Theonomy in Christian Ethics* (Nutley, N.J.: The Craig Press, 1979), 34.

3. Ibid., "Preface to Second Edition," xvii.

4. This is the underlying assumption of the whole book, *Theonomy in Christian Ethics*, but especially see the second preface, xi-xix, and 251f.

5. John M. Frame, "*The Institutes of Biblical Law*: A Review," *The Westminster Theological Journal* 38 (Winter 1976):200-01.

6. Rousas J. Rushdoony, *The Institutes of Biblical Law*, vol. 1 (Phillipsburg, N.J.: Presbyterian & Reformed Publishing Co., 1973), 3.

7. Ibid., 3.

8. Ibid., 760.

9. Bahnsen, *Theonomy*, 46, and elsewhere as this is a common theme in theonomy.

10. Ibid., xviii; he references Deuteronomy 4:6-8 and Leviticus 18:24-27.

11. Rushdoony, *Institutes*, 8-9; and in many other theonomist writings.

12. Ibid., 8.

13. Rushdoony, in the foreword to Bahnsen's *Theonomy*, ix.

14. "An Interview with Greg Bahnsen," *Journey*, November-December 1986, 10.

15. Rushdoony, *Institutes*, 7.

16. Rushdoony is so entrenched he will not even allow that Peter's vision in Acts 10 in any way abrogated Mosaic dietary restrictions. He does, however, make a qualified concession of this point in other passages. See *Institutes*, 301.

17. Douglas Moo, "Jesus and the Authority of the Mosaic Law," *The Best in Theology*, vol. 1, ed. J. I. Packer, 107.

18. Rushdoony, *Institutes*, 14. He cites no such declarative Scripture to support this claim.

19. Ibid., 8-9. See also p. 3: "The law, as given through Moses, established the laws of godly society, or true development for man under God"; and p. 679.

20. Ibid., 4. Two problems may be noted: Elsewhere, Reconstructionists say that God would never give his people, the church, a job which he would not see that they accomplished. On this ground the theonomists berate dispensational "pessimism." Yet such a mission is just what Rushdoony seems to be saying that God gave to Israel. Second, where in Scripture was Israel given the explicit command to subdue the entire planet? To "create the society God requires" has to be international, according to the Adamic covenant theory.

21. Developed in Douglas G. Chismar and David A. Rausch, "Regarding Theonomy: An Essay of Concern," *Journal of the Evangelical Theological Society* 27 (September 1984):315-16. Also note Paul B. Fowler, "Theonomy: An Assessment of Its Implications for Church and Society," unpublished paper, 3.

22. Greg L. Bahnsen, "Ten Theses of Theonomy," *Journey*, November-December 1986, 8.

23. Bahnsen, *Theonomy*, 52.

24. Ibid., 70.

25. Ibid., 72.

26. Lorne A. McCune, "Theonomy: A Critique of the Use of Matthew 5," unpublished syllabus for Th.D. diss., Dallas Theological Seminary, 1984, 3. See also chapter 2, "Feudalism and Federalism," in Rousas J. Rushdoony, *This Independent Republic* (Fairfax, Va.: Thoburn Press, 1978).

27. Chismar and Rausch, "Regarding Theonomy," 322.

28. McClune, "Theonomy," ch. 4, p. 2.

29. Rushdoony, *Institutes*, 6.

30. Bahnsen, *Theonomy*, xxix, xvii, 217, xxv, xviii, respectively.

31. Ibid., xvii and xviii, respectively.

32. Ibid., xxv.

33. Rushdoony, *Institutes*, 10-12.

34. For example, compare Bahnsen, *Theonomy*, xx, xvii, with Rushdoony, *Institutes*, 11. It should be noted that many Christians would agree with the Reconstructionists' view of such internal distinctions in the Old Testament law. The controversy centers around the use of these categories and as to whether only the ceremonial portion of the law was abrogated.

35. Bahnsen, *Theonomy*, 207-8; see also Rushdoony, *Institutes*, 304.

36. Bahnsen, *Theonomy*, 207.

37. Ibid., 208-9. It is astonishing that Bahnsen sees this truth so clearly regarding the ceremonial law, but not the rest of the law. Did not "Christ's obedient life" and "sacrificial death" fulfill the entire law for us? If not, we are still in our sins! Yet if Christ's fulfillment of the moral and case laws on our behalf does not relieve us of the requirement to obey them in sanctification, as Bahnsen contends, then neither does Christ's fulfillment of the ceremonial laws on our behalf relieve us of these. Either we are required to

obey them *all* as a pattern of sanctification, or we are not; anything less is inconsistent. Bahnsen simply misses the point that both the typological and nontypological aspects of the law were of temporary purpose "until the seed should come" (Galatians 3).

38. It should again be observed that many non-Reconstructionists have little problem with the theonomist view of the ceremonial law, only with their inconsistent nonapplication of it.

39. Rushdoony, *Institutes*, 23.

40. Ibid., 700.

41. Ibid., 732.

42. Bahnsen, *Theonomy*, 217.

43. Ibid., xvi.

44. Rushdoony, *Institutes*, 50-58. Also, only one of the three tithes is said to be required today. The reasoning seems somewhat arbitrary: the two thirds meant for social financing is today assumed by the state.

45. Bahnsen, *Theonomy*, 215.

46. Ibid., 216.

47. Greg Bahnsen, *By This Standard* (Tyler, Tex.: Institute for Christian Economics, 1985), 137-38.

48. Cf. Bahnsen, *Theonomy*, 445, and Rushdoony, *Institutes*, 77.

49. North's strongest and most extensive statement on the sabbath is found in North, *The Sinai Strategy* (Tyler, Tex.: Institute for Christian Economics, 1986), 228f. Bahnsen supports the continued observance of the sabbath on the first day of the week minus purely "ceremonial" regulations such as offerings; but the basic keeping of the first day of the week is said to be connected with "God's moral law." Presumably, this is why he lists it among capital crimes regarding which contemporary Christians are admonished to "adjust their attitudes." (*Theonomy*, 228-30, 445-46).

50. Bahnsen, *Theonomy*, 35.

Chapter 3

Christian Reconstructionism and Future Things

*T*he two major areas of disagreement between Reconstructionists and the authors of this book are theonomy and postmillennialism. These two aspects were called *ethics* and *eschatology* in a recent debate between Reconstructionists Gary North and Gary DeMar and non-Reconstructionists Dave Hunt and Thomas Ice. Gary DeMar later said, "Hunt and Ice emphasized eschatology, while we stressed ethics. . . . Contrary to what Dave Hunt says, the debate topic was not on eschatology."[1] Actually ethics and eschatology are not as unrelated as DeMar implies. One's view of eschatology, to a large extent, determines what kind of ethics one develops and practices. It is our contention that Reconstructionist eschatology, more than any aspect of their theology, is the greatest determining factor in shaping the distinctive features of dominion theology.

POSTMILLENNIAL ESCHATOLOGY

End Time Influence upon Present Times
    R. J. Rushdoony, the patriarch of Reconstructionism, believes that the "kind of faith we have governs the whole of

our lives . . . theology is a seamless garment, and a man's view of the end times is inseparable from his view of God."[2] It is one's view of the future and the end times which greatly impacts the way he lives his life in the present. It is not a matter of either ethics or eschatology, but how eschatology impacts ethics. Rushdoony explains the dynamic interaction of eschatology and ethics:

> I shall be motivated very much differently from either a premillennial or an amillennial believer. Thus, we cannot hold that these differing doctrines of eschatology are a matter of indifference. They make a very great difference in how we view the world and our work and future in it. There are said to be at least 40 million Christians in the United States who profess to believe that the Bible is the infallible word of God. If these people believe that the end is near, and the rapture at hand, their impact on the world is very different from that of 40 million who believe that they shall conquer the world. In the one situation, people are preparing to leave the world, and to snatch other brands from the burning before they leave. In the other, they are preparing to conquer the world and assert the *"Crown Rights of King Jesus."*[3]

We are not saying that eschatology is *the* major area of theology, but it makes a significant difference, producing two very different versions of Christianity. What is it that makes Reconstructionist eschatology so different from not only premillennialism but amillennialism as well?

Amillennialism and postmillennialism have much in common. The major area of criticism postmillennialists have against amillennialism is its pessimistic view toward the progress of the gospel in the current age. In fact, some Reconstructionists call themselves "optimistic amillennialists."[4]

On the other hand, there is a greater discontinuity between premillennialism, especially the dispensational version, and postmillennialism. However, both premillennialism and post-millennialism do share a common view of Christ's earthly victory. Amillennialism sees only a heavenly victory.

The place to start in our understanding of Reconstructionist eschatology is to consider an extensive statement about what this new postmillennialism believes.

Creation and Fall

To understand Reconstructionist views of the end, we must go back to the beginning. Reconstructionists see a symmetry between the fall of Adam in Paradise and the restoration through the Second Adam ascending to Paradise restored. The creation and fall of man goes something like this:

> Adam was created a king. He was to subdue the earth and have dominion over it. His kingship, however, was not absolute; Adam was a subordinate ruler, a king (prince) under God. He was a king only because God had created him as such and ordered him to rule. God's plan was for His image to rule the world under His law and oversight. As long as Adam was faithful to his commission, he was able to have dominion over the earth.

> But Adam was unfaithful. Unsatisfied with being a subordinate ruler in God's image, applying God's law to creation, he wanted autonomy. He wanted to be his own god, making up his own law. For this crime of rebellion he was cast out of the Garden. But . . . this incident did not abort God's plan for dominion through His image. The Second Adam, Jesus Christ, came to accomplish the task which the First Adam had failed to do.[5]

Shortly after the fall, the Lord promised a struggle between the seed of the woman and the seed of the serpent. In the long run, the kingdom of God would crush the kingdom of man (Satan).

Israel and the Coming Messiah

After the fall, God's plan was to restore man through all the biblical covenants which "were provisional re-creations, looking forward to the definitive New Creation: the New Covenant."[6] The history of the world was building toward the coming of Messiah. Abraham was chosen as patriarch and father of the promise. Israel had the special goal of being a kingdom of priests with the special responsibility of providing Jesus Christ—the Messiah—for the nations. So it was that Israel's history was moving toward the coming of Messiah and his kingdom.

Throughout the Old Testament, God raised up deliverers to save his people and to secure the blessings of life under God's rule. All of these, however, failed to bring lasting peace and order. In the incarnation of the Son, the King himself comes into the world to conquer the enemy once and for all. Jesus came as the Greater Joshua, who makes war against God's enemies, and as the Greater Son of David, who rules the world in righteousness.[7]

The Victory of the Resurrection

"The war between the Seed of the Woman and the seed of the Serpent climaxed at the Cross and Resurrection."[8] The resurrection is the basis for "a proper understanding of the progressive conquest of the effects of evil and the curses of God over nature."[9] In other words, the power of the resurrection is a model and enablement for the kind of progressive conquest of the world by redeemed humanity which postmillennialism envisions. The kingdom has been established, but it needs to expand and grow through the faithfulness of Christians.

Salvation for Reconstructionists is viewed as "re-creation." David Chilton sees this re-creation progressively being fulfilled as salvation "restores man to his original calling and purpose, and guarantees that man's original mandate—to exercise dominion under God over the whole earth—will be fulfilled."[10]

Thy Kingdom Come

When Jesus came to earth two thousand years ago, it was not "merely to save men from eternal death and punishment, as important as that is. He came to establish the Kingdom of God. . . . He came to reassert God's rule."[11] Reconstructionists see the kingdom "established *definitively* in the finished work of Christ," while it is at the same time currently being "established *progressively* throughout history (until it is established *finally* on the Last Day)."[12]

Reconstructionists often feel misunderstood by others who characterize them as believing that the church is to bring in the kingdom.[13] Perhaps this perception exists, in part, because of Reconstructionism's trifold explanation of the coming of the kingdom. Reconstructionists clearly teach that Christ established the kingdom at his first coming. Chilton said, "Jesus is the King, and His Kingdom has arrived."[14] However, "the trouble is there are some Reconstructionists who speak in terms of a take over."[15] (See appendix C for more examples.) Rushdoony has asked: "How is Christ's Kingdom to come?"[16] He later answers his own question by declaring that "God has a plan for the conquest of all things by His covenant people."[17] George Grant makes it clear that the kingdom is viewed by Reconstructionists as still coming. "Christ's disciples were to be world-changers. . . . They were to work for the coming of the Kingdom."[18] He then adds the following: "World conquest. That's what Christ has commissioned us to accomplish."[19]

There is justification for saying that Reconstructionists use "bringing in the kingdom" language in some of their literature. However, in fairness, more recent works have attempted to explain their position more clearly. The kingdom must be seen in three different perspectives. First, it is definitively established in the life, death, resurrection, and ascension of Jesus Christ. Second, it increases and advances progressively from that time to the end of the world. Finally, it is established fully at Christ's second coming.[20]

The Great Commission

Christ's command to make disciples of all the nations is viewed by Reconstructionists as their "marching orders" which "God has set forth to His people concerning their earthly responsibilities for constructing His Kingdom."[21] Reconstructionists see the Great Commission (Matthew 28:18-20), with the added empowering of the Holy Spirit, as the resource for fulfilling the original Dominion Mandate (Genesis 1:26-28). Only this time it will be worldwide in scope. "Christians must be obedient to the mandate God has given to extend His Kingdom to every sphere of life, to every corner of the globe (Gen. 1:26-28; Matt. 28:18-20)."[22]

Reconstructionists believe this calling will be achieved by Christ through his people because of his resurrection, his ascension to heaven, and his current mediatorial reign from the throne of heaven. Heaven is to be gradually brought to earth by the empowerment of the Holy Spirit—heavenizing the earth.

This power is brought to us by the Spirit of the Risen Christ. When he entered heaven, Christ received the Spirit, and poured it out on his people (Acts 2:33). The Spirit brings to the church the power and blessing of the kingdom.[23]

Faithfulness to the preaching of "the gospel and adherence to the Bible as the standard and means of advancing the kingdom on earth"[24] demonstrate the Reconstructionist's reliance upon God. While Christ is the reigning King in heaven—sovereignly and secretly ("behind the scenes") administering his top-down rule—Christians are to be submissively and openly applying a bottom-up approach through humiliation. "Christians are meant to rule, to be leaders. But we are to lead by service, not by domination."[25] Faithful and humble service to God will result, over the long haul, in God entrusting earthly power to his people. At some point, the world will see this exhibit of godly character and the majority will submit to God. Thus, from the human perspective the growth of the kingdom is bottom-up.

Is Satan Alive and Well on Planet Earth?

Satan and his demons were "definitively defeated and bound"[26] by Christ's atonement, resurrection, and ascension. This is explained within their definitive, progressive, and final framework, similar to the way their view of the kingdom functions. Since Satan has been definitively defeated, all he can do now is slow down the Christianization of the world if believers are ignorant and unfaithful enough to allow this defeated foe to deceive them in this way.[27] Chilton expounds,

> Before the coming of Christ, Satan controlled the nations; but now his death-grip has been shattered by the Gospel, as the good news of the Kingdom has spread throughout the world. . . . That Satan has been bound does not mean that all his activity has ceased. The New Testament tells us specifically that the demons have been disarmed and bound (Col. 2:15; 2 Pet. 2:4; Jude 6)—yet they are still active. It is just that their activity is restricted. And, as the Gospel progresses throughout the world, their activity will become even more limited.[28]

Israel

In contrast to the eventual faithfulness and empowerment by the Holy Spirit of the church, "ethnic Israel was excommunicated for its apostasy and will never again be God's Kingdom."[29] (See appendix B for a list of biblical references which speak of Israel's restoration.) Postmillennialists have always believed that the majority of ethnic Jews will one day be converted to Christ. (This is not surprising since a majority of the world will be converted anyway, according to postmillennialists.) However, "the Bible does not tell of any future plan for Israel as a special nation."[30] The church is now that new nation (Matthew 21:43) which is why Christ destroyed the Jewish state. "In destroying Israel, Christ transferred the blessings of the kingdom from Israel to a new people, the church."[31]

Related to the judgment of God upon Israel in A.D. 70 are a number of events which the Reconstructionist, preterist (past) interpretation of prophetic literature produces, making their eschatology unique.

PROPHETIC EVENTS RELATED TO THE A.D. 70 JUDGMENT UPON JERUSALEM

The Olivet Discourse and the Book of Revelation

The Olivet Discourse (Matthew 24-25, Mark 13, and Luke 17, 21) is one of the major teaching sections of Christ's ministry. How it is handled is a major factor in any eschatology. David Chilton is quite clear in his understanding of when it was fulfilled. "The Olivet Discourse is not about the Second Coming of Christ. It is a prophecy of the destruction of Jerusalem in A.D. 70."[32]

The Book of Revelation is viewed by all students of eschatology to be an expansion of Christ's teachings in the Olivet Discourse. Chilton is also clear in stating his understanding of that section of God's Word:

> The Book of Revelation is not about the Second Coming of Christ. It is about the destruction of Israel and Christ's victory over His enemies in the establishment of the New Covenant Temple. In fact, as we shall see, the word *coming* as used in the Book of Revelation never refers to the Second Coming. Revelation prophesies the judgment of God on apostate Israel; and while it does briefly point to events beyond its immediate concerns, that is done merely as a "wrap-up," to show that the ungodly will never prevail against Christ's Kingdom. But the main focus of Revelation is upon events which were soon to take place.[33]

Understanding these portions of Scripture in a preterist way is radically different from the viewpoint of most amillennialists and all premillennialists.

Why a Preterist Interpretation?

Reconstructionists interpret these eschatological passages as preterist events for the following reasons: *First*, the canon of Holy Scripture was entirely completed before Jerusalem fell.

> The death, resurrection and ascension of Christ marked the end of the Old Covenant and the beginning of the New; the apostles were commissioned to deliver Christ's message in the form of the New Testament; and when they were finished, God sent the Edomites and the Roman armies to destroy utterly the last remaining symbol of the Old Covenant: the Temple and the Holy City. This fact alone is sufficient to establish the writing of the Revelation as taking place before A.D. 70. . . . There would be no further special revelation once Israel was gone. To return to the point: the Book of Revelation definitely was written before A.D. 70, and probably before A.D. 68.[34]

Second, both the Olivet Discourse and Revelation are dealing with issues and events which had to be fulfilled for the contemporaries of that day. Chilton supports this by appealing to the phrase in Revelation 1:1, "the things that must *shortly* take place."

> The Book of Revelation . . . is a prophecy of the period known in Scripture as "the Last Days," meaning the last days of the covenantal nation of Israel, the forty-year "generation" (Matt. 24:34) between the Ascension of Christ (A.D. 30) and the Fall of Jerusalem to the Romans (A.D. 70). It foretells events that St. John expected his readers to see very soon.[35]

Third, their approach to interpretation is said to be "the fusion of covenant and symbol."[36] This means that "much of the Bible is written in symbols. A helpful way to understand this, perhaps, would be to speak of these symbols as a set of patterns and associations."[37] Therefore, Reconstructionists stress the primacy of symbolism in prophetic interpretation, rather than a more literal approach.[38]

This Generation

Matthew 24:34 is the pivotal passage for the Olivet Discourse: "Truly I say to you, this generation will not pass away until all these things take place." Chilton concludes, "This means that everything Jesus spoke of in this passage, at least up to verse 34, took place before the generation then living passed away."[39]

This approach means that passages such as Matthew 24:30, "and they will see the Son of Man coming on the clouds of the sky with power and great glory," is not a reference to the future Second Coming, as most Christians have traditionally understood. Instead, this event is seen by Reconstructionists to have been a part of Christ's First Coming.

> In Matthew 24, therefore, Jesus was not prophesying that he would literally come on the clouds in A.D. 70 (although it was figuratively true). His literal "coming on the clouds," in fulfillment of Daniel 7, took place in A.D. 30, at the beginning of the "terminal generation." But in A.D. 70 the tribes of Israel would see the destruction of the nation as the result of His having ascended to the throne of heaven, to receive His Kingdom.[40]

The Reconstructionist, preterist approach means that many personalities, events, and places referred to prophetically in the Scriptures have already been fulfilled. Rather than references to "things to come," they are explained as "things that came." What are these items and how were they fulfilled?

The Middle of History, Not the End of History

Reconstructionist postmillennialists are unique, in relationship to most amillennialists and all premillennialists, in that they see most of their eschatology being fulfilled in the middle of history, rather than toward the end. "As Christ pointed out in Matthew, the Great Tribulation was to take place, not at the end of history, but in the middle."[41] This preterist understanding greatly affects events, personalities, and chronologies. Note the following list of important terms:

The Great Tribulation "took place in the Fall of Israel. It will not be repeated and thus is not a future event."[42]

The Great Apostasy "happened in the first century. We therefore have no Biblical warrant to expect increasing apostasy as history progresses; instead, we should expect the increasing Christianization of the world."[43]

The Last Days "is a Biblical expression for the period between Christ's Advent and the destruction of Jerusalem in A.D. 70: the 'last days' of Israel."[44]

The Antichrist "is a term used by John to describe the widespread apostasy of the Christian Church prior to the Fall of Jerusalem. In general, any apostate teacher or system can be called 'antichrist'; but the word does not refer to some 'future Führer.'"[45]

The Rapture is "the 'catching up' of the living saints 'to meet the Lord in the air.' The Bible does not teach any separation between the Second Coming and the Rapture; they are simply different aspects of the Last Day."[46]

The Second Coming "coinciding with the Rapture and the Resurrection, will take place at the end of the Millennium, when history is sealed at the Judgment."[47]

The Beast "of Revelation was a symbol of both Nero in particular and the Roman Empire in general."[48]

The False Prophet "of Revelation was none other than the leadership of apostate Israel, who rejected Christ and worshiped the Beast."[49]

The Great Harlot of Revelation was "Jerusalem which had always been . . . falling into apostasy and persecuting the prophets . . . [it] had ceased to be the City of God."[50]

The Millennium "is the Kingdom of Jesus Christ, which He established at His First Advent . . . the period between the First and Second Advents of Christ; the Millennium is going on now, with Christians reigning as kings on earth."[51] "Other postmillennialists interpret the millennium as a future stage of history. Though the kingdom is already inaugurated, there will someday be a greater outpouring of the Spirit than the church has yet experienced."[52]

The First Resurrection of Revelation 20:5 is a "Spiritual resurrection: our justification and regeneration in Christ."[53]

The Thousand Years of Revelation 20:2-7 is a "large, rounded-off number . . . the number ten contains the idea of a fullness of quantity; in other words, it stands for manyness. A thousand multiplies and intensifies this (10 X 10 X 10), in order to express great vastness. . . . [It] represents a vast, undefined period of time. . . . It may require a million years."[54]

The New Creation "has already begun: The Bible describes our salvation in Christ, both now and in eternity, as 'a new heaven and a new earth.'"[55]

The New Jerusalem "the City of God, is the Church, now and forever."[56]

The Final Apostasy refers to Satan's last gasp in history (Revelation 20:7-10). "The Dragon will be released for a short time, to deceive the nations in his last-ditch attempt to overthrow the Kingdom."[57] This will be "in the far future, at the close of the Messianic age,"[58] shortly before the Second Coming.

Armageddon "was for St. John a symbol of defeat and desolation, a 'Waterloo' signifying the defeat of those who set themselves against God, who obey false prophets instead of the true." "There never was or will be a literal 'Battle of Armageddon,' for there is no such place."[59]

The above snapshots help give an idea of the distinctive aspects of Reconstruction eschatology. Now we will look at the postmillennial vision concerning how the expansion of the kingdom will take place.

Blessing and Cursing

"How is Christ's Kingdom to come?"[60] According to Rushdoony:

Scripture is again very definite and explicit. The glorious peace and prosperity of Christ's reign will be brought about only as people obey the covenant law. In Lev. 26, Deut. 28, and all of Scripture, this is plainly stated. There will be peace and prosperity in the land, the enemy will be destroyed, and men will be free of evils only "If ye walk in my statutes, and keep my commandments, and do them" (Lev. 26:3). The obedience of faith to the law of God produces irresistible blessings: "And all these blessings shall come on thee, and overtake thee, if thou shalt hearken unto the voice of the Lord thy God" (Deut. 28:2). On the other hand, disobedience leads to irresistible curses: "But it shall come to pass, if thou wilt not hearken unto the voice of the Lord thy God, to observe to do all his commandments and his statutes which I command thee, this day, that all these curses shall come upon thee, and overtake thee" (Deut. 28:15).

According to these and other declarations of Scripture, the determination of all things within time is in terms of obedience and disobedience to God's law. This is plainly spelled out for the various areas of life. *First*, national, rural, and urban prosperity and success are conditional upon obedience to God's law. *Second*, human fertility is similarly an area where God's curse and blessing are operative, and we are either cursed or blessed in the fruit of our bodies. *Third*, agricultural fertility and prosperity are also tied to the law. *Fourth*, the weather is likewise related to the law, so that God judges and blesses by means of the rain, hail, snow, dew and sun. *Fifth*, our relationship to our enemies is again conditional upon obedience. *Sixth*, our personal lives and activities are blessed or cursed in terms of our obedience to God's law.[61]

Within the above stated framework, as God brings increasingly more people to redemption in Christ (special grace), this leads increasingly to more obedience to God's law (common grace), resulting in greater blessings affecting society and an increasing restraint of evil.[62] "Through generations of obedience, the godly will increasingly become competent and powerful, while the ungodly will grow weak and impotent."[63] As this process crescendos the "wicked are 'raptured' first (i.e., driven out of the earth and disinherited), as the righteous increasingly come into possession of all things."[64]

Divisions within the Camp

While most Reconstructionist postmillennialists agree with each other on most issues, there has developed a growing split over some aspects of their eschatological system. Reconstructionist Doug Wilson has warned fellow postmillennialists of potential dangers in adopting James Jordan's "Interpretive Maximalism," which Chilton has done in his commentary on Revelation, *Days of Vengeance*.[65] Wilson warns that "the approach to the Bible [Jordan] advocates is extremely dangerous."[66]

Gary North sounds a note of division between the "Tyler" approach to eschatology and the direction of fellow postmillennialist Greg Bahnsen:

> We in Tyler are nervous about its self-conscious separation of theonomy (ethics) from postmillennialism. We argue for postmillennialism in terms of the ethical cause-and-effect system of God's judgments in history (Deut. 28): righteousness wins, evil loses. We think we hear a time bomb ticking in *Theonomy*. (Maybe it's just a metronome.) We also are more interested in pursuing biblical theology and biblical symbolism than he is.[67]

Greg Bahnsen, in a book review of Chilton's *Days of Vengeance*, said that he "cannot recommend my friend David's commentary on Revelation." He cited three major reasons: (1)

It embodies an unsound, imaginative hermeneutic; (2) it is confused about the book's structure and meaning; and (3) it is guilty of considerable errors in history and interpretation.[68]

These differences, which have only surfaced in the last few years, should be watched to see if this rift leads to major differences within Reconstructionist postmillennialism. Since this viewpoint has only been revived within the last few decades, it is still in its infancy. However, the rich polemical environment will most likely produce a variety of flowers in the postmillennial garden.

CONCLUSION

Reconstructionist postmillennialism differs from its close cousin, amillennialism, and from its more distant relative, premillennialism, in its "belief that Scripture teaches the success of the great commission in this age of the church."[69] The distilled essence of postmillennialism is understood to be "its essential optimism for the kingdom in the present age. This confident attitude in the power of Christ's Kingdom, the power of its gospel, the powerful presence of the Holy Spirit, the power of prayer, and the progress of the great commission sets postmillennialism apart from the essential pessimism of amillennialism and premillennialism."[70]

Chapter 3, Notes

1. Gary DeMar, *American Vision*, June 1988.

2. R. J. Rushdoony, *God's Plan For Victory: The Meaning of Post Millennialism* (Fairfax, Va.: Thoburn Press, 1977), 3.

3. Ibid., 2.

4. Gary DeMar and Peter Leithart, *The Reduction of Christianity* (Fort Worth: Dominion Press, 1988), 41.

5. David Chilton, *Paradise Restored: An Eschatology of Dominion* (Tyler, Tex.: Reconstruction Press, 1985), 67.

6. David Chilton, *The Days of Vengeance* (Fort Worth: Dominion Press, 1987), 583.

7. DeMar and Leithart, *Reduction*, 209.

8. Chilton, *Days of Vengeance*, 584.

9. Gary North, *Is The World Running Down?* (Tyler, Tex.: Institute for Christian Economics, 1988), 163.

10. Chilton, *Paradise*, 25.

11. DeMar and Leithart, *Reduction*, 209.

12. Chilton, *Paradise*, 73.

13. DeMar and Leithart, *Reduction*, 192.

14. Chilton, *Paradise*, 73.

15. David Chilton, television interview with Bill Moyers, "God and Politics," part 3 on *Moyers*.

16. Rushdoony, *God's Plan*, 54.

17. Ibid., 57.

18. George Grant, *The Changing of the Guard: Biblical Principles for Political Action* (Fort Worth: Dominion Press, 1987), 90.

19. Ibid., 51.

20. DeMar and Leithart, *Reduction*, 160.

21. Gary North, "Editor's Introduction" in George Grant, *Changing of the Guard*, xxxi.

22. Gary DeMar, *Ruler of the Nations: Biblical Principles for Government* (Fort Worth: Dominion Press, 1987), 184.

23. DeMar and Leithart, *Reduction*, 218.

24. Ibid., 42.

25. Ibid., 221.

26. Chilton, *Paradise*, 224.

27. Gary North, *Healer of the Nations: Biblical Principles for International Relations* (Fort Worth: Dominion Press, 1987), 218-19.

28. Chilton, *Vengeance*, 503.

29. Chilton, *Paradise*, 224.

30. Ibid.

31. DeMar and Leithart, *Reduction*, 213.

32. Chilton, *Paradise*, 224.

33. Chilton, *Vengeance*, 43.

34. Chilton, *Paradise*, 159-60.

35. Chilton, *Vengeance*, 51-2.

36. Gary North, "Stones and Cornerstones in Christian Reconstruction," *Christian Reconstruction,* March-April 1988, 2.

37. Chilton, *Paradise*, 18.

38. See Chilton, *Vengeance*, 27-39.

39. David Chilton, *The Great Tribulation* (Fort Worth: Dominion Press, 1987), 2.

40. Ibid., 25.

41. Ibid., 14.

42. Chilton, *Paradise*, 224.

43. Ibid., 225.

44. Ibid.

45. Ibid., 224.

46. Ibid., 148.

47. Ibid.

48. Ibid., 225.

49. Ibid., 183.

50. Ibid., 188, 225.

51. Ibid., 225, 195.

52. DeMar and Leithart, *Reduction*, 41-42.

53. Chilton, *Paradise*, 225.

54. Chilton, *Vengeance*, 506-7.

55. Chilton, *Paradise*, 226.

56. Ibid.

57. Chilton, *Vengeance*, 519.

58. Ibid., 526.

59. Chilton, *Great Tribulation*, 144, 142.

60. Rushdoony, *God's Plan*, 54.

61. Ibid., 54-55.

62. See Gary North, "Common Grace, Eschatology, and Biblical Law," Appendix C in Chilton, *Vengeance*, 623-64; Gary North, *Dominion and Common Grace: The Biblical Basis of Progress* (Tyler, Tex.: Institute for Christian Economics, 1987).

63. Chilton, *Paradise*, 223.

64. Ibid., 223-4.

65. For an explanation of "Interpretive Maximalism" see Chilton, *Vengeance*, 36-39.

66. Doug Wilson, *Law and Love: Constructive Criticism for Reconstructionists* (Moscow, Idaho: Ransom Press, n.d.), 10.

67. North, "Stones and Cornerstones," 2.

68. Greg L. Bahnsen, "Another Look at Chilton's *Days of Vengeance*," cited by the editor of *The Counsel of Chalcedon*, July 1988, 3.

69. Greg L. Bahnsen, "The *Prima Facie* Acceptability of Postmillennialism," *Journal of Christian Reconstruction* 3 (Winter 1976-77):68.

70. Ibid., 66.

Chapter 4

What Would a Christian Reconstructed America Be Like?

The year is 40,255 A.D.[1] The place is the reconstructed American republic. A sample of cases from a local public record might include the following.

Case 1: Frank has an oak tree near the corner of his 120 acre flat, unfenced lot. A twelve-year-old boy, Nick, has fallen from the tree and died of a head injury. When the local magistrates investigate to determine if restitution is to be owed the family of the boy, they find that another young climber had also fallen from the tree five years earlier, with only a minor injury. Yet another incident had occurred seven years before involving Frank's son, who suffered a slightly separated shoulder. Frank had been warned by a local elected civil elder, Bob, after the second accident, to take measures to prevent any further injury. So Frank grudgingly put up a warning sign, which had long since become weathered and unreadable.

Frank is convicted of criminal negligence by a local court and an appeals court. George, Nick's father, hears a remorseful public plea by Frank for acceptance of restitution for the crime, based upon Exodus 21:30. But the young lad was his father's only son, and his oppressive grief cannot be overcome. On a prescribed date, Frank is led into a municipal plaza and beaten to death with hundreds of rocks hurled from a crowd of men. George, Bob, and another witness to the fall are there to throw the first three stones.[2]

Case 2: Marge, age 33 and a passive non-Christian, voluntarily sold herself three years ago to become the slave of Elton and his family, as restitution for totaling their only vehicle. Her job is to garden and help Elton's semi-invalid wife with the cooking. In four years she will be released from slavery at the sabbath year. One day, she mistakenly instructs a hired landscaper to cut the lower branches from Elton's favorite pepper tree. Elton, an embittered man known for a volatile and violent temper, flies into a rage when he learns of this. He picks up a three-foot-long branch from the pile of freshly cut limbs and strikes Marge several times on her head, shoulders, back, and legs, causing deep welts and bruises and a badly swollen left eyelid.

A local civil elder called by a neighbor checks on the situation and prepares release papers for Marge based upon Exodus 21:26. But two days after the beating, Marge's eye is better and she is well able to resume her routine. Elton is judged to have been penalized by losing Marge's work for two days. Marge remains his property and no action is taken against him.[3]

THE LIMITATIONS OF LOOKING INTO THE FUTURE

The above scenarios are very plausible according to the stated interpretations and applications of leading Reconstructionist writers. Yet there are inherent limitations whenever one engages in projecting what life would be like under the implementation of any ideology. One constraining factor in trying to envision a theonomist society is the disagreement within the theonomist school itself. As noted in chapter 2, some advocate strict sabbath-keeping on Sundays, some are more lenient. Some have detailed fiscal and agricultural policies from the law, while others demur from such a course. Another limitation is that not every Reconstructionist, and not every aspect of Reconstructionist thought, can be examined. The present chapter will review only significant highlights.

A third limitation is that most theonomists forecast Christian dominion as being ushered in through education and conversion. They admit, however, that not everyone will be converted. It is safe to assume that a relatively large segment of the population of a hypothetical theonomistic country could be pagan or nominally Christian. Even a figure of 5 to 20 percent would represent an immense number of people. Also, the theonomist government would treat some groups differently in the final state of global conquest than it would during the transition phase, with some "heretics" reclassified from targets for conversion to targets for prison.

Finally, it must also be said that even if a country such as the United States became a "reconstructed" society, this would not necessarily confirm postmillennial eschatology—revivals have happened before without ushering in the millennium. With these caveats in mind, this chapter examines the kind of society the Reconstructionists desire us to have.

THE FINAL WORLD CONDITION

Immediately before Christ returns to rule, what might a Reconstructed world look like? The most prominent terms describing the Reconstructionists' ideal order are these: international, republican, decentralized, substantially regenerated, and under biblical (mainly Mosaic) law. David Chilton offers this succinct outline:

> The Christian goal for the world is the universal development of Biblical theocratic republics, in which every area of life is redeemed and placed under the Lordship of Jesus Christ and the rule of God's law.[4]

He elsewhere calls for "a world of decentralized theocratic republics."[5] Greg Bahnsen describes it as "the Kingdom of God, an international community of faith," which "comes by the Spirit's gracious power working through evangelistic preaching and Christian nurture."[6] Although most Reconstructionists see America as a potentially significant player in worldwide Christian Reconstruction, due to its heavily Christian roots and heritage, "America is not God's chosen nation."[7]

When will this goal be completed? Chilton estimates that it will take a minimum of thirty-six thousand more years before Christ is ready to return and anoint the finished conquest, according to his calibration of biblical prophetic terminology (see endnote 1). Not many of his fellow Reconstructionists would place it that far into the future.

A "RECONSTRUCTED" NATION

Narrowing the question to the national level, then, What is the Reconstructionist vision of one of these future "theocratic" republics, and how might this vision evaluate, and suggest changes in, the United States of America?

The fundamental superstructure of the ideal theonomic nation is found in the concept of diversity within unity. Borrowing a term from Calvin, Reconstructionists see all of society as ordered by God into different *spheres* or *institutions*. Diversity is located in these multiple spheres which operate within society. Each plays a unique and constructive role and is administered by a hierarchy of authorities. Unity is supplied by God through his law, which tells the authorities within each institution how it should function internally and in relation to the other institutions in society.

Multiple Social "Spheres"

Among the spheres mentioned by Rushdoony are "art, science, church, family, business, agriculture, everything. . . ."[8] More recently he has compacted these into six general areas:

self, family, institutional church, businesses/vocations, private associations, and civil government.[9] In the ideal theonomic nation, the spheres are to be completely autonomous, yet individually oriented toward the central fact of God and his revelation. God provides the unifying umbrella under which mankind's institutions harmoniously exist. Each sphere is seen as playing its prescribed role in benefiting society and glorifying God within the strict limitations laid down by God's Word, modeled in the Old Testament law.

> No institution is exempt: church, state, family, economy, school, farm, etc. Every institution has a structure of responsibility and standards of performance. . . . If the civil government bears the sword, then it should bear the sword in terms of God's law. If a corporation makes a profit, then it should make a profit in terms of God's law. If a farm plants a crop, then it should plant it in terms of God's requirements for agriculture.[10]

Although there must obviously be interaction, encroachment by one sphere into the area of another (or abdication of responsibilities by an institution, leading to imbalance) is a sign of breakdown. On the other hand, the spheres also serve to check and balance each other. Since a person's life crosses over many areas, if he is treated unjustly in one institution he may appeal to governing authorities in another.[11]

Decentralized Governing Hierarchies within Each Sphere

The crucial Old Testament passage used by Reconstructionists as a blueprint for government within the spheres is Exodus 18:15-26 (NIV):

> Moses answered him, "Because the people come to me to seek God's will. Whenever they have a dispute, it is brought to me, and I decide between the parties and inform them of God's decrees and laws."

Moses' father-in-law replied, "What you are doing is not good. You and these people who come to you will only wear yourselves out. The work is too heavy for you; you cannot handle it alone. Listen now to me and I will give you some advice, and may God be with you. You must be the people's representative before God and bring their disputes to him. Teach them the decrees and laws, and show them the way to live and the duties they are to perform. But select capable men from all the people—men who fear God, trustworthy men who hate dishonest gain—and appoint them as officials over thousands, hundreds, fifties and tens. Have them serve as judges for the people at all times, but have them bring every difficult case to you; the simple cases they can decide themselves. That will make your load lighter, because they will share it with you. If you do this and God so commands, you will be able to stand the strain, and all these people will go home satisfied."

Moses listened to his father-in-law and did everything he said. He chose capable men from all Israel and made them leaders of the people, officials over thousands, hundreds, fifties and tens. They served as judges for the people at all times. The difficult cases they brought to Moses, but the simple ones they decided themselves.

DeMar seeks to explain how this concept was codified in view of life in the promised land:

Local governments were designated as "towns." Every town (literally, "gate") had its own court system with its own rulers and administrators. Affairs of the towns were to be handled by the officials of the town selected "out of all the people" from the town (Deuteronomy 16:18).[12]

The key to governing the future theocratic republic, according to the Reconstructionists, is that this pattern of authority will now be applied not only within the church, and not only in the limited sphere of civil government, but in every sphere and subsphere (such as an individual industry within the greater sphere of business). Every sphere will have its own court system, applying the appropriate case laws and case law principles and ruling on disputes and problems arising within the sphere. Each industry, each business within an industry, each neighborhood, each association—everything—would have such a grassroots based ruling hierarchy. As North puts it, "Each institution acts as a miniature court."[13] As mentioned previously, potential injustice can be checked by appealing to a court in another, but perhaps related, sphere or by appealing to a higher court within the sphere if a case is deemed to be difficult to decide.

The officials (also called "judges" or "elders"), would be elected by those in the sphere over whom they are to govern. Presumably they would have expertise in their respective fields. Rushdoony suggests that qualifications for candidates might be those for church eldership in the pastoral epistles. He sees the eldership structure in the sphere of the institutional church as a close copy of that given to national Israel, and a model for leadership in all spheres in the future reconstructed republic. His contention is that Paul did not explicitly apply this rule to other spheres because at the time the epistles were written, such an extension was socially unfeasible.[14]

Decentralization and delegation are key elements in theonomy, because such an arrangement recognizes the dangers inherent in man's sinful nature and the damage created by power-wielding despots and institutions. Not only would the world be decentralized into many nations, but each nation would be decentralized geographically. Within each sphere, the disbursement of power would be augmented by the related exercise of delegation. Sticking tenaciously to the Mosaic blueprint, DeMar comments that "God structured the nation of Israel . . . by dividing the land among the twelve tribes.

No one tribe could dominate the entire nation because of the influence of the other eleven tribes. This would tend to dilute the power of any one tribe."[15]

Jurisdictions would not necessarily coincide with the Old Testament formula of "thousands, hundreds, fifties and tens," but would be variable according to culture and technology. There would be major authorities to decide the difficult cases, but apparently no unifying ruler or elite council. Because of the pervasive, standardizing influence of the law, the theonomic ideal would be "management by exception," rather than the accretion of a huge volume of case law red-tape.[16]

As mentioned in previous chapters, both North and Rushdoony draw favorable parallels between the ideal reconstructed state and the medieval feudal pattern of life. Whether one agrees with the accuracy of their comparison, North envisions a final system

> of complementary, competing authorities. The Bible tells us: 'Where no counsel is, the people fall: but in the multitude of counsellors there is safety' (Proverbs 11:14). In a multitude of lawful sovereigns there is also safety, in time and on earth. Each authority has its assignments, defined by God's law, but no single authority has absolute authority in any given sphere of life. Only God has absolute sovereignty. Therefore, the Bible establishes a system of checks and balances, and God's law provides the pivot point.[17]

A CLOSER LOOK AT SOME SIGNIFICANT INSTITUTIONS

The spheres most extensively commented upon by Reconstructionists are family (and the closely related area of education), church, state (or civil government), and business/economics.

Self

The key building block of society is said to be the individual. Therefore, true Christian conversion by the masses is a prerequisite for reconstruction. Only the regenerated are "self-governed" individuals. Only they have God's Spirit and are capable, according to DeMar, of governing themselves and others. Non-Christians cannot rule themselves and therefore must be excluded from a government under God's law.[18]

Family and Education

The family is called the "first governing institution" (of more than one person), and the "training ground for future leaders."[19] Parents must assume the direct and ultimate responsibility for educating their children. State schools are seen as a blatantly antibiblical intrusion upon the sphere of the parents, and to some extent upon that of the institutional church. DeMar commendably states that the product of education "should be a completely developed biblical worldview where all of life is seen through the corrective lenses of the world of God."[20] Which sphere will run the schools? Rushdoony indicates the acceptability of schools operated in some connection with the institutional church, although the family must remain in responsible control: "The Christian school is a manifestation of the visible church, and at the same time, an extension of the home."[21]

The Institutional Church

Reconstructionists vehemently deny that they are advocating control over society by the institutional church, since the church is only one of many spheres. They claim that critics misrepresent their position to be one of "ecclesiocracy" (theonomists use this word to speak of government by the visible church) rather than their true position in favor of "theocracy" (rule by God through universal church members governing the various spheres according to God's law).

Most Reconstructionist descriptions of the ideal church follow conspicuously Reformed and especially Presbyterian formulas in areas of organizational structure and sacraments. The fate of any Christian unwilling to conform to those strictures is not stated, although the clear implications of flouting God's "law-order" will be examined below. Following the general social pattern of decentralization, the church is envisioned chiefly as a local unit. The visible church is to be heavily endowed through the tithe and freewill offerings. Financing is important in view of the added responsibilities of education and welfare of the truly needy, such as widows—functions currently held by the civil government.

The proper functions of the institutional church include: (1) Restraining people from sin through preaching of the Word of God; (2) protecting members from doctrinal error; (3) spreading awareness of the need for repentance; (4) excommunicating unrepentant sinners and exercising other forms of church discipline; (5) turning civil offenders (in this case certain unrepentant sinners) over to the state; (6) resolving disputes between members; and (7) providing for various forms of welfare, thus drastically reducing the mischievous role of the state. In the words of David Chilton, "The church is the divinely appointed minister of grace," as distinguished from the state, which is "the divinely appointed minister of justice."[22]

The State

Reconstructionists see the modern state as engaged in a Satanic encroachment into the functions of almost every other sphere. It is described as the major institutional block to the fulfillment of the dominion mandate and the establishment of functionally balanced theocratic republics. Where God's law is seen to favor private property rights, the state is viewed as socialistic. Where God is seen to require decentralization and delegation through the multiple sphere system, the state is viewed as greedily hoarding power to its own highly centralized sphere. Where God desires private Christian philanthropy through the tithe, the state promotes a demoralizing civil welfare edifice. Where God's law is seen as the formula for property and freedom, the demonic state is seen as stifling initiative and efficiency, thus driving men into despair and subverting the theonomic directive. As Gary North words it, "Satan is a consummate bureaucrat."[23] Finally, the modern state is seen as an instrument of evil because it is an inherently religious tool and is mainly in the hands of humanists who seek to boost its power for their own unrighteous ends, such as abortion, homosexuality, and the repression of Christianity.

The only legitimate functions of the state according to Reconstructionist thought are: (1) Restraining civil evil; (2) punishing evil; (3) protecting the law abiding; and (4) defending the nation (in the period before global reconstruction is completed). This should be administered through a hierarchical system of elders or judges with extreme emphasis upon the local governing units, as with the other institutions in society.

One of the most controversial elements of theonomy is the advocacy of re-establishing the Mosaic penal system. What would this mean? Most prominently, the death penalty for at least the following crimes: murder, gross negligence resulting in the death of another, rape, adultery, apostasy, homosexuality, bestiality, gross incorrigibility in children, idolatry, and perhaps sabbath-breaking. As mentioned in chapter 2, the issue of capital punishment for sabbath-breaking has stirred some apparent disagreement among theonomists, not an insignificant issue should their hopes ever come to fruition.

Another controversy is the issue of stoning. Many Reconstructionists allow for the modernization of the method of execution. Not, however, Gary North. He argues forcefully for the role of stoning as an integral part of the Mosaic penal code. His reasoning covers economic, sociological, and psychological ground, and includes the following points: First, stones are plentiful at almost no cost. Second, no single blow can be traced to any person, reducing feelings of guilt. Third, it displays collective responsibility for crime prevention. Fourth, executions should be public and personal. Fifth, it is symbolic of God's crushing the head of Satan, as prophesied in Genesis 3:5.[24]

A prominent plank of the theonomists' criminal justice platform is the emphasis on restitution as opposed to incarceration. The Old Testament law generally penalized offenders according to the principle of "eye for eye, tooth for tooth." A thief, vandal, or criminally negligent individual had to pay back the victim in monetary measure for the loss, or in time and labor as a slave. In a reconstructed republic, updated Old Testament restitution would be the backbone of the criminal and civil justice system.

Questions and concerns abound for Reconstructionists regarding exactly how the Mosaic civil regulations are to be transferred into the future godly society. Must men wear Jewish borders and fringes on their garments, in strict obedience to Deuteronomy 22:11-12? Absolutely yes, says Rushdoony, to preserve unity and holiness.[25] For the same reason, no one should be allowed to wear clothing of mixed material: such an "unnatural union is to despise the order of God's creation."[26] No hybridization is to be allowed, because again this arrogantly seeks to improve upon God's creation.[27] There are other controversial justice issues in the theonomist agenda, such as citizenship and civil rights. These will be examined in the following section on theonomic implications for the U. S. Constitution and the Bill of Rights.

How would the government be financed? Taxation would remain the principal method of civil income, yet the tax rates and amounts would be much less, according to Reconstructionists. The decrease would be due to the shift in the welfare burden and other social costs away from the government to more appropriate spheres such as the church. Also, the increased economic efficiency of a privatized theonomic nation would relieve many of the social ills currently treated by the government.

A final question logically asked of Reconstructionists concerns constitutional monarchy. If Israel is to be our model, then can we not have a king such as Saul, David, Solomon, and the rest of the royal line? The answer often given is that the Jewish king was allowable for Israel only because he was typological of Christ, the permanent and eternal King. As an earthly system, however, the godly, reconstructed polity is viewed as republican: it must be elected in keeping with the pattern given to Moses.[28]

Business and Economics

For Reconstructionists, "there is only Christian economics."[29] Any attempt to operate an economy on principles not grounded in Scripture's view of reality violates implacable moral and economic laws and will ultimately lead toward poverty. With this opinion many non-Reconstructionist Christians agree. However, the Reconstructionists do not merely advocate an economy based on a general biblical worldview, but presuppose the Mosaic law as the boilerplate for any economy at any time.

Private property rights, for example, are held to be biblically endorsed by the very fact that theft is divinely prohibited (theft implies the legitimate concept of ownership). Yet Reconstructionists call for a system which would be, were it not for stringent moral sanctions, virtually libertarian. Indeed, Rushdoony has classified himself as "close to being a libertarian."[30] Why? Because they see the Mosaic pattern of autonomous spheres as reducing the public sector; it becomes only one sphere of many, and even that sphere is limited to clear-cut issues of justice as described above. Industrial and other business spheres would be administered privately within their respective zones of expertise, unless exceptional cases called for a second opinion.

Gary North, a trained economist and the foremost Reconstructionist economic theorist, claims to see a marked correspondence between the Old Testament social order and the classical dicta of free market economics (concepts which, he and others have noted, were systematized from the Reformation culture):

We see the "privatized" nature of the biblical social order in the eighth commandment: "Thou shalt not steal." But we also find the foundational principles of a free economy in all the other nine commandments. The ten commandments are as fine a statement of the principles of liberty, including . . . voluntary exchange, as we can find anywhere in the history of man. The Old Testament is an anti-statist document. . . . Limited civil government is one of the two political preconditions of a free market economy. The other precondition is predictable law which places limits on civil government, which the ten commandments and the case laws also provide.[31]

North's broad principles for economic prosperity would raise few qualms from any morally-oriented, classic conservative political economist. His basic formula is that biblical ethics and social cooperation, a spirit of servanthood, and legal predictability will inevitably produce God's blessings of prosperity.[32] Controversy or uncertainty arises when he and others attempt to speculate on how specific points of the Mosaic law should be transferred from the ancient Hebrew culture into the future theocratic republic. For example, must each farmer rest the land during the sabbath year? North says no; only the principle should be retained. Land should be rested one year in seven, but this should not be uniformly enforced; the sabbath should be rotated among farmers. The same is true of sabbath year and jubilee debt cancellation.[33] The reasoning seems to be pragmatic—such a scheme fits more easily into a modern economy. Yet one may ask, Can pragmatism be put over God's law? Why did God not originally give North's revised form of the sabbath when speaking to Moses?

Significant changes in a reconstructed society from today's economic landscape would be:

Banking and finance would have tight limitations on debt.

Thirty-year mortgages would be outlawed.

There could be no reserve banking system, and no un-backed or partially-backed paper money. The most probable outcome would be a monetary system based on the gold standard.[34]

Harsh penalties would be instituted for lying and slander, since free-market business needs a reliable framework and honest ground-rules.

The tithe, not public taxes, would finance most social welfare.

And voluntary slavery would be allowed for reasons ranging from restitution to the simple desire of some for financial security.

WHAT WOULD HAPPEN TO THE U. S. CONSTITUTION?

Perhaps the most interesting paradox in contemporary theonomist literature is their view of the U. S. Constitution. On the one hand, the founding of the American republic and its political culture is praised because of the Puritan contribution. And the Constitution is lauded as an example of biblical principles in action, practically applied to the building of a new society. Yet a serious reading of Reconstructionism raises monumental doubts about the compatibility of its vision with the guarantees of liberty found in the Constitution, and even with the basic three-part structure of the U. S. Government. Would the Constitution even survive a theonomic reconstruction?

The first ten amendments would appear to face the quickest overhaul. The Bill of Rights is often applauded by theonomists, such as Gary DeMar.[35] But there would obviously need to be drastic modifications, especially in the First Amendment, which reads:

> Congress shall make no law respecting establishment of religion, or prohibiting the free exercise

thereof; or abridging the freedom of speech, or of the press; or the right of the people peaceably to assemble, and to petition the Government for redress of grievances.

The truly radical nature of the Reconstructionist agenda for America can be seen by simply comparing their positions with the first two points of the amendment. Although the theocratic nation would contain many who were not Christians, free exercise of their religion would be hazardous and unthinkable. Bahnsen, Rushdoony, and others typically list apostasy and idolatry as capital crimes and blasphemy as a major offense. Their definition of such acts is quite broad. Would a Buddhist be allowed to erect a public shrine? Would there be synagogues and mosques?

A larger question is the fate of many now considered orthodox Christians—dispensationalists, for example. To Greg Bahnsen, "Dispensationalism is as antagonistic as modern Protestantism and Romanism, though for different reasons, to the law of God."[36] Roman Catholicism, of course, is considered to be apostate by virtually all Reconstructionists. Yet here it is equated to dispensationalism in an adversary relationship to God's law. How serious a charge is this? Dispensationalists are seen by Reconstructionists such as Bahnsen to be antagonistic to God's law-order because they claim that the Mosaic law has been replaced with a new system and they totally repudiate the theonomic hermeneutic of abrogation (see chapter 2). Rushdoony declares that all who oppose the law-order in a theonomic society, including criminals and dissidents, are at war with the law-order and with society. Nothing is more heinous in a theocratic society than to openly question the law-order. The legitimate institutions must therefore react with "destruction" or other appropriate punishment to those with whom they are at war.[37]

Would dispensationalists, then, be welcome in any church? According to Rushdoony, dispensationalism is "unbelief and heresy."[38] Unrepentant dispensationalists would certainly be excommunicated. They would claim that the sabbath was no longer a requirement; that many social regulations were "legalism" and not now required by God. Many would be handed over to the civil authorities as those "at war" with the law-order. In other words, they would be criminals. Perhaps their crime would not be ruled as deserving of death. Even so, in a theonomic republic those considered to be criminals lose citizenship and many attendant rights. Rushdoony notes that in Puritan New England, exclusive citizenship was often based upon church membership.[39] In his words, "The right have the rights."[40]

Why do Reconstructionists not advocate taking present action against dispensationalists and other religious groups? In the postmillennial strategy, the law can only be applied in nations which are officially under the law and substantially reconstructed. Open societies are considered to be "missionary situations." The heretic is a candidate only for conversion until the nation is reformed.[41] How and when victory is declared is not stated, and is an interesting question in itself. But at the point at which the law is instituted, heresy is apparently transformed from a nonpunishable crime into "treason." From that moment, the First Amendment provision for religious pluralism would be a thing of the past for dispensationalists, amillennialists, and many other Christians, as well as for all non-Christian religious groups.

"Congress shall make no law . . . abridging the freedom of speech, or of the press. . . ." Would a public sermon interpreting Galatians 3 to refer to sanctification as well as justification be allowed? Would this not be an open declaration of war on the law-order? What about a newspaper editorial questioning the requirement against wearing shirts made with mixed types of thread or in favor of reserve banking? The answers to all such questions are the same: opposing the law-order must be met by criminal sanction. Forget the First Amendment.

These examples show the poor prospects for survival of the Bill of Rights in a theonomic America. But what of the main body of the Constitution? While separation of powers and federalism are definitely in harmony with Reconstructionism, many stipulations would obviously be rewritten to conform to the Mosaic law. Congress might retain the power to lay and collect taxes, but only within the limits set by the law. Even this might be heavily localized. The executive branch would perhaps undergo the most profound alteration. Some might see the president as analogous to Moses' role as the supreme judge. But then what of the Supreme Court? Also, many Reconstructionists might fear in the presidency the specter of human kingship, usurping the role of Christ.

The potential for endless debates by Reconstructionists over the fate of the Constitution is evident. The certainty is that the present document would not easily conform to any scheme attempting to graft it together with the theonomic ideal. To equivocate on this point is neither honest with the Old Testament nor with American historical and political reality.

CONCLUSION

No one really knows what a country controlled by Reconstructionists would be like. There are always questions of how many holding this viewpoint would be needed to really enforce it and how consistent with the theology those in power would be. As premillennialists, we much prefer to have the Lord Jesus himself ruling over the nations directly rather than have those who, however sincere, believe they are to rule on his behalf.

Chapter 4, Notes

1. Using David Chilton's prophetic time scale. David Chilton, *Paradise Restored: An Eschatology of Dominion* (Tyler, Tex.: Reconstruction Press, 1985), 221.

2. The plausibility of this scenario is based upon the combined interpretations by Gary North and Rousas J. Rushdoony of Deuteronomy 22:8; Exodus 21:38-42; Deuteronomy 17:7 and 21:21; see North, "In Defense of Stoning," *The Sinai Strategy* (Tyler, Tex.: Institute for Christian Economics, 1986), 122-25, and Rushdoony, *Institutes of Biblical Law*, vol. 2 (Vallecito, Calif.: Ross House Books, 1982), 350. Basically, the Deuteronomy 22 law requiring railings on rooftop porches is connected with liability laws and

penalties regarding habitually dangerous oxen. Then North's argument for the perpetual use of stoning as the divinely mandated form of execution is applied.

3. See Rushdoony, *Institutes*, vol. 2, 350-52. Rushdoony's interpretation of Exodus 21:20-27 is applied here, although on p. 352 he apparently reads the passage such that no punishment is taken even if the slave dies after lingering one or two days.

4. Chilton, *Paradise*, 226.

5. Ibid., 219.

6. Greg Bahnsen, *Theonomy in Christian Ethics* (Phillipsburg, N.J.: Presbyterian & Reformed Publishing Co., 1977, 1984), xx.

7. Ibid., xxi.

8. Rousas J. Rushdoony, *Intellectual Schizophrenia* (Phillipsburg, N.J.: Presbyterian & Reformed Publishing Co., 1961), 61.

9. Cited in Gary DeMar, *God and Government*, vol. 1 (Atlanta: American Vision Press, 1982), 29.

10. Gary North, *Unconditional Surrender* (Tyler, Tex.: Geneva Press, 1981), 221-22.

11. Ibid., 203-4.

12. DeMar, *God and Government*, 36.

13. North, *Unconditional Surrender*, 204.

14. Rousas J. Rushdoony, *The Institutes of Biblical Law*, vol. 1 (Phillipsburg, N.J.: Presbyterian & Reformed Publishing Co., 1973), 740f.

15. DeMar, *God and Government*, 36.

16. North, *Unconditional Surrender*, 228. Considering the practice of case law "principles" being constantly recodified to stay current with changing cultural and technological contexts, as Bahnsen and others advocate (see chapter 2), it is difficult to see how a ponderous bureaucracy would not be the result.

17. Ibid., 204.

18. DeMar, *God and Government*, 13.

19. Ibid., 14.

20. Ibid., 16.

21. Rushdoony, *Intellectual Schizophrenia*, 42.

22. Chilton, *Paradise Restored*, 229.

23. North, *Unconditional Surrender*, 206.

24. North, *Sinai Strategy*, 121-22.

25. Rushdoony, *Institutes*, vol. 1, 23.

26. Ibid., 87.

27. Ibid., 255.

28. DeMar, *God and Government*, 82.

29. Gary North, *Moses and Pharaoh* (Tyler, Tex.: Institute for Christian Economics), 1985, ix.

30. In an interview with Bill Moyers, aired 23 December 1987; transcript p. 5.

31. North, *Sinai Strategy*, 15.

32. For instance, see North, *Sinai Strategy*, 212-13, 227, 203, 125; and *Inherit the Earth* (Fort Worth: Dominion Press, 1987), 59.

33. North, *Sinai Strategy*, 85.

34. See Moyers's interview with Rushdoony, transcript p. 4.

35. DeMar, *God and Government*, 134. Much of the Bill of Rights was derived from natural law theory. North totally rejects natural law; see North, *Moses and Pharaoh*, 235ff.

36. Bahnsen, *Theonomy*, 21.

37. Rushdoony, *Institutes*, vol. 1, 92-94.

38. See Foreword to the second edition of Bahnsen's *Theonomy*.

39. Rushdoony, *Institutes*, vol. 1, 98-100.

40. Ibid., 92.

41. Ibid., 39.

PART 2

THE USE OF THE MOSAIC LAW IN THE CHURCH AGE

Chapter 5

An Evaluation of Reconstructionist Arguments on Theology and History

*I*n the following chapters we will examine the philosophical, theological, and historical arguments of theonomy. Then we will look at theonomy in light of the Old Testament covenants and law, the meaning of Matthew 5:17-20, as well as the teaching of Paul on the law. Finally we will examine whether Christians have a mandate from God, based on Genesis 1-2 and Matthew 28:18-20, to rule the earth, using "biblical law" during the present age.

The Excluded Middle

Bahnsen's relegation to antinomianism of all persons who reject his view is oversimplistic reductionism. He posits false extremes and then expects us to embrace theonomy to stay away from the deadly practice of antinomianism, even though he himself vacillates on what he means by law. But Christians are not restricted to a choice between two extremes, for there is a third position, the middle one, that Bahnsen excludes from his discussion. This choice is the law of Christ in the current age. This law is consistent with the law of God, even as the Mosaic law was, but its expression and application differ from previous manifestations of God's law. The charge of antinomianism can rightly be applied to those who reject all the commandments of God, but the rejection of the specific commands of the Mosaic codes along with their punishments does not a law-rejecter or law-breaker make. We shall see how this is so in the coming sections.

THEONOMY AND THE CHARACTER OF GOD

Tying the law to the nature of God is an important emphasis of theonomy and one we readily accept. All Christians should love and obey the law of God because the law reflects his character. As we previously stated, the issue is not whether Christians are to be obedient to the law of God but rather to which manifestation of his law are they to be obedient. There are different manifestations of the law of God given to different groups: to Israel and to the nations. Some of these laws are identical or at least similar, but the peoples of Israel and the nations are not under the provisions of the others' laws.

For example, if you were to go to an attorney with a friend to have a contract on land drawn up for each of you and you later examined each other's contract, you would find that many of the terms and provisions of the contracts were very similar if not identical. However, you are not bound to your friend's contract with its terms any more than that friend is bound to yours. You are bound to the specific contract that you made. Noah made a contract for the nations as their representative that has many provisions identical or similar to the terms of agreement which Israel adopted under Moses. The nations are not under the contract with God under Moses, however, but under the contract with God under Noah.

This is not to say that you cannot obey the laws given to Moses, but you are not obligated to them in order to be faithful to God. For example, if you lived in a state that had a speed limit of 55 miles per hour and you moved to a state that had a 65 miles per hour limit, you might still decide that 55 is a safer speed for you to drive. But you have no obligation to drive 55 in your new state, and by driving that speed you are not being obedient to the jurisdiction of your old state. You have simply applied the ideas of your old state to your new situation. In the same way, the law of Moses forbade certain foods which separated the Israelites from the Canaanites. Jesus and Paul said that all foods were clean, but you may decide to abide by some of the food laws of Israel for health reasons.

Moreover, the idea that the unchangeableness of God requires that the specific details of the Mosaic code be transferred to all times and cultures simply does not follow.[1] God expects his creation in general and his people in specific to conform to his character, for to fall short of God's character is sin (Romans 3:23). Beginning in the garden, God instructed mankind to obey his will (Genesis 2:15-17), and God's will or law was repeatedly revealed to mankind through divine visitations prior to Sinai. In addition, the conscience of man provided a general understanding of the demands of God upon his creation (Romans 2:12-16). In reaffirming his promise to bless Abraham and his descendants, God makes clear to Isaac that Abraham had been obedient to a pre-Mosaic revelation of God's law:

> "I will make your descendants as numerous as the stars in the sky and will give them all these lands, and through your offspring all nations on earth will be blessed, because Abraham obeyed me and kept my requirements, my commands, my decrees and my laws." (Genesis 26:4-5 NIV)

The later Mosaic covenant became a more specific expression of many provisions of God's will observed in the patriarchal period. But every revelation of God's law reflects his character, regardless of when it was given. Moreover, there is a basic consistency in God's law, with variations based only on cultural factors and God's purposes for mankind at the time the law is given.

Let us expand on this important point. It is agreed, as mentioned, that God's character never changes, and his law for man at any time flows from his perfect character. Willing obedience conforms to his character in that it conforms to his law. Revealed law contains many instructions—both principles and specific directives—which remain the same despite changes in temporal factors such as time, place, dispensation, or immediate divine purpose. These are continuities.

But God's law at any time also contains many instructions which are indeed specific to temporal factors. It is noteworthy that these factors, and the instructions connected with them, were contained within God's perfect purposes from eternity past. Because these specific, varying laws flow from God's eternal purposes, the fact that they vary cannot be inconsistent with his eternal nature. Rather than being inconsistent with his character, each expression of his law is perfectly suited to the unique period and circumstances into which he speaks it, whether one considers either the continuous or discontinuous aspects. Even the theonomists implicitly affirm this truth by admitting that God may reveal "abrogations" of previous commands. Theonomists would never claim that such abrogations—changes in God's instructions—deny God's immutability.

To use a human example, if a certain man is an excellent farmer and wishes to teach his son to follow in his footsteps, what will he teach him? Obviously, he will tell him that he must always work hard in any season; this is a continuity and is consistent with the father's character. (Likewise, God has never told man to stop worshiping him or loving one's neighbor.) But the farmer will also teach his son to express his constantly diligent work in different ways according to the season and the crop. He will not tell the son to plough and plant corn in the autumn or to try to harvest in winter. This would be absurd. He teaches him to plough in the season made for ploughing, and harvest in the season made for harvesting. To teach this is also obviously in keeping with the father's character. In the same way, Scripture shows God revealing different expressions of the law appropriate for different times; expressions and times which are segments of God's overall plan for history, a plan set in the unchanging granite of God's immutable nature. Conforming to God's will requires enough discernment of the Scriptures on our part not to attempt to plough when God has told us the season for ploughing is finished.

Let us now illustrate the previous idea by a few examples from Scripture. The taking of innocent human life was always a violation of God's standard for man. Genesis 9 tells us that the murderer's life is to be taken expressly because the murder of another human made in the image of God is a crime demanding the severest judgment. However, we observe God earlier in man's history not exacting that penalty from Cain. Though murder was still wrong, God did not demand a life for life there, but instead made Cain a vagabond.

The law of God given to Israel forbade adultery and required death by stoning for those guilty of its violation. This law and its penalty are clearly spelled out in the codes of Israel. But in the New Testament Jesus did not exact such a penalty on the woman caught in adultery. Rather he forced her accusers to look at their own sins. He was not fervent concerning the law as they desired.[2] Moreover, the apostle Paul did not ask the church to stone the man living with his father's wife, nor to turn him over to the civil magistrate, but instead to withdraw fellowship from him until he repented. At another place, Paul did not demand that the church or civil magistrate put to death heretics. No such leniency was provided in Israel.

The codes of Israel reflect the character of God in ceremonial, moral, and civil expressions; none of these manifestations are ever presented as superior to the others nor severable. These three are inseparable parts of the law of God for Israel. Paul in Colossians 2:16-17 states that Christians are not to allow themselves to be judged regarding the law, either in dietary practices of the law or the observance of the sabbath day. The writer of Hebrews says in chapters 4 and 10 that not only the "ceremonial law" is fulfilled in Christ but also the sabbath. The whole law was fulfilled in Christ, not just part of the law; it stands or falls as a whole.

This does not mean that Christians do not have law. But the basic laws of respect toward God and neighbor—continuities—demanded by the Mosaic law—discontinuities—are not expressed in the same way in the church age nor do they always exact the same penalty. Nowhere in the nations is capital punishment obligatorily extended beyond the penalty for taking human life, whereas in Israel this penalty was exacted for various crimes as may be seen from the enumeration given by Davis:

> In the Mosaic law the death penalty was prescribed for eighteen different offenses: murder (Exod. 21:12-14); causing the death of a pregnant woman, and possibly for causing the death of her child (Exod. 21:22-25); killing a person by a dangerous animal that had killed before, yet was not kept caged (Exod. 21:28-30); kidnapping (Exod. 21:16); rape of a married woman (Deut. 22:25-29); fornication (Deut. 22:13-21); adultery (Lev. 20:10); incest (Lev. 20:11-12, 14); homosexuality (Lev. 20:13); sexual intercourse with an animal (Lev. 20:15, 16); striking a parent (Exod. 21:15); cursing a parent (Exod. 21:17); rebelling against parents (Deut. 21:18-21); sorcery and witchcraft (Exod. 22:18); cursing God (Lev. 24:10-16); attempting to lead people to worship other gods (Deut. 13:1-16); avenging a death despite acquittal by the law (Deut. 17:12); intentionally giving false testimony against someone in jeopardy of the death penalty.[3]

THE HISTORICAL INTEGRITY OF
CHRISTIAN RECONSTRUCTIONISM

Modern theonomists are "sensitive to the charge of novelty,"[4] that is, that their view lacks historical precedent. This accounts for their appeals to Calvin, the Puritans, and the Westminster Confession as supportive of Reconstructionist theonomy. Do these three sources add credence to the Reconstructionists' claims?

Calvin

The evidence for such support from Calvin is, at best, mixed. Despite his controversial efforts to theocratize Geneva, Calvin called "stupid and false" and "perilous and seditious" the view that a government is not "rightly framed" if it does not follow "the law of Moses." Calvin's appeal to "the common law of nations" as a basis for state rule is rejected by Rushdoony, who accuses Calvin of "classical humanism," and "silly and trifling reasoning."[5]

It is clear that Calvin appealed repeatedly to the "law of God" and his "righteousness" as the essential premise of state rule.[6] However, it is unclear that Calvin and his reformation colleagues insisted on the articulation of Mosaic case law, with its penal enforcements, as mandatory for the state. Bahnsen approvingly quotes this statement of Calvin:

> Because the mortal lawgiver's jurisdiction extends only to the outward political order, his ordinances are not isolated, except when actual crimes are committed. But God, whose eye nothing escapes, and who is concerned not so much with outward appearance as with purity of heart, under the prohibition of fornication, murder, and theft, forbids lust, anger, hatred, coveting a neighbor's possessions, deceit, and the like.[7]

Bahnsen goes on to quote a similar passage from Luther, also approvingly. Bahnsen's conclusion, however, is that although "only God is in a position to judge and preside internal or personal sins," the Mosaic law calls for punishment not only of social crimes (murder, theft, etc.), but of personal sins committed publicly (blasphemy, rebellion to parents, etc.):[8]

> It is in the public realm of human society that the magistrate bears not the sword in vain. It would be

vain for him to assume the prerogative of judging
and punishing any and all sins, as if he were like
God and could know men's hearts. However, there
is firm grounding and good purpose in the magistrates' use of the sword for those crimes against
which God prescribes it. . . . [9]

It is unlikely that either Luther or Calvin would have
accepted Bahnsen's essential presupposition: that all the commandments of the Mosaic code, unless directly abrogated, are
applicable today. Indeed, such a conclusion runs counter to
their explicit statements. Note Luther on false teachers:

Temporal power does not force men to believe, but
simply prevents them from being misled by false
doctrine; otherwise, how could heretics be prevented
from preaching? I answer, this the bishops should
do, to whom, and not to the princes, such deity is
entrusted. [10]

Such statements fail to endear Luther to the Reconstructionists. Rushdoony comments that "the law suffered badly at
the hands of Martin Luther." Rushdoony, in fact, is disgusted
with virtually all the early Protestant leaders: "The Reformation
was . . . stillborn. . . . Such [antitheonomic] ideas common
in Calvinistic and Lutheran circles, and in virtually all churches,
are still heretical nonsense."[11]

But what of Calvin's efforts to theocratize Geneva? Those
efforts were significant for several reasons. Foremost is the
fact that his efforts failed:

Calvin's efforts to reform Geneva and the Genevans
naturally led to internal conflict. Not all the inhabitants were Calvinists, and even some of those who
agreed with him at times felt he carried his rigorous
demands too far. [12]

As noted by Earle E. Cairns, "Calvin used the state to inflict
. . . severe penalties. Such penalties proved to be much too
severe, 58 people being executed and 76 exiled by 1546."[13]

Calvin clearly distinguished between church and state. Although the state's authority in punishing crimes extended to areas considered by virtually all of Protestantism to be beyond the scope of its legitimate power, Calvin's Ecclesiastical Ordinances noted:

> let all be done in such a manner as to keep from the ministers [of the church] any civil jurisdiction whatever, so that they may use only the spiritual sword of the Word of God as St. Paul ordered them. Thus the consistory [spiritual leadership] may in no wise take from the authority of the officers of civil justice.[14]

The Ecclesiastical Ordinances go on to state that whereas the church may try spiritual offenders, the secular council "shall deliberate and then pass judgment according to the merits of the case."[15]

The Reconstructionist theonomists do not eliminate the state, either, though such a distinction appears superficial. The theonomic ideal is that the institutional church and the state are to be autonomous, coequal spheres within a theocentric context. In practice, however, the clergy would determine that theological context; anything else would risk doctrinal anarchy, or at least instances of conflict and crisis. The primacy of the visible church would be essential in areas of open heresy or false teaching. The reality is that in these and other instances, the state becomes merely an extension of both the invisible *and the visible* church. It punishes what the church condemns. This is what happened to Geneva, and it serves to underscore the tension between theonomic theory and hard reality.

One cannot help but conclude that Calvin's own thinking on church-state relations was confused. Calvin opposed implantation of the Mosaic law into civil life, yet advocated a government that could try and condemn heretics. Therefore, to infer historical precedent from Calvin's thinking and practice for modern theonomistic teaching is to ignore the ambivalence in Calvin himself.[16]

The Puritans

Reconstructionists consider the Puritans the decisive illustration of a Christian society. Bahnsen asserts that the premise of Puritan social policy was theonomic:

> the penal commandments of the law of God needed to be enforced by godly magistrates, for to fail in this matter was to violate God's righteous demand. The positive attitude of the Puritan's toward every stroke of God's law led them to oppose antinomianism in both theology and politics.[17]

Similar comments are made by James Jordan ("[the Puritans] turned unanimously to the judicials of Moses for their civil order") and Gary North ("The New England Puritans set forth the Old Testament law as the ideal for civil government, the family and the church").[18]

Though it is true the Puritans were generally theonomistic in outlook,[19] they found the system unworkable and eventually ended their quest to establish a theocratic society. Interestingly, the Puritans appealed to inner piety as the premise upon which a holy society could be built. Yet personal pietism is the target of some of the Reconstructionists' most vicious invective. Rushdoony labels pietism an "infection" and "paganism," and North and Chilton have called pietists "mush-mouthed, spineless, lily-livered, milksops."[20]

Some Reconstructionists champion obedience as the only concern of true Christianity. Bahnsen and Jordan seem more sympathetic to the view that the inner life has merit, and Reconstructionist Michael R. Gilstrap has warned, "It is my fear, however, that in our beehive of dominion activity, we often neglect the more personal and individual aspects of personal piety."[21] But Rushdoony, North, and their compatriots were ferocious in belittling it.

It is noteworthy that not all the Puritans were theonomists. Such Puritan luminaries as Henry Billinger and Samuel Rutherford argued that, in Billinger's words, "we should seem to show ourselves more than half mad" to seek to "thrust on and apply" Moses' judicial law "to other nations."[22]

It cannot be stressed too strongly that the Puritans themselves left mixed messages regarding the nature of theonomy. They did not always echo an identical theonomic perspective. Further, Puritan theocracy presupposed a community of the redeemed. The fact that the Puritan state collapsed into the influx of non-Puritan immigrants to the colonies testifies to the ineffectiveness of Puritan evangelism and, at least to a certain extent, the unattractiveness of Puritan society.

There were three Puritan sects: The *Nomists*, who maintained "an excessive adherence to the law"; *antinomians*, who asserted a "rejection of mandatory law-keeping"; and *orthodox Puritans*, who adopted a more moderate position.[23] While Reconstructionists give tacit admission to such diversity, they seem uncomfortable with it. Such diversity underscores the dubious nature of their claim to historical precedent, in that it reveals that there were cracks in Puritan society even before its downfall.[24]

While it cannot be denied that some Puritans were theonomistic, the movement as a whole was never in wholehearted agreement. Indeed, when the second colonial charter for the Massachusetts Bay Colony was approved in 1691, it "enlarged the franchise [electorate] beyond church membership, forced religious toleration, provided that the English crown appoint the governor, and allowed for popular election of councilmen (but anyone or all could be denied the election by a note from the governor)."[25] These are hardly the clarions of a theocratic state, and indicate that within some seventy years of the famous Puritan arrival at Plymouth, the dream of an American theocracy was evaporating.

As will be mentioned later, the Puritans, unlike the Reconstructionists, did not base their theocratic convictions on Matthew 5:17-20.[26] The Puritans' identification with Israel resulted in their fusion of church and state into a theocratic government. Matthew 5, the Reconstructionist text of texts, is not a Puritan prooftext.

The Westminster Confession

Greg Bahnsen devotes thirty-one pages of *Theonomy in Christian Ethics* to his argument that the historic Westminster Confession conforms to Reconstructionist theonomy. Of crucial importance to his study is understanding the revisions of the 1643 confession that took place in 1788. Those revisions fundamentally altered the original confession's position on the role of government. First, we must consider the original confession itself. The Westminster Confession of 1643 charges the civil magistrate to ensure that:

> unity and peace be preserved in the church, and that the truth of God be kept pure and entire, that all blasphemies and heresies be suppressed, all corruptions and abuses in worship and discipline prevented or reformed, and all the ordinances of God duly settled, administered, and observed.[27]

The confession goes on to state that the civil magistrate could call and be present at synods, and "provide that whatsoever is transacted in them be according to the mind of God."[28] The 1643 confession is clearly a theocratic, theonomic statement that assures a Christian government. The magistrate "may not assume" the "administration of the Word and sacraments, or the power of the keys of the kingdom of heaven," but is given freedom to do just about everything pertaining to the functioning of the church.

The 1788 Revisions. By 1729, the American Presbyterian church had grown wary of theonomy. Their 1729 Synod, according to A. A. Hodge, affirmed the Westminster Confession except for some clauses in the twentieth and twenty-third chapters, "Concerning the Civil Magistrate."[29] The 1788 Presbyterian General Assembly revised three chapters of the 1643 Confession, all of which related to the civil magistrate:

> The purpose of these revisions was to deny to the magistrate the right and power: (1) to proceed in judgment against individuals who would hold views

contrary in worship; (2) to suppress heresies and corruptions in worship; or (3) to call ecclesiastical synods, etc.[30]

The effect of the revisions was to carefully prescribe the relationship of state to church, to remove from the state any interference in ecclesiastical matters, and to prohibit the state from acting as the servant of the church.

In spite of these substantial changes, Bahnsen makes the astounding claim that "the new [1788] outlook was not significantly different from the older viewpoint."[31] To equate the American Presbyterians of 1788 with the English Puritans of 1643 is a remarkable and inaccurate rendering of history and reveals Bahnsen's shaky historical premise. It also reveals his unwillingness to deal with the facts. The 1788 revision directly changed the very specific theonomic contentions of the 1649 Confession.

In addition to his view of the text and intent of the Westminster Confession's church-state sections, Bahnsen and James Jordan also offer an unusual interpretation of the Westminster concept of "general equity" in the application of Israel's judicial laws.[32] "General equity" as used here is usually defined as the underlying principles of a text. The Reconstructionists carry it much further:

> Perhaps the best interpretation of [the concept of general equity] is to see it as affirming the necessity to apply the illustrations given in the Old Testament case laws to changed, modern situations and new social circumstances. . . . God has not stopped requiring social righteousness and justice; the law which He gave to define this justice has permanent validity. . . . So the civil magistrate is still required to execute just recompense upon criminals as dictated in the law of God (cf. Heb. 2:2), even if the crimes committed may have to be understood within a different set of social circumstances that pertain in modern America.[33]

Bahnsen concedes that "particular cultural expression"[34] found in the case laws is irrelevant to contemporary application, and Jordan also admits that "the confession is in error . . . in assuming that the Mosaic case laws were designed as a civil code for any nation."[35] However, neither writer is dismissing the case laws as such. Jordan asserts that the case laws were "explanations of the moral law, and thus form a foundation for civil codes,"[36] and Bahnsen's view of the concept of general equity is that "only the cultural connotations are invalid. We are still obligated to apply these case laws as illustrations cross-culturally to society today."[37] For example, the electric chair would be a relevant cultural means of implementing the death penalty, whereas stoning would not.

This understanding of general equity is controversial to say the least. It "contrasts with the reformed consensus that 'general equity' was referring not to the specific case laws as illustrations, but to the general moral principles underlying the case law as summarized in the Ten Commandments."[38]

THEONOMY AND THE ELEMENTS OF THE LAW

The general equity question gives rise to another issue: What elements of the Old Testament law do the theonomists wish to apply? The usual interpretation of the Mosaic code allows for three essential divisions: ceremonial law, civil law, and moral law.

The *ceremonial laws* are most often viewed as symbols of various aspects of the atonement made by and in Christ, and thus no longer practicable or relevant in the church today. Bahnsen takes a similar view and agrees with Calvin that "the meaning of the ceremonies is eternal, while their outward form and use are temporal; consequently Christ continues even the ceremonial law."[39] Bahnsen's use of "confirm" is unconventional and somewhat alters the traditional understanding that Christ, in his atonement, eliminated the need for the ceremonial practices (this will be discussed further in chapter 6). Nonetheless, Bahnsen concurs with mainstream orthodox thought that the ceremonial codes are inapplicable today.

Bahnsen also notes that "special imperatives" were given to specific individuals in certain situations (for example, Abraham's offering of Isaac). According to Bahnsen, however, to justify God's immutability, Abraham was always bound to offer Isaac whenever the "conditions are met."[40] It is unclear how Abraham would know when those identical conditions recurred.

Bahnsen's major argument relates to *moral law*, which he says reflects "God's absolute righteousness and judgment, but not showing the means of salvation 'per se' for sinners."[41] Bahnsen and Rushdoony believe the moral law should be divided into two categories, *summary laws*, which are broad and general (i.e., do not steal), and *case laws*, "which illustrate, define, and in some ways qualify the summary laws."[42] Whereas case laws have been traditionally understood to be strictly applicable to theocratic Israel and merely illustrative of general principles, Bahnsen and his colleagues would apply them today on a national basis:

> the governments of the world today should be guided in their judicial decisions by all the legislation of the Old Testament and, in particular, should assess the Old Testament penalties for any infraction to those laws, whether civil or religious.[43]

Rushdoony agrees with Bahnsen. In the words of R. Laird Harris, Rushdoony affirms that "if the moral law is binding . . . then the civil law is binding too, and upon governments and institutions as well as individuals."[44] As noted earlier, the application of case laws would, in Fowler's words, be "minus their cultural expressions." However, the necessity of their institutionalization would be absolute.

Beyond this, the multitude of questions and problems connected with the definition of the elements of the law has been examined in chapter 2.

As we have mentioned, in the view of the theonomists the judicial codes of the Old Testament are to be enforced by civil authorities. This is an extension of the Reconstructionists' view that Israel was not, in any unique way, a theocracy:

> Church and state are separated as to their functions in both Testaments of God's Word; thus the law which was valid in the older Testament cannot be invalidated in the New Testament on the basis of the principle of church/state separation. . . . Since Scripture speaks of Christ establishing justice in the earth we can speak of the Old Testament theocracy becoming in the New Testament a Christocracy with international boundaries.[45]

In this matter the theonomists are correct. Israel was not a strict theocracy with direct rule by God. Instead, it was a constitutional monarchy. The Mosaic code served as a constitution, the king as the executive of the civil law, the priests as the mediators of the religious law. The legal elements of these parts were not always strictly separated.

But this is not the essential question for whether the civil law of Israel should be practiced in contemporary nations. The real question is whether the Mosaic law given to Israel is to be practiced by any other nation not under the covenant. The answer is no! Certainly nations are to gain wisdom from observing Israel (Deuteronomy 4), and nations are to practice righteousness, commending good and punishing evil (Romans 13). But influencing a nation to follow the law of God and influencing a nation to follow the law of Moses are two different things (this matter is taken up further in chapter 7). God's law found in general revelation and special revelation may provide proper guidance for any people, and as Christians we should seek to have justice and righteousness prevail. But there is no call to make a modern Israel in America or in any other nation.

Chapter 5, Notes

1. For many years Old Testament scholars have recognized that the Mosaic covenant reflects a particular form of covenant that existed throughout the Near Eastern world, when a superior made an agreement with an inferior. This covenant was bilateral, with requirements posed on both sides of the agreement. The covenant would become void with a violation on the part of one of the parties, or if it were superseded by another covenant. The sabbath was probably the seal of the covenant and would remain in force so long as the covenant was in force. Christ has instituted a new covenant with a new law, though this law reflects the character of God even as the Mosaic covenant with Yahweh did. See the studies by Meredith Kline (*The Treaty of the Great King*, *By Oath Consigned*, and *The Structure of Biblical Authority*), Dennis J. McCarthy (*Treaty and Covenant*, *Old Testament Covenant*) and William J. Dumbrell (*Covenant and Creation*).

2. Theonomists have argued that Jesus' actions accord with Numbers 5:11-31, the procedure for a woman accused by her husband of adultery. However, as Moo demonstrates for several other instances in the Gospels, the presence of the Law-giver opens the possibility of "abrogation of laws" depending upon their "relationship to Jesus' teaching and to the new situation which his coming inaugurates." Douglas J. Moo, "Jesus and the Authority of the Mosaic Law," in *The Best in Theology* , ed. J. I. Packer.

3. John Jefferson Davis, *Evangelical Ethics* (Phillipsburg, N.J.: Presbyterian & Reformed Publishing Co., 1985), 198.

4. Ibid., 3.

5. Rousas Rushdoony, quoted in Lorne A. McCune, "Theonomy: A Critique of the Use of Matthew 5," Th.D. diss., Dallas Theological Seminary, 1984, 5-7.

6. Greg Bahnsen, *Theonomy in Christian Ethics* (Phillipsburg, N.J.: Presbyterian & Reformed Publishing Co., 1977, 1984), 2-4.

7. Ibid., 382.

8. Ibid., 381-83.

9. Ibid., 382.

10. Martin Luther, *Secular Authority: To What Extent It Should Be Obeyed*, in *Martin Luther: Selections from His Writings*, ed. John Dillenberger (Garden City, N.Y.: Anchor Books, Doubleday and Co., 1961), 389.

11. Rushdoony, quoted in McClune, "Theonomy," 6.

12. W. S. Reid, "Calvin," in *The New International Dictionary of the Christian Church*, ed. J. D. Douglas (Grand Rapids: Zondervan Publishing House, 1978), 178.

13. Earle E. Cairns, *Christianity Through the Centuries* (Grand Rapids: Zondervan Publishing House, 1981), 311.

14. John Calvin, *Ecclesiastical Ordinances*, in *The Protestant Reformation*, ed. Hans J. Hillerbrand (New York: Harper and Row, 1969), 178.

15. Ibid., 178.

16. McCune, "Theonomy," 2, n. 2.

17. Bahnsen, *Theonomy*, 549-53.

18. McCune, "Theonomy," 43-44.

19. Bahnsen, *Theonomy*, 549-53.

20. McCune, "Theonomy," 43-44.

21. Michael R. Gilstrap, "Dominion from Our Knees," *The Geneva Review*, March 1987, 2.

22. McCune, "Theonomy," 5, n. 4.

23. Ibid., 57-58.

24. Ibid., 8.

25. Ibid., 52.

26. Ibid., 69.

27. Quoted in David L. Neilands, "Theonomy and the Westminster Standards," *Journey Magazine*, November-December 1986, 13.

28. Ibid., 13.

29. Ibid.

30. Ibid., 14.

31. Bahnsen, *Theonomy*, 542-43.

32. This phrase is found in chapter 19, section 4: "To [Israel] also, as a body politic, [God] gave sundry judicial laws, which expired together with the state of that people: not obliging any other now, further than the general equity thereof." (Westminster Confession, quoted in Neilands, "Theonomy," 12.)

33. Bahnsen, *Theonomy*, 540-41.

34. Bahnsen, quoted in Paul Fowler, "God's Law Free from Legalism: Critique of *Theonomy in Christian Ethics*" (unpublished paper, n.d.), 3.

35. James Jordan, "Calvinism and the Judicial Law of Moses," *Journal of Christian Reconstruction* (Winter 1978-79):40.

36. Neilands, "Theonomy," 12.

37. Fowler, "God's Law," 3.

38. Ibid.

39. Bahnsen, *Theonomy*, 48-49.

40. Bahnsen, quoted in Douglas Chismar and David Rausch, "Regarding Theonomy: An Essay of Concern," *Journal of the Evangelical Theological Society* 27 (September 1984):319.

41. Bahnsen, *Theonomy*, 214.

42. Bahnsen, quoted in Chismar and Rausch, "Regarding Theonomy," 319-20.

43. R. Laird Harris, "Theonomy and Christian Ethics," *Covenant Seminary Review* 5 (Spring 1979):1, quoted in R. P. Lightner, "Theonomy and Dispensationalism," *Bibliotheca Sacra* (January-March 1986):27.

44. Harris, "Theonomy," 2.

45. Rushdoony, *The Institutes of Biblical Law* (Phillipsburg, N.J.: Presbyterian & Reformed Publishing Co., 1973), 739-81.

Chapter 6

Are Christians under the Mosaic Law?

THE MEANING OF MATTHEW 5:17-20: CHRIST FULFILLS THE LAW

The *Locus Classicus* of Jesus' Teaching on the Law

No passage of the New Testament is more important to theonomists than Matthew 5:17-20 (NIV):

> "Do not think that I have come to abolish the Law or the Prophets; I have not come to abolish them but to fulfill them. I tell you the truth, until heaven and earth disappear, not the smallest letter, not the least stroke of a pen, will by any means disappear from the Law until everything is accomplished. Anyone who breaks one of the least of these commandments and teaches others to do the same will be called least in the kingdom of heaven, but whoever practices and teaches these commands will be called great in the kingdom of heaven. For I tell you that unless your righteousness surpasses that of the

Pharisees and the teachers of the law, you will certainly not enter the kingdom of heaven."

The reason for this is that the coming of Christ appears
to bring a new order in New Testament teaching, and even
various statements and actions of Christ in the Gospel accounts
seem to indicate his rejection of a literalistic obedience to the
law (John 7:53-8:11; Matthew 12:1-14).

Bahnsen sees this Matthean text as the most important
for the thesis that the Mosaic law remains in force today for
Christians:

> The *locus classicus* pertaining to Jesus and the law
> is Matthew 5:17-20: in this familiar section Jesus
> speaks openly of His relation to the law of the Older
> Testament, the status of that law, and what the re-
> sponse of His disciples should be to that law. The
> theonomy of true kingdom righteousness is the heart
> of His teaching here.[1]

If Bahnsen's view on this passage is wrong, then his entire
thesis is in doubt. The interpretation of Matthew 5:17-20 centers
on at least five major questions:[2] (1) What is the message of
Matthew's Gospel? (2) What is the central thrust of the passage?
(3) What is the meaning of "Law and Prophets" in the text?
(4) What did Christ mean by his having come to "fulfill"? and
(5) How do verses 18-20 relate to verse 17?

The Message of Matthew's Gospel
In understanding the message of the Gospel of Matthew
one may discern that his work is deeply rooted in the Old
Testament. His Gospel has a primary function in proving Jesus
to be the Messianic King foretold in the Old Testament.
Matthew presents Jesus as the fulfillment and realization of all
that the Old Testament anticipates. With these points in view
one may better understand the meaning of Matthew 5:17-20
and how Jesus has "fulfilled" the Law and the Prophets.

Christ begins with a strong denial that he had come as a rebel, a rejecter of law, though he was often accused of being a lawbreaker (Mark 2:24; Luke 6:2). As Randy Gleason has said, "His sweeping modifications of three important institutions of the Mosaic Law (i.e. divorce—5:32; oaths—5:34; talion—5:39), his claim to stand in the place of Yahweh as lawgiver (7:24f), and his direct contrasts between the old and new (9:16f), all could easily lead to the mistaken notion that he was completely canceling the Law of Moses."[3]

Rather than being a rejecter of law, Christ had come to fulfill the law. Matthew's good news about Jesus is anchored, or is rooted, in the Old Testament. Matthew quotes more than fifty times from the Old Testament, mainly from the prophets. These Old Testament quotes and allusions reveal an intense interest in how Jesus fulfilled the purposes of God as Messiah-King. Matthew desires to show that the major events in Christ's life took place in fulfillment of prophecy.

Moreover, Matthew presents Jesus as the Messianic King. He begins (2:2) and ends (27:37) his book with reference to Jesus as the "King of the Jews." He is announced in Matthew 25:1-4 as the King who will judge the nations. He is also seen as the one who will rule as the Davidic King. The genealogy of the book set forth his royal lineage, demonstrating his right as David's descendant to sit on the throne. All of this is in fulfillment of the Messianic prophecies (e.g., Isaiah 9:7; 16:5; 32:1-4; Jeremiah 30:9).

Matthew's major purpose is to prove that the major events in the life of Jesus were in fulfillment of prophecy.[4] Other New Testament writers speak likewise, but Matthew is the most pronounced in this message that Jesus is the fulfillment of the Messianic hopes of the Old Testament. Because of this Matthew has been rightly called "the gospel of fulfillment."[5]

So then, when we look at Matthew's presentation of the Sermon on the Mount, we need to see that event, including 5:17-20, in light of the "fulfillment" motif.

The Significance of "I Have Come"

When Christ said "I have come" (5:17), he seeks to reveal his eschatological mission.[6] This is the major idea in verse 17 and is reflective of the theme of the Gospel of Matthew. This eschatological emphasis may be observed in Christ's consciousness of fulfilling the Old Testament and is surely setting the tone of 5:17-20 as a prophetic statement rather than a legal statement as is thought by the theonomists.

Jesus asserts that he had not come to *destroy* (or "abolish")[7] the Old Testament Scriptures (often identified as the Law and Prophets in the days of Christ)[8] but to fulfill them. The emphasis in 5:17 is not personal disobedience by "breaking the law" but rather the issue of "abrogating the law" as a system.[9] The "law" in this passage has prophetic import. Jesus does not mean that he is not moving beyond the law as a rule of life. In saying that he has not come to set aside the Old Testament Scriptures, Christ reveals his desire to stay within the history of redemption[10] rather than producing a movement with no Old Testament connection.

The Meaning of "the Law or the Prophets"

The expression "the Law or the Prophets" in Matthew 5:17 refers to the whole of the Old Testament canon.[11] This was a standard meaning during the fifth to third centuries B. C., as well as during the Maccabean period and at the Dead Sea community at Qumran.[12] "Law and/or Prophets" is used ten times in the New Testament in reference to the Old Testament.[13] Luke used Moses as a metonymy for the law three times when referring to the Old Testament (i.e., "Moses and the prophets," 16:29; 16:31; 24:27). Occasionally the Pentateuch, historical books, and prophetic books, and the wisdom and poetical books are referred to as "the Law of Moses, the Prophets and the Psalms" (Luke 24:44).

Bahnsen insists that the use of law in Matthew 5:17 refers to ethical stipulations. Several problems exist for this position. Most often in the New Testament "the Law and the Prophets" are "cited for their prophetic value as witnesses to the Messiah and the eschatological fulfillment He brings."[14] The message of the Gospel of Matthew suggests that "the Law or the Prophets" in Matthew 5:17 is to be understood in the prophetic sense. Lastly, the meaning of *plēroō*, discussed below, and its attachment to "the Law or the Prophets" favors the prophetic over the ethical use of the phrase.

In Matthew 5:17, the idea of "Law" in the prophetic sense should not surprise us. The Pentateuch is replete with prophetic elements. The proto-evangel (Genesis 3:14-15) prophesied of Jesus, declared Paul (Galatians 4:4). The Abrahamic Covenant includes prophecy referring to Christ (Genesis 12:1-3; 13:15; 17:8), a point that Paul substantiates in Galatians 3:16. Christ fulfilled Messianic predictions by Jacob (Genesis 49:10) and Moses (Deuteronomy 18:15-19). The Levitical offerings referred to Christ according to the writer of Hebrews (10:1f; cf. 8:4-5; 9:8-9, 23). The Passover was fulfilled by Jesus through his death (Luke 22:16; cf. 1 Corinthians 5:7; John 1:29). Last, Jesus himself said he fulfilled what was spoken of in the Law (Luke 24:44).

So then, though the use of the phrase "the Law and the Prophets" may carry an ethical connotation, usually it refers to the Old Testament with its promises in view.[15] This is not to deny that the ethical demands of the law are included within this statement, but the fulfillment is prophetic rather than ethical.

The Meaning of "Fulfill" and "Abolish"
Bahnsen argues that "fulfill" means to "confirm and restore in full measure." He says that Jesus established and restored the law to full measure as the rule of life for believers as well as society. He contends this is the meaning found in some Septuagint references and in four New Testament passages (Romans 15:19; 2 Corinthians 10:6; James 2:23; Revelation 3:2).

The way in which Jesus came to fulfill the Law and the Prophets is different from that envisioned by Bahnsen. The basic meaning of the Greek word *plēroō* is to "fill," in the sense of filling a bottle with water.[16] It may also mean to finish or complete something already begun. Prophecies or promises[17] and God's will[18] are all things that may be "fulfilled." Bahnsen's argument that *plēroō* means "to establish" or "to confirm" does not agree with the evidence.[19] *Plēroō* is never used in the Septuagint to render the Hebrew word *qûm*, meaning to "establish" or "confirm."[20] Rather, about seventy times in the Septuagint *plēroō* translates the Hebrew word *mâlê'*,[21] literally meaning "fill, be full."[22] A study of a concordance for the Septuagint reveals that none of the Hebrew terms for "confirm" are translated by any of the Greek terms for "fulfill" and none of the Hebrew terms for "fulfill" are translated by any Greek term for "confirm." More significantly, there are no examples in the New Testament which clearly indicate "confirm" as a possible meaning.[23]

The predominant use of "fulfill" in Matthew's Gospel denotes the fulfillment of divine prophecies in the Old Testament. Of the sixteen times that Matthew uses *plēroō*, twelve are undeniably used in a prophetic sense.[24] Other than 5:17, the three other debatable occurrences of "fulfill" are 3:15, 13:48, and 23:32. In Matthew 3:15, the idea of prophetic fulfillment is most likely since other words were used by Matthew for "obey" (*pŏein*: 5:19; 7:12, 21, 24; 8:9; 12:50; 19:16; *tērein*: 19:17; 23:3; 28:20; and *phylassein*: 19:20). The baptism of Christ did not fulfill any Old Testament command. His baptism, and attendant theophanies of 3:16-17, allude to Messianic prophecies (Isaiah 42:1; 44:2; Psalm 2:7); the sense of "fulfill" at Christ's baptism is probably eschatological.

Matthew 13:48 has "fulfill" signifying the filling of a net with fish. Here the term has a nontheological meaning (though the parable is one of eschatological significance). Matthew 23:32 refers to the Pharisees "filling up" the measure of sin that their fathers did (though here there is a reference to the prophets). Thus, even these two noneschatological uses of "fulfill" may have been used due to the eschatological context in which the word is found.

Even the non-Matthean examples do not necessarily mean "confirm." James 2:23 probably means "perfected" or "completed" since *plēroō* and *teleioō* are synonyms in the New Testament. Abraham's faith was completed by his obedience, in that his obedience gave evidence to his faith. In 2 Corinthians 10:6 and Revelation 3:2, "fulfill" means to "carry out" or "bring to completion" acts of obedience. Romans 15:19 talks of Paul "filling up" the area from Jerusalem to Illyricum with the gospel by his preaching. Even the example of 1 Kings 1:14 probably does not carry the meaning "confirm" in Bahnsen's sense of "restore" or "reestablish." The Hebrew term here, *mâlê'*, may be translated "fill in." By filling in Bathsheba's words Nathan would be substantiating her words but not reestablishing them.

Jesus should be seen as saying that contrary to the thoughts of some that he was a novel messiah in rebellion to the Scriptures, he was in the flow of God's redemptive work. He had not come to set aside the Old Testament Scriptures, but was the divine "fulfiller" of them.

Apart from the lexicographical considerations of *plēroō*, Bahnsen seeks to support his claims for "confirm" by contrasting the term "fulfill" with the antonym "abrogate": "the thought of confirming (or establishing) constantly recurs in this catalogue of antonyms for abrogate. . . ."[25] Furthermore, Bahnsen says, "ou . . . alla" indicate that *plēroō* and *kataluō* must be directly contrary in meaning.[26]

Bahnsen has jumped to a hasty and incorrect conclusion concerning the nature of opposites. Grammatical contrasts often merely speak of differences, not exact opposites. For example, Jesus' statement, "Do not lead us into temptation, but deliver us from the evil one," does not contrast exact opposites. Under Bahnsen's system, the Greek word for "deliver" cannot mean the obvious, but must be the exact opposite of "lead" ("to mislead, delude,") rather than the proper antonym, "follow."

We should understand the expression of Jesus as a Hebraistic manner of speaking, in which one of two alternatives is negated but not negated absolutely; it is negated for comparison, with another alternative given more emphasis or importance.[27] For example, Hosea 6:6 says, "I desire mercy, not sacrifice" (NIV). We should not, however, understand Hosea to be saying that Yahweh did not want sacrifice at all, but that he more greatly desired mercy.

A good comparison to the usage of Matthew 5:17 is the statement of Jesus in Matthew 10:34: "Do not think that I came to bring peace on the earth; I did not come to bring peace, but a sword." Here we have a close parallel to Matthew 5:17, including the eschatological "I have come." Moreover, like 5:17, it is introduced by the same "never think that" prohibition (including *ou*), and the adversative "but" (*alla*), contrasting "peace" and a "sword." Surely this passage is not saying Jesus in no way came to bring peace (cf. John 16:33). "Peace" and "sword" are not exact opposites. "Sword" is used to symbolize the opposite of "peace" only in the sense of persecution.

Likewise, "to abolish" in Matthew 5:17 in contrast with "to fulfill" does not prohibit the idea that by fulfilling "the Law and the Prophets" Jesus could not still in some sense set aside the law. If "abolish" is used in the absolute sense, then the Old Testament could not be set aside in any way, in contradiction to several New Testament passages (e.g., Romans 10:4; Hebrews 10:9; 8:6; 7:12; 8:13; 2 Corinthians 3:10) and even contrary to the thinking of many theonomists on the passing away of the ceremonial law.

Bahnsen's contention that the setting aside of the law in Romans 10:4 is setting aside the law as a way of righteousness[28] does not follow since the law was *never* a means of attaining righteousness.

Lastly, Jesus on several occasions during his earthly ministry changed aspects of the law. In Mark 7:19 he repeals the dietary laws (Leviticus 11) of the Old Testament. In the context he explains that defilement has nothing to do with what a man eats but the source of true defilement is the heart: "Thus he declared all foods clean," clearly abrogating the distinction between clean and unclean animals.

Bahnsen has said, "The Christian shares responsibility not only for promoting obedience to God's law but also for its enforcement."[29] However, Jesus does not deal with sinners in such a way. For example, in his contact with the Samaritan woman, an adulteress (cf. John 4:17f), he desires to bring her forgiveness, not the stoning of the Mosaic requirements (Leviticus 20:10; Deuteronomy 22:21, 23) The sinful woman in the house of Simon (Luke 7:36-50), most likely a prostitute, should have received the same punishment. Jesus did not endeavor to make sure the Mosaic penalty would be exacted, but he should have done so according to the logic of Bahnsen's position. Deuteronomy 12:5-14 makes clear that the place of worship was to be strategic to Israel's worship, but Christ rescinds this in John 4:21-24. Deuteronomy 18:20 teaches that false prophets were to be stoned, but Matthew 13:27-30 teaches that true and false were to be allowed to grow together until the angels do the judging (13:41). Other examples could be provided.

Bahnsen's Argument for the Enduring Nature of the Law in Matthew 5:18

Concerning the jot and tittle of 5:18, Bahnsen says, "Not even the very least extensive number of the very least significant aspect of the Older Testamental law will become invalid until heaven and earth pass away!"[30]

He believes that the two clauses "until heaven and earth pass away," and "until all things come to pass" are functional equivalents. He translates the verse, "For truly I say to you, until heaven and earth pass away (i.e.) until everything has taken place, not one iota or one horn will by any means become invalid."[31]

The Temporal Nature of the Mosaic Law in Matthew 5:18: An Answer to Bahnsen

A major problem with Bahnsen's position is his translation of the Greek verb *genetai* as "invalid." This translation is simply unwarranted according to its lexical definition. The word means to "become," or here "pass away."[32]

A better interpretative translation would be: "Until heaven and earth pass away [i.e. within that time span], not one jot or tittle shall pass away from the law until all things [jots and tittles of God's whole Old Testament counsel] come to pass [or are realized, fulfilled]."[33] Within the framework of all time, not the smallest detail of the law will pass away until everything is fulfilled; at this time it can then pass away.

How Do Christians Outperform the Pharisees?

Obedience to the commandments. Until such time that all is accomplished, however, persons are to keep the commandments of the Old Testament, but this is not just the law. God's requirements were in force until the "Lord of the law," brought a better testament or covenant. Then the disciples were to keep whatever he commanded them (Matthew 28:20).

Righteousness beyond the Pharisees. This passage was a rebuke to the Pharisees but no doubt was demoralizing to the disciples. How could anyone outperform the law? The Pharisees were meticulous in observance of the law of Moses, but then Jesus in 5:21-28 shows that they fell short of the inward observance of the heart. Christ sought to cause the disciples to see their spiritual inability to obey the law. The first beatitude identified the essential element needed by the faithful, "recognition of one's own spiritual incapacity to save oneself." Christ's commandments were beyond the demands of any legal system and no one could obey them. One could only stand in Christ's righteousness, not one's own. It is to the righteousness found in Christ that Paul referred when he considered his righteous observance of the law as a Pharisee to be rubbish (Philippians 3:5-6). He had found another righteousness: "But now apart from the Law the righteousness of God has been manifested, being witnessed by the Law and the Prophets" (Romans 3:21).

CHRISTIANS ARE NOT UNDER THE LAW
ACCORDING TO THE APOSTLE PAUL

Paul Taught that the Law of Moses
Has Been Set Aside

Paul says that the law of Moses has been set aside with the completed work of Christ. The Jews understood him to be "persuading the people to worship in ways contrary to the Law," and that he was teaching "all the Jews who live among the Gentiles to turn away from Moses" (Acts 18:13; 21:20-29). Though Paul's accusers may have misunderstood him, the accusation surely is based on statements and actions of Paul that gave rise to such thinking, even as the declaration of the Jews against Jesus' claim to deity was based on his words and actions that gave them reason to understand him in that way. We shall look at various texts from the Pauline writings to determine to what extent his teachings and actions confirm what his enemies thought.

The first major text to examine is Romans 6:14f. Bahnsen says that this passage is "the most 'sloganized' verse in the dispensationalist's polemic."[34] Bahnsen says that Paul's expression about not being under law "is to take a legal system and its demands *for your reckoning* before God."[35] However, if this were true, then even Israel was not under law since no one has ever been saved by the law but always by grace.

The Hebrew word for grace, *chen* (the major translation of *charis* in the Septuagint), occurs twenty-seven times in the Pentateuch. Certainly Yahweh was gracious toward Israel and they were saved by grace, but they are never said to be under grace; however, they were, Paul argues in Galatians 3:25, under law (*hupo nomon*). Though they were not under law as a means of justification (Galatians 3:21), they were under it as a rule of life. If under law means in Romans 6:14 what it means in 3:23, Christians are not "under the law" as a rule of life.

In Romans 7:4-6, the apostle Paul indicates that Christians have died to the law in order that we might belong to another, the resurrected Lord, and thus live in the Spirit. In the analogy of verses 1-4, the first husband is the Lord before his death and resurrection, before the age of the Spirit, before he had fulfilled all things. The second husband is the resurrected Lord after which the law was no longer in force. The law was ordained by God and was good, but this "old way" was a written code, while the new way is by the Spirit (7:6).

In Romans 10:4 Paul indicates that "Christ is the end of the law so that there may be righteousness for everyone who believes" (NIV). Bahnsen interprets the passage as saying,

> this verse declares, not that Christ terminates any and all obligation to the law of God, but that Christ is the end of the law as a way of righteousness. The believer is imputed with the righteousness of Christ which comes by faith; he does not earn it by the works of the law, for if righteousness came through the law, then Christ died needlessly (Gal. 2:21). Law-righteousness is terminated by faith-righteousness, but Paul does not say that the law is terminated in all respects for the believer (only as a personal way to justification).[36]

The apostle, however, is *not* saying that Israel was ever made righteous by the law before Christ. Instead he argues that some did not accept the righteousness that comes from God (10:3) and sought to use the law as a means. The word "end" is the Greek word *telos* so that this is almost an exact parallel with Matthew 5:17, since *telos* probably should be translated "goal" or "fulfillment."[37] Bahnsen's statement that Christ is the "termination" of the law as a way of righteousness will not hold since the idea that it ever was such is totally absent in, and contrary to, the text.

Paul in 1 Corinthians 9:19-23, especially verse 20, expresses his willingness to put himself under the law (clearly the whole Mosaic law), though he was not under it, to be able to reach those under the law. Surely this is not law as a means of righteousness, for Paul would not contradict his very gospel through such acts by pretending that legal observance would gain standing with God. To be under the law, then, must mean obedience to law as a rule of life. Even though he was not under the law as a requirement (he could follow it or not as he desired), he was always under the law of Christ, obviously different from the Mosaic law. Interestingly, Bahnsen deals little with this passage in his brief four mentions of parts of it.

Bahnsen and Rushdoony often make the point that one cannot be justified by observing the law, but one is sanctified by observing the law. For example, Bahnsen says, "the Christian is obligated to keep the whole law of God as a pattern of sanctification. . . ."[38] Rushdoony argues, "Salvation is by the grace of God through faith, and sanctification is by law."[39] Galatians 2:19-3:5 teaches otherwise:

> For through the law I died to the law so that I might live for God. I have been crucified with Christ and I no longer live, but Christ lives in me. The life I live in the body, I live by faith in the Son of God, who loved me and gave himself for me. I do not set aside the grace of God, for if righteousness could be gained through the law, Christ died for nothing!

> You foolish Galatians! Who has bewitched you? Before your very eyes Jesus Christ was clearly portrayed as crucified. I would like to learn just one thing from you: Did you receive the Spirit by observing the law, or by believing what you heard? Are you so foolish? After beginning with the Spirit [rather than by observing the law], are you now trying to attain your goal by human effort [by observing the law]? Have you suffered so much for nothing—if it really was for nothing? Does God give you his Spirit and work miracles among you because

you observe the law [present tense], or because you
believe what you heard? (NIV)

The law cannot justify according to 2:16, but as 2:19
says, "I die to the law to live to God." Galatians 3:2 says we
began the Christian life (justification) by faith and are not able
to continue the Christian life (continuance of Spirit's work
among you) by observing the law. No, it too is by faith. As
Russell Bowers says, "'an adoption of the Jewish cycle of
feasts and fasts,' i.e., adoption of the Mosaic Law as the
pattern for sanctification, is totally out of place."[40]

Christ came under the law to redeem those under the law
(Galatians 4:4-5). When we were children (under the law) we
were in slavery under the basic principles of the world. Paul
is afraid the Galatians were in the process of turning back to
these "weak and miserable principles." What were these? They
appear to be the "flesh" and the "law" (cf. Romans 8:3):

> What then were the 'elements of the world' to which
> the Jews, prior to the 'fulness of time,' were in
> bondage? In light of our previous discussion of
> *stoicheia*, we may put the question in this form:
> What did Paul regard as basic forces inherent in the
> world, considered as a temporary structure of things
> and ineffectual for salvation, to which the Jews were
> in bondage? It would appear that there are especially
> two such forces in the mind of the Apostle, namely,
> the Law and the Flesh. This is already suggested by
> Gal. 6:14, the only other place where Paul uses the
> term 'world' in this letter, where both of these factors
> must be considered as structurally involved in the
> world to which he had been crucified, the Law as
> represented by circumcision and the Flesh as that
> in which Paul's opponents wished to glory (12,
> 13). . . . It seems probable, therefore, that Paul re-
> gards the law and the flesh as the two fundamental
> cosmical forces to which the Jewish Christians, prior
> to Christ's redemption, had been in bondage, and

from which they were now redeemed by Christ and through Him given a new existence in the Spirit.[41]

In Ephesians 2:14-22, Paul reminds the Gentiles that they were once excluded from Christ, citizenship in Israel, and the covenants. What kept them on the outside was the "dividing wall of hostility" caused by "the law with its commandments and regulations." Bahnsen attempts to prove that only the ceremonial law (laws concerning sacrifices, temple, priesthood, and so on) is in view. But the text nowhere implies only the ceremonial law. Acts 15:19-21 shows that more than the ceremonial law caused division, and Acts 10:9-16 demonstrates that it was not the only segment which was abolished. Second, the law in Scripture is viewed as a unit; in reality the so-called civil, moral, and ceremonial laws often become difficult to separate from one another. Hogg and Vine perceptively state: "The law is not to be conceived of as a bundle of separate strands, whereof if one be broken the rest may still remain intact, but rather as a sheet of glass which, if it be broken in any part, is broken as a whole.[42] Sanders elucidates further:

> When Paul says that the law kills or that Christians die to the law, the statements include all the law. He does not distinguish between the ritual law (to which one dies) and the moral law (which remains). Nor does he distinguish between the law as abused through self-righteousness and the law as fulfilled in the right spirit. It is not a precise statement of Paul's view to say that one dies to only one function of the law.[43]

Paul tells the Colossian Christians that Christ on the cross "canceled the written code, with its regulations." Thus they should let no one judge them on what to eat or drink, religious festivals, or Sabbath days (all being matters of the Mosaic law). Again he uses the phrase "basic elements of the world," tying it to not submitting to rules of "do not handle, do not taste, do not touch."

**Paul Set Aside the Enforcement
of the Law in His Ministry**

Bahnsen argues for the duty of the Christian to enforce the law through the civil magistrate:

> The Christian must take it upon himself to encourage, exhort, and demand obedience to God's holy standards of morality in home, church, society, place of employment, and nation. . . . The Christian shares responsibility not only for promoting obedience to God's law but also for its enforcement. . . . They must also exhort governmental officials to enforce God's righteous law by imposing divinely prescribed punishments upon violators of God's law.[44]

The law of Moses teaches that "if a man sleeps with his father's wife . . . the man and the woman must be put to death" (Leviticus 20:11). In 1 Corinthians 5 this sin occurred, but Paul's punishment is to turn the man over to Satan (5:5) by expulsion from the church (5:7, 13). He even says judgment of those outside the church is not the church's business (5:12). If the sinner of 2 Corinthians 2:5-11 is the same person, then the church was ultimately supposed to restore him to fellowship. Such would have been impossible had the Mosaic penalty been carried out.[45]

Deuteronomy 18:20 says if a prophet "presumes to speak in my name anything I have not commanded him to say . . . [he] must be put to death." However, in the New Testament Hymenaeus and Philetus "wandered away from the truth," saying "that the resurrection has already taken place" and so destroying the "faith of some" (2 Timothy 2:17f); yet Paul does not urge their death. Rather he wishes that they will come to their senses and escape the trap of the devil (2 Timothy 2:24-26).

CONCLUSION

The Christian is to love the law of God. Grace does not free the believer from obedience to the will of God. However,

Christians are not under the expression of the law as it was given to Israel. Instead, we may use the Mosaic legislation as examples of how we may respond individually and corporately; we may gain wisdom from it. Christians are, however, to obey the will of God as it is expressed in the New Testament—the law of Christ—and the law revealed in the Adamic and Noahic covenants.

Chapter 6, Notes

1. Bahnsen, *Theonomy in Christian Ethics* (Phillipsburg, N.J.: Presbyterian & Reformed Publishing Co., 1973), 39.

2. Acknowledgment is given to Randy Gleason, a doctoral student in Wayne House's seminar on Theonomic Ethics, for his delineation of these.

3. Randy Gleason, "A Critique of the Theonomic Use of Matthew 5:17-20" (unpublished paper, 1988), 6, in paraphrasing John P. Meier, *Law and History in Matthew's Gospel* (Rome: Biblical Institute Press, 1976), 66.

4. Donald Guthrie, *New Testament Introduction* (Downers Grove, Ill.: InterVarsity Press, 1970), 25.

5. Lorman M. Peterson, "Gospel of Matthew," *The Zondervan Pictorial Encyclopedia of the Bible*, 5 vol., ed. Merrill C. Tenney (Grand Rapids: Zondervan Publishing House, 1976), 4:128.

6. John P. Meier, *Law and History in Matthew's Gospel* (Rome: Biblical Institute Press, 1976), 66.

7. William F. Arndt and F. Wilbur Gingrich, *A Greek-English Lexicon of the New Testament and Other Early Christian Literature* (Chicago: The University of Chicago Press, 1979), 414.

8. Meier, *Law and History*, 70.

9. The closest parallel to the idea of "rescindment" of law rather than disobedience to it is found in 2 Maccabees 2:22; 4:11; and 4 Maccabees 5:33.

10. D. A. Carson, "Matthew," in *The Expositors Bible Commentary*, vol. 8 (Grand Rapids: Zondervan Publishing House, 1984), 142.

11. John Murray, *Principles of Conduct* (Grand Rapids: Wm. B. Eerdmans Publishing Co., 1957), 149; usually the word *Law* means the Pentateuch. Hermann Kleinknecht and W. Gutbrod, *Biblical Key Words from Gerhard Kittel's Theologisches Worterbuch zum Neuen Testament: Law* (London: Adam & Charles Black, 1962), 79.

12. Norman L. Geisler and William E. Nix, *A General Introduction to the Bible*, rev. ed. (Chicago: Moody Press, 1986), 247.

13. Four times in Matthew: 5:17; 7:12; 11:13; 22:40; once in Luke: 16:16; once in John: 1:45; three times in Acts: 13:15; 24:14; 28:23; once in Paul: Romans 3:21.

14. Meier, *Law and History*, 71. Cf. Matthew 11:13; Luke 16:16; 24:27; 24:44; John 1:45; Acts 13:15 in context; 24:23; 28:23; Romans 3:21.

15. Kleinknecht and Gutbrod, *Biblical Key Words*, 79.

16. Gerhard Delling, "Plēroō," *Theological Dictionary of the New Testament*, vol. 6, ed. Gerhard Kittel and Gerhard Friedrich (Grand Rapids: Wm. B. Eerdmans Publishing Co., 1964-1976), 286.

17. Arndt and Gingrich, *Greek-English Lexicon*, 670-72.

18. Reinier Schippers, "Fullness," *The New International Dictionary of New Testament Theology*, vol. 1, ed. Colin Brown (Grand Rapids: Zondervan Publishing House, 1975), 734.

19. See Bahnsen, *Theonomy*, 67-68. The only exception is one reference in 1 Kings 1:14 (LXX). Schippers, "Fullness," 1:734.

20. Delling, "Plēroō," 293; and Robert Banks, *Jesus and the Law in the Synoptic Tradition* (London: Cambridge University Press, 1975), 210.

21. Delling, "Plēroō," 287.

22. Francis Brown, S. R. Driver, and Charles A. Briggs, *A Hebrew and English Lexicon of the Old Testament* (Oxford: Clarendon Press, 1906), 569-70.

23. See Carson, "Matthew," 142-44.

24. 1:22; 2:15, 17, 23; 4;14; 8:17; 12:17; 13:14 (*anaplēroō*), 35; 21:4; 26:54, 56; 27:9.

25. Bahnsen, *Theonomy*, 67. Delling should be given careful consideration when he says, "The meaning of [*plēroō*] in Matthew 5:17 cannot be determined simply by the contrast with [*katalpsoosi*]."

26. Ibid., 65.

27. Gary D. Long, *Biblical Law and Ethics: Absolute and Covenantal* (Rochester, N.Y.: Backus Book Publishers, 1981), 20- 22.

28. Bahnsen, *Theonomy*, 223.

29. Ibid., 476.

30. Ibid., 73.

31. Ibid., 81.

32. Arndt and Gingrich, *Greek-English Lexicon*, 160-61.

33. Paul Fowler, "God's Law Free from Legalism: Critique of *Theonomy in Christian Ethics*" (unpublished paper, n.d.), 78.

This suggested translation is based upon several understandings of the Greek grammar. First, *pante* ("all things") finds its antecedent in "one jot or tittle" of the law. The third singular verb *parelthe* suggests that "jot [neuter] and tittle [feminine]" were collectively considered to be a neuter plural because a neuter plural subject takes a third singular verb. Thus "jot and tittle" serves as the antecedent to *pante*, a neuter plural substantive, functioning as an adjective.

The verb *genetai* ("come to pass") is used in the sense of "coming to pass of prophesied events." (Meier, *Law and History*, 54.) It is used this way in Matthew several times (1:22; 21:4; 24:6, 34; 26:54, 56). For example a parallel to 5:18 is 24:34, "This generation will not pass away until all these things take place." *Genetai* (5:18) is parallel to *pleroo* (5:17), reiterating the same basic thought of prophetic fulfillment. A similar passage is Matthew 1:22 where the two verbs are used together: "Now all this took place (*genetai*) that what was spoken by the Lord through the prophet might be fulfilled (*pleroo*)."

Thus both terms describe together how Jesus fulfilled Scripture by his coming. There are, then, two temporal clauses. The first, "until heaven and earth disappear" simply means "never, until the end of time," but is qualified by the second temporal clause, "until everything is fulfilled." Within the framework of all time, not the smallest detail of the law will pass away until everything is fulfilled; at this time it can then pass away.

Finally, the "Law" probably refers to more than the Mosaic legal codes (Arndt and Gingrich include Matthew 5:18 among the verses listed for *nomos* standing for the entire Old Testament [Arndt and Gingrich, *Greek-English Lexicon*, 543]) since it is in the same verse with "the Law and the Prophets" in verse 17; it probably refers to the entire Old Testament (cf. John 10:34; 12:34; 15:25; 1 Corinthians 14:21; Romans 3:19; Luke 16:17). The prophetic portions of the law concerning the Messiah would eventually be fulfilled, and then the Old Testament as a rule of life would be replaced by the law of Christ (1 Corinthians 9:21; Galatians 6:2).

34. Bahnsen, *Theonomy*, 221. Interestingly neither the Old Scofield nor the New Scofield nor the Ryrie Study Bible has a note on this verse.

35. Ibid.

36. Ibid., 223.

37. See the studies on the meaning of *telos*: John E. Toews, *The Law in Paul's Letter to the Romans: A Study of Rom. 9:30-10:13* (Ann Arbor, Mich.: University Microfilms International, 1978), 220-21; Robert Badenas, *Christ the End of the Law: Romans 10:4 in Pauline Perspective*, Journal for the Study of the New Testament Supplement Series:10 (Sheffield: JSOT Press, 1985); F. F. Bruce, *Paul: Apostle of the Heart Set Free* (Grand Rapids: Wm. B. Eerdmans Publishing Co., 1977), 190-91.

38. Bahnsen, *Theonomy*, 34.

39. Rousas J. Rushdoony, Foreword to Bahnsen, *Theonomy*, vii.

40. Russell H. Bowers, Jr., "Paul on the Law and the Christian," (unpublished paper, n.d.), 23, interacting with a statement from Ernest DeWitt Burton, *A Critical and Exegetical Commentary on the Epistle to the Galatians*, International Critical Commentary (Edinburgh: T & T Clark, 1921), 132.

41. A. J. Bandstra, *The Law and the Elements of the World: An Exegetical Study in Aspects of Paul's Preaching* (Kampen: J. H. Kok, 1964), 60-61.

42. C. F. Hogg and W. E. Vine, *The Epistle to the Galatians* (Fincastle, Va.: Bible Study Classics, 1959), 240-41.

43. E. P. Sanders, *Paul, the Law, and the Jewish People* (Philadelphia: Fortress Press, 1983), 83.

44. Bahnsen, *Theonomy*, 475-76.

45. Rushdoony, Bahnsen, and others have contended that Paul would have ordered that the congregation turn the man over to the civil authorities, but refrained because he knew the unrighteous authorities would have done nothing because they did not obey the law. This fails because it is inconsistent: under theonomy, Christians are said to be responsible to call an unrighteous government to account. The Corinthians should at least have made the gesture

of attempting to have the sinner punished by the authorities. Israel's prophets, when surrounded by an unrighteous government, confronted the rulers with their disobedient neglect of the civil law (e.g., 1 Kings 18:18). Paul doesn't even hint at such an action. A new law system has replaced the old.

Chapter 7

Should the Nations Be under the Mosaic Law?

THE UNIQUENESS OF THE MOSAIC LAW

Continuity of the Law

Theonomists believe there is a moral continuity between the Old Testament and the New Testament, so that we are to submit to the entire Old Testament law unless it has been specifically discontinued by God. Three questions are raised by this theonomic approach: (1) What exactly is meant by the Old Testament law? (2) Is it possible to hold to a moral continuity between the Old and New Testament when considering the specific purposes of the law as given within the Sinaitic Covenant? (3) Is the law of the Sinaitic Covenant the only way that God's holy character can be expressed in a law code?

Theonomy's Dilemma

Bahnsen states the dilemma that theonomists face in connecting the Mosaic law with New Testament law:

> Should general discontinuity be established between the doctrine of the state as it applies to Older Testament Israel and the doctrine of the state applying

123

to either (1) the nations outside of Israel during the former dispensation or (2) the civil governments of the New Testament era, then there would be reason to question whether the law binding Israelite rulers properly continues to direct civic leaders today.[1]

This being the case, theonomists must demonstrate:

1. That the Sinaitic Covenant was intended to be primarily applicable to more than just Israel;
2. That other nations were not distinguished within the covenant from Israel;
3. That in the Old Testament God held other nations accountable to the specific terms (including the ceremonial) of the Sinaitic Covenant; and
4. That the office of magistrate was indeed distinguished under the covenant from the function of the cult.

In order to understand whether the covenant made with Israel, with its accompanying commandments, should still be practiced by Christians or nations today we must have a basic knowledge of covenants in the ancient world.

The Nature and Types of Covenants in the Old Testament World

Covenants in the Old Testament have certain components that are uniform among the various types. There was a solemn promise made binding by an oath. This oath could be a verbal formula or a symbolic action. The parties making the oath were obligated to the contract. The covenant had legal force and became the basis for relationship between the parties and defined the nature of ethical standards between them.[2]

There were three types of covenants in the ancient Near East: the Royal Grant Treaty, the Suzerain-Vassal Treaty, and the Parity Treaty. The *Royal Grant Treaty* was a promissory type of covenant that arose out of the king's desire to reward a loyal servant. The reward usually was grants of land, a dynasty, or a priesthood. Biblical examples of this kind of treaty include the Abrahamic and Davidic covenants.

That the Abrahamic Covenant was this type may be seen from a careful examination of the expressions found in Genesis 26:5 compared with parallel expressions in the ancient Near East. Genesis 26:5 says of Abraham's response to his covenant with Yahweh: "Abraham obeyed Me and kept My charge, My commandments, My statutes, and My laws." The term *law* is from the Hebrew *torah* which basically means "to direct, teach, or instruct." The verbs of Genesis 26:5 are "obeyed" (similar terminology found at Amarna in covenant contexts) and "kept" (paralleling an Assyrian grant where Ashurbanipal rewarded his servant Bulta with a grant because he "kept the charge of my kingship").[3] Both of these verbs indicate a personal relationship rather than a legal code of ethics. Thus, obedience to *torah* comes from the relationship of covenant. The covenant Yahweh initiated with Abraham came not out of compulsion to some legislation but as a response to God:

> A close examination of the context reveals no covenant stipulations which could be viewed as pure legislative or ethical codes. What the context does reveal is that God has praised His servant Abraham because he has been faithful to do whatever the Lord instructed him to do. He did it not out of compulsion to legislation, but in a faith response to the instruction of God.[4]

A popular form of covenant was the *Suzerain-Vassal Treaty*, which bound an inferior vassal to a superior suzerain and was binding only on the one who swore. This treaty has some distinct characteristics:

1. Identification of participants.
2. Recollection of previous relations.
3. Terms or obligations of the treaty.
4. The deposit and public reading of the treaty.
5. List of witnesses, usually before the gods.

6. Blessing for obedience to suzerain or curses for disobedience.[5]

There are several biblical examples of this treaty form, including Jabesh-Gilead serving Nahash (1 Samuel 11:1) and the kings in the valley who served Chedorlaomer (Genesis 14). The most notable and perspicuous example, though, is the covenant between Yahweh and Israel at Sinai.

The *Parity Treaty* is of minor importance to our analysis on the law. This treaty bound two equal parties. Biblical examples include treaties between Jacob and Laban (Genesis 31:44-50), Abraham and Abimelech (Genesis 21:25-32), and Joshua and the Gibeonites (Joshua 9:3-27).

Four major covenants attract our attention: the covenant established originally with Adam and Eve, the reestablishment of that covenant with Noah, the covenant between Abraham and Yahweh, and the covenant between Israel and Yahweh at Sinai.

The Covenant with Adam and Eve

Although Genesis 1:26-28 does not use the term *covenant*, the parallel with the covenant idea of Genesis 9 strongly suggests a covenant that Yahweh (the suzerain) made with Adam and Eve (the vassals). Yahweh defined man's character and gave a statement of duties, with accompanying blessings for obedience and curses for disobedience.

Yahweh put the man into the garden to serve and to keep. The Hebrew is problematic, but the terms regularly have covenantal significance (Exodus 3:12; Numbers 28:2; Genesis 26:5) and maybe should be understood in this passage as referring to God putting Adam into the garden to serve him and keep his covenant.

The Renewal of the Covenant with Noah

Yahweh announced to Noah that he would destroy the earth because of "violence." The Hebrew word for violence (*chamas*) may refer to acts of bloodshed and violence (Ezekiel

7:23), but it has a broader meaning in contexts of covenantal unfaithfulness, contexts in which there is a violation of the image of God.

In contrast to the people of the earth falling under God's judgment, Genesis describes Noah as a "just" man. This "justness" was not referring to legal righteousness as in the New Testament but obedience within a covenant relationship already established. The text, then, gives no indication of a new covenant being established. There is no phrase "to cut a covenant," but instead the word *qûm*, to "establish." Other instances of this word refer to a covenant which has already been established and a guarantee of its continuation (cf. Genesis 6:18; 9:9, 11, 17; 17:7, 19, 21; 26:3; Ex. 6:4).

The statement of covenant renewal rather than covenant initiation is also seen as one observes the parallel of Genesis 1-2 and Genesis 9. Both give man instruction to be fruitful and multiply. In both, man's role as image bearer is emphasized. Lastly, stipulations of the covenant are given, which include blessings (food that can be eaten) and curses (death for certain actions).

The Noahic Covenant is perpetual. It serves as a basis of God's relationship and the standards imposed upon the nations. The rainbow is provided by Yahweh as a sign of the covenant. This is a fitting sign for it is not limited to any particular locality or any specific time; all nations can observe the covenant sign under which they have responsibility to Yahweh.

Yahweh's Covenant with Israel Is Unique

Israel's future is tied to their obedience to the Abrahamic Covenant (Exodus 19:3-6).[6] The Sinaitic Covenant further defines the Abrahamic Covenant. The Suzerain-Vassal Treaty at Sinai is built upon a Royal Grant Treaty to Abraham, an unconditional covenant given as a reward for loyalty. Several proofs lead to this conclusion. Abraham was already a vassal to Yahweh (Genesis 14:17-15:1) before the covenant ceremony (Genesis 15). Abraham became such when he was in Ur (Acts 7:2-3 with Joshua 24:2-3). Abraham was faithful like his ancestor Noah. God would give him a great name (contrast the attempt of the unfaithful of Genesis 11:4 to make themselves a great name), and a great nation. Exodus 19:5 and 6:4 strongly tie in the Sinaitic Covenant with the Abrahamic Covenant of Genesis 15.

Not only is Israel's covenant unique, but Israel is to be distinguished from the rest of the nations. Although all the earth is the Lord's, Israel is a special possession, property set aside for personal use. Israel would be a kingdom of priests, a special mediator between God and the nations. Israel would be a holy nation (*goy*). *Goy* is rarely used of Israel but is used here and in the Abrahamic Covenant of Genesis 12:2, lending support that Moses had in view the Genesis passage when speaking of the covenant with the nation Israel.

The purpose of Israel's covenant with Yahweh clearly indicates that it was not shared with the nations around it. The ethical stipulations of Israel in Exodus 20-33, et al, are given not to establish a covenant but are an explanation (instruction) of how they are to live in view of their prior covenant. Grace then preceded the law, and the stipulations of Sinai were not for the nations in general but to a people under grace.

The nations surrounding Israel were never called to adopt the law of Moses; rather Israel's obedience to the law would attract the nations. Deuteronomy 4:6-8 says the surrounding nations would be attracted to Israel and consider it wise. The Queen of Sheba came to Solomon (1 Kings 10:1-13), but there is no evidence she established Israel's law in her kingdom. Only Israel had direct revelation from God, so only through it could the other nations receive God's revelation (Deuteronomy 4:7-8). Psalm 147:19-20 says that Yahweh only gave to Israel his law. Moses, in his rehearsal of God's dealings with Israel, indicates the uniqueness of Israel (Deuteronomy 32). So then, the nations are bound to the Noahic Covenant, not the Sinaitic Covenant.

Since the nations around Israel were not called to adopt

the Mosaic Covenant, it seems evident that the pagan nations would not be judged by the law of Moses. Contrarily, theonomists reject both these theses and contend that the pagan nations were to assume Israel's law and would be judged even as Israel for disobedience to the law of Moses.

Bahnsen, in his discussion of Romans 1 and 2, seems to distinguish the moral law from the written law given to Moses: "Even though they did not have the advantage of a written (and hence redemptive) revelation of this law as did Israel, nevertheless no Gentile can claim ignorance or exemption from responsibility to God's law."[7]

By this statement Bahnsen appears to consider the written and unwritten law as direct equivalents. Not to delineate between these two expressions of the law allows Bahnsen to move quickly from one to the other without explaining what it is persons are to be in obedience to. For example, Bahnsen says,

> The deliverance of the law to Israel in written form will not hinder God from punishing sin in non-Israelites (or even non-Israelite rulers), nor should it be thought to contradict its [the Mosaic law's?] world wide application.[8]

And again he says,

> Accordingly, the Mosaic law was a standard by which unredeemed Canaanite tribes were punished (Lev. 8:24-27) and which "non-theocratic" rulers were called to obey (Ps. 119:46; Prov. 16:12) or prophetically denounced for violating (Isa. 14:4-11; Jer. 25:12; Ezek. 28:1-10; Amos 2:1-3; etc.).[9]

He concludes, then, that the entire world should be under the law of Moses and is judged for violation of the specifics of that law. The law here is the Mosaic law. But the law written on the hearts of the Gentiles does not have the specificity or clarity of the law written on tables of stone.

The Basis of Judging the Nations

Misunderstanding the nature of judicial authority. Theonomists misunderstand the nature of judicial authority under the Noahic Covenant. Judicial authority before the flood was exercised directly by God and in direct communion with God (cf. Adam and Eve, Cain, Enoch). With the reestablishment of the covenant with Noah as the head of the (new) race, man was now given a duty to execute judicial authority over men who violated the image of God by taking the life of another (Genesis 9:6). Rebellion against Yahweh in Genesis 11:4 may be seen as a rebellion by the vassal against the suzerain, which caused him to scatter them throughout the world (the nations).

Confusion of the law of God. Sometimes theonomists seem to speak of the law of God as the moral law in the heart of man, whether Israelite or Gentile, and sometimes as the written law at Sinai. They jump back and forth between these two with no clarification. It is true that nations are commanded to be just, but never are specific regulations given to them as they were to Israel. Paul in Romans 2:14-15 argues that the nations have a law written in their hearts even though they do not have the stipulations of the Mosaic law.

Since a law is given within the context of a covenant, the nations could not be given the Mosaic Law since they are not under the covenant of Sinai; instead they are under the Noahic Covenant. Probably part of the confusion is that many stipulations of the Noahic Covenant are identical to the Sinaitic Covenant, though they are not as detailed. For example, capital punishment is mandated under the Noahic and Mosaic covenants for the taking of human life; under Israel, however, capital punishment was extended further to include crimes such as Sabbath breaking and children reviling parents. In contrast, Gentiles were given all animals for meat whereas Israelites were prohibited from certain types of animals.

Failure to recognize the unique role of Israel. Israel as a kingdom of priests and a holy nation under the Abrahamic Covenant had a unique role as a mediator:

Their role thenceforth would be to mediate or intercede as priests between the holy God and the wayward nations of the world, with the end in view not only of declaring his salvation, but providing the human channel in and through whom that salvation would be effected.[10]

As priests for the nations they were given more detailed instructions for living than were the nations. This parallels in many ways the situation of priests within Israel, who were given more detailed instructions than the people in general. Israel may serve as a model for the nations, but this does not require that the nations follow in exact detail all or most of the commands given to Israel, even as the priests were models for the people but Israelites were not expected to follow in detail the commands given to the priests.

ARGUMENTS FOR THE ENFORCEMENT OF THE MOSAIC LAW IN MODERN SOCIETIES

Christian Reconstructionists believe not only that the Mosaic law should be practiced by individual Christians for sanctification but that Christians are responsible to have the civil magistrates enforce it in its detail in each society in which they live. Democratic societies are considered contrary to the enforcement of biblical law since this would be rule by the people rather than rule by God. Moreover, the position is held because of belief in the perpetual nature and universality of biblical [Mosaic] law. Connected to this perspective is the view that the civil magistrates of the nations have the perpetual function under God to enforce the Mosaic law.

Should Christians Do Away with Democracy?

Democracy as the enemy of Christianity. Rushdoony has often stated that democracy is unacceptable to a proper view of biblical law:

democracies . . . are at war against orthodox
or Biblical faith. The consequence of such a deser-
tion by the state of its calling as the ministry of
justice can only be finally the fall of the state. The
state which ceases to be a terror to evil-doers and
becomes a terror to the godly is committing
suicide.[11]

Democracy is "vox populi, vox dei." There is no
standard other than the will of the people, which
can include all things. It is "the people, yes. . . .

Supernatural Christianity and democracy are inevitably enemies, as Dewey recognized. . . . [Dewey
said] "I cannot understand how any realization of
the democratic ideal as a vital moral and spiritual
ideal in human affairs is possible without surrender
of the conception of the basic division to which
supernatural Christianity is committed."[12]

Rushdoony seems to mean in his use of the term *democ-*
racy the idea of "total democracy" in which there is no other
standard than the whim of the people, no true truth, no real
values, no absolute ethic: "Total democracy means total 'equality' and the end of morality and values as divisive and aristo-
cratic."[13] Again he says, "Absolute monarchy and democracy,
statism in other words, came into existence as revivals of
paganism and as anti-Christian movements, whatever their os-
tensible claims otherwise."[14]

An Evaluation of Rushdoony's
Perspective on Democracy
We concur with much of Rushdoony's treatment on democracy. Unbridled democracy not guided by justice and morality
is one of the worst systems of government. It leads either to
an anarchic form of government, such as the French Revolution
(representative of the thinking of Jean Jacques Rousseau), or

to a statism that destroys individual rights and private association in the name of equality and freedom.

The framers of the Constitution rejected this perspective
of democracy and the concurrent forms of socialism and pre-
Marxism of their day.[15] Instead they created a republican form
of government, maintaining balance of power in government
but not totally trusting the power of the masses either.[16]

However, in accepting much of Rushdoony's insightful
critique of contemporary democracy and equalitarianism, there
is not an imperative within Christian theology to abolish
pluralism and seek to establish a monolithic form of government
in which the Mosaic laws and consequent penalties in toto are
enforced. The requirement for the nations is to establish justice,
and this may approximate aspects of the moral and/or civil law
found in Israel, but there is no mandate to codify the Mosaic
law as the law of the land.

Is the Mosaic Law Perpetual
and Universal in Scope?

The perpetual nature of the Mosaic law. Christian Reconstructionists are very serious about the eventual enforcement
of the law of Israel in every nation of the earth. Bahnsen states:

> Not even the very least extensive number of the
> very least significant aspect of the Older Testamental
> law will become invalid until heaven and earth pass
> away! This statement is underscored in its impor-
> tance by the double negative (*ou me*) and use of
> amen at the head of the sentence [Matthew 5:17].
> It is hard to imagine how Jesus could have more
> intensely affirmed that every bit of the law remains
> binding in the gospel age.[17]

> If every jot and tittle of the Older Testamental law
> is confirmed for the New Testament era, and if God
> commands that certain criminals be executed accord-
> ing to His law, then those criminals [adulterers, in-

corrigible children, sabbath breakers, sorcerers, and blasphemers] are to be executed during the New Testament era (by the civil magistrate—Rom. 13:1-4).[18]

Ambiguity of the term law. A major difficulty with Bahnsen and other theonomists in the discussion of whether Christians and the nations are to obey the law is their lack of clarity on which law is being discussed. For example when Bahnsen says that every jot and tittle of the law is to be obeyed, the statement seems absolute. Yet he would not argue for the ceremonial to be enforced in all its details. Another example apart from the ceremonial law was the requirement to keep the Sabbath. The Sabbath was practiced on Friday evening through Saturday afternoon, and yet theonomists would not contend for this practice, instead substituting the Christian resurrection day, Sunday. Nowhere is Sunday indicated in the New Testament to be a substitution for Saturday. The aspects of the Mosaic law—ceremonial, civil, and moral—are not easily divided and often overlap. What standards must one use to decide which are to be continued and in what detail they are to be practiced?

SHOULD THE CIVIL MAGISTRATE ENFORCE THE MOSAIC LAW?

Theonomists offer the following arguments for the perpetual nature of the civil magistrate enforcing the Mosaic law:

1. God sovereignly appoints and removes rulers.
2. Rulers, as God's appointees, are not to be resisted.
3. Rulers bear religious titles.
4. Hence, rulers are God's viceregents, avengers of his wrath.
5. The magistrate must deter evil but honor the good.

6. The magistrate must rule, then, according to God's law.
7. Therefore, the magistrate is subject to criticism and judgment for lawlessness.

The Duty of Civil Magistrates within the Nations: An Answer to the Theonomists

Their first postulate is that God sovereignly appoints and removes rulers.[19] We do not contend with this view. Clearly even pre-Mosaic and post-Mosaic rulers all serve by the permission and will of God, including Pharaoh, Herod, Pilate, Nebuchadnezzar, and Cyrus.

The second view is that rulers, as God's appointees, are not to be resisted.[20] Little here is to be contested. Authority belongs to God, and the Noahic Covenant indicates that judicial authority has been given to men (cf. Romans 13:2-5). Whenever someone rebels against those authorized by God to express his authority then this is rebellion against God.

Bahnsen sees significance in the perspective that rulers bear religious titles. He contends that while these terms may be mundane, they also "could . . . bear religious connotation."[21] He does not explain what this means. Use of such titles as "my servant" and "my shepherd" when speaking of rulers such as Nebuchadnezzar and Cyrus indicates no more than covenantal relationship with them under the Noahic Covenant.

Since rulers are servants of God, rulers are God's vice-regents, avengers of his wrath.[22] Clearly Israel's rulers had this function under the Sinaitic Covenant. Nations have no such function under the Sinaitic Covenant. Paul in Romans 13:1-2 states that rulers have this function, but he never ties it into the law of Moses.

The fifth point that Bahnsen makes is that the magistrate must deter evil but honor the good. Again, this is a duty included in the Noahic Covenant. Bahnsen gives several passages to support this view (Proverbs 10:9, 29-30; 13:6; 28:18), but none of these passages are directed to Gentiles. Instead, they are directed to Israel, which is under the Sinaitic Covenant.

The last two points of his argument is where Bahnsen develops his major theses. First, based upon the previous points, the magistrate must rule according to God's law.[23] Bahnsen argues that David desired to bring the nations under his kingship and under the stipulations of the Sinaitic Covenant (2 Samuel 22:21-25, 44-50; Psalm 18:43-50). However, the passages really reveal that David desired to exercise his responsibility to defeat these enemies of God, not rule over them. Nowhere is there a statement of seeking to impose the Mosaic code on the nations. Bahnsen also says that God's judgment of Sodom and Nineveh was due to their disobedience of the Mosaic law. Gary DeMar argues similarly that God's judgment on the nations is evidence that he expected for them to obey God's civil law:

> Even nations outside Israel were required to follow the law as it was given to the nation Israel. This is a controversial statement. If the nations of the OT world were supposed to obey God's civil law, then it becomes more difficult to argue that nations of the NT world are not under the same obligation. But what is the evidence that nations in the OT were to be governed by God's law? The best evidence is this: GOD JUDGED THEM.[24]

However, Sodom was destroyed at least four hundred years before Sinai, and Nineveh's judgment is stated to be because of their wickedness and evil ways, specifically their violence, shown earlier to be God's reason for judgment on the pre-flood world.

Lastly, Bahnsen argues that the Canaanites were destroyed because of their failure to follow the law of God (Leviticus 18:24-27). But God's judgment against them dated back at least to the time of Abraham (Genesis 15:16). Never were they judged for direct violation of a Mosaic code.

Bahnsen's final argument is that "the Magistrate is subject to criticism and judgment for lawlessness."[25] He gives several examples of God's sovereignty over the nations for this position, but this is not the issue. The question is whether the nations are judged under the Sinaitic Covenant or the Noahic Covenant. In the prophets the nations are judged for idolatry (Jeremiah 46:25), arrogance toward God (Jeremiah 48:42), hostility toward Israel (Jeremiah 49:25), immorality (Isaiah 13:19), and violence (Jonah 3:8). All of these are nonspecific laws that are included in the Noahic violation of the image of God as well as being in the Sinaitic Covenant. However, Israel is clearly judged for violation of the Sabbath (Daniel 9:1-15). All of the judgments of the nations mentioned in the prophets may be seen as judged by God at Eden, Babel, Sodom, and the pre-diluvian world, long before Sinai.

The law as it was given to Israel was unique based upon a specific relationship they bore to the Abrahamic Covenant. The nations of the world, other than Israel, have no such relationship. Instead, the nations have their mandate from the Abrahamic and Noahic Covenants, a point established in the preceding chapter. Since this is true, God judges the nations based upon their adherence to their commitment to the covenant with Noah. The judicial authority of the civil magistrate to enforce God law is legitimate, but it is not the specific expression of the law of God as it was given to Israel. Certainly many of the practical expressions of the law God gave to Israel, and the particular penalties, may be used as a model for establishing civil laws for society, but there is no requirement to do so, and the failure to do so, other than the will of God in the conscience and given through Noah, will not necessarily bring the wrath of God.

Chapter 7, Notes

1. Greg Bahnsen, *Theonomy in Christian Ethics*, 2d ed. (Phillipsburg, N.J.: Presbyterian & Reformed Publishing Co., 1984), 319.

2. On the nature of covenants see the studies by William J. Dumbrell, *Covenant and Creation* (Nashville: Thomas Nelson Publishers, 1984); O. Palmer Robertson, *Christ and the Covenants* (Phillipsburg, N.J.: Presbyterian & Reformed Publishing Co., 1980); Thomas Edward McComiskey, *The Covenants of Promise* (Grand Rapids: Baker Book House, 1985); George Mendenhall, "Covenant," *International Dictionary of the Bible* (Nashville: Abingdon Press, 1962), 1:714; Eugene H. Merrill, "Covenant and the Kingdom: Genesis 1-3 as Foundation for Biblical Theology," *Criswell Theological Review* 1 (Spring 1987):295-308.

3. M. Weinfeld, "The Covenant of Grant in the Old Testament and in the Ancient Near East," *Journal of the American Oriental Society* 90 (1970):185.

4. Robert L. Dean, Jr., "Theonomy, the Mosaic Law, and the Nations," (unpublished paper, n.d.), 13.

5. Mendenhall, "Covenant," 714-15.

6. Cf. "to keep a covenant" in Genesis 17:9-10; 1 Kings 11:11; Exodus 17:14; Psalm 78:10; 103:18; 132:12, referring to fidelity to a prior covenant.

7. Bahnsen, *Theonomy*, 340.

8. Ibid., 342.

9. Ibid., xviii.

10. Eugene H. Merrill, *Kingdom of Priests* (Grand Rapids: Baker Book House, 1988), 80.

11. Rousas J. Rushdoony, *Institutes of Biblical Law*, vol. 1 (Phillipsburg, N.J.: Presbyterian & Reformed Publishing Co., 1973), 62.

12. Rousas J. Rushdoony, *This Independent Republic* (Tyler, Tex.: Thoburn Press, 1964), 122.

13. Ibid., 131.

14. Ibid., 15.

15. H. Wayne House, ed., *Restoring the Constitution* (Dallas: Probe Books, 1987), 7.

16. Ibid., 4-6.

17. Bahnsen, *Theonomy*, 73-74

18. Ibid., 446.

19. Ibid., 343.

20. Ibid., 345-48.

21. Ibid., 348.

22. Ibid., 349.

23. Ibid., 387.

24. Gary DeMar, *Ruler of the Nations: Biblical Principles for Government* (Fort Worth: Dominion Press, 1987), 86.

25. Bahnsen, *Theonomy*, 363.

Chapter 8

Is the Great Commission a Command to Dominate the World?

*D*ominion Theology is often used as a synonym for the Christian Reconstruction movement. Dominion means "rule." To rule was God's stated purpose for the creation of Adam (Genesis 1:26). Adam was commissioned two verses later to "be fruitful and multiply, and fill the earth, and subdue it; and rule over . . . the earth" (1:28).

The Hebrew word for rule is a military term yielding the idea "to trample," "to put under foot," "to conquer."[1] *Subdue* is a sister word appearing in the text along with rule meaning "to bring into bondage," "to bring under control." The *Dominion Covenant* or the *Cultural Mandate* are two well-known theological titles denoting God's charge to Adam to rule and subdue the creation.

WHAT IS THE DOMINION MANDATE IN GENESIS 1:28?

David Chilton says that spirituality's basic characteristic is dominion: "Spirituality does not mean retreat and withdrawal from life; it means *dominion*."[2] Gary North expands on this:

> Satan has run many things on earth ever since the
> Fall of man, because Adam defaulted on his assign-
> ment. . . . Dominion is still God's assignment to
> man, not to Satan. God's assignment to man to
> exercise dominion across the face of the earth is
> still in force. . . . God is in charge, waiting for His
> people to challenge the rulers of the earth and take
> the steering wheel from them. . . . The battle for
> the earth is currently going on.[3]

One's understanding of future events, or biblical prophecy
(eschatology), impacts the way one views Christ's dominion.
It is not a matter of dominion vs. no dominion. Rather, it is
an issue of *how* dominion is worked out by God through man
in history and *when* it will be established and *who* or *what*
man is called to rule over. The premillennialist sees Christ
intervening catastrophically in a moment of history, resulting
in an establishment of his mediatorial rule. This is when the
passages that refer to the victory of God's people over the
social, political, economic, and legal realms will be successfully implemented—not during this current age as Reconstructionists believe. Reconstructionist Kenneth Gentry makes the
issue of their belief clear when he states,

> The point of Christian reconstructionism that is a
> main bone of contention in the wider debate today,
> is not that it teaches the victory of God's kingdom
> on earth (most standard dispensationalists teach that
> there will be almost 1000 years of victory), but that
> it teaches the victory on earth during and continuous
> with our present era.[4]

Alva J. McClain is typical of a premillennialist in terms
of understanding the charge of dominion given to Adam by God:

> In the Genesis account of the creation of man, the
> very first of the divine injunctions laid upon him
> was regal in character: "Let them have dominion,"

says the Creator, "over all the earth". . . . Thus, among other important likenesses to his Creator, man was given a limited sovereignty in relation to the earth.[5]

In a recent debate with Reconstructionists Gary North and Gary DeMar, non-Reconstructionist Dave Hunt argued that man was given dominion in Genesis 1:26-29 and still has it. He also noted that "Adam did not lose 'dominion,' he lost his relationship to God and his place in Eden. . . . Even after the Fall man retains his God-given dominion, which is simply a stewardship responsibility to care for the earth."[6] He does not have to try to regain it since Psalm 8:6-8 restates that man has dominion over the creation. Calvinist John Robbins agrees. The Dominion Mandate "clearly gives mankind dominion over the animals and the earth. It does not give men dominion over men."[7]

Yet Reconstructionist George Grant insists that our calling is "world conquest. That's what Christ has commissioned us to accomplish." He adds, "Thus, Christian politics has as its primary intent the conquest of the land—of men, families, institutions, bureaucracies, courts, and governments for the Kingdom of Christ."[8]

The Reconstructionist view of dominion is misdirected. Only the God-Man, Jesus Christ, is destined to rightfully rule over the people of this earth. "Hallelujah! For the Lord our God, the Almighty, reigns" (Revelation 19:6b).

Both the Reconstructionist and the premillennialist agree that godly dominion will one day be exercised in the name of Christ by his redeemed people, because "the God of peace will soon crush Satan under your feet" (Romans 16:20a). But how this is accomplished and when it takes place is a major point of difference between the two systems. Eschatology accounts for the differences between the premillennial view of dominion and the postmillennial vision.

Postmillennial dominion sees the church's mission as expanding Christ's rule in the present age, with Christ mediating his rule from heaven through the church. Then Christ will return and receive his kingdom after the church has expanded the rule of God over the whole earth. This view sees a large majority of the earth's population being converted and reigning on the earth for an indefinite length of time. Kenneth Gentry has summarized this view as follows:

> The present age is the New Covenant Era, or the kingdom age, promised in the OT prophecies. The Church is spiritual Israel. . . . Christ is currently ruling and reigning in the affairs of men from heaven. . . . World conditions will gradually improve in the long run as the Spirit-empowered converts faithfully and vigorously begin applying the whole counsel of God to all of life. Before the Lord's return the world will be dominated by the Christian message and the vast majority of mankind will be converted. After an extensive era of righteousness and peace, Satan will be loosed and will incite a brief rebellion among the non-converted. The rebellion will be repressed by the glorious Second Coming of Christ.[9]

Premillennial dominion, on the other hand, will be initiated at Christ's second coming, when he will mediate his rule from the New Jerusalem as the Sovereign over a hierarchical structure. Believers will reign with Christ for one thousand years, when a majority of the earth's population will most likely be converted and go yearly to worship Christ in person.

Both views see a short time of apostasy and rebellion led by a loosed Satan, who is instantly judged and removed from the stage of history forever. Then the eternal state begins.

DOES PREMILLENNIALISM BELIEVE IN DOMINION IN HISTORY?

Both postmillennialism and premillennialism believe that Christ will be victorious in history by establishing his earthly rule as the Second Adam. However, Reconstructionists often picture premillennialists as not believing in a victorious end to history, as typified by the following remarks:

> In short, the plan of God points only to the defeat of his church in history. . . . The gospel in history is doomed to failure. In premillennialism . . . the issues of history will be settled in Christ's favor only through a final physical confrontation between God and Satan. The history of the church is therefore irrelevant: the conflict of the ages will be settled from the gospel, ethics, and the dominion covenant issued to Adam (Gen. 1:26-28), Noah (Gen. 9:1-17), and the church (Matt. 28:18-20).[10]

Many other accusations that premillennialism necessitates defeatism within history and a pessimistic vision could be given. For example,

> we have given up the belief that we are supposed to work for victory on this earth . . . to expect the eventual "takeovers" of cultural institutions . . . for the bringing of every "high thing" into obedience to Christ, the King. Oh, we believe that these "victory" Scriptures are true, all right, but we "spiritualize" them, and relegate their main fulfillment to some future age, after Christ comes back. And so we take the heart belief right out of God's people, the belief that they are called to take dominion of the land, as Joshua was called of God to conquer Canaan for Christ, and replace it with one of a kind of "holding action," winning as many people as possible, and building as many local churches as possible, and all the while waiting for some future time till Christ comes back so that we can really see the Kingdom built![11]

Two points need to be made in opposition to such Reconstructionist broadsides. First, it may come as a surprise to some postmillennialists that premillennialists do believe in victory within history. The millennium is still within history for the premillennialist. There are still people being born, dying, and believing the gospel during the millennial period. Even after the Second Coming history will still be moving toward the final end.

Today when a premillennialist speaks of "the end," he is speaking in a way that must have been similar to the way Noah spoke. Noah had 120 years to prepare for God's judgment on the world. Noah and family may have spoken of "the end," that is, when the flood would come. However, the flood did not bring an end to history, but an end to the world as they knew it and the end of an era. This period of judgment was their passage into a new world. So it is with the premillennial understanding of the end of this age. It prepares the way for the next age to come—the millennium, not the end of history.

Reconstructionists believe we are not living in the "last days" before Christ's return. They believe the last days have already occurred. According to Chilton,

> the expression the last days, and similar terms, are used in the Bible to refer, not to the end of the physical world, but to the last days of the nation of Israel, the "last days" which ended with the destruction of the Temple in A.D. 70.[12]

Chilton then interprets all of the last days passages in the New Testament as events that have already taken place.

This approach does not accord with Old Testament teaching; moreover, it takes large portions of the New Testament and makes them inapplicable to believers today since many passages revolve around instructions for believers in light of the last days (1 Timothy 4; 2 Timothy 3).

One passage, among many, which does not fit into such Reconstructionist thinking is Hosea 3:5: "Afterward the sons of Israel will return and seek the LORD their God and David their king; and they will come trembling to the LORD and to

His goodness in the last days." This is something which has not yet been fulfilled.

Reconstructionists do not believe in the restoration of Israel to their covenant status, since they believe that God has finished with them and divorced them. They believe that the church takes over the not yet fulfilled promises made to Israel as the new Israel under the new covenant. They do believe, however, that one day in the future many individual Jews will be converted to Jesus as their Messiah. The difficulty for Reconstructionists is that if the last days events prophesied in the Bible have already happened (in A.D. 70), how can they then maintain that one of those events is still future, namely the conversion of the Jews?

Reconstructionists tend to miss the fact that Premillennialists do believe in victory within history.

> Historical future means "in-time" future, just as historical past means "in-time" past. . . . Dispensational premillennialists maintain that the goal of history should be within history. And historical ends are within time.[13]

Leading Premillennialists have always asserted that the victorious reign of Christ is the only fitting climax to history within time.[14]

Additionally, the gospel in history is not doomed to failure. The extent of the success of the gospel during this current age is dependent upon God's sovereign purpose for it. So to argue, in principle, that premillennialists do not believe in the victory of the gospel is to distort the real issue about God's purpose for the gospel.

Scripture indicates that a majority of people will not come to Christ during the church age.[15] On the other hand, the Scriptures do say that a greater number will come to Christ during the seven year tribulation period (Revelation 7:9). Before the tribulation comes to an end, the gospel "shall be preached in the whole world for a witness to all the nations" (Matthew 24:14). This will be a continuation of the course begun during the church age. The extent of the gospel's success is currently having a worldwide impact. But it will continue to become greater during the next two periods of God's plan— the tribulation and the millennium. Walvoord declares that during the millennium "it is safe to assume that the majority of the earth's population will be saved in contrast to all previous generations where only a comparatively few ever come to know the LORD."[16]

Since Satan will not be present during the millennium to deceive the nations (Revelation 20:3), it will be the greatest time of blessing and knowledge of the Lord (Isaiah 11:6-9; Jeremiah 31:34; Micah 4:1-8; Zechariah 14:9-21). So premillennialists believe that the gospel will be victorious. We simply see a different timing from that advocated by postmillennialists.

Whether the preaching of the gospel succeeds or fails is not an issue. The Bible does not speak in terms of whether or not the gospel will succeed. The real question is whether or not God will accomplish his plan in history. It is God who causes the gospel to be effective. Premillennialists believe that the gospel will fully accomplish God's plan for man and the world. During this current church age, God's plan is to call out a people for his own name. This goal the gospel is accomplishing.

PREMILLENNIAL DOOM AND GLOOM

Christian Reconstructionists often misrepresent the premillennial view by saying that our position is inherently a pessimistic one. In contrast, those familiar with the Christian Reconstruction movement will readily agree that some of the most pessimistic literature of the last fifteen years has come from the pens of Gary North, R.J. Rushdoony, and others in the movement. They speak about how God judges periodically in history and then brings salvation out of judgment. They say that God is currently judging apostate western culture, much as he did the Roman Empire. Out of the rubble of this current judgment, a remnant of believers will step forward and rebuild a Christian society which will fulfill the biblical mandate. Let's look at an example from Gary North:

> Consider the dimensions of our losses. In the last fifty years, the Moslem religion has increased in size 500%; Hinduism by 117%; Buddhism by 63%, and Christianity by a mere 47%. Not only have we lost two-thirds of the globe since 1917 to the Marxists, but we are currently losing the religious populations as well. It is obvious that Christians are losing ground, figuratively and literally.[17]

North would say that it is not going to be this way in the days ahead. During chapel services at a small Christian college a few years ago, Gary North spoke on economics and the dismal days ahead for the American economy. The reaction of many of the students was that North was the most negative and pessimistic speaker they had ever heard. One student in particular told me, "I like to think that we have a better future than that!" In response, North would likely say, "I was speaking of the short run. In the long run we have a great future." But apart from specifics, how is this really different from the premillennial outline of history?

Premillennialists say that the tribulation is followed by a time of blessing. This is basically the same general scenario as the one envisioned by postmillennialists. Why are they not being pessimistic and defeatist when they speak this way? Why are they not the ones who are just holding on and waiting until God finally, but slowly, in the distant future brings victory? Why are they not experiencing the kind of victory for which they chide premillennialists? Their accusations are inappropriate.

Reconstructionists have a place for trials and tribulation in their scheme. They should not argue in principle that premillennialists are pessimistic without applying the same standards to themselves. How is their pessimism different from premillennialists? They would reply, "It is because we are optimistic about the future." Well, so are premillennialists! Within our view the kingdom has the potential for being fully established within a decade; their kingdom, however, would take much longer, even given a "best case" scenario. The main difference is they believe Christ is already reigning now through the church, while we believe he is currently the victorious and Sovereign Head of the church, which is gathering many citizens for his coming reign.

Premillennialism, when fairly considered, is not a pessimistic system. However, when the question is asked about God's plan for this age in relation to the social and political success of the church, the biblical text has several pessimistic themes. (We hasten to affirm that there will be different levels of success in promoting Christian values and ideas in society and government, but millennial standards await Christ's victorious return.) It is pessimistic about many things, usually related to man's sin and rebellion. It is very pessimistic about man's saving himself. It is pessimistic about Cain's mastery over sin (Genesis 4:6-8. It is pessimistic about the heart and nature of man before the flood (Genesis 6:5), as well as after the flood (Genesis 8:21). It is pessimistic about Israel's ability and desire to obey God's covenant (Deuteronomy 29:4). It is pessimistic that Israel could avoid being defeated by their enemies because of their violation of the covenant (Jeremiah 27-29). The Bible is even pessimistic about redeemed man establishing the kingdom in this age.

This is why the real issues boil down to dealing with specific scriptural passages, not just generalized arguments about the supposed outworkings of your opponents' views. This is why those critical of theonomic postmillennialism have challenged them to produce collaborating exegesis.[18] They are long on stating their views, but short on establishing from Scripture the foundation upon which the superstructure is supported. While both theology and exegesis are important, exegesis must be the basis on which proper theology is grounded.

One of the slogans of the Reformation was the Latin phrase *Sola Scriptura* (Scripture alone). It was supposed to remind Christians that only the Bible was the church's authority and measure in determining truth. The Roman Catholic church stressed a dual authority: Scripture and church tradition. When the two conflict, the track record is that men tend to let the man-made authority interpret the Bible. Fellow Reconstructionist Doug Wilson claims that some within the Reconstructionist movement have made their dual authority the Bible and theology. James Jordan has said, "We have to say that the check and balance on interpretation is the whole rest of Scripture and of theology."[19] While our theology must flow from Scripture, it must be noted that "Scripture and theology are not co-regents."[20] Wilson's sober warning concerning the danger of allowing the theological tail to wag the scriptural dog must be heeded.

> If our theology is allowed, in any measure, to regulate how the Scriptures are handled, then humanistic dross is inserted into the pure Word of God. Do we want some sort of Protestant magisterium? God forbid! Theology must never regulate Scripture. Scripture must regulate theology.[21]

At best, the Reconstructionist system is built upon a theological inference, from which they try to develop a large body of Scripture. If certain things are assumed about the Bible, a Reconstructionist can make his system appear to work within the biblical framework, especially to the naive. However, this system can never be derived from specific biblical passages.

What passages do Reconstructionists base their eschatology upon? Where does the Bible teach that we, not Christ, are the instruments to establish Christ's earthly kingdom? Where does the Bible say that we are to be involved in the social, political, and economic aspects of society during the church age in the way Reconstructionists affirm? Failure to answer such questions reveals the weakness of Christian Reconstructionist dogma when examined under the light of the Scriptures alone.

THE GREAT COMMISSION AND THE DOMINION MANDATE

When asked for passages that teach their view, Reconstructionists will usually cite the Great Commission of Matthew 28:18-20. To Reconstructionists, the Great Commission is merely an extension and New Covenant update of the Cultural or Creation Mandate of Genesis 1:26-30.

> The Creation Mandate is consequently undergirded by the restorational activity of God by means of the New Creation [Great Commission] power. Therefore, kingly dominion by man is reflected in evangelistic enterprise. . . . No Christian should doubt the necessity of soul-winning in a fallen world. But what about culture-winning? Cultural Christianization.[22]

Evangelism has certainly been added to the Cultural Mandate by the Christian Reconstruction movement, but their real goal is the Cultural Christianization of the world:

> Personal redemption is not the do-all and end-all of the Great Commission. Thus, our evangelism must include sociology as well as salvation; it must include reform and redemption, culture and conversion, a new social order as well as a new birth, a revolution as well as a regeneration. Any other kind of evangelism is short-sighted and woefully impotent. Any other kind of evangelism fails to live up to the high call of the Great Commission.[23]

Chilton echoes this:

> The Great Commission to the Church does not end
> with simply witnessing to the nations. . . . The king-
> doms of the world are to become the kingdoms of
> Christ. They are to be discipled, made obedient to
> the faith.[24]

And North adds the following:

> This assignment by Christ is simply a recapitulation
> of the dominion assignment given to Adam and Noah
> by God. It is the same assignment. Now Christ
> announces His power over history, for He has suf-
> fered in history: "And Jesus came and spoke unto
> them, saying, All power is given unto me in heaven
> and in earth" (Matthew 28:18). This is the historical
> foundation for His recapitulation of the original
> dominion assignment.[25]

Did Jesus have in mind the implications the Reconstructionists bring to the Great Commission, or have they read
something into the text that does not belong? No one doubts
that in the Great Commission the intent of the preaching of
the gospel is salvation from sin. The question is whether or
not additional ideas, such as the Reconstructionist view of
dominion, are stated explicitly or implicitly. Let's look at the
Great Commission in order to determine the scope of Christ's
command. There are a number of passages which record our
Lord's instruction: Matthew 28:18-20, Mark 16:14-18, Luke
24:44-49, John 20:21-23, and Acts 1:3-8. We will examine the
nature and tone of these passages taken as a group.

Mark 16:15 is the passage which most directly parallels
the Matthew commission. "Go into all the world and preach
the gospel to all creation." Clearly these words refer exclusively
to Christian evangelism and soteriological salvation. The same
is evident in the Luke account when Jesus says that "the Christ
should suffer and rise again from the dead the third day; and

that repentance for forgiveness of sins should be proclaimed in His name to all the nations, beginning from Jerusalem" (24:46-47). The soteriological gospel is even spelled out in the Luke passage—"repentance for the forgiveness of sins." There is no language or tone in either of these passages that would support the notion of Christianizing the world.

In Acts, Luke takes this commission ("repentance for forgiveness of sins should be proclaimed in His name to all the nations, beginning from Jerusalem") and uses it as his outline (1:8). The disciples are to be witnesses of the death and resurrection of Messiah for soteriological salvation, from Jerusalem to all the nations. Throughout Acts, the proclamation is always the soteriological gospel. Never are the apostles and evangelists involved in the Christianization of the culture. This does not mean that a by-product of the gospel was not some degree of Christianization of their culture, but this was never advocated in Acts. The Christian missionaries certainly had many opportunities to speak like modern Reconstructionists if this had been included in their divine agenda. Certainly the pagan Roman Empire was in as much need of Christianization, and probably more so, than is America and the rest of the world today. If the early church was called to be involved in the Christianization of the culture it would have been recorded. They did change much of Roman society, but the mandate to do so is not seen.

The empowerment of the Holy Spirit in Acts 1:8 was given to Christ's disciples to enable them to preach salvation from sin. John's version of the Great Commission confirms this: "'Peace be with you; as the Father has sent Me, I also send you.' And when He had said this, He breathed on them, and said to them, 'Receive the Holy Spirit. If you forgive the sins of any, their sins have been forgiven them; if you retain the sins of any, they have been retained'" (John 20:21-23). In a similar way to Matthew 16:19, the Lord says that forgiveness of sin is given to the church in the form of the gospel. Those who believe it have their sins remitted. This is once again soteriological in nature. The empowerment by the Holy Spirit, in both Acts and John, enables Christ's messengers to boldly preach the gospel, in spite of the opposition.

However, Reconstructionists often point to three factors they believe carry the day for their "Dominion Commission." First is the word "disciples" (Matthew 28:19). Gary North gives us insight into what the Reconstructionist means by discipleship:

> Step by step, person by person, nation by nation, Christians are to disciple the nations. This means that they are to bring men under the discipline of the legal terms of God's covenant. . . . How can we disciple the earth if we are not involved in running it?[26]

According to North, a disciple is more than a mature believer in Christ; he is also a social and political activist.

This idea of a disciple does not hold up under close scrutiny. The Greek word *mathētēs* simply means "learner" or "pupil,"[27] and is one of the general terms used to describe a believer in Christ: "The name was carried over into Acts, where it frequently has the general sense of Christian."[28] For example, Acts 14:21 says, "after they had preached the gospel to that city and had made many disciples, they returned to Lystra." It is clear that a person's conversion to Christ constituted the making of a disciple. In the next verse the text says, "strengthening the souls of the disciples, encouraging them to continue in the faith." Those who had become disciples are now partaking of the ongoing ministry of the Great Commission as they are strengthened in the faith.

The Reconstructionist implication that discipleship includes a social and political aspect of running things is not supported by biblical usage. A disciple is anyone who is a believer, who is learning God's Word and is growing.

Several points require mentioning in connection to Matthew 28:19-20. First, Reconstructionists say that the phrases "teaching them to observe all that I commanded you" (28:20) and the "all" in "all authority" (28:18) refer to every sphere of life. For the Reconstructionist the Christian life is not just some mystical Jesus in your pietistic little heart. George Grant declares, "We are to make disciples who will obey everything that He has commanded, not just in a hazy zone of piety, but in the totality of life."[29] But the debate is not over whether or not believers are to be totally committed to our Lord Jesus Christ or if we are to obey some, not all, of his commands. Rather, the controversy is over the scope of what Christ has commanded.

Reconstructionists say that since it is God's will to bring both personal and social salvation before Christ returns, it is necessary to redeem institutions as well as people. Those outside the Christian Reconstruction movement say that God's will is individual salvation now and social salvation at the coming of Christ. Thus, the "all" refers to the directives given to the church to carry out its mission of individual evangelism and teaching in order to build up believers to live in faithfulness to our Lord during this dark age.

Kenneth Gentry lists three categories of teaching which the "all" encompasses: "First . . . it included all new material. . . . Second . . . all previous teaching of Scripture. . . . Third . . . the yet-future teaching of the apostles."[30] It is not debated that past, present, and future revelation is for the believer today. Certainly all Scripture is given to build up believers in this age. But how is the believer to understand and apply the various portions of Scripture? According to Gentry:

> Those who neglect the social and cultural ramifications of New Testament teaching are relegating Scripture to irrelevance. It should be obvious that the New Testament has much to say on social and other affairs. It is concerned with divorce (Matt. 5:27-32; Luke 16:18), the rich man's duty to the poor (Luke 16:19-25; 2 Cor. 8:13ff), employer-employee relationships (Eph. 6:5-9; Luke 10:17), honest wages

(I Tim 5:18; Luke 10:7), godly citizenship and the function of the state (Rom. 13:1-7), finances (Rom. 13:8; Matt. 15:14ff), and so on. To overlook these social instructions, one would have to confine his Biblical studies to the exegesis of "Genuine Cowhide" on the cover of his Bible."[31]

Premillennialists believe that the New Testament does have social and cultural ramifications. But they also believe that the emphasis on social and cultural issues reflects the purpose God has for this age, namely the individual duties of a Christian before a watching world, rather than the redemption and conversion of institutions. A look at Gentry's examples in the above citation tells how individual believers are supposed to behave in relationship to the different spheres of life: marriage, charity, employer-employee relationships, citizenship, and finances. Nowhere in the New Testament does it teach the agenda of Christianizing the institutions of the world.

When the New Testament speaks of the believer interacting with this current evil world system, it is never a challenge to take it over. Rather, it is defensive (separate from the darkness of evil, Romans 13:12; 2 Corinthians 6:14), as well as offensive (exposure of that evil with the light, Ephesians 5:11). But it is not a conquering of evil. Christ has already done that and will complete it at his second coming. Our job is to be a faithful witness to those in the darkness of Plato's cave. We are to shine the light of God's word on current issues in order to remove the shroud of darkness cast over this world system by Satan.

The Greek word *elegchete* translated "expose" in Ephesians 5:11 means "to show someone his sin and to summon him to repentance."[32] We are to give the biblical perspective on "the unfruitful deeds of darkness" so that a person will repent of sin and leave the kingdom of darkness. Paul had a perfect opportunity to tell the troops to get out and Christianize the darkness, but he did not. Instead he admonishes them to awake from sleep (5:14) and live a godly life (5:15), resulting in worship to God (5:19-20) and submitting properly to authority (5:21-6:9). This type of enlightened lifestyle will draw the fire of the servants of darkness (6:12).

If ever there was a wide open door where Paul could tell the believer to give Satan a black eye, it is here. Rather, Paul tells us to take up the full armor of God and "stand firm." Reconstructionists are telling us to charge when God has told us to take up a defensive posture against the enemy (6:13-14). The offensive weapon is absent since the commander's orders are given three times to stand and resist (6:13-14). The believer is given the shield to protect against Satan's offensive. The sword is for a counterattack in resisting the evil one's attempts to overtake your defensive position. This counterattack enables the Christian to follow the orders of his commander to stand. It is the Christian who is under attack by "the flaming missiles of the evil one" (6:16). It is Satan who is on the prowl. When Satan is resisted, he will flee.

Satan's "flaming missiles" (6:16) are described as "schemes of the devil" (6:11). Earlier in the epistle (4:14), Paul gives the believer the antidote to such schemes. It is a mature believer who has been equipped by gifted men with God's word, enabling him to solve deceitful schemes by "speaking the truth in love" (4:11-15). So it is that the Christian warrior, clothed with Christ's provision, is not moved as the shield of faith extinguishes the missiles. The sword of the Spirit—God's Word—enables him not to be deceived by the assaulting schemes of Satan's twisted perspective. During this whole battle, the faithful believer is depending upon Jesus Christ himself to fight the battle, as is illustrated by his constant prayer (6:18).

What is the battle of Ephesians 6 all about? Is it the struggle to roll back humanism and regain the glory days of the Christian West? George Grant declares that "The army of God is to conquer the earth, to subdue it, to rule over it, to exercise dominion. Christians are called to war."[33] However, the apostle Paul taught that the war was to subdue the world, the flesh, and the devil so that the believer could "walk in a manner worthy of the calling with which you have been called" (4:1).

This same battle is spoken of by Paul in at least two other passages. Romans 7:15-25 describes the conflict which all believers encounter, while 2 Corinthians 10:1-9 has many parallels to the Ephesians 6 passage. It is important, once again, to note that the battle of 2 Corinthians 10 is a war against the flesh and the believer's temptation to be taken captive to Satan's justifications for not walking in a holy manner. But we do not need to fall for that trick, since God has made a divine provision (10:4). Satan approaches us with the temptation to partake of depraved, speculative thought (10:5). This is why, in the battle to live a godly life before God, we have the weapon of healthy doctrine to give us proper direction and also the Divine enabling of our will, so we will be able "to punish all disobedience, whenever your obedience is complete" (10:6).

This is not a passage telling us to develop a Christian worldview,[34] as commendable as that may be. (Perhaps Romans 12:2 is grounds for that.) It is encouraging us in the struggle against the temptations to sin which are offered by the world, the flesh, and the devil. It is true that all of God's Word is implied in the "alls" of the Great Commission. But since the Reconstructionists' view of the commission is misdirected, those in the movement end up trying to do what God has decreed he will accomplish: the establishment of the kingdom. Our calling is not to "construct a KINGDOM ENVIRONMENT,"[35] as one Reconstructionist put it, but rather to be involved as God's instruments for calling out the Bride of Christ for the coming, future kingdom.

Next, sometimes Reconstructionists teach that not only are individuals outside of the nation of Israel to be evangelized, but the national structure (or government) is also to be converted. "Individuals are, of course, included in the commission. But the commission includes men in their social and political associations as well."[36] They do not deny that the normal use of the Greek word *ethnē*, used in Matthew 28:19, means "the peoples outside of Israel,"[37] but they believe this use of "nations" includes the making of "Christian nations."

Gary North gives the following as one of the requirements for a nation becoming Christian: "Each nation must publicly ally itself with Christ."[38] But he cites no scriptural basis for such a statement. Still another Reconstructionist says,

> He did NOT tell us to go out and "make SOME disciples of all the nations" . . . gathering them into little groups here and there, and then waiting for the rapture . . . but rather He said to "make ALL NATIONS disciples" . . . which is quite another thing![39]

Earlier in Matthew's Gospel, Jesus had commissioned the disciples to "go only to the lost sheep of the house of Israel" (10:6). But upon the Jewish rejection of Jesus as their Messiah (Matthew 12), our Lord's command is to now go to all the peoples, not just Jews alone (Matthew 28). But does this mean that the national, political institutions are included in this Great Commission? No!

Passages such as Revelation 7:9 tell us more specifically the result of taking the gospel to the nations. Those who will believe will form "a great multitude which no one could count, from every nation and all tribes and peoples and tongues." The Reconstructionist notion that the whole world is to be converted before Christ's return cannot be supported from this verse. When the gospel is preached to the nations (i.e., all the peoples of the world) then some "from" or "out of" every nation will believe.

The same language is used in Acts 15:14 when James says that "God first concerned Himself about taking *from among* the Gentiles a people for His name." Further, the word *Gentiles* is the English translation of the same Greek word used in Matthew 28:19 and translated "nations." The grammar of the text does not support a notion such as Christianizing the world.

Rather, the preaching of the gospel draws out a people from among the peoples or nations of the world—a group of people called the church, a spiritual nation from among the nations.

It is easy to see that we are told to preach the gospel to every nation, to every creature, but passages like Revelation 7:9 and Acts 15:14 tell us the purpose and response of this command. In addition, our English word "church" is a translation of the Greek word *ekklēsia*, which means "called out ones." Just as God called Abraham out of Ur of the Chaldeans, so Christ is calling out of the nations a people for his own name—the Body of Christ.

Some Old Testament passages do teach that the nations will one day serve Messiah, but this is during the millennium (Isaiah 2:2-3; Amos 9:12; Micah 4:2; Zephaniah 3:9-10). Since, as shown elsewhere, this present age is not the kingdom, these passages are speaking of a future time and not the present. The conversion of the nations will not take place before the coming of the Lord.

The Cultural Mandate has not been withdrawn since its giving and restatement as the Noahic Covenant in Genesis (1:28-30; 9:1-3). The Cultural Mandate was given to Adam and to all of humanity, whether redeemed or unregenerate. This explains why even unbelievers still contribute to the advancement of the Mandate. This is in part what Ecclesiastes 2:26b means when it says, "to the sinner He has given the task of gathering and collecting so that they may give to one who is good in God's sight." The unbeliever, even in rebellion against his Maker, is still accomplishing God's will. The Cultural Mandate is still a directive to all mankind.

However, the Great Commission is given to the redemptive institution, the church, as a directive. Rather than interpreting the Great Commission by the Cultural Mandate, as Reconstructionists do, it is better to see the Great Commission, with its soteriological thrust, as something we are able to further with the aid of the fruit of the Cultural Mandate. Mankind has fulfilled, and is fulfilling, the Cultural Mandate, even though it is by the sweat of his brow and in rebellion against God. Christ, during the millennium, will lead his people toward further progress in fulfilling the Dominion Mandate.

One further reason for the erroneous view that the Great Commission is a call for worldwide Christianization flows from the mistaken notion that we are now in the kingdom. This is often referred to as "Kingdom Now" teaching:

> Reconstructionists insist that the will of God is being denied by those who say the kingdom of God is not now operating and that it cannot expand as Christians obey God and get to work to disciple the nations. God's will is that His kingdom come, that His will be done on earth as it is in heaven (Matt. 6:10).[40]

Christians are to pray that Christ will return and bring with him the kingdom. Then God's will in heaven will be brought to earth. But not until Christ rules physically from Jerusalem.

Worldwide evangelism is the calling of the church in this age, not Cultural Christianization. Sadly when the two are combined the result is not the bright and shining city on a hill; rather it is Babylon the great, spoken of in Revelation 18, which God will judge in the future. This is the great danger of having a wrong view of the future—it affects your view of the present and how to be involved in present issues.

We do not mean that Christians are to abandon responsibilities toward individual and societal concerns such as helping the poor or protesting abortion. We only question the permanent success of our efforts or the ability to significantly alter the social structures of this world until Christ the King installs his government in the millennium.

If history is any indication, we can expect Reconstructionists to become more entangled with institutions of this world in a way that will be displeasing to our Lord. In addition, the idea of trying to take over the world will also lead to the church being distracted from its primary calling of evangelization. Tragically, this will contribute to the further unfaithfulness of the church in these last days before the return of Messiah.

Chapter 8, Notes

1. William L. Holladay, *A Concise Hebrew and Aramaic Lexicon of the Old Testament* (Grand Rapids: Wm. B. Eerdmans Publishing Co., 1971), 333.

2. David Chilton, *Paradise Restored: An Eschatology of Dominion* (Tyler, Tex.: Reconstruction Press, 1985), 4.

3. Gary North, *Liberating Planet Earth* (Fort Worth: Dominion Press, 1987), 23-24.

4. Kenneth L. Gentry, Jr., "*The Reduction of Christianity*: A Review Article," *The Counsel of Chalcedon*, April-May 1988), 31.

5. Alva J. McClain, *The Greatness of the Kingdom* (Winona Lake, Ind.: B M H Books, 1959), 42-43. It is significant to also notice that McClain sees, even in the creation account, a glimpse of premillennial eschatology. "The plural 'let them have dominion,' on this view, could have some reference to Adam and his wife Eve; for in the antitype the Last Adam also has a 'wife' who, though subject to her divine Head, will nevertheless sit regally with Him in His Mediatorial Kingdom (Rev. 19:7; 20:6)" (p. 43).

6. Dave Hunt, *CIB Bulletin*, May 1988, 1.

7. John W. Robbins, *Pat Robertson: A Warning to America* (Jefferson, Md.: The Trinity Foundation, 1988), 93.

8. George Grant, *The Changing of the Guard: Biblical Principle for Political Action* (Fort Worth: Dominion Press, 1987), 50-51.

9. Kenneth L. Gentry, Jr., "Searching Scripture," *The Counsel of Chalcedon*, March 1982, 15.

10. Gary North, "Christianity and Progress," *The Journal of Christian Reconstruction* 11 (May-June, 1987):2.

11. Raymond P. Joseph, "Kingdom Victory," *The Counsel of Chalcedon*, August 1982, 22-23.

12. Chilton, *Paradise*, 112.

13. Ramesh P. Richard, "The Premillennial Interpretation of History," *Bibliotheca Sacra* 138 (July-September 1981):204, 208.

14. An example of another premillennialist who argues that history needs the millennium in order for it to come to a satisfactory conclusion is McClain, *Greatness of The Kingdom*, 527-31.

15. This can be seen in Romans 11:15, "Now if [Israel's] transgression be riches for the world and their failure be riches for the Gentiles, how much more will their fulfillment be!" The current church age is the time of Gentile blessing as the gospel has gone to the nations because of Israel's transgression. However, an even greater time of gospel blessing will result in Israel's fulfillment (during the millennium). Therefore, since the millennium is future to this present age, a greater number will come to Christ. Therefore, a minority will be saved during the present time.

16. John F. Walvoord, *The Millennial Kingdom* (Grand Rapids: Zondervan Publishing House, 1959), 316-17.

17. North, *Liberating Planet Earth*, 24-25.

18. North, "Publisher's Preface" in David Chilton, *The Days of Vengeance* (Fort Worth: Dominion Press, 1987), xxiii.

19. James Jordan, *Judges: God's War Against Humanism* (Tyler, Tex.: Geneva Ministries, 1985), xiii.

20. Doug Wilson, *Law and Love: Constructive Criticism for Reconstructionists* (Moscow, Idaho: Ransom Press, 1988), 12.

21. Ibid., 11.

22. Kenneth L. Gentry, Jr., "The Greatness of the Great Commission," *The Journal of Christian Reconstruction* 7 (Winter 1981):39.

23. George Grant, *Bringing in the Sheaves* (Atlanta: American Vision Press, 1985), 70.

24. Chilton, *Paradise*, 213.

25. Gary North, *Unconditional Surrender: God's Program for Victory* (Tyler, Tex.: Geneva Press, 1981), 218.

26. North, *Liberating Planet Earth*, 9.

27. William F. Arndt and F. Wilbur Gingrich, *A Greek-English Lexicon of the New Testament and Other Early Christian Literature* (Chicago: University of Chicago Press, 1957), 486.

28. R. S. Rayburn, s.v. "Christians, Names of," Walter A. Elwell, ed., *Evangelical Dictionary of Theology* (Grand Rapids: Baker Book House, 1984), 216.

29. Grant, *Sheaves*, 68.

30. Gentry, "Great Commission," 41.

31. Ibid., 40.

32. Friedrich Buschsel, s.v. "elegcho," *Theological Dictionary of the New Testament*, vol. 2, Gerhard Kittel, ed. (Grand Rapids: Wm. B. Eerdmans Publishing Co., 1964), 474.

33. Grant, *Sheaves*, 97-98.

34. "We are to 'take captive every thought to make it obedient to Christ' (2 Corinthians 10:5). . . . In other words, we are commanded to have a Biblical worldview." (Ibid., 93.)

35. Raymond P. Joseph, "Kingdom Victory: The Historical Aspect," *The Counsel of Chalcedon*, August 1982, 3.

36. Gary DeMar and Peter Leithart, *The Reduction of Christianity: Dave Hunt's Theology of Cultural Surrender* (Fort Worth: Dominion Press, 1988), 180.

37. Hermann Cremer, s.v. "ethnos," *Biblico-Theological Lexicon of New Testament Greek* (Edinburgh: T. & T. Clark, 1895), 227.

38. North, "What Is a Christian Nation?" *The Geneva Review*, September 1987, 10.

39. Joseph, "Kingdom Victory, 22.

40. DeMar and Leithart, *Reduction*, 323.

Chapter 9

God's Purpose for the Church Age

*T*he first major controversy in the early church touched upon the issue of God's purpose for the church age. The Jewish believers held that Gentiles had to become converts to Judaism before they could trust Christ as their Savior. This meant that they had to be circumcised and keep the Mosaic law.

The apostles in the Jerusalem church convened a council to settle this dispute. Among those present was the apostle Peter, who boldly affirmed, "But we believe that we are saved through the grace of the Lord Jesus, in the same way as [the Gentiles] also are" (Acts 15:11). The council concluded that one did not have to become a proselyte to Judaism in order to be saved through the grace of the Lord Jesus. This was the council's decision concerning obedience to the law.

Following this decision, James gave an explanation of the apostles' thinking on the matter. His clarification of their rationale seems to have included a desire to soothe the Jewish element weakened by the verdict. This was not a compromise but rather a focusing on God's long range plan which would give hope to Jews concerning their calling as God's elect nation. The question raised in this Council concerning Gentiles, Jews, and salvation was further explained by learning God's purpose for this age, how it related to past ages (Israel), and the role of the future age (the millennium). It makes sense that James is interested in clarifying God's purpose for this new church age which has just begun.

IS THE CHURCH TO TAKE OVER?

In the process of his explanation, James reminds his hearers "how God first concerned Himself about taking from among the Gentiles a people for His name" (15:14) and cites an Old Testament prediction of Gentile inclusion among God's people (Amos 9:11-12). According to the postmillennialists, the purpose of God in the gospel is to convert the Gentiles (or nations). Chilton has said, "the New Testament interpretation of [Amos 9:11-12] explains it as a prophecy of the conversion of the nations under the government of Christ (Acts 15:14-19)."[1] However, the language is very clear: God's intent for this age is to "take out" from among the nations a people for his name, not to convert the nations and make them into Christian republics. This may be on the Reconstructionists' agenda, but there is no evidence it is on God's agenda during this age.

Here is one of the many opportunities a New Testament spokesman had to affirm that "Christianity is destined to take over all the kingdoms of the earth. God has given His people a 'covenant grant' to take possession and exercise dominion over His creation."[2] But James did not. Rather, he talked about "taking out," not "taking over."

This language of "taking out from among" fits the pattern the rest of the New Testament paints concerning God's goal for the church. She is called the "bride of Christ." Believers saved during this age will take on the name of Christ through marriage. This fits into the scriptural motif of selecting out of many possible options a woman to be one's bride. This spiritual bride is being made ready by Christ himself, for the purpose of presenting her to himself on their wedding day (Ephesians 5:25-27).

Moreover, the Scriptures, not just premillennialists, say the church has a heavenly destiny and is a heavenly people (Colossians 3:1-4). During the current age she is to make herself ready for the day when her groom comes from heaven and takes her to rule with him in the heavenlies in his kingdom. This involves evangelism, or the numerical completion of the Bride, as well as the call to godly living in the present because of her future destiny. Robert Saucy summarizes the purpose of the church in this present age as that of a *witness*:

> Believers are here to witness to the coming kingdom, not to inaugurate the kingdom rule. They are here as ambassadors of the King, to urge people to transfer their citizenship to the future kingdom by coming into a relationship with the King today. This focus of "witness" is clearly evident in the words of the Lord's so-called "great commission" (Luke 24:47-48) as well as in the purpose of the coming of the Spirit summed up in Jesus' words, "He will bear witness of Me, and you will bear witness also" (John 15:26-27).[3]

This summary best fits the New Testament perspective of the current purpose of the church in relation to the future kingdom. Saucy notes the two major areas in which the power of the future kingdom is at work in believers today:

> First, the primary thrust of kingdom power relates to the inner person. While any genuine transformation of the inner person must certainly affect outward behavior, the blessings of the kingdom for today focus on the spiritual aspect of life and not the material. . . . In short the concern is for power for the three great marks of the church—faith, hope, and love.[4]

Earlier in Acts the apostles raised the question of when the kingdom would be restored to Israel (1:6). This question came after a forty day period when Christ spoke "of the things concerning the Kingdom of God" (1:3). It is important to notice that their question assumes that it is a matter of *when* the kingdom would be restored to Israel, not *if* it would be restored. Reconstructionists teach that when God established the church, he abandoned Israel as a nation forever because of their unbelief. If God had taken the kingdom from Israel and not just postponed it, then surely such an important point would have been covered by our Lord when he taught the apostles about the kingdom of God during their forty day learning period. Yet, their view that a future in the kingdom remains for Israel as a nation is clearly unshaken.

Christ did not instruct his disciples to take over the world in the way the Reconstructionists teach. Instead of telling the troops to charge, he told them to be "witnesses" (1:8). The nature of this witnessing is evident by observing what the early evangelists said and did as they went from Jerusalem to Judea and Samaria and then to the remotest part of the earth. They preached the gospel of forgiveness of sins, but never said a word about taking over Rome for Jesus. Yet Gary North has said, "[Christians today] have lost the vision of victory which once motivated Christians to evangelize and then take over the Roman Empire."[5]

The purpose and calling of the church is faithful preaching of the gospel in the present while waiting eagerly for Christ to come from heaven. These activities are showing the world of darkness what the light of God's kingdom is like.

The Great Commission also supports the fact that the church's basic calling is evangelism to all the nations. This calling and hope of the church is seen in the gifts and ministries to which the church is called. During the church age the believer receives the first of two installments which prepare him for the coming kingdom. They center around the two ways the Bible uses the word *redemption*: (1) Redemption from sin which is obtained by trust in the gospel (Colossians 1:14); and (2) redemption of our bodies (Romans 8:23). The first is indicated by the down payment of the Holy Spirit (Ephesians 1:14), which is the guarantee for the second and final installment—the redemption of the body. This is what Paul writes about in Romans 8:23: "And not only this, but also we ourselves, having the first fruits of the Spirit, even we ourselves groan within ourselves, waiting eagerly for our adoption as sons, the redemption of our body." We long for the outer man or body to catch up to the inner man or our regenerated spirit.

Since Reconstructionists combine the kingdom and the present age, they also end up misunderstanding the two phases of redemption. Kenneth Gentry has said, "We have entered the kingdom (Col. 1:13) and are to proclaim it to others (Acts 28:19). The whole creation awaits the godly dominion of the New Creation saints of God (Rom. 8:19-23)."[6] Gentry twists the language of Romans 8:23 from something that will happen in an instant in the future to a process in the present. Such are the kinds of exegetical mistakes that will be made if one begins with the premise that the purpose of the church age is taking over the world.

The church age is a time of development, but not the kind Reconstructionists advocate. It is a time that stresses development of the inner spiritual life, something Christ constantly noted as missing from Pharisaic Judaism (Matthew 5-7, 23).

> The thrust of the apostolic concern for believers can be seen in Paul's prayers for their inner experience. Paul's desire is for the power of "steadfastness and patience" (Col. 1:11), the power of sustaining hope while they wait for their inheritance (Eph. 1:18-19; cf. Rom. 15:13), and the power of faith and love (Eph. 3:16). Similarly Peter wrote about the power of protection for the believer in a hostile world (1 Pet. 1:5).[7]

Saucy's second area of present kingdom power during the current church age is "fundamentally a power displayed through outer weakness (cf. 2 Cor. 12:9-10)."[8] This is the "strength through weakness" theme which the world cannot

even begin to understand. We question whether or not Reconstructionists have a grasp of this clear New Testament doctrine.

> Far from giving believers today the kingdom power
> that will someday crush all its enemies, the church
> today, as Ladd has said, "is like other men, at the
> mercy of the powers of this world." Though Christ
> has overcome the strong man (Luke 11:21-22) and
> believers are overcomers in Him, the enemy is yet
> given provisional power to overcome the saints (I
> Pet. 5:8; cf. Rev. 11:7). . . .
>
> The nature of the present kingdom power is nowhere
> more clearly displayed than at the cross of Christ.
> From the outward viewpoint there is no greater dis-
> play of weakness than the Cross. Recognizing this,
> the people mockingly called for a display of overt
> power by Christ to save Himself. But God's purpose
> at that time called for the power of God to be manifest
> through the weakness of the Cross. This is the power
> Paul boasted of in his own life and what he taught
> the early church.[9]

It is sad to say it, but Reconstructionists, like Christ's
enemies in his day, are calling for an invalid and premature
display of power by claiming that the present church age is a
time for the church "to work for the coming of the Kingdom."[10]
The kingdom will not be brought in until the period of the
church's humiliation is completed and the church has filled up
"that which is lacking in Christ's afflictions" (Colossians 1:24).
Then Christ will burst on the scene with "power and great
glory" (Matthew 24:30) at his second coming in much the
same way that he unexpectedly was raised from the grave.

Since our calling in the present age is primarily
evangelism and discipleship, we are to shine brightly by following a Christian lifestyle. In Titus 2:12-14, Paul instructs us "to
deny ungodliness and worldly desires and to live sensibly,
righteously and godly in the present age, looking for the blessed

hope and appearing of the glory of our great God and Savior, Christ Jesus; who gave Himself for us, that He might redeem us from every lawless deed and purify for Himself a people for His own possession, zealous for good deeds." This is the purpose of believers today, to glorify Christ in the darkness of this world by doing good deeds, "which God prepared beforehand, that we should walk in them" (Ephesians 2:10).

James continues his explanation of the Jerusalem council's decision by quoting this Old Testament promise concerning the restoration of Israel: "After these things I will return, and I will rebuild the tabernacle of David which has fallen, and I will rebuild its ruins, and I will restore it" (Acts 15:16). This language fits the premillennial picture of God returning to deal with Israel after the Rapture. It is during the tribulation period and the millennium that this verse will be fulfilled. God's unconditional promises to Abraham and Israel will yet be fulfilled, but it will be after the current church age is completed.

This is also the picture painted by Paul in Romans 11. He teaches that Israel's rejection has led to the gospel coming to the Gentiles, even though God still maintains a remnant of elect Israel during this present age. God will restore Israel to a place of blessing after the church age is completed. Romans 11 teaches that the salvation of Israel (the rebuilding of the tabernacle of David) will result in even greater gospel blessing for the whole world. "Now if [Israel's] transgression be riches for the world and their failure be riches for the Gentiles, how much more will their fulfillment be!" (Romans 11:12).

This is the point: once Israel is restored to the place of blessing and the tabernacle of David is rebuilt, then will follow the third phase in the plan of God. That period will be the time of the millennium, when the nations will indeed be converted and ruled over by Christ. If Israel's disobedience led to the calling out of many Gentiles to be part of the bride of Christ, think of what will happen when Israel is converted. It will lead to mass conversion of the Gentile nations: "'In order that the rest of mankind may seek the Lord, and all the Gentiles who are called by My name,' says the Lord, who makes these things known from of old" (Acts 15:17-18). As Romans 11:32 declares, "For God has shut up all in disobedience that He might show mercy to all."

Reconstructionists mix God's future program with his present program. This results in at least two major errors: (1) Reconstructionists neglect the emphasis God has for this present age, and (2) they try to bring about what God has planned for a future era, but which only he can accomplish in his timing and by his direct agency.

What is the emphasis God has for this present age? He is calling out of the sons of darkness, through evangelism, a people for his own name. He is demonstrating that, unlike Adam and Israel, this new people, the church, will be faithful to him even though it is their lot to suffer persecution and conflict during the darkness of this present age. Paul, the apostle to the Gentiles, is typical of the church's calling. At his conversion his calling was "to bear My name before the Gentiles and kings and the sons of Israel; for I will show him how much he must suffer for My name's sake" (Acts 9:15-16).

It is not the plan of God for the church to conquer the world. We are not going to rule the governments and institutions of this world. God has kept this prerogative for himself. He will magnify himself by putting down evil, for the greater the opposition, the greater is the glory of the one who puts it down.

How does God put down evil? By wearing Saul's heavy armor? By matching evil at its own game? No! A thousand times no! God's ways are not the ways of fallen man's, nor is his wisdom and power. He does it as David did, with a small sling and a stone. Paul says, "when I am weak, then I am strong." So it was with David. So it was with Christ. And so it is with his church.

Who would have ever thought that someone would be a Savior by dying? What weakness! The world's logic would never have devised such a plan. Messiah's suffering likewise proved to be a stumbling block for Israel, which is why they rejected the Man of Sorrows—Jesus—the nobody from Nazareth.

Since the church is being prepared to be the bride of Christ, she is, like Christ, learning "obedience from the things which He suffered" (Hebrews 5:8). This suffering completed Christ's preparation to become "a high priest according to the order of Melchizedek" (Hebrews 5:10). Christ's earthly suffering, even though temporary, prepared him for a future ministry. He showed his faithfulness to God by enduring hardship in light of his future goal.

The same is true for the church. Since she is called Christ's body, she is experiencing some of the things he did in his humiliation. This is what Paul had in mind in Colossians 1:24: "Now I rejoice in my sufferings for your sake, and in my flesh I do my share on behalf of His body (which is the church) in filling up that which is lacking in Christ's afflictions." The church's sufferings certainly do not add in any way to the atonement Christ alone secured. Therefore, the purpose for which the church is "filling up" Christ's sufferings is related to the parallel plan and purpose God has for teaching the church through suffering, just as Christ also learned though suffering.

It was God's plan for Christ to first be humiliated and then to be exalted to the throne of rulership (Philippians 2), demonstrating that exaltation comes by humbling oneself before his sovereign. God will exalt the church to rulership only after she has been made fit to rule by humiliation and suffering. The kingdom of God is not to be taken by force; rather God will establish it in his own time, which according to the Bible is yet future. The church is to be the faithful steward. When her Lord returns he should find her doing the things put in her charge.

The New Testament pictures the believer as a ray of light during the present darkness. He is to shine the light of the gospel because Messiah has not yet returned to set up his kingdom. Paul develops the light/dark motif in 1 Thessalonians 5:1-11. He tells us that "the day of the Lord will come just like a thief in the night" (v. 2). Therefore, since we are "sons of light" (those who will inherit the kingdom), our behavior is to reflect our future even though we are living in the night (the period before the coming in of the kingdom). Christians are working the "night shift," waiting for the sunrise.

The dawn is the Second Coming of Christ, which is why he is called the "morning star" (2 Peter 1:19). Our job on the "night shift" is clarified by Paul in Ephesians 5:7-14 when he says we are to expose evil (bring it to light), not conquer it as Reconstructionists insist. Christ will conquer it at his coming, which is the reason for the definitive judgment upon his return.

These are some of the major reasons for this present church age, reasons that are not related to Israel's kingdom. Instead the present age is to be a time of gathering the body of Christ out of the present world, so that she may be made ready as his bride during the future kingdom. It will be a kingdom that is established and ruled by Jesus Christ and his people.

THE DISPENSATION OF GRACE

Ephesians 2 and 3 is probably the most extensive passage in the New Testament explaining the nature and purpose of the church age. However, in the volumes of Reconstructionist literature, there are only a few faint references to this aspect of these crucial passages. In the second half of Ephesians 2, Paul tells the Ephesian believers that God has taken Jews and Gentiles and made them into one body (2:16). This resulted in the breaking down of barriers between the two groups (2:13-19). The purpose of this new work was that the church might be "a dwelling of God in the Spirit" (2:22).

God's plan has been broadened to include the redemption of the whole world. Since Paul has argued in chapters 1 and 2 that salvation is solely on the basis of God's sovereign and electing grace, we can affirm the following two aspects of the grace of God during the church age: "(1) the blessing is entirely of grace and (2) that grace is for all."[11]

So then, when someone says that this is the age of grace, it does not mean that God was not gracious in saving others during previous times, but that the intensity and extent of his grace has been expanded. God is no longer dealing primarily with one nation, Israel; instead he is taking out from among the nations a people he is forming into a new nation.

In the parable of the landowner and the vineyard (Matthew 21:33-46), Christ said, "the Kingdom of God will be taken away from [Israel], and be given to a nation producing the fruit of it" (v. 43). Jesus then proceeds to tell the parable of the wedding feast (22:1-14), showing that the Jews would reject the gospel while the Gentiles would accept it. The ones who make up the new nation which produces fruit are the Gentiles, who are gathered out of the nations during the age of grace.

This does not mean that God is forever finished with Israel as a nation, as Reconstructionists insist. Ray Sutton teaches that God divorced Israel.[12] In explaining the parables of Matthew 21 and 22, he says, "For the next several chapters, one section after another pronounces judgment and total discontinuity between God and Israel . . . total disinheritance."[13] But J. Dwight Pentecost better represents what God did when the whole of Scripture is taken into account: "Christ did not announce a judgment terminating Israel's hope, but He did announce a postponement of the realization of that hope until some future day."[14]

Sutton builds his case upon the thesis that "Matthew follows Deuteronomy's covenant structure. Without a doubt, the structure of the two books is parallel."[15] And one can go to Deuteronomy and find many passages which tell of God's cursing of the nation of Israel (Deuteronomy 28-32).

However, if one steps back and takes in the whole picture, he sees that there will indeed be a time within the history of Israel when they will be cast out of the land and even dispersed among the nations. Yet passages such as Deuteronomy 30:1-10 note that one day Israel will return to the Lord their God with all their heart, "then the LORD your God will restore you from captivity, and have compassion on you, and will gather you again from all the peoples where the LORD your God has scattered you" (30:3).

This passage was written at the beginning of Israel's history, before it became apostate. It is important to note that it lays out the career of Israel in advance, including its yet future regathering from the nations, conversion, and the inheritance of all her blessings which God promised in the Abrahamic covenant.

Many passages in the Old Testament speak of Israel's sin and disobedience toward God, but just as many speak of God's restoration of his chosen nation in the last days (Deuteronomy 4:27, 30-31; 30:1-10; Isaiah 11:11, 16; Jeremiah 23:3; 31:31-34; Ezekiel 36-37; Hosea 5:15-6:3; Micah 5:6-7; 7:18-20; Zechariah 8:3-8). These are ignored by Reconstructionists. In addition, no passages speak of God totally abandoning Israel. The only way anyone can come up with such a view from the Bible is to be selective. When all of Scripture is taken into account, there is only one conclusion: God is not yet finished with Israel as a nation.

For Sutton to say that persistent disobedience results in God forever cutting Israel off from promises such as the land is inconsistent with the grace of God. As Dave Hunt once said,

> Israel has been involved in idolatry and wickedness since the very beginning, yet God has forgiven her in the past and all of her sins of the future were known to God at the time He made His promises. At what point did her sins become so bad that God had to go back upon His Word, nullify His promises, and reject Israel?[16]

Reconstructionists are Calvinists. They believe God predestines who will be saved. They believe God controls history. Why, therefore, would they deny that in the future God will cause and enable Israel to believe and bless them with the full complement of the original blessing made to Abraham (Genesis 12:1-3)? If they do not acknowledge this, in effect they are saying that God elected the nation of Israel on the basis of grace alone (Romans 9:6-24), but the nation was rebellious enough to forfeit their election. Either Reconstructionists will have to give up their belief in predestination and election, or they will have to become consistent with it and give up their view that God is finished with Israel as a nation. In this case, it makes sense that soteriology and eschatology both are based upon unconditional election.

Premillennialists believe the Bible teaches that Israel is currently being disciplined, as the Mosaic covenant called for, because of disobedience. In addition, while Israel is in the "woodshed," God is being gracious to the Gentiles. When "all Israel" believes, which is a condition for blessing, God will complete the promises to Abraham, which include a land forever. We find this same pattern in the sanctification of an individual believer. When the believer sins, he is disciplined, not divorced. We may not be faithful, but our God certainly is. God does not let a believer continue in sin without correcting him. Israel's current status is one of discipline. Then, God is going to restore Israel through chastisement and his grace. They will, by God's grace, accomplish God's will.

Sutton is projecting the ungodly behavior of sinful men— divorce—upon God. Believers should be thankful that God is faithful even though we are not. The constant theme of the Old Testament prophets was that Israel had severely disobeyed God's law and would be punished for it. But always, there was the hope of future blessing and eventual fulfillment of God's promises in full to his people. Both aspects need to be considered.

We have already noted above that Acts 15 and Romans 11 speak of Israel being temporarily set aside because of their rejection of Messiah. However, these two passages also provided the rest of the story: God will keep his original promises to the fathers and will one day convert and place Israel as the head of the nations.

We are in full agreement with Sutton and Reconstructionists that Israel was, and currently remains, under the curse due to her national rejection of Messiah. Individual Jews who convert to Christianity find acceptance in Christ. But it should be pointed out that after Christ speaks parables of judgment and pronounces woes upon the nation and its leaders (Matthew 22-23), he also says: "Behold, your house is being left to you desolate! For I say to you, from now on you shall not see Me until you say, Blessed is He who comes in the name of the Lord!" (23:38-39) The word of judgment is there but so is the hope. Our Lord's pattern is similar to that of the Prophets and Deuteronomy when they speak about Israel's future restoration.

This is further supported in the Olivet Discourse (discussed in chapter 13) which speaks of the destruction of Jerusalem in A.D. 70 (Luke 21:20-24), and the similar, yet very different, future event of Israel's deliverance shortly before the Second Coming of Jesus (Matthew 24). In Luke 21:24, in speaking of the A.D. 70 judgment, Jesus says, "they will fall by the edge of the sword, and will be led captive into all the nations; and Jerusalem will be trampled under foot by the Gentiles until the times of the Gentiles be fulfilled." This parallels the prediction of Deuteronomy 28:64: "the LORD will scatter you among all peoples, from one end of the earth to the other end of the earth," and Deuteronomy 30:3-4: "the LORD your God will restore you from captivity . . . and will gather you again from all the peoples where the LORD your God has scattered you. . . . From there the LORD your God will gather you, and from there He will bring you back."

The scattering of the nation of Israel occurred in A.D. 70, when about one million Jews were killed and another two million sold into slavery (in addition to those who were already in the dispersion). Luke 21:24 says that this scattering will continue "until the times of the Gentiles be fulfilled." So the passage is looking beyond the destruction of Jerusalem in A.D. 70 to some future date. This future time is the Second Coming of Christ (vv. 25-28).

GOD'S MYSTERY NOW MADE CLEAR

Paul speaks in Ephesians 3:5 of a mystery "which in other generations was not made known to the sons of men, as it has now been revealed to His holy apostles and prophets in the Spirit." This mystery—something now revealed which was hidden or unknown in the past—is identified by Paul to be, "that the Gentiles are fellow heirs and fellow members of the body, and fellow partakers of the promise in Christ Jesus through the gospel." As Ryrie notes, "This equality is the point of the mystery revealed to the apostles and prophets in New Testament times."[17]

Paul, the apostle to the Gentiles, says of his calling that it was "to bring to light what is the administration [dispensation] of the mystery which for ages has been hidden in God" (Ephesians 3:9). In his epistles, Paul revealed many of the new and unique doctrines relating to the church. He says this mystery was created so that "the manifold wisdom of God might now be made known through the church to the rulers and the authorities in the heavenly places. This was in accordance with the eternal purpose which He carried out in Christ Jesus our Lord" (Ephesians 3:10-11). Paul is saying that the church age is one aspect, in contrast to Israel, of the single plan or decree of God. One of its purposes is a heavenly one: to teach the angels something about God. Therefore, the purpose of the church age is to show in history another aspect of the plan of God.

Therefore, it is not wrong, in the light of Scripture, to say that God has one single plan which encompasses in its unfolding different and progressive stages. Israel is one stage or aspect and the church is another. There is continuity and discontinuity between the ages.

This is what Paul wrote about in Galatians 3 and 4 where he says that the promises made to Abraham were not fulfilled by the works of the law but by faith in God's grace (3:10-4:11). Moreover, "Christ redeemed us from the curse of the Law, having become a curse for us . . . in order that in Christ Jesus the blessing of Abraham might come to the Gentiles, so that we might receive the promise of the Spirit through faith" (3:13-14).

In order to explain the latter truth, Paul develops an analogy using three distinct elements: (1) the promise to Abraham, (2) the law, and (3) the fulfillment of the promise of the Spirit through faith, called the inheritance. The first aspect of the analogy is how the promise made by God to Abraham will be fulfilled. It is not going to be fulfilled by keeping the law. Paul says, "for if the inheritance is based on law, it is no longer based on a promise; but God has granted it to Abraham by means of a promise" (3:18). If not by law, then what was the purpose of the law?

The law was given so that it might add transgressions (3:19), not to make men righteous (3:21). It was given to "shut up all men under sin, that the promise by faith in Jesus Christ might be given to those who believe" (3:22). The law was to act as our tutor to lead us to Christ (3:23-24). In this analogy, the time spent under the bondage of the law is compared to a son who is to receive an inheritance when he reaches maturity (4:1-2). A slave is told what to do by someone over him: when to get up in the morning, what to eat, what to wear, what to do during the day, how to do it, when to quit, whether or not he can be married, and so on. Likewise, a son who is not yet mature is given similar instruction, but this is to prepare him for when he comes of age, so that he will be a responsible heir.

The period of the law is compared to that age of childhood, immaturity, and legalistic instruction (3:24). It is a time when the tutor—the law—tells us how to act. But the tutor cannot receive the inheritance, nor can the child until he comes of age (4:2). The coming of age is called the "fullness of the time" when Christ came and redeemed us from the law and brought believers into sonship (4:4-5).

The coming of age is analogous to the church age (4:6-7). This is a time when, by means of the Holy Spirit (the sign of life given to those composing the body of Christ), God's plan moves from a period when his people were motivated as a child (by the external standards of the law) to maturity in Christ. As an adult properly trained by the tutor, the heir acts responsibly and from internal (Spirit) motivation. He no longer needs the law, since he has an internal motivation to please the father. This mature person knows what to do and does it without the aid of his tutor, just as a mature person today provides for his family, works on the job, and does the things he needs to without anyone telling him to do it. He is an internally motivated person. This is what Paul means when he said, "if you are led by the Spirit, you are not under the Law" (5:18).

Even though the law is temporary, it shows us our sin and need for a Savior. The law is a dead, external force which could never create in us the desire to want to be pleasing to the Father. It is the Holy Spirit who creates the desire to please the father. This new motivation is called "the law of Christ" (6:2; 1 Corinthians 9:21), which consists of an attitude of love, manifested by "others oriented" activity, such as bearing one another's burdens. The law of Christ is known by other names in other contexts: the perfect law, the law of liberty (James 1:25), the royal law (James 2:8), the whole law (James 2:10), and the law of love (Romans 13:8-10).

Paul teaches that the essence of the law is "through love serve one another" (5:13), and he echoes Christ's teaching when he says, "the whole law is fulfilled in one word, in the statement, 'You shall love your neighbor as yourself' " (5:14).

> Paul was not suggesting that New Testament believers are obligated to keep the Mosaic Law. Instead he was saying that since both the Mosaic Law and the law of Christ are founded on God's moral law, one who fulfills the law of Christ is in essence fulfilling the heart of the Mosaic law.[18]

This gets to the whole point: the church age is a period of progress from Promise, to Law, to Grace. The purpose of the church age is to show that believers will do God's will because they love God, the result of his first loving us (1 John 4:10) and giving us this new nature. "If you love Me, you will keep My commandments" (John 14:15). The church age is a final answer to the question Satan asked God concerning Job:

"Does Job fear God for nothing?" (Job 1:9). God answers back in history, "Yes, men made new will serve me and remain loyal even through suffering and deprivation. Look at the church, my bride!"

DOES THE CHURCH INHERIT THE BLESSINGS AND CURSINGS OF ISRAEL?

In Romans 12:1, Paul urges the Roman believers on the basis of "the mercies of God, to present [their] bodies a living and holy sacrifice, acceptable to God." What are the mercies of God? They are explained in the previous eleven chapters of Romans as God's marvelous plan of salvation. These eleven chapters constitute the longest sustained theological discourse in the New Testament, and show the greatness of God's mercies toward us. In the concluding chapters Paul lays out commands or standards for believers to follow. The motivation Paul uses is that we have been blessed, therefore let's renew our mind in accordance with God's mercy.

Contrary to the New Testament approach to blessing, Reconstructionists want to put us back under the law's approach. They believe the blessing and cursing section of Deuteronomy 28 is the model for the church. George Grant declares, "In the heart of the Pentateuch, God lists the covenant blessings that He will shower upon any society that is faithful to Him and His Word."[19] Then Grant asks, "How could any Christian walk away from these blessings? How could any Christian seriously believe that none of this can happen in history, now that Satan's defeat at Calvary is behind us?"[20]

In Psalm 147:19-20, the Lord makes a clear statement in regard to the recipients of the law:

> He declares His words to Jacob,
> His statutes and His ordinances to Israel.
> He has not dealt thus with any nation;
> And as for His ordinances, they have not known
>   them.

Grant is wrong to say that the covenant blessing will be showered upon "any society" that is faithful to God and his Word. The nations are under the jurisdiction of the Noahic covenant, not the Mosaic covenant. The blessing and cursing section is clearly addressed to Israel. Grant would have to note specific reasons within the text for expanding its application beyond the borders of Israel. This he cannot do since those factors are not there. Deuteronomy 27:9, an introduction to a cursing section, tells Israel, not the church, that this "day you have become a people for the LORD your God." The charge to obey the Lord God and "do His commandments and His statutes" is given to Israel in verse 10. The rest of the chapter uses specific language addressing Israel, Moses, Levi, Judah, Joseph, Benjamin, Mount Ebal, and the Levites, to name only some of those mentioned in this cursing section.

The concluding context also supports the clear notion that God was speaking with Israel and not leaving it open-ended for the church. Deuteronomy 29:1-2 says that these "are the words of the covenant which the LORD commanded Moses to make with the sons of Israel in the land of Moab . . . and Moses summoned all Israel." Therefore, one has to spiritualize the text in order to say with certainty that God will do this to "any society faithful to Him and His Word." God may give those blessings to others or he may smite a people with these curses, but there is no scriptural evidence that such an action is the result of a cause/effect relationship from Deuteronomy 28. Rather, God's blessing and cursing is the result of his sovereign plan.

Acts 14:16-17 says, "And in the generations gone by He permitted all the nations to go their own ways; and yet He did not leave Himself without witness, in that He did good and gave you rains from heaven and fruitful seasons, satisfying your hearts with food and gladness." This is one of the two major aspects of common grace. The other aspect is that God restrains evil. God has been and continues to be gracious to the nations, but not because they have obeyed him. Their track records show they haven't even come close. God is blessing them simply because he has chosen to as a part of his sovereign plan.

FROM BAD TO BETTER?

Gary North also applies the Mosaic law broadly with his rationalistic, cause/effect view of common grace. He too teaches that it is the specific basis for blessing and cursing:

> What we are told is that the law of God restrains men. They do the work of the law written on their hearts (Rom. 2:14-15). This law is the primary means of God's external blessings (Deut. 28:1-14); rebellion against His law brings destruction (Deut. 28:15-68). Therefore, as the reign of biblical law is extended by means of the preaching of the whole counsel of God, and as the law is written in the hearts of the regenerate men (Jer. 31:33-34; Heb. 8:10-11; 10:16), and as the unregenerate come under the sway and influence of the law, common grace must increase, not decrease.[21]

If common grace has been increasing, why has sin progressed so far? Why has the church become so diluted in her faith and practice? If this is victory, what would defeat be like? Why has Christianity declined, just about any way you want to measure it, from its glorious beginnings in America? If common grace and progress were truly on the rise, then how does one account for decline? If Reconstructionists say it is because we cannot handle blessing and therefore have become unfaithful, then they have proved the point—we have experienced decline, not progress.

This issue surfaces the schizophrenia of many Reconstructionists. On the one hand, they preach progress and increasing victory. Yet when non-Reconstructionists note that circumstances in the world do not bear this out, we are scolded for looking at the world and not Holy Writ and lectured on the great progress of Christianity when the big picture is viewed. It must be a very big picture indeed. Since the Bible is true, there should be a discernible correspondence between what it teaches and what is going on in the world. Non-Reconstructionists are not guilty of looking at the world and reading it back into the Bible, at least not on this issue. Because the Bible speaks of things progressing from "bad to worse," of men "deceiving and being deceived" (2 Timothy 3:13), we look out at our world and see how bad things really are.

On the other hand, Reconstructionists, as a group, are the leaders of a pessimistic critique of the modern scene. This does not make sense if things were so great during the time of the Reformation and the Puritans that we need to get back to those times. If special grace and common grace have been increasing, as North says, then he either really does not believe that we have made true progress today or the Reformers and Puritans were not as great as Reconstructionists generally boast.

Common grace is on the decline, especially God's restraint of evil. This accounts for the rising apostasy and the decline of Christianity. North is wrong and Van Til is right on this issue. In fact, one day God will remove the restrainer and hell on earth will be the order during the tribulation. It's going to get bad before it gets worse.

Acts 17:26 also speaks of God's sovereign rule and plan as the reason for Gentile history. God "made from one, every nation of mankind to live on all the face of the earth, having determined their appointed times, and the boundaries of their habitation." There is no mention of the blessing and cursing framework of Reconstructionists.

The New Testament is the portion of the Bible that tells the church what her blessings are and that believers will be motivated by God's grace to respond in a way pleasing to him. True grace does not lead to license and passivity; rather it provokes to righteous activity. Colossians 3:1-12 presents an argument similar to Romans and Ephesians in its appeal to live for Christ. Paul reminds the Colossians of the greatness of their heavenly blessings (3:1-4) and then calls for them to "consider the members of your earthly body as dead" to sin and an ungodly lifestyle (3:5-8). In its place, believers are to "put on the new man" which is being renewed in accordance with the Head—Jesus Christ (3:9-12).

This tone and attitude of Paul, Christ, and the entire New Testament is quite different from the improper attempt at mixing the Old Covenant with the New as expressed in Reconstructionism:

> What the Church needs to point to is real answers for society. . . . We must view the law given to Moses and the prophets as the revealed will of God for men of all ages. Our culture needs Christian reconstruction, but we can only supply it if we look to God and His Law-Word as God's eternal will for man and his culture.[22]

The non-Reconstructionist Christian is not saying that we hate God's law or that it cannot give us counsel for today. He is saying that he is not under the law as a rule of life; rather we are under the law of Christ. Since we are regenerate believers, we love the law and want to obey it because the law is good (Romans 7:12). However, the law is accomplished indirectly, as a by-product, as we walk "according to the Spirit" (Romans 8:4). "His commandments are not burdensome" (1 John 5:3), since we are new creatures who love the things of God.

Often Reconstructionists make it sound as though being under the law for sanctification is an either/or situation: "Logically the only alternative to God's law is humanism. One will either follow the law of God as a blueprint . . . or man will follow a humanistic set of values."[23] One of the problems with this statement, which is typical within Reconstructionist circles, is to make all the law of Scripture a generic whole they call "Biblical law." Therefore, if you are against placing Christians under the Mosaic law, you are accused of being against all law. This is not necessarily the case. Those of us living in Texas are not under the traffic laws of California, even though there may be great similarity between the two systems. If I speed in Texas and am ticketed, it is because I broke the Texas speeding law, not the California speeding law.

As Christians we live not under Moses but Christ. Some of the commandments are the same, but they are in force because they are the stipulations required under the particular covenant. It is the covenantal arrangement which makes the law of a given contract binding upon the subordinate parties. Christ has freed us from the law for salvation or sanctification.

When it comes to developing wisdom in the various areas of life, we do have to look to the law for insight. Cornelius Van Til has correctly observed that there is no neutrality between the believer and unbeliever when it comes to what the options in life are: "There are two, and only two, mutually exclusive philosophies of education. These are involved in two mutually exclusive philosophies of man. . . . "[24] The believer finds his direction in God's Word, while the unbeliever finds it in himself and in the philosophies of man.

> The Christian has his standard in the revealed will of God. This standard is absolute. The non-Christian finds his standard in human experience. So also the Christian seeks to realize his ideal by following his standard through the power of faith given him by God. The non-Christian, be he realist, idealist or pragmatist, seeks to realize his ideal in his own power.[25]

The believer is not to adopt viewpoints in any area of life that are the product of the world system. He is to attempt to develop and hold to a biblical view of government, economics, family, education, and so on. We are children of the light, and we are to shine in the current darkness. However, since it is not the plan or will of God for the kingdom of God to take over in this age, we are to be like Daniel—standing for biblical standards while waiting for God's intervention in history to be realized. This could be called a "wisdom approach," as opposed to the Reconstructionist "law approach." The biblical model is Proverbs. As one studies the book of Proverbs, it soon becomes apparent that the wisdom of Proverbs is largely the product of Solomon meditating upon the law of Moses. He then uses the wisdom literature format to pass this on to his son and to the next generation.

Wisdom differs from law in that law provides the legal stipulations which regulate the covenantal agreement and can be enforced by civil penalties. Law can govern any area of life, such as civil, family, personal, and religious institutions. On the other hand, wisdom is advice with no legal penalties attached. Wisdom tells the naive "the end of a matter" so that the pitfalls of life may be avoided. Wisdom admonishes all to follow after her because living by wisdom is right and yields certain practical benefits. Wisdom also applies to every area of life.

Adultery is treated in similar yet different ways in the law and wisdom literature. The law says, Thou shalt not . . . (Deuteronomy 5:18) and in certain situations the law's violation carries the death penalty (Deuteronomy 22:22). Wisdom gives insight into why one should not commit adultery and even appeals to the student to follow the way of wisdom (Proverbs 7:6-23). But it does not legislate civil penalties. Wisdom says that if a wise person will walk in her way, certain benefits will follow. No wonder Paul told Timothy "that the Law is good, if one uses it lawfully" (1 Timothy 1:8). In the church age, a wisdom approach to the Mosaic law is a good and lawful use of the law.

Deuteronomy 4:6-8 appeals to a wisdom and understanding given exclusively to Israel, which the other nations would observe:

> "So keep and do them, for that is your wisdom and your understanding in the sight of the peoples who will hear all these statutes and say, 'Surely this great nation is a wise and understanding people.' For what great nation is there that has a god so near to it as

is the LORD our God whenever we call on Him? Or what great nation is there that has statutes and judgments as righteous as this whole law which I am setting before you today?"

Though given to Israel, this wisdom is evident to outsiders who would likely seek to imitate this wisdom. This has been the approach taken by many of the Gentile nations during the current church age when Christians have been able to exert influence.

For a Christian to function in one of these areas, he would want to apply specific Old Testament laws meant for Israel in order to develop a wise approach in those areas. But it is wisdom and not law. Reconstructionists might say, "If it is not law then it is not binding, and no one would have a motive for obeying it." This is true, Israel's law is not binding on the nations. The Noahic covenant is. However, the believer made new will want to be mature and apply the wisdom he learned during his childhood (under the law). There is a big difference between law and wisdom, though often the net effect will be the same since the regenerate believer will want to apply the wisdom of God's law. But the fact remains that the Mosaic Covenant and the laws attached to it were made with Israel and no one else.

Gary North is critical of premillennialists who use resources such as Rushdoony's *Institutes of Biblical Law* as a "reference work on the Old Testament case laws."[26] There is not much difference in how one approaches the Old Testament case laws, whether as law binding for today or as wisdom. Since both views hold that the law is, in some measure, applicable today, adjustments for our current situation must be made for either law or wisdom. Quite frankly, Rushdoony has some good insights into this area. However, the framework in which one views these Old Testament passages is what makes the real difference. Reconstructionists cannot apply the Mosaic law directly since much of it is tied to the physical land of Israel. Therefore, they make modifications similar to those made by someone treating the law as wisdom.

If the proper purpose and role of the church is taken into account, then one takes the case laws as wisdom. If not, then they are wrongly taken as law binding on us today.

It is wrong to conclude from the wisdom view that its advocates hate the law of God or are antinomian pietists. It is not a question of law or no law, but the nature of law and how it is to be used under the new covenant. The wisdom view loves the law; Christians are regenerate and do the law because we walk in the Spirit and fulfill the law of Christ.

God's purpose for the church age is to call out from among the nations a people for his name, to be his Son's bride. The purpose for this age is different than the previous one. Therefore, while there is continuity between the ages, there is also discontinuity. God's purpose is not Christianization of the world but evangelization. The church is the instrument for calling the peoples of the world to repent and believe the gospel. Those who respond are to be built up by the Word of God which he has given to his church. We are involved in tireless activity while our Master has gone on a long journey; we are eagerly waiting for his Son to come from heaven and deliver us from the wrath to come. This is the purpose and goal of this present church age.

Chapter 9, Notes

1. David Chilton, *The Days of Vengeance: An Exposition of the Book of Revelation* (Fort Worth: Dominion Press, 1987), 462. Chilton does not even deal with the Acts 15:14 passage in his book on eschatology, *Paradise Restored*. This is not surprising, since this is a passage which speaks directly to the issue of the purpose of this age, which does not include the establishment of God's kingdom.

2. Chilton, *Vengeance*, 587.

3. Robert L. Saucy, "The Presence of the Kingdom and the Life of the Church," *Bibliotheca Sacra* 145 (January-March 1988):46.

4. Ibid., 44-45.

5. Gary North, *Liberating Planet Earth: An Introduction to Biblical Blueprints* (Fort Worth: Dominion Press, 1987), 142.

6. Kenneth J. Gentry, Jr., "The Greatness of the Great Commission," *Journal of Christian Reconstruction* 7 (Winter 1981):47.

7. Saucy, "Presence of the Kingdom," 45.

8. Ibid.

9. Ibid.

10. George Grant, *The Changing of the Guard: Biblical Principles for Political Action* (Fort Worth: Dominion Press, 1987), 90.

11. Charles C. Ryrie, *Dispensationalism Today* (Chicago: Moody Press, 1965), 63.

12. Ray R. Sutton, *That You May Prosper: Dominion By Covenant* (Tyler, Tex.: Institute for Christian Economics, 1987), 242.

13. Ibid., 243.

14. J. Dwight Pentecost, *The Words and Works of Jesus Christ: A Study of the Life of Christ* (Grand Rapids: Zondervan Publishing House, 1981), 385.

15. Sutton, *That You May Prosper*, 244.

16. Personal letter from Dave Hunt to Thomas Ice, 21 December 1987.

17. Ryrie, *Dispensationalism*, 134.

18. Wayne G. Strickland, "Preunderstanding and Daniel Fuller's Law-Gospel Continuum," *Bibliotheca Sacra* 144 (April-June 1987):192.

19. Grant, *Changing of the Guard*, 106.

20. Ibid., 107.

21. Gary North, *Dominion and Common Grace: The Biblical Basis of Progress* (Tyler, Tex.: Institute for Christian Economics, 1987), 94.

22. R. J. Rushdoony, "Against Much Praying," *Chalcedon Report*, November 1987, 15.

23. T. Mark Duncan, "The Five Points of Christian Reconstruction from the Lips of our Lord," *The Counsel of Chalcedon*, July 1988, 31.

24. Cornelius Van Til, *Essays on Christian Education* (Phillipsburg, N.J.: Presbyterian & Reformed Publishing Co., 1971), 36.

25. Cornelius Van Til, *The Defense of the Faith*, 3d ed. (Phillipsburg, N.J.: Presbyterian & Reformed Publishing Co., 1967), 66.

26. Gary North, "Publisher's Preface" in Chilton, *Vengeance*, xxvi.

PART 3

WHAT THE FUTURE HOLDS

Chapter 10

Is Premillennialism a Heresy?

*I*s premillennialism *heresy*? This is what some Reconstructionists think. R.J. Rushdoony associates it with such heresies as Manichaeanism, racism, Arminianism and Pharisaism,[1] and says, "premillennialism existed as a heresy in the church, rising and falling in various eras, long before John Darby."[2] Rushdoony sees premillennialism leading to the "Pharisaism which crucified Christ and which masqueraded, as it still does, as the epitome of godliness. There can be no compromise with this vicious heresy."[3] These are strong words.

Since heresy is "a deliberate denial of revealed truth coupled with the acceptance of error,"[4] it is a serious matter to accuse someone of believing and spreading heresy. Throughout church history, many have been put to death for real and perceived heresy. Is premillennialism a heresy that is finally being exposed for what it really is? We will examine such claims after first defining the three major views of the end times.

THREE MAJOR VIEWS OF ESCHATOLOGY

There are three major views of eschatology, and each revolves around its view of the return of Christ in relation to

193

the millennium or the kingdom of God. The three systems are premillennialism, amillennialism, and postmillennialism. While these terms are widely used and are the accepted labels for the three viewpoints, they can be misleading if not understood properly. It will be helpful for us to hear a brief description by a proponent of each category.

Premillennialism

John F. Walvoord describes his *premillennial* faith as "an interpretation that the Second Coming of Christ will occur before His literal reign of one thousand years on earth."[5] After his victorious intervention into history, Christ will personally reign from Jerusalem producing a time of peace, prosperity, and righteousness. Premillennialists identify the present era as the church age, a work separate and distinct from that of Israel in God's plan. Christ's redemptive work is the only basis for salvation for the believer regardless of the period of time in which he lives.

Amillennialism

Amillennialism is described by Floyd E. Hamilton as the view "that Christ's millennial kingdom extends from His Resurrection from the tomb to the time of His Second Coming on the clouds at the end of this age."[6] There is no literal, future reign of Christ on the earth. "On earth, Christ's kingdom 'is not of this world,' but He reigns esp. in the hearts of His people on earth . . . for a 'thousand years,' the perfect, complete time between the two comings of Christ."[7] After the future second coming of Christ, believers from all of history will enter into heaven for eternity immediately following the final judgment of all mankind.

Postmillennialism

The Christian Reconstruction movement advocates the postmillennial prophetic perspective. Norman Shepherd defines *postmillennialism* as "the view that Christ will return at the end of an extended period of righteousness and prosperity (the millennium)."[8] Like the amillennialist, the postmillennialist considers the current age the kingdom of God. However, the reign of Christ is not just in the hearts of believers today; it also has an impact on society.

> [The postmillennialist] expects a future period when revealed truth will be diffused throughout the world and accepted by the vast majority. The millennial era will therefore be a time of peace, material prosperity, and spiritual glory.

> The millennium will be of extended duration though not necessarily a precise 1,000 years. Because it is established through means presently operative, its beginning is imperceptible. Some postmillennialists provide for a gradual establishment of the millennium; others for a more abrupt beginning. Most, but not all, allow for a brief apostasy or resurgence of evil just prior to the advent and in preparation for the judgment. Even during the millennium, the world will not be entirely without sin, and not every person will be converted.[9]

Postmillennial and Amillennial Similarities

Since the following discussion will concentrate on the debate between premillennialists and postmillennialists, the amillennial position will not be discussed further. However, it should be pointed out that amillennialists and postmillennialists have more in common with each other than they do with premillennialists. Walvoord believes that "premillennialism is obviously a viewpoint quite removed from either amillennialism or postmillennialism."[10] This is so, he maintains, because premillennialists are more consistently literal in their hermeneutical approach than the other two.

Reconstructionists have noted their closer kinship with their amillennialist brethren as well. David Chilton links amil-

lennialists and postmillennialists together because of their common belief that the kingdom or millennium is the current age.
Premillennialists see it as future. He declares, "orthodox Christianity has always been postmillennialist. . . . At the same
time, orthodox Christianity has always been amillennialist (i.e.,
non-millenarian)."[11] More to the point Chilton declares, "What
I'm saying is this: Amillennialism and Postmillennialism are
the same thing. The only fundamental difference is that 'post-
mils' believe the world will be converted, and 'amils' don't.
Otherwise, I'm an amil.[12] Ray Sutton claims that Rushdoony
took Princeton professor Geerhardus Vos's *The Pauline Eschatology* and used this amillennial system to restructure his
brand of postmillennialism.[13]

As can be expected, there is a spectrum of postmillennialism represented by various voices within the Christian Reconstruction movement, but it would not be improper to label
this synthesized version of the two systems "neopostmillennialism." Most within the movement have added an innovation
or two, rather than adopting the classical version.[14]

PREMILLENNIALISM CHARGED WITH HERESY

A striking characteristic of the Reconstructionists is their
tendency to argue that many aspects of history have been distorted or dropped out by modern revisionists.[15] While Reconstructionists are correct concerning their overall philosophy of
history and much of the time on many points of history, on
occasion they have been guilty of the same charge they level
at the revisionists. One major example is the misguided charge
that premillennialism is heresy. David Chilton boldly claims:

> The notion that the reign of Christ is something
> wholly future, to be brought in by some great social
> cataclysm, is not a Christian doctrine. It is an unor-
> thodox teaching, generally espoused by heretical
> sects on the fringes of the Christian Church.[16]

The Supposed Link with Cerinthus

Chilton more specifically charges that premillennialism "seems to have been originated by the Ebionite arch-heretic Cerinthus, a 'false apostle.'"[17] This charge cannot in any way be supported; it is a pure fabrication. There are no records from church history that lead to such a conclusion. Chilton needs to find a historian outside of his own camp who will support his claim. If premillennialism was the heresy of Cerinthus, then why were the early church fathers who opposed and defeated Cerinthus also premillennial?

Chilton's use of the word *seems* is particularly disturbing. One should have a well-documented case before calling heretical a major segment of the orthodox Christian church down through the years. Some modern writers have called dispensational premillennialism heretical, but Chilton and company are alone in calling all forms of premillennialism unorthodox. Rushdoony is correct in noting that one's religious philosophy so often determines how he views the past. Let's look at the charge by Chilton.

Cerinthus. Cerinthus (c. 100) was certainly the Ebionite arch-heretic which Chilton notes. Cerinthus was a gnostic. He taught that the world was not created by God but by an angel. He also taught that Jesus was just a man, but he had more wisdom and righteousness than other men. Cerinthus held that the Christ spirit descended on Jesus at his baptism and departed before his crucifixion. Thus Jesus was not really God.[18]

Even though Cerinthus was indeed a heretic, Chilton is wrong in implying that Cerinthus was the originator of premillennialism. Chilton completely misconstrues a quote by Irenaeus where he speaks of Cerinthus as a heretic by claiming that Irenaeus's objections were against premillennialism. As we look into the life of Irenaeus, we will see that Chilton has twisted quotes about Cerinthus from the pen of Irenaeus.

Irenaeus. Contrary to Chilton's statement, one of the earliest premillennialists was Irenaeus (130-202), who as a boy probably studied under Polycarp, who in turn was a disciple of the apostle John.[19] Irenaeus is one of the sources Chilton uses to link premillennialism to Cerinthus. Yet Irenaeus did not say or imply that Cerinthus and the Ebionites originated premillennialism.

The fourth-century historian Eusebius does say that Cerinthus believed in "an earthly reign of Christ." However, let us look at the full statement of Eusebius and see if this is really the kind of premillennialism that Irenaeus or any of the fathers taught. Irenaeus did not disassociate himself from Cerinthus because Cerinthus was within the broad spectrum of premillennialism; on the other hand, he did disassociate himself from Cerinthus because of his errant views on the person of Christ.[20]

> For this is the doctrine of Cerinthus, that there will
> be an earthly reign of Christ; and as he was a lover
> of the body, and altogether sensual in those things
> which he so eagerly craved, he dreamed that he
> would revel in the gratification of the sensual appe-
> tite, i.e. in eating and drinking, and marrying; and
> to give the things a milder aspect and expression,
> in festivals and sacrifices, and the slaying of vic-
> tims.[21]

This "earthly reign of Christ" is more like the Muslim or Mormon view of carnal banqueting, and it is consistent with the Gnostic tendency of Cerinthus. But would Irenaeus, a clear and strong premillennialist, be speaking against premillennialism in general, or the misguided extremes of this early heretic?[22] Irenaeus is attempting to clarify the truth on the matter, as a premillennialist, not arguing against premillennialism per se. It is wrong for Chilton to link all the premillennialists of the early church with Cerinthus's view. If that were the case then Irenaeus himself is guilty. Irenaeus clearly believed in a future, literal, thousand-year reign of Christ on the earth, but he did not think it would be a drunken orgy as did Cerinthus. Modern premillennialists would join with amillennialists and postmillennialists in speaking out against such a view of the kingdom.

Another issue should be raised regarding this matter. Early premillennial fathers such as Irenaeus do not portray Cerinthus as a heretic because of his "drunken orgy" view of the millennium. This charge is made later by antimillennialists such as Eusebius, whom Chilton quotes as his source. In fact, it is highly probable that Cerinthus was not a millennialist, since it would clearly conflict with his gnosticism.

Consider this for a moment: What gnostic, who did not believe that the Christ had a physical body in his first coming, would believe that there was going to be a physical, literal kingdom on earth in the future with carnal orgies? So it is debatable whether Cerinthus even held to a premillennial view. It would certainly be inconsistent with his Christology. George Peters has said this concerning the Cerinthian issue:

> For it must ever be borne in mind that what we know of Cerinthus [as holding Chiliasm] comes from the bitter adversaries of Millenarianism, while the Chiliastic opposers of Cerinthus never mention his holding so grossly to a carnal Millennium. . . . Neander doubts the Chiliasm of Cerinthus as reported simply because it would be antagonistic to his own system and . . . adds: "It may be a question, indeed, whether he entertained such gross and sensual notions of this Millennial Sabbath as Caius and Dionysius imputed to him; for such views would hardly be in keeping with his system as a whole.[23]

The Supposed Link with Paganism

Chilton concludes his "documentation" of the charge that premillennialism is heresy by quoting from the French Catholic, Louis Bouyer. Bouyer suggests that "premillennial literalism" is a pagan product, while the more symbolic view of the millennium is a later mature development of the church.[24] This apologist is typical of the Catholic position on eschatology. Since the Roman Church is supposed to be the mother of all historic orthodoxy, the fact that she is out of step with the early church on eschatology is one glaring discontinuity. Since Rome follows the later development of Augustine and the church's shift away from premillennialism in the fifth century, Catholics have argued that Augustine's view was a maturity in the primitive church away from childish chiliasm.

It is also not surprising to see Chilton have to resort to a Roman Catholic scholar as his only scholarly support for his historical misinterpretation. Scholar Hans Bietenhard, after noting how the early church was solidly chiliastic until the time of Augustine, says,

> Today, it is admitted on all hands—except for a few Roman Catholic exegetes—that only an eschatological interpretation [in the context meaning chiliastic one] is consistent with the text. If the question is still open whether the hope is to be maintained or not, it will now be decided by other than exegetical and historical considerations.[25]

Chilton has found in Louis Bouyer one of those few Roman Catholics who still hold to a distorted view of the early church's eschatology. Ironically, if one examines the logic of Chilton closely, he proves too much, for he adds proof to the well established fact that it was allegorical hermeneutics which led to the decline of early premillennialism.

First, in an earlier reference, Bouyer says that the early church fathers' view of eschatology shows "clearly that the strangeness of so many of the characteristics of sub-apostolic Christianity does not necessarily mean heresy."[26] Chilton uses Bouyer's analysis to support his point that premillennialism is heresy, whereas Bouyer clearly says that it is not.

Second, Bouyer admits that premillennialism has a line of descent from the apostles themselves: "Millenarianism, born, it would seem, in Asiatic circles, among those 'presbyters,' those 'ancients,' themselves disciples of the Apostles, whose sayings Papias gathered together . . . soon spread far more widely."[27]

Rather than explaining it as coming from a heathen background, just the opposite is more likely true. Since Papias (c. 60-130), one of the earliest sources for premillennialism, is one of the fathers said to have been a hearer of the apostle John in Asia (author of the Revelation), it makes better sense to see premillennialism as coming from an apostolic rather than a heathen source. Asia would have better access to the Revelation of John and thus was more influenced by its fruit—premillennialism.[28]

Third, Bouyer, by arguing against "premillennial literalism," is arguing for a nonearthly kingdom. This would rule out the type of postmillennial kingdom Chilton envisions: "Christians rule with Christ in His Kingdom now, in this age . . . and Christianity is destined to take over all the kingdoms of the earth."[29] For Chilton to have a kingdom in this present age requires a literal kingdom, which means he would partake of the "literalism" which Bouyer objects to.

Fourth, Chilton summarizes Bouyer as saying, "some early Church Fathers (e.g. Justin Martyr) adopted premillennial literalism because of their heathen background, to which the Biblical literary genres and imagery were unfamiliar."[30] Though Bouyer is admitting that the early church was indeed premillennial, the source for this eschatology is mistaken. The earliest times of the church were in many ways some of the least pagan of all church history, since the church at her birth was almost totally Jewish and often purged by persecution. It is as the church became more Gentile, and consequently more pagan, that the pagan idea of *spiritualization* began to take root, and orthodoxy moved from premillennialism to Augustinian amillennialism. One writer put it this way:

> And I must say again that I am glad of such unexceptional testimony as Jerome's to the fact that this was the judgment of the 'Jewish Church,' and that to hold the Millenarian doctrine was to 'Judaize!' It would not be difficult to show that this ancient doctrine of the Church was maintained, and unim-

pugned, until the Christian Church began to HEATHENIZE."[31]

It is true that Justin Martyr was heavily influenced by Greek philosophy, but that only means that his premillennialism was cast in a more pagan vein. In other words, he took the orthodoxy of his day, premillennialism, and cast it to some degree into a non-Christian framework.[32] He did not develop it out of that kind of framework. If anything, most scholars believe it was Augustine's eschatology, not the early church's premillennial eschatology, that was influenced by pagan philosophy.

Fifth, why would such strong premillennialists such as Irenaeus, Tertullian, and Hippolytus argue against the philosophically influenced views of Justin as a defense of premillennialism, if premillennialism is the product of these early pagan influences? In fact Justin was arguing against the Jewish notions of his day, while Irenaeus, Tertullian, and Hippolytus argued against Justin and supported the Jewish thought.[33]

PREMILLENNIALISM'S PROMINENCE IN THE EARLY CHURCH

The Belief of the Church Fathers

Premillennialism was the pervasive view of the earliest orthodox fathers. This is the consensus of both liberal and conservative scholars in historical theology. J.N.D. Kelly, acknowledged internationally as an authority on patristic Christian thought, is typical of the scholarly opinion on this question and notes that the early church was chiliastic or millenarian in its eschatology. Speaking of the eschatology of the second century he observes:

> The clash with Judaism and paganism made it imperative to set out the bases of the revealed dogmas more thoroughly. The Gnostic tendency to dissolve Christian eschatology into the myth of the soul's

upward ascent and return to God had to be resisted. On the other hand millenarianism, or the theory that the returned Christ would reign on earth for a thousand years, came to find increasing support among Christian teachers. . . . This millenarian, or 'chiliastic,' doctrine was widely popular at this time.[34]

Kelly asserts further that premillennialism or chiliasm was dominate through the middle of the third century: "The great theologians who followed the Apologists, Irenaeus, Tertullian and Hippolytus, were primarily concerned to defend the traditional eschatological scheme against Gnosticism. . . . They are all exponents of millenarianism."[35]

Still another historian says,

Primitive Christianity was marked by great chiliastic enthusiasm. . . . By chiliasm, strictly speaking, is meant the belief that Christ was to return to earth and reign visibly for one thousand years. That return was commonly placed in the immediate future.[36]

Further insight into the eschatology of the early church is noted by Kelly:

Irenaeus, for example, treats the hope of a resplendent earthly Jerusalem as traditional orthodoxy, and protests against attempts to allegorize away the great texts of the Old Testament and Revelation which appear to look forward to it. Tertullian likewise, after establishing the reality of Christ's heavenly kingdom, adds that this by no means excludes an earthly kingdom also. In fact, the latter is due to come before the former, and it will last for a thousand years.[37]

If all forms of premillennialism are heresy, then Chilton is willing to wipe out the first two and a half centuries of orthodox fathers. Harry Bultema said, "Except for Cerinthus, who apparently expected some sort of a millennium as the Mormons do today, it was the most pernicious sects such as the Alogi and the Gnostics who opposed this doctrine [of premillennial eschatology]."[38]

Premillennialism was not contradicted by a single orthodox church father until the beginning of the third century, when Gaius (Caius) first launched an attack. Gaius is the first one in recorded church history who interpreted the thousand years symbolically. Additionally, he also rejected the Book of Revelation, holding that it was written by Cerinthus and should not be in the canon.[39] But even with Gaius' appearance, premillennialism was still very much the eschatology of the day.

Some Early Opposition

Premillennialism was attacked by the Alexandrian school in Egypt during the middle of the third century, and Augustine's influence prevailed against it by the fifth century.

> During the third century the belief in chiliasm as a part of the Church's faith died out in nearly all parts of the Church. It did not seem called for by the condition of the Church, which was rapidly adjusting itself to the world in which it found itself. The scientific theology, especially that of Alexandria, found no place in its system for such an article as chiliasm. The belief lingered, however, in country places, and with it went no little opposition to the "scientific" exegesis which by means of allegory explained away the promises of a millennial kingdom.[40]

Clement of Alexandria and his pupil Origen popularized not so much another view as an antichiliastic polemic. In fact, Origen and his viewpoint are accused of having destroyed the Eastern churches.

> The attack against Chiliasm by these dissenters cannot meet with our approval, for they placed their

speculation above the Word of God and distorted it according to their grandiloquent ideas, denying the resurrection of the body and the future glorification of the material world, which was also created by God; for according to them the material world, matter, contained sin from which the spirit of man must liberate itself. It was only natural and a matter of course that they were very much against Chiliasm, but they threw away, as a German saying goes, with the bath water the baby also. They were a kind of Hymenaeus and Philetus who had departed from the truth, saying the resurrection was past already (2 Tim. 2:17). The success of the pernicious principles of this school was the first and chief cause of the decline of Chiliasm (emphasis added).[41]

Fellow Reconstructionist Greg Bahnsen has accused David Chilton and his hermeneutical mentor, James Jordan, of an overly speculative hermeneutic.

Jordan finds esoteric meaning in the fact that the word "mother" is used exactly six times in Judges 17:1-6. Karl Hubenthal . . . duly criticized this as allegorizing the text. Jordan's "defense" . . . was two-fold: (1) Cassuto also reasons in this way [so what?], and (2) this was an "ancient literary device." Well, the ancient world certainly did sport many hermetic, esoteric, and especially allegorical works (e.g., Philo), but I find it strange that Jordan makes the Bible one of them! Interpretive Maximalism leaves the interpreter with an unsure game of "guessing" (as the end of Jordan's letter admits), rather than a confident "thus saith the Lord."[42]

Since Chilton, Jordan, and many other Reconstructionists handle the Scriptures in a manner described by Bahnsen as "allegorical," is it any wonder to find them in league with historical traditions of the same stripe?

Supported by the Council of Nicaea

The Council that decided the Arian controversy, the Council of Nicaea (A.D. 325), is said by Philip Schaff to be "the most important event of the fourth century."[43] In the expanded form of the Nicene Creed which grew out of this Council (A.D. 381), it reads, "We look for the resurrection of the dead, and the life of the world to come. Amen."[44] The Council provided the following explanation for this article:

> The world was made less on account of God's providence, for God knew beforehand that man would sin. For that reason we look forward to new heavens and a new earth according to the Holy Scriptures: the appearance in the Kingdom of our great God and Savior, who will become visible to us. And as Daniel says, "The holy ones of the Most High shall receive the Kingdom." And there will be a pure and holy earth, the land of the living and not of the dead, of which David, seeing with the eye of faith, is speaking (Ps. 27:13): "I believe that I shall see the goodness of the Lord in the land of the living"— the land of the meek and humble.[45]

Notice that although the word *millennium* is not used, the creed is clearly referring to a future, not present, kingdom; a future, not present-age resurrection. This early church statement came over three hundred years after the kingdom is said by postmillennialists to have been instituted. Not only is the postmillennial view not even hinted at in the early traditions, but the premillennial view can be clearly and strongly identified.

The premillennialism of this first church council is acknowledged by the founder of postmillennialism himself, Daniel Whitby (1638-1726). Whitby, speaking of premillennialism, lists many of the early fathers who held it and includes "the first Nicene Council."[46] In fact Whitby clearly believed that the early church held to a premillennial eschatology.

> The doctrine of the Millennium, or the reign of the saints on earth a thousand years, is now rejected by all Roman Catholics, and by the greatest part of Protestants, and yet it passed among the best of Christians for two hundred and fifty years for a tradition apostolical; and as such is delivered by many Fathers of the second and third century, who spake of it as the tradition of our Lord and his apostles, and of all the ancients that lived before them; who tell us the very words in which it was delivered, the Scriptures, which were then so interpreted, and say that it was held by all Christians who were exactly orthodox.[47]

With an admission like this from an opponent, premillennialism has nothing to fear in arguing against postmillennialism.

The Pagan Influence in
Premillennialism's Decline

Pagan philosophy was evident in the denial of the resurrection in at least two instances in the ministry of Paul. The sermon on Mars Hill in Acts 17 shows their violent reaction as Paul preached "the resurrection of the dead" (v. 32). A more extensive defense of the Christian resurrection is given by Paul in 1 Corinthians 15. Because of the Greek denial of the importance of the physical realm, they denied the whole idea that resurrection was possible. This bias against the physical was the basis for rejection of a future physical kingdom of God on earth, and Greek philosophy was the conduit.

> In the early Christian centuries Chiliasm first weakened with the strengthening among the Christians of Greek philosophical thought. . . . Greek sentiment and thought opposed even the conception of a final historical drama and a real Millennial kingdom on this earth.[48]

Reconstructionist Distortions of the Historical Record

What Chilton "seems" to think is true concerning the earliest beginnings of premillennialism is in reality wrong. In fact it is the postmillennial view that has early ties with paganism. Furthermore, not only do the experts in this field, including postmillennialists, [49] not agree with Chilton's conclusion, they do not even acknowledge his view. Chilton will have to show specific documentation to win support for his case. Even Chilton's Reconstructionist colleague Gary North is not as extreme in his analysis of the church's early eschatology:

> Historically, the church has had defenders of all three positions. The early church fathers were mainly premillennial or postmillennial. The Roman Catholics after Augustine (early fifth century) became mainly amillennial, although there were occasional postmillennial revivals. [50]

At least North admits the historic origin and standing of premillennialism. However, who are the early church fathers who were postmillennial? There are none. Who led those "occasional postmillennial revivals"? They are not there.

Chilton is so anxious to cast aspersion on premillennialism's origins that he severely misstates the evidence. In the same vein, Chilton tries to improve the historical image of the postmillennial position. He redefines some of the issues "broad enough" so that he can hitch the more recent postmillennialism to the wagon of amillennialism and say that this historic orthodox position of the church includes his view. [51]

Postmillennialism: Bringing up the Rear

Postmillennialism was in fact the last of the three major eschatological systems to be developed. It is true that postmillennialism maintained some features of the older amillennialism, but if postmillennialism is to be considered different from the amillennial view, which postmillennialists maintain, then it has to be recognized as just that—a distinct system. It did not originate as a system until the early 1700s. This is the understanding of seemingly all except certain Reconstructionists such as Chilton.[52] Clouse summarizes the historical development of postmillennialism:

> As the popularity of premillennialism waned, postmillennialism rose to prominence. First expressed in the works of certain Puritan scholars, it received its most influential formulation in the writings of the Anglican commentator Daniel Whitby. It seemed to him that the kingdom of God was coming ever closer and that it would arrive through the same kind of effort that had always triumphed in the past. Among the many theologians and preachers who were convinced by the arguments of Whitby was Jonathan Edwards. Edwardsean postmillennialism also emphasized the place of America in the establishment of millennial conditions upon the earth.[53]

This view of the late development of postmillennialism is supported by the postmillennialist John J. Davis. He notes that John Calvin "paved the way for the full flowering of the postmillennial view in English Puritanism," and he acknowledges that the system was popularized "through the writings of the Anglican commentator Daniel Whitby."[54] So Davis, a postmillennialist, concurs with the mainstream thinking that postmillennialism originated shortly after the Reformation.

A New Hypothesis

Daniel Whitby first put forth his views in a popular work entitled *Paraphrase and Commentary on the New Testament* (1703). It was at the end of this work that he first set forth what he calls in his own words "A New Hypothesis" on the millennial reign of Christ. Thus, the system called postmillennialism was born in the early 1700s as a hypothesis. Whitby and his modern followers present their arguments and explanations based upon unproved assumptions—assumptions resulting in a hypothesis rather than something which is the fruit of the study of Scripture or even the voice of the church.

CONCLUSION

The three views of the millennium did not all appear at the same time in church history. Premillennialism was first held by the early church fathers who were the closest to the original apostles. As the allegorical interpretation of the Book of Revelation became entrenched during the time of Augustine, the amillennial view arose and gained almost exclusive dominance until the Reformation. At this time, literal interpretation regained ascendancy, producing a revival of premillennialism, with the birth and development of postmillennialism following closely behind. Postmillennialism rose to dominance during the nineteenth century, while premillennialism made a strong comeback following the Civil War. Amillennialism also saw a revival as many during the last one hundred years moved from the postmillennial position to the amillennial camp. The last twenty years has seen an upsurge of postmillennialism. In fact, the premillennial position is probably more on the decline at the present time than the other two views.

Obviously what the church has believed down through her history is important to Chilton since he makes such strong claims about the historic orthodoxy of postmillennialism and equally strong assertions of heresy toward his opponents. Yet the historical evidence is just not there to support his strong charges.

A recent *Christianity Today* poll revealed that 9 percent of that magazine's readership held to essentially a postmillennial view.[55] This is an optimistic turn of events. Clouse has theorized, "Whenever the United States has faced a time of crisis, there have been those who have revived civil postmillennialism as a means to encourage and comfort their fellow citizens."[56]

This describes well the state of the church in the United States today and could account, at least to some degree, for the desire among many evangelicals to see revival and a victorious church during this age, rather than the end time plan of God. This dominion eschatology seems to be especially gaining among the more politically active evangelicals and the positive confession charismatics. After all, it is easier to rally the troops if you can say convincingly, "We're going to win." In addition, those in the positive confession wing of the charismatic movement have realized that if they can make good things happen in their personal lives by applying their theology, why not in the larger social and political realms?

The debate between premillennialism and postmillennialism will not be settled by examining each other's pedigree. However, since Chilton and other Reconstructionists have tried to use the historical argument to their advantage, we've had to examine their argument to expose their misrepresentations of the historical record.

This mishandling of history also influences Chilton's handling of the Bible; he interprets those passages that speak of a future reign of Christ in light of his misunderstanding of history. Chilton says at the beginning of his chapter on Revelation 20 that one must have the proper historical understanding before engaging in exegesis: "If we wish to gain an understanding of the orthodox position, we must understand that the answer to this precise question cannot be determined *primarily* by the exegesis of particular texts."[57]

Historical understanding is an aid to correct interpretation, but the exegesis of the text is the *most essential* ingredient for gaining a proper understanding of the Bible on any subject. We must resist the temptation to introduce extratextual factors when the text itself does not yield our preconceived interpretation. If we fail to do so the text, seen in the resulting readjusted light, will too easily yield our twisted view.

Even fellow postmillennialist Greg Bahnsen acknowledges that in the debate over eschatology "the opponents must get down to hand-to-hand exegetical combat on particular passages and phrases."[58] This is why careful searching of the Scriptures is essential for a proper understanding of the millennial reign of Christ. Once again, postmillennialist Davis says it well: "The decisive factor in any determination should be biblical exegesis, not some attempt to read the 'signs of the time.' "[59]

Chapter 10, Notes

1. R. J. Rushdoony, *Thy Kingdom Come: Studies in Daniel and Revelation* (Fairfax, Va.: Thoburn Press, 1970), 134.

2. R. J. Rushdoony, *God's Plan for Victory: The Meaning of Post Millennialism* (Fairfax, Va.: Thoburn Press, 1977), 5.

3. Rushdoony, *Thy Kingdom Come*, 134.

4. M. R. W. Farrer, s.v. "Heresy," in *Evangelical Dictionary of Theology*, ed. Walter A. Elwell (Grand Rapids: Baker Book House, 1984), 508.

5. John F. Walvoord, s.v. "Premillennialism" in *The Zondervan Pictorial Encyclopedia of the Bible*, ed. Merrill C. Tenney (Grand Rapids: Zondervan Publishing House, 1975), 4:845-6.

6. Floyd E. Hamilton, s.v. "Amillennialism," in *The Zondervan Pictorial Encyclopedia of the Bible*, 1:129.

7. Ibid.

8. Norman Shepherd, s.v. "Postmillennialism," in *The Zondervan Pictorial Encyclopedia of the Bible*, 4:822.

9. Ibid.

10. John F. Walvoord, *The Millennial Kingdom* (Grand Rapids: Zondervan Publishing House, 1959), 6.

11. David Chilton, *Days of Vengeance: An Exposition of the Book of Revelation* (Fort Worth: Dominion Press, 1987), 494.

12. Personal letter from David Chilton to Thomas Ice, 17 December 1986.

13. Ray Sutton, "Studies/ Book of Daniel I," taped message 4,022 from Geneva Ministries, Tyler, Texas, n.d.

14. See a presentation of the more classical version by Loraine Boettner, *The Millennium* (Phillipsburg, N.J.: Presbyterian & Reformed Publishing Co., 1957). More recently Boettner's "Postmillennialism," in *The Meaning of the Millennium: Four Views*, ed. Robert G. Clouse (Downers Grove, Ill.: InterVarsity Press, 1977), 117-52. Rushdoony has noted, "I was delighted when I found that position [postmillennialism] in Dr. Loraine Boettner, who really is the father of modern postmillennialism, though unfortunately he does not combine it with a theonomist position" (Michael D. Philbeck, "An Interview with R. J. Rushdoony," *The Counsel of Chalcedon*, October 1983, 14).

15. R. J. Rushdoony, *The Biblical Philosophy of History* (Phillipsburg, N.J.: Presbyterian & Reformed Publishing Co., 1969). Here Rushdoony applies his Van Tilian approach to history. He rightly points out that one's religious philosophy governs his view of history. This is abundantly illustrated with brilliant Van Tilian rigor, that modern views of history are suicidal, implicitly desiring an end of history. This mentality carries over into the movement. Reconstructionists believe that premillennialists are wrong, and often say they are historically heretics, but they do so without backing it up from the specifics of history. This polemical use of history is an ideological projection of the way they think history should have been: it is not based on observations of the way it really was.

16. Chilton, *Vengeance*, 494.

17. Ibid., n. 2.

18. G. L. Carey, s.v. "Cerinthus," in *The New International Dictionary of the Christian Church*, ed. J. D. Douglas (Grand Rapids: Zondervan Publishing House, 1974), 207.

19. D. F. Wright, s.v. "Irenaeus," in *The New International Dictionary of the Christian Church*, 516.

20. Irenaeus was certainly not a postmillennialist or an amillennialist. In fact it is not an overstatement to note that Irenaeus was one of the strongest and most extensive premillennialists of the early church. Amillennial and postmillennial views are later developments in church history.

21. Eusebius, *Ecclesiastical History*, vii.xxv.2-3.

22. Irenaeus wrote against Cerinthus in *Against Heresies*, Book 1, Chapter 26.

23. George N. H. Peters, *The Theocratic Kingdom*, 3 vols. (1884; reprint, Grand Rapids: Kregel Publications, 1972), 1:454.

24. Chilton, *Vengeance*, 494.

25. Hans Bietenhard, "The Millennial Hope in the Early Church," *Scottish Journal of Theology* (1953):30. Special thanks to Doug Riggs for providing this article.

26. Louis Bouyer, *The Spirituality of the New Testament and the Fathers* (New York: Desclee Company, 1963), 171.

27. Ibid., 171-2.

28. See G. W. H. Lampe, "Early Patristic Eschatology," in *Eschatology: Four Papers Read to The Society for the Study of Theology* (Edinburgh: Oliver & Boyd LTD., 1953), 31-32.

29. Chilton, *Vengeance*, 587.

30. Ibid., 494.

31. Eruvin, as quoted by Nathaniel West, *The Thousand Years in Both Testaments* (New York: Revell, 1880), 388.

32. Postmillennialists also have had advocates with whom they have not been pleased. Many premillennialists have made the charge over the years that postmillennialism included the liberal Social Gospel movement of the late 1800s and early 1900s. (Hal Lindsey, *The Late Great Planet Earth* [Grand Rapids: Zondervan Publishing House, 1970], 176.) While this is said by postmillennialists to be unfair—the linking of conservative postmillennialists with liberal postmillennialists—the fact remains that there is a liberal version of postmillennialism. David Chilton has cried foul on this issue:

> The dominion outlook is equated with the liberal "Social Gospel" movement of the early 1900s. Such an identification is utterly absurd, devoid of *any* [emphasis added] foundation whatsoever. The leaders of the Social Gospel movement were evolutionary humanists and socialists, and were openly hostile toward Biblical Christianity. It is true that they *borrowed* [emphasis original] certain terms and concepts from Christianity, in order to pervert them for their own uses. (Chilton, *Paradise Restored: An Eschatology of Dominion* [Tyler, Tex.: Reconstruction Press, 1985], 228.)

Chilton begins his reaction by declaring, "Such an identification is utterly absurd, devoid of any foundation whatsoever." Well, if that exclusive statement is correct, why does Chilton start to admit a couple of sentences later that there is after all some basis? "It is true that they borrowed certain terms and concepts from Christianity." So if they "borrowed" then there is some foundation after all, not "devoid of any foundation whatsoever."

33. See J. N. D. Kelly, *Early Christian Doctrines* (San Francisco: Harper & Row, 1978), 465-9.

34. Ibid., 465.

35. Ibid., 467, 469.

36. Joseph Cullen Ayer, *A Source Book for Ancient Church History: From the Apostolic Age to the Close of the Conciliar Period* (New York: AMS Press, 1970), 25.

37. Kelly, *Early Christian Doctrines*, 469.

38. Harry Bultema, *Maranatha! A Study of Unfulfilled Prophecy* (Grand Rapids: Kregel Publications, 1985), 294.

39. "Gaius," in *The Oxford Dictionary of the Christian Church*, ed. F. L. Cross (London: Oxford University Press, 1957), 535.

40. Ayer, *Source Book*, 219.

41. H. Hoekstra, cited by Bultema, *Maranatha!*, 296.

42. Greg Bahnsen, "Another Look At Chilton's *Days of Vengeance*," *Journey Magazine*, March-April 1988, 12.

43. Philip Schaff, *Nicene and Post-Nicene Christianity*, vol. 3 of *The History of the Christian Church* (Grand Rapids: Wm. B. Eerdmans Publishing Co., 1910), 631.

44. Philip Schaff, *The History of Creeds*, vol. 1 of *The Creeds of Christendom* (Grand Rapids: Baker Book House, 1919), 29.

45. Cited by Bultema, *Maranatha!*, 243-4.

46. Cited by Daniel T. Taylor and H. L. Hastings, *The Reign of Christ on Earth or The Voice of the Church in All Ages Concerning the Coming and Kingdom of the Redeemer* (Boston: H. L. Hastings, 1881), 228.

47. Ibid.

48. Erich Sauer, *From Eternity to Eternity* (Grand Rapids: Wm. B. Eerdmans Publishing Co., 1954), 141.

49. A recent postmillennialist, John Jefferson Davis, recognizes the historic roots of premillennialism: "The more pessimistic premillennial outlook was popular in the first three centuries of the Christian church, when believers were periodically threatened with persecution, were social outcasts, and exercised little influence within the political system." (John Jefferson Davis, *Christ's Victorious Kingdom: Postmillennialism Reconsidered* (Grand Rapids: Baker Book House, 1986), 118.)

50. Gary North, *Unholy Spirits: Occultism and New Age Humanism* (Fort Worth: Dominion Press, 1986), 381.

51. Chilton, *Vengeance*, 493-8.

52. Some of the major works on the matter include Iain Murray, *The Puritan Hope: A Study in Revival and the Interpretation of Prophecy* (Carlisle, Penn.: The Banner of Truth Trust, 1971); J. A. De Jong, *As the Waters Cover the Sea: Millennial Expectations in the Rise of Anglo-American Missions 1640-1810* (J.H. Kok N.V. Kampen, 1970); Greg Bahnsen, "The *Prima Facie* Acceptability of Postmillennialism," *The Journal of Christian Reconstruction* 3 (Winter 1976-77):48-105. Bahnsen tries to make Calvin a postmillennialist, which is doubtful. By simply observing the era from which almost all the postmillennial quotes cited by Bahnsen are taken, it shows that they were from about 1600 on. This is when the majority of scholars say postmillennialism arose as a system. In this way, Bahnsen's article supports the standard view of historians that postmillennialism is a post-Reformation, Puritan development. Peter Toon, editor, *Puritans, The Millennium and the Future of Israel: Puritan Eschatology 1600 to 1660* (London: James Clarke & Co., 1970). See especially the contributions of Toon and R. G. Clouse. Bryan W. Ball, *A Great Expectation: Eschatological Thought in English Protestantism to 1660* (Leiden: E. J. Brill, 1975).

53. R. G. Clouse, s.v. "Millennium, Views of the," *Evangelical Dictionary of Theology*, 717.

54. Davis, *Christ's Victorious Kingdom*, 16-17.

55. "Readers Poll," *Christianity Today*, 6 February 1987, 9-I.

56. Clouse, "Millennium," 718.

57. Chilton, *Vengeance*, 493.

58. Bahnsen, "*Prima Facie* Acceptability," 57.

59. Davis, *Christ's Victorious Kingdom*, 127.

Chapter 11

Thy Kingdom Not Yet Come

"Christians rule with Christ in His Kingdom now, in this age . . . and Christianity is destined to take over all the kingdoms of the earth."[1]

"Jesus is the King, and His Kingdom has arrived. . . . The Kingdom was established when Christ came. But it has not yet reached its full development."[2]

"Christ ushered in the kingdom of God."[3]

"Now His kingdom is of this world. Now His followers do fight for His honor . . . His kingdom is now visible in this world through His people."[4]

"But the church age (kingdom age) had been in operation for 40 years by 70 A.D."[5]

Reconstructionists clearly believe this current age is the kingdom age predicted by the prophets in the Old Testament. However, they often speak as well of the coming of the kingdom. Gary DeMar and Peter Leithart advocate the importance for Christians to pray for the coming of Christ's kingdom:

All opposition in all areas will be overcome by the King. And as it is, it will be an indication that the Messianic kingdom is coming. Christ taught His disciples to pray: "Thy kingdom come, thy will be done, *on earth* as it is in heaven" (Matt. 6:10). That prayer is a continual reminder to us that the coming of the kingdom means the doing of God's will, and that the reign of Christ (His kingdom) through our obedience comes precisely here on earth.[6]

DeMar and Leithart also say that "the kingdom could be *both* present *and* future."[7]

But are the church age and the kingdom age to be equated? Is the kingdom spoken of in the Old Testament and this age the same? Or is one aspect of the kingdom operating now, with another aspect yet to be fulfilled after Christ's coming?

In terms of the universal kingdom, God has and always will rule his world by his sovereignty. But in terms of the Messianic kingdom we believe it has not yet arrived because Messiah has not returned to earth. We offer the following as a tentative definition of the kingdom: "The kingdom is the rule of God through Christ upon the earth."

There are two distinctives which *kingdom* denotes: (1) the act of ruling, and (2) the sphere or territory ruled. Reconstructionist Peter Leithart says, "understood abstractly, it would mean something like 'rule' or 'reign.' If concrete, it would mean 'realm.'"[8] The context of a passage will determine whether the act or sphere is being stressed.

Premillennialist Alva J. McClain lists three essential elements: "first, a ruler with adequate authority and power; second, a realm of subjects to be ruled; and third, the actual exercise of the function of rulership."[9]

Reconstructionists and premillennialists usually do not disagree greatly on abstract definitions of "rule" and "kingdom." DeMar and Leithart have said, "Our view of the Kingdom, oddly enough, has been well summarized by the Dispensationalist theologian Herman Hoyt of Grace Theological Seminary."[10] However, the "major differences between Hoyt's position and ours are 1) the question of timing, and 2) whether or not Christ will be physically present during the millennium."[11]

IN WHAT WAY IS GOD'S KINGDOM PRESENT?

God is sovereign and eternally in control of his creation (the universal kingdom). However, he clearly decreed that the fall and sin would be a part of that plan. Therefore, his kingdom does not eliminate disobedience by the creature. God is working in history to reestablish his kingdom over his creation. He is clearly working through man, especially the Second Adam—Jesus Christ. But that does not mean that his rule is manifested fully at all times in history. It is implemented in different forms. Reconstructionists would agree with this statement.

Premillennialist George Ladd has popularized among evangelicals a view that "the Kingdom of God is in some sense both present and future."[12] Ladd's "already, not yet" approach says that if we understand the kingdom as

> the reign of God, not merely in the human heart but dynamically active in the person of Jesus and in human history, then it becomes possible to understand how the Kingdom of God can be present and future, inward and outward, spiritual and apocalyptic.[13]

Among those who hold to this approach, there has been debate over just where to draw the line between the present form of the kingdom and the future. Often a determining factor is whether the abstract quality of the kingdom is stressed. Leithart emphasizes this aspect when he defines the kingdom as "Christ's saving rule, which produces a sphere of blessing, privilege, and responsibility."[14] Because Reconstructionists stress the present reality of the kingdom, it makes sense that they would opt for a definition which places the emphasis on "rule" rather than "sphere." This is not to say that Reconstructionists do not believe that kingdom includes a realm, but it is to say that they stress the abstract instead of the concrete. Reconstructionists would agree that "it is impossible to reduce the Kingdom concept to the idea of dominion or reign without including the realm in which that reign is exercised."[15]

In recent years there has been a trend for some dispensationalists to adopt a conservative version of an "already, not yet" approach to the kingdom. Dispensationalist Robert Saucy has said, "The kingdom was in some way present in the person of Christ and His words and deeds; yet the primary teaching at the close of His earthly life still looked forward to the kingdom."[16] Saucy is saying that some form of the Messianic kingdom is present, although the theocratic aspects are yet future. However, we believe that whatever dynamic God has given believers today does not mean that the Messianic kingdom is here. We see it as totally future.

David Chilton has said, "Jesus is the King, and His Kingdom has arrived. . . . The Kingdom was established when Christ came. But it has not yet reached its full development."[17] Reconstructionists see Christ's kingdom as having a program, stages, or development involved in it, similar to the argument of dispensationalists. This is clearly seen in the language they use to talk about the kingdom. Gary North asks, "What is God's earthly Kingdom?"[18] The adjective "earthly" distinguishes it from another kind of kingdom.

Premillennialists speak in the same way. McClain called the earthly kingdom the "Mediatorial Kingdom" (method of rule) and contrasted it with the "Universal Kingdom" (extent of rule).[19] McClain calls our attention to the wide scope of how the kingdom of God is spoken of in the Bible:

> First, certain passages present the Kingdom as something which has always existed; yet in other places it seems to have a definite historical beginning among men. (Compare Ps. 10:16 with Dan. 2:44.)

> Second, the Kingdom is set forth in Scripture as universal in its scope, outside of which there is no

created thing; yet again the Kingdom is revealed as a local rule established on earth. (Compare Ps. 103:19 with Isa. 24:23.)

Third, the Kingdom sometimes appears as the rule of God directly, with no intermediary standing between God and man; yet it is also pictured as the rule of God through a mediator who serves as channel between God and man. (Compare Ps. 59:13 with 2:4-6.)

Fourth, it has been noted that often the Bible describes the Kingdom as something wholly future; whereas in other texts the Kingdom is said to be present reality. (Compare Zech. 14:9 with Ps. 29:10.)

Fifth, the Kingdom of God is set forth as an unconditioned rule arising out of the sovereign nature of Deity Himself; yet, on the other hand, it sometimes appears as a Kingdom based on a covenant made by God with man. (Compare Dan. 4:34-35 with Ps. 89:27-29.)

Some of the above distinctions, if not all, have been noticed by Biblical scholars and attempts have been made to explain them; sometimes by asserting the existence of one kingdom with two aspects or phases; or by the assumption of two kingdoms.[20]

Premillennialists believe that God's universal kingdom exists today. It is God who is in charge of the world. God has and always will be providentially at the wheel. But on the other hand, it is the mediatorial kingdom (John Walvoord calls it the millennial kingdom or theocratic kingdom)[21] that Christ will set up at his coming. Charles Ryrie describes this future kingdom as:

the period of a thousand years of the visible, earthly reign of the Lord Jesus Christ, who, after His return

from heaven, will fulfill during that period the promises contained in the Abrahamic, Davidic, and new
covenants to Israel, will bring the whole world to
a knowledge of God, and will lift the curse from
the whole creation.[22]

McClain says that the mediatorial kingdom includes three
elements:

(a) the rule of God through a divinely chosen representative who not only speaks and acts for God but
also represents the people before God; (b) a rule
which has especial reference to the earth; and (c)
having as its mediatorial ruler one who is always a
member of the human race.[23]

Reconstructionists also believe in various stages or
periods of development within the kingdom. Perhaps Chilton
says it clearest as he explains their version of what could be
called an "already, coming, and not yet" view:

Jesus is the King, and His Kingdom has arrived. . . . Things will never be "perfect" before
the Last Judgment. . . . Although the Kingdom was
established definitively in the finished work of
Christ, it is established progressively throughout history (until it is established finally on the Last Day).[24]

Reconstructionists believe the kingdom has been established, but it has not reached the "millennial" stage of its
development. Postmillennialist Loraine Boettner makes a distinction between the kingdom in the present and the millennium
which will come at the end of the present kingdom:

We have defined Postmillennialism as that view of
the last things which holds that the Kingdom of God
is now being extended in the world through the
preaching of the Gospel and the saving work of the
Holy Spirit in the hearts of individuals, that the
world eventually is to be Christianized, and that the

return of Christ is to occur at the close of a long period of righteousness and peace commonly called the "Millennium."[25]

Reconstructionists are constantly mocking premillennialists for not having a victorious view of the kingdom, since we believe that God has predestined total victory in a way that differs from theirs. Who in the Christian Reconstruction movement could say it more colorfully and boldly than Gary North?

> Who said anything about a utopia? Only the pessimists, who use the word in order to ridicule people who preach that Christians are not foreordained to be losers in history. Why is civilization more helpless than the soul of any sinner? The gospel saves sinners, after all. Why should we expect no major social improvements in history? . . . Why shouldn't we expect widespread social and institutional healing in history?
>
> If God is willing to put up with the victory of evil, then there is nothing that Christians can do about it except try to get out of the way of victorious sinners if they possibly can, while handing out gospel tracts on street corners and running rescue missions. The question is: Is God really willing to put up with the the triumph of sinners over His church in history? Yes, say premillennialists and amillennialists. No, say postmillennialists.[26]

It is not that premillennialists do not believe in the triumph of God's people in history. Rather, we see the Bible teaching a different character and timing to the kingdom than do Reconstructionists. "Though there is a rule of God in the present age which can properly be described by the word kingdom, it is not the fulfillment of those prophecies that pertain to the millennial reign of Christ upon the earth."[27]

What is the proper view of this present aspect of the kingdom, and what is the nature of the future, mediatorial kingdom? Moreover, how does this differ with the Reconstructionist postmillennial view? Postmillennialist David Chilton has phrased the problem well: "In essence, the question of the Millennium centers on the mediatorial Kingdom of Christ: When did (or will) Christ's Kingdom begin?"[28] So then, is this present age the kingdom? This is really one of the most crucial questions which divides the premillennialists from both the postmillennialists and most amillennialists.[29]

We equate the mediatorial kingdom with the kingdom in general. We believe that when the Bible speaks of Christ's kingdom, it is the mediatorial kingdom. "Every time the term kingdom is used theologically . . . it refers to the same thing, the kingdom yet to come on this earth inaugurated and governed by the Messiah."[30] E. R. Craven has said concerning the timing of the establishment of the kingdom of God that there "is no critically undisputed passage in the Scriptures which declares, or necessarily implies, even a partial establishment in New Testament times."[31]

The New Testament often refers to the kingdom as something future rather than synonymous with the present age, as the following discussion will show.[32]

Paul puts in the future both the "appearing" of our Lord and "His kingdom" in his charge to Timothy to preach the word (2 Timothy 4:1). Therefore, the kingdom is said to arrive at a point in the future when the Lord appears at his second coming. The passage also links his judgment with this event.

Verse 18 of the same chapter speaks of the Lord's deliverance "from every evil deed, and will bring me safely to His heavenly kingdom." Certainly this deliverance from every evil deed is future. And since it is, then so is his heavenly kingdom.

> This expression is not a synonym for heaven, but rather indicates that the long-awaited Messianic Kingdom will be "heavenly" in origin and character as contrasted with earthly kingdoms. It is the closest approximation to the familiar phrase "kingdom of heaven" so frequently used in Matthew's Gospel.[33]

After being stoned in Derbe, Paul and Barnabas returned to some of the cities they had previously visited and sought to give the newly converted disciples some advice: "Through many tribulations we must enter the kingdom of God" (Acts 14:22). If they were in the kingdom, this statement would make no sense. Since they were not in the kingdom, nor are we, they spoke of it as yet future.

Reconstructionists often cite the Lord's prayer as a mandate for bringing in their postmillennial kingdom. They believe this is their calling to "heavenize" the earth.

> Restoration begins by realizing that we live in the midst of God's kingdom. God's pattern for godly living is established in heaven. In the Lord's Prayer we petition God, "Thy Kingdom come. Thy will be done, on earth as it is in heaven" (Matthew 6:10). God has not called us to forsake the earth, but to impress heaven's pattern on earth.[34]

Premillennialists pray this prayer as well and see it being answered at the second coming when Christ returns and sets up the kingdom that he will rule with a rod of iron. This does not mean that the kingdom is to gradually be brought in by the current resources the church has, as Reconstructionists teach. The passage does not state or imply the means by which this prayer will be answered.

Gary North argues that some of the parables of Matthew 13 (vv. 24-30 and 36-43) refer "to the building of the kingdom of God."[35] However, it is better to see them representing "certain conditions related to the Kingdom which are contemporaneous with the present age. But nowhere in Matthew 13 is the establishment of the Kingdom placed within this age."[36] North further argues that the angels remove the unrighteous at the end of the kingdom or at the end of the world.[37] This can better be understood to be a reference to the Lord removing the unrighteous before the kingdom has begun. Verses 41-43 present the following picture: (1) The Son of Man sends his angels to gather out of his kingdom the unrighteous (v. 41),

(2) the unrighteous are thrown into the furnace of fire (v. 42), and (3) "*Then* the righteous will shine forth as the sun in the Kingdom of their Father" (emphasis added). It is after the judgment and separation that the kingdom begins, since the righteous are left to shine in the kingdom. This also confirms that the current age is not the kingdom.

Dr. McClain gives an excellent summary of the significance of the purpose of the parables in Matthew 13 and how they relate to the kingdom and this present age:

> What is certain in the teaching of these difficult parables is that the present age, viewed from the standpoint of the Kingdom, is a time of preparation. During this period the Son of man is sowing seed (vs. 37), generating and developing a spiritual nucleus for the future Kingdom, a group called "sons of the kingdom" (vs. 38, ASV). At the same time He is permitting a parallel development of evil in the world under the leadership of Satan (vss. 38-39). It is the purpose of God to bring both to a "harvest," when the good and bad will be separated, and then to establish the Kingdom in power and righteousness (vss. 41-43, 49).[38]

Notice what Christ said in Matthew 25:31-32, "But when the Son of Man comes in His glory, and all the angels with Him, then He will sit on His glorious throne. And all the nations will be gathered before Him. . . ." This passage clearly says that Messiah returns first from heaven and then rules in the kingdom of glory.

Peter joins Paul and Jesus in making these kinds of statements. Shortly before his death, Peter said that believers are "to make certain about His calling and choosing you" (2 Peter 1:10). The reason he gave was "in this way the entrance into the eternal kingdom of our Lord and Savior Jesus Christ will be abundantly supplied to you" (1:11). If he was already in the kingdom when he wrote this in A.D. 66, why then did he put it in the future? It is doubtful that Peter had in mind the more recent artificial categories of "now, not yet." If the kingdom were here and only needed further development in order to bring it to full maturation, then he surely would have used different language. However, if the kingdom is yet in the future, as premillennialists hold, then the passage is well put to convey that notion. The kingdom of God is yet future.

In dealing with the pseudo-wisdom of the Corinthians, Paul said, "Yet we do speak wisdom among those who are mature; a wisdom, however, not of this age, nor of the rulers of this age, who are passing away; but we speak God's wisdom . . . which none of the rulers of this age has understood. . . . " (1 Corinthians 2:6-8). The word *age* is used by Paul, not *world*. If this age and the kingdom were synonymous, as post-millennialists insist, then this description does not fit the conditions of an age where the knowledge of the Lord will cover the earth as the water does the sea. That kind of knowledge does not exist during this present evil age.

In Galatians 1:4 Paul says that Christ "gave Himself for our sins, that He might deliver us out of this present evil age." Again, he does not say *world* but *age*. This age is the age of darkness. The future age is the age of the light of the kingdom. "The New Testament views the present aeon or age of the world as essentially heathenish, which we cannot love without forsaking Christ."[39] When the kingdom comes believers will love that age, since it will be a time of the rule of Christ in every area of life.

George Peters declares, "The object of Christianity is not so much to Christianize the present world as to save souls out of it, so as not to be condemned with the world . . . but to rule with Him in His Millennium."[40] John Calvin made a similar statement when he said, "There is no reason, therefore, why any person should expect the conversion of the world, for at length—when it will be too late, and will yield them no advantage."[41]

Paul had the hope of ruling with Christ at his second

coming when he declared in Philippians 3:20, "For our citizenship is in heaven, from which also we eagerly wait for a Savior, the Lord Jesus Christ." Paul says that our citizenship is located in heaven. Not that we are to heavenize the earth and then make the earth heaven, but that we are waiting for Christ's return and his taking us to be with him. This is not to deny responsibilities that we have while on earth to do good or promote justice. But our hope is to be on the coming of Christ, not in Christianizing the institutions of society in anticipation of Christ's return.

Gary North asks the question: "Why can't Christians be citizens of two countries?"[42] The simple answer is that the Bible only teaches a single citizenship. It is not a matter of whether one can possibly imagine a scheme (which North has attempted) which allows Paul's statement in Philippians 3:20 to stand and at the same time say that we have a dual citizenship: earthly and heavenly. We are warned in James 1:6-8 about the dangers of being double-minded; it leads to instability. We have a single citizenship no matter where we are in God's creation as believers.

The parable of the nobleman in Luke 19:11-27 is another example of how Jesus spoke of the future nature of the kingdom.[43] Jesus was in Jericho, shortly before the triumphal entry into Jerusalem and his final rejection. Within this setting verse 11 gives us great insight as to why the people were so excited to see Jesus enter Jerusalem—they thought he was going to finally bring in the kingdom they sought. "He went on to tell a parable, because He was near Jerusalem, and they supposed that the kingdom of God was going to appear suddenly."

In contrast to this popular expectation, Christ spoke of a nobleman who went on a long journey to a far country. Since the context is clear that the nobleman is referring to Jesus, then it means that "he will not exercise his kingly authority until his return in the second advent, and then the scene of the exercise of this regal authority is the same place as that from which the king departed, namely, the earth."[44] It is thus on the return of the king that the kingdom will be set up. So Christ did not set up the kingdom during his first coming; it awaits his return.

Only two chapters later, Luke relates when the kingdom of God will come. "Even so you, too, when you see these things happening, recognize that the kingdom of God is near" (21:31). In 18:11 he corrected the people who "supposed that the Kingdom of God was going to appear immediately." Then in 21:31 he says that it will come when they "see the Son of Man coming in a cloud with power and great glory" (21:27). This will be during the future second coming.

Christ's own words in Luke 18:8 give a clear corrective to the false notion of the postmillennialists that this age is the kingdom and that it will progressively manifest faith in Christ. The passage says, "when the Son of Man comes, will He find faith on the earth?" This is "an inferential question to which a negative answer is expected."[45] So this passage is saying that at the second coming Christ will not find, literally, "the faith" upon the earth. It is this lack of faith which leads to his judgment of the world. John Calvin recognized this when commenting on the passage:

> Christ expressly foretells that, from his ascension to heaven till his return, unbelievers will abound; meaning by these words that, if the Redeemer does not so speedily appear, the blame of the delay will attach to men, because there will be almost none to look for him.[46]

Rushdoony attempts to give an interpretation which will allow for his postmillennialism:

> it must not be assumed that the word "cometh" applies only to the second coming at the end of the world. It applies to the Lord's every coming in judgment against men and nations. . . . Heretics love to push this question away from themselves and to hold that it has reference to a great supposed falling

away from the faith before the end of the world. The question, however, was asked of disciples who would face the judgment on Jerusalem, and they were asked as individuals to face up to this question, even as we are. This question is not for the end time but for us now. . . . False eschatologies have turned a great parable of hope and victory into a parable of despair. . . . [47]

Rushdoony's explanation simply will not satisfy the evidence. It is not an assumption that the word "cometh" applies only to the second coming at the end of the world, since the text of the passage links it to Messiah's judgment. Throughout the New Testament Christ's coming and judgment are universally linked to his future second coming. Rushdoony is guilty of the sin he speaks against. He assumes that "cometh" is some periodic coming in judgment at different times in this current age. Where does he find Scripture to support such a notion? Rushdoony is calling people like John Calvin heretics for holding to the interpretation which has been taken universally by the church.

Further, he abstracts the idea of judgment and makes it apply to the present and not to the second coming. Yet the passage speaks of a historic event not an idea. How can he say that premillennialists take the parable to be not one of hope and victory, but one of despair? We believe the second coming of Christ to judge the world on behalf of the elect is a parable of great hope and victory. But it is not a victory parallel to Rushdoony's perspective.

The time of Christ's return and lack of "the faith" upon the earth parallels other passages which speak of the great apostasy. One such passage is 2 Peter 3:1-18, which teaches that the leaven of unbelief has reached such a degree "that in the last days mockers will come with their mocking, following after their own lusts, and saying, 'Where is the promise of His coming? For ever since the fathers fell asleep, all continues just as it was from the beginning of creation'" (3:3-4). Peter is not saying that these "mockers" will deny the second coming; instead they will deny the promise of an "any-moment," sudden, or cataclysmic coming. The mockers attempt this by replacing the apocalyptic, any-moment nature of Christ's return with their false uniformitarian notion that "ever since the fathers fell asleep, all continues just as it was from the beginning of creation" (3:4). This amounts to the replacement of an apocalyptic hope for a present process. The seriousness of the charge that the Lord is slow about his promise to return (3:9) is well stated by Peters:

> Esteemed men of ability and usefulness, are certainly assuming grave responsibility in this matter, when in books, etc., they teach that Christ's Advent is not to be watched for as He commanded, but teach that it is still postponed for many, many long centuries, and that, instead of incoming wrath and tribulation, the Church is to anticipate triumph and continued progress.[48]

Yet in spite of the many passages in the New Testament admonishing us to look for Christ's coming, Reconstructionists often chide the notion as escapism and pietism. They are not looking for the any-moment return of Jesus Christ. They say that he cannot come and will not come for at least a thousand years or more. (David Chilton has said, "It may require a million years.")[49] Reconstructionists say the kingdom will be brought in progressively through current processes, not through the any-moment intervention of God. This noncataclysmic view of progress is parallel to the mockers' view of slowness in 2 Peter 3. However, Peter's analogy is suddenness: like creation, which was sudden, and like the flood, which was sudden, so will be the coming of Christ. This will totally catch the ungodly off guard, since they are not looking for Christ's coming. We pray it will not catch Reconstructionists off guard as well.

Contrary to this New Testament teaching, Reconstructionists believe that someone who is looking for Christ's coming is detrimental to establishing the kingdom in the present. They are right in this belief. North says,

> The shortening of men's time horizons as a result of both premillennialism and amillennialism has contributed to a decline in competence among Christian workers and an increase in reliance upon the miraculous. If men do not believe that they have a lifetime to develop their skills and capital, let alone to pass down both skills and capital to later generations, they must become dependent upon God's miracles to advance their causes. As men's time horizons shrink, their quest for "the big pay-off" increases, since only through such a discontinuity can they expect to advance themselves significantly in a brief period of time.[50]

Are non-Reconstructionists to be chided for believing in magic because they are relying upon Christ to save them miraculously from their sin, rather than working to accomplish that over a long period of time? "Of course not," the Reconstructionists reply, "you have misapplied the principle." We respond in kind that their whole eschatology goes against the admonitions of Scripture for the church to be eagerly awaiting Christ's any-moment coming.

Reconstructionists do not deny the second coming; they believe most of the passages on the second coming refer to something else. But Peter says that believers are looking for, not working toward, a new heaven and a new earth (3:13). The righteousness of the future age will come suddenly and in a moment (3:10-13)—"like a thief" (3:10). The language of Scripture, once again, does not support the Reconstructionists' position, but rather the cataclysmic interventionism of premillennialism.

That the kingdom is yet future is also implied in a number of passages which speak of the church inheriting this kingdom (1 Corinthians 6:9-10; 15:50; Galatians 5:21; Ephesians 5:5;

James 2:5). McClain notes that "Paul not only sees this inheritance of the Kingdom in future time but definitely excludes it from the present age by placing it after the resurrection and rapture of the Church."[51]

The biblical teaching on inheritance includes at least two items: (1) Since God is sovereign and trustworthy, he is able to guarantee the future deliverance of his promise, and (2) the promise is made within a covenantal or contractual framework; therefore, some aspects of the promise (i.e., regeneration) are given up front, while other phases are delivered in the future. The time of future payment corresponds with the setting up of the kingdom. So it is that both the payment and the kingdom are yet future. The two phases are seen in the two references to the word *redemption*: "We have redemption, the forgiveness of sins" (Colossians 1:14), and "waiting eagerly for . . . the redemption of our body" (Romans 8:23).

This is why many believers will receive a new physical body in the resurrection before the thousand-year kingdom is begun. The removal of most aspects of the curse will be evidenced by a change in the human body and in the earth as well. Since man is the steward who introduced the curse upon creation, when man is redeemed and receives the full installment of God's redemption, then the creation will reflect the changed status of mankind by no longer groaning and laboring under the curse brought by man (Romans 8:18-26). This will happen in an instant, not over a long evolution of the environment, as Reconstructionists teach.

Rushdoony has taught, "According to St. Paul, the very creation around us groans and travails, waiting for the godly dominion of the children of God (Rom. 8:19-23)."[52] Gary DeMar adds, "The curse of sin and death is removed as more and more people come under the preaching of the gospel (Rom. 8:18- 25)."[53] These statements blatantly ignore the language of the text: "waiting eagerly for our adoption as sons, the redemption of our body" (Romans 8:23). Paul is waiting for an event, not a process. He is looking for the resurrection when

234 What the Future Holds

the redemption of the body will occur. Paul says nothing about "the godly dominion of the children of God," or the gradual removal of "the curse of sin and death."

One of the apostle Paul's biggest problems in his ministry was dealing with the Corinthians. The two epistles reveal that they had a wrong view of the Gospel which lead to a wrong view of the Christian life. They were often found to be blending their former pagan practices and ideas of spirituality with radically different Christianity. At one point in his interaction with this spiritual elitism, Paul chided, "You are already filled, you have already become rich, you have become kings without us; and I would indeed that you had become kings so that we also might reign with you." McClain cogently observes the implications of this passage:

> For, to the apostle, that glorious prospect would mean an end of all hunger and thirst, reviling, persecution, defamation, uncertainty of dwelling-place, and danger of life itself (vss. 9-13). But since believers are not yet fit to reign, they must be careful to "judge nothing before the time, until the Lord come" (vs. 5). In the meantime, the present sufferings have a beneficent purpose in relation to the future Kingdom: "If we endure, we shall also reign with him" (II Tim. 2:12, ASV).[54]

McClain draws out the true import of this present age. The present age is a time of preparation for the coming kingdom, just as was Christ's first coming. It is a time of humiliation and often suffering, just as was Christ's former ministry. Paul makes mention of this in 1 Corinthians 4:9: "God has exhibited us apostles last of all, as men condemned to death; because we have become a spectacle to the world, both to angels and to men." But when God has finished completing his bride, then will this glorious church reign with her Savior in the coming kingdom. McClain accurately summarizes the plan of God:

At His first coming our Lord was exalted to be both
Lord and Messianic King (Acts 2:36); but not until
His second coming will He establish His Kingdom
on earth as the rightful successor to the throne of
His father David. In the interim He is gathering to
Himself a body of people, distressed and debtors
because of sin, who are destined to be associated
with Him in the coming Kingdom.[55]

The picture is that of David who was anointed King of
Israel but did not attain the throne for some time after. It was
during this time between his anointing as king and his actual
ascent to the throne that he gathered to himself, out of Saul's
kingdom, a band of men in distress and debt. The men developed a great loyalty during the fugitive years to David and
were the core of his leadership when David ruled from
Jerusalem.

Christ is following a similar pattern during the church
age. He has been anointed King in his ascension and given
the place of honor at the right hand of God. But the church
age is a time in which Satan and his rebellious court refuse to
give up their rule. In the meantime, Christ is drawing out of
Satan's kingdom (fallen humanity) a band of loyal followers.
Messiah will yet return to defeat the usurper and will be installed
and take over rule in Zion. This present age is a time of preparation for the church, his bride, which will rule with him at
that time. Samuel J. Andrews has pointed out the relationship
between Christ's present status and his future role:

It is as its Head that He rules over [the Church],
not as its King; for this latter title is never used of
this relation. Nor is His rule over His Church legal
and external, like that of an earthly king. . . . The
relation between Him, the Head, and the Church,
His Body, is a living one, such as nowhere else
exists, or can exist; His will is the law, not merely
of its action, but of its life. . . . He rules in the
Church though the law of a common life. . . .[56]

Christ as head of the church (1 Corinthians 12:12-32; Ephesians 1:18-23; Colossians 1:18) is different than Christ as King. He is both, but now his ministry as a priest after the order of Melchizedek is primary (Hebrews 7:1-27). At a future time, his ministry as King will become central. Just as David had been anointed king, but did not rule immediately from Zion, so it is that Christ is certainly King, but not yet in fullness and unveiled glory.

Believers are affected in a similar and corresponding way. While we are by covenant and future blessing a people who are destined to rule, our current status is that of strangers and pilgrims in a far country. We are to be people who are calling to the citizens of this world to flee from the wrath to come by fleeing to Christ. As children of light, we are not to be asleep, but are to shine the light of the gospel on a hill. This age is the night and the call is to come and join the group who will one day rule when the day comes at the second coming. But we are not now ruling in this manner. Andrews notes some of the dissimilarities between this age and the one to come:

> Had it been the purpose of God to set the Son at His ascension as the King of the nations, He would in some way have made His kingship so plain that the nations could not have been ignorant of it, and of the duty of allegiance and homage. There must, also, have been in every land those publicly invested with His authority to act as His representatives, and with power to give commands and to compel obedience . . . but [today] He does not appoint their princes, nor dictate their laws, nor is His hand seen in judgment.

> To affirm that mortal and sinful men are already admitted to have part in His functions of universal rule, and are empowered by Him to govern the nations, is a proud and presumptuous antedating of the Kingdom. His kings must be first made like

Him, immortal and incorruptible. When the earthly
in them is changed into the heavenly, then can they
exercise His heavenly authority.[57]

Gary North reacts to the premillennial claim that this is
not the kingdom but a time of preparation for the coming
kingdom by charging us with the belief that Christ is not all-
powerful during this age. It is not that we believe that Christ's
power to establish his kingdom is limited during this age; rather
we believe it is not his will to have his church establishing the
kingdom. North complains,

> Christ's earthly power can only be manifested when
> He returns physically to set up a top-down bureau-
> cratic kingdom in which Christians will be respon-
> sible for following the direct orders of Christ, issued
> to meet specific historical circumstances. The pre-
> millennialist has so little faith in the power of the
> Bible's perfect revelation, empowered by the Holy
> Spirit, to shape the thoughts and actions of Chris-
> tians, that Jesus must return and personally issue
> millions of orders per day telling everyone what to
> do, case by case, crisis by crisis.[58]

Premillennialists plead guilty to the desire to have "a top-
down" kingdom. We eagerly look forward to Jesus Christ's
earthly reign. It is interesting that someone like North, who
preaches in so many other places the centrality of hierarchy to
proper covenantal relationships, would complain about a top-
down kingdom, especially with Jesus Christ at the top. In fact,
fellow Reconstructionist James Jordan, who at the time of this
writing works for North, favors the top-down approach: "Americans (evangelicals) like to believe the myth that society is
transformed from the bottom up and not from the top down.
This flies squarely in the face both of history and of Scripture."[59]

Jordan, a postmillennialist, believes the church should
bring in the kingdom via a top-down approach. So the issue
is not that premillennialists are top-down and postmillennialists

are bottom-up; rather, the issue is when and how the kingdom will be implemented. Premillennialists believe the church age is not the Kingdom, thus the character of the church age is different from the kingdom. As a result, the agenda for each age differs. This is why premillennialists are (or at least should be) involved in different kinds of things than are postmillennialists.

Since premillennialists are not working to establish the kingdom, it only follows that we not be involved in the same way as those working toward that goal. This is why so many of North's arguments, in fact most, assume his position and then chide premillennialists for being consistent with their theology. His attack should be primarily an exegetical and theological one, since it is not a sin not to be working toward bringing in the kingdom if God's Word does not teach us to do so.

Herein lies a major danger in the Reconstructionist movement. If this is not the kingdom and God is currently only "heal[ing] souls, not institutions,"[60] then Satan is still in control (even though temporarily) of institutions. It means that God has not willed a total control by Christians of various divinely established institutions. Certainly we can have influence during the church age, much as Daniel had influence within the providence of God. But Daniel did not take over the Babylonian Empire and make it an Israelite Empire. Our involvement should be tempered with the knowledge that we will never totally reform society, while at the same time realizing we have a duty to be true to God and not participate in evil. Christians are to stand for godly standards within society as a testimony to the God who will one day establish his righteous kingdom. We do love God's law and his standards.

We should point to the evil in our day and tell the world that this is the product of man's rebellion against God. We should admonish unbelievers to acknowledge that their sin has put them under a curse and to trust Christ's work on the cross as the payment for their sin. Believers should be faithful stewards during this life, while at the same time waiting "for His Son from heaven, whom He raised from the dead, that is Jesus, who delivers us from the wrath to come" (1 Thessalonians 1:10). Waiting for Christ is not a sin; it is what you are doing while waiting that is important.

Robert Saucy identifies two major implications of the postponement of the kingdom and the effect it has on us now:

> First, the primary thrust of kingdom power relates to the inner person. While any genuine transformation of the inner person must certainly affect outward behavior, the blessings of the kingdom for today focus on the spiritual aspect of life and not the material. . . .
>
> Second, the present kingdom power is fundamentally a power displayed through outer weakness (cf. 2 Cor. 12:9- 10).[61]

Not only are Reconstructionists and postmillennialists wrong about the timing of the kingdom, but they also have to lower the high standards the Bible teaches will characterize the kingdom. In order for them to argue that the kingdom is present in this age, they have to lower the quality of Christ's glorious reign. They end up with more of a "millennial ghetto" than a glorious kingdom.

How, on a gradualist basis, are people going to live a thousand years (Isaiah 65:20, 22)? North says, "the kingdom of God becomes truly worldwide in scope. This involves the beginning of the restoration of the cursed world. The curse will then be lifted progressively by God. One result is longer life spans for man."[62] This gradualism is in stark contrast to the interventionist perspective; with Christ's intervention, the curse can be reversed in the same way it was implemented—in a moment.

How do Reconstructionists explain the gradual removal of the curse upon animals, ending the fear and strife between animals and between animals and man (Isaiah 65:25)? This will be removed in an instant at the second coming and at the interventionist inauguration of the kingdom.

At what point will sickness be removed in the gradualist kingdom? Isaiah 33:24, speaking of a millennial condition says, "And no resident will say, 'I am sick.'" This is no problem for premillennialists, since Christ's coming will bring about a sudden change in these conditions, just as the curse was introduced in the moment of Adam's fall.

A kingdom set up by the personal intervention of Messiah and ruled over by him will have the highest possible quality of existence until the eternal state. In addition it will have the personal presence of Messiah himself, which will certainly add to the glory and greatness of the period. Within the Reconstructionist framework, Messiah is in heaven and only present mystically in his kingdom. His absence from the earth during his kingdom reign robs Messiah of his moment of earthly glory and exaltation. It is a truncated reduction of the true reign of Christ. Since the first phase of Christ's career, his humiliation, was spent physically upon the earth, it follows that there should be a corresponding display of his great glory through his reign on the earth. Dispensationalist John Pilkey has noted that postmillennialists

> suppress the future millennial career of Jesus Christ, transferring to moral mankind what belongs to Him. Control of the last thousand years of world history belongs to the Risen Christ, as immediate theocratic agent, and to His brethren, the "sons of the resurrection"—not to any combination of well-intentioned mortals in an ecclesiastical status quo development.[63]

Romans 8:18-25 uses catastrophic/interventionist language. That is to say, the old world becomes a new world because of the second coming. This is opposed to the gradualism of this current age, which Reconstructionists teach. Once again the language is that of "waiting eagerly" (8:23) rather than establishing the kingdom.

One premillennialist raises two major objections to equating this current age with the millennium:

(1) The interaction between group, individual and environment evidently is a lot more profound than even sociologists are willing to admit, so profound in fact that a catastrophic alteration is required for the "perfect" social order; (2) This being the case, even total regeneration of the human race would not be far reaching enough to establish the "millennial vision." The physical environment must be totally changed (Rom. 8:19-22).[64]

Only the premillennial, futurist viewpoint does justice to the Bible's descriptions of the radical changes Christ's kingdom will truly bring.

Dispensationalists are often accused of being defeatist, just sitting around waiting for the rapture. It is unfortunate but true that pietism[65] has infected many in the dispensational camp. However, social and cultural impotence is not organic to dispensationalism. The believer is called to a ministry of exposing evil during the night (Ephesians 5:11). We are the light of the world shining in the current darkness, a testimony to those of the night as to what the day will be like.

The New Testament points out that the apostolic church centered its ministry around the words and deeds of Christ and were told to do as he did. "As the Father has sent Me, I also send you" (John 20:21). Robert Saucy notes how the early disciples of Christ lived according to this pattern:

They displayed their Lord and proclaimed the coming kingdom through a bold witness of word and an excellent behavior that involved a life of supernatural love and good deeds to others. They lived out the presence of the kingdom in the personal principles of righteousness, peace, and joy as witness to the accomplished victory of the King over sin. Subsequent church history reveals the tendency of the church to veer away from this course through either the temptation to withdraw from the world or the temptation to rule the world. The apostolic church, which must be the norm, succumbed to neither temptation.[66]

The church of the twentieth century must follow the lead of the apostolic church on this matter. We must not turn to the right or to the left. We are not to withdraw from the world, but are to continue preaching the gospel and warning men to flee from the wrath to come until Christ comes. We cannot go in the other direction, which Reconstructionists are advocating, to rule this present world. Both pietism and dominion theology are wrong and can be corrected by a healthy dose of biblical instruction.

We are not establishing the kingdom during this age. Our primary mission is evangelism, while looking for the coming of Christ. It is a mission of calling men to prepare for the coming Kingdom by becoming citizens of heaven through faith in Christ. The proper attitude is often described in Scripture as that of a steward who is left with a job to do in the absence of the owner of the house (Matthew 24:45-51; 25:14-30). His current motivation is a future event—the desire to be found faithful upon the return of the householder. The faithful servant is motivated by the future. Because the hopes and aspirations of the believer are ahead, it helps him discipline and sacrifice in the present for future goals and rewards. This is exactly what properly applied premillennialism produces.

A dispensational premillennial theory of the current social order has been proposed by Charles Clough:

A major insight of dispensational premillennialism is the picture it gives of the dynamics of evil. There are three factors involved: (1) the impact of regenerated and spiritually active people relative to the impact of the remainder; (2) the restraining ministry of the Spirit during the Church Age in suppressing total evil domination of basic social structures; (3) all pervading domain of Satan over both the social order and its physical environment. Factor (2) is relatively stable and factor (3) in the realm of the social order appears to vary approximately inversely with factor (1). As is commonly recognized, then, the basic variable is the impact of the church.

But the unique contribution of this eschatology is how it establishes realistic upper and lower limits on the variation of Satanic domination in the present social order. The upper limit of which the pretribulational rapture is an integral part states, in effect, that no matter how small the church is in the world the general social order of the world will be graciously kept from total Satanic control until the rapture. Satan's plans are held in temporary suspension while the human race is given opportunity to trust Christ (II Pet. 3:9). The lower limit of which Satan's reign over physical creation is an integral part states, in effect, that no matter how many are won to Christ in the world the general social order of the world will still remain under the influence of a corrupt physical environment. Christ must return and redeem physical creation for elimination of this influence. . . . Thus dispensational premillennialism sets forth data from which it is possible to deduce a realistic picture of the working of evil in the social order today and why the "perfect" social order must be future to a supernatural realignment of the basic factors.[67]

The result of this view is a certain degree of social and political involvement during the church age. Because the servant does not know when his Master is going to return, he desires to be a faithful steward going about the business of his Lord. If dispensationalists are not properly involved in issues today, it is not inherent to their theology; rather it is unfaithfulness to their calling. Dispensationalists are not involved in the same ways that Reconstructionists are, since their views of the future differ. But dispensationalists are involved and active.

Dispensationalists believe in victory in history in every sphere of life. In fact, we believe in dominion theology! Just as salvation is accomplished immediately by Christ's work as the author of a whole new race, so will the consummation be immediate, not mediate as Reconstructionists preach. Alva J. McClain also notes that there is a carry-over of many accomplishments during the church age into the kingdom:

> The premillennial philosophy of history makes sense. It lays a Biblical and rational basis for a truly optimistic view of human history. Furthermore, rightly apprehended, it has practical effects. It says that life here and now, in spite of the tragedy of sin, is nevertheless something worth-while; and therefore all efforts to make it better are also worth-while. All the true values of human life will be preserved and carried over into the coming kingdom; nothing worth-while will be lost. Furthermore, we are encouraged in the midst of opposition and reverses by the assurance that help is on the way, help from above, supernatural help— "Give the king thy judgments, O God. . . . In his days shall the righteous flourish . . . all nations shall call him blessed" (Ps. 72:1, 7, 17).[68]

Since the present age is not the kingdom and the kingdom is yet future, the biblical premillennialist is watching and waiting for our coming King, while going about the tasks he has commissioned us to do. At the same time, our prayer is "Come, Lord Jesus."

Chapter 11, Notes

1. David Chilton, *The Days of Vengeance* (Fort Worth: Dominion Press, 1987), 587.

2. David Chilton, *Paradise Restored* (Tyler, Tex.: Reconstruction Press, 1985), 73-74.

3. R. J. Rushdoony, *Thy Kingdom Come* (Fairfax, Va.: Thoburn Press, 1970), 196.

4. Gary North, *75 Bible Questions Your Instructors Pray You Won't Ask* (Tyler, Tex.: Spurgeon Press, 1984), 170.

5. Ibid., 188.

6. Gary DeMar and Peter Leithart, *The Reduction of Christianity: Dave Hunt's Theology of Cultural Surrender* (Fort Worth: Dominion Press, 1988), 356.

7. Ibid., 151.

8. Peter Leithart, "The Rule of Christ," *The Geneva Review*, May 1988, 7.

9. Alva J. McClain, *The Greatness of the Kingdom* (Winona Lake, Ind.: BMH Books, 1959), 17.

10. DeMar and Leithart, *Reduction*, 207.

11. Ibid.

12. George Ladd, *The Presence of the Future* (Grand Rapids: Wm. B. Eerdmans Publishing Co., 1974), 3.

13. Ibid., 42.

14. Leithart, "Rule of Christ," 7.

15. Robert L. Saucy, "The Presence of the Kingdom and the Life of the Church" *Bibliotheca Sacra* 145 (January-March 1988):33.

16. Ibid., 34.

17. David Chilton, *Paradise Restored* (Tyler, Tex.: Reconstruction Press, 1985), 73-74.

18. Gary North, "Editor's Introduction" in George Grant, *The Changing of the Guard: Biblical Principles for Political Action* (Fort Worth: Dominion Press, 1987), xii.

19. McClain, *Greatness of the Kingdom*, 21.

20. Ibid., 19-20.

21. John F. Walvoord, *The Millennial Kingdom* (Grand Rapids: Zondervan Publishing House, 1959), 297.

22. Charles Ryrie, *The Basis of the Premillennial Faith* (Neptune, N.J.: Loizeaux Brothers, 1953), 145-46.

23. McClain, *Greatness of the Kingdom*, 41.

24. Chilton, *Paradise Restored*, 73.

25. Loraine Boettner, *The Millennium* (Phillipsburg, N.J.: Presbyterian & Reformed Publishing Co., 1957), 14.

26. Gary North, "Christianity and Progress," *Christian Reconstruction*, May-June 1987, 1, 3.

27. Walvoord, *Millennial Kingdom*, 297.

28. Chilton, *Vengeance*, 493.

29. There is a more recent brand of amillennialism which makes the eternal state the kingdom and not the present age. See Anthony A. Hoekema, *The Bible and the Future* (Grand Rapids: Wm. B. Eerdmans Publishing Co., 1979). The more traditional Augustinian amillennialism saw this present age as the kingdom.

30. Stanley D. Toussaint, "The Kingdom and Matthew's Gospel," *Essays in Honor of J. Dwight Pentecost*, ed. Toussaint and Charles H. Dyer (Chicago: Moody Press, 1986), 19-20.

31. E. R. Craven, "Excursus on the Basileia," Lange's *Commentary on Revelation* (Grand Rapids: Zondervan Publishing House, 1960), 95.

32. Much of the material for this discussion is taken from McClain, *Greatness of the Kingdom*, 432-41.

33. Ibid., 433.

34. Gary DeMar, *Ruler of the Nations: Biblical Principles for Government* (Fort Worth: Dominion Press, 1987), 122-23.

35. Gary North, *Dominion and Common Grace: The Biblical Basis of Progress* (Tyler, Tex.: Institute for Christian Economics, 1987), 66.

36. McClain, *Greatness of the Kingdom*, 441.

37. North, *Dominion and Common Grace*, 66-67.

38. McClain, *Greatness of the Kingdom*, 441.

39. George N. H. Peters, *The Theocratic Kingdom* (Grand Rapids: Kregel Publications, 1972), 1:589.

40. Ibid.

41. John Calvin, *Commentary on a Harmony of the Evangelists, Matthew, Mark, and Luke* (Grand Rapids: Baker Book House, n.d.), 17:147.

42. Gary North, "Foreword" in DeMar and Leithart, *Reduction*, xiii.

43. Saucy is to be credited for calling our attention to this argument in "Presence of the Kingdom," 35.

44. George E. Ladd, *Crucial Questions about the Kingdom* (Grand Rapids: Wm. B. Eerdmans Publishing Co., 1952), 71.

45. Randolph O. Yeager, *The Renaissance New Testament* (Gretna, La.: Pelican Publishing Co., 1978), 7:149.

46. John Calvin, *Harmony of the Evangelists*, 16:201.

47. Rousas J. Rushdoony, *Salvation and Godly Rule* (Vallecito, Calif.: Ross House Books, 1983), 416-17.

48. Peters, *Theocratic Kingdom*, 3:166.

49. Chilton, *Vengeance*, 507.

50. Gary North, *Backward, Christian Soldiers? An Action Manual for Christian Reconstruction* (Tyler, Tex.: Institute for Christian Economics, 1984), 251.

51. McClain, *Greatness of the Kingdom*, 433.

52. R. J. Rushdoony, *The Institutes of Biblical Law* (Phillipsburg, N.J.: Presbyterian & Reformed Publishing Co., 1973), 451-52.

53. DeMar, *Ruler of the Nations*, 171.

54. McClain, *Greatness of the Kingdom*, 433.

55. Ibid., 440.

56. Samuel J. Andrews, cited by McClain, *Greatness of the Kingdom*, 437.

57. Ibid., 438.

58. Gary North, "Christianity and Progress," *Christian Reconstruction*, May-June 1987, 2.

59. James B. Jordan, *The Sociology of the Church* (Tyler, Tex.: Geneva Ministries, 1986), 17.

60. North, "Christianity and Progress," 2.

61. Saucy, "Presence of the Kingdom," 44-45.

62. Gary North, *Unconditional Surrender: God's Program for Victory* (Tyler, Tex.: Geneva Press, 1981),˙199.

63. Personal letter from John Pilkey to Thomas Ice, 23 March 1988.

64. Charles A. Clough, "Dispensational Premillennialism and the Present Social Order" (unpublished paper, Dallas Theological Seminary, 1966), 11.

65. Pietism has been defined by Reconstructionists as restricting Christianity only to the internal dimension of "Christ in your heart," to the exclusion of Christ ruling over the external world. They believe true piety includes both. (See David Chilton, "Piety and Christian Reconstruction," *The Biblical Educator*, June 1981.) Dispensationalists agree that it is wrong to limit God to only the spiritual or inner realm. This is why we so strongly believe in a literal kingdom of Christ, which will encompass his rule over every area of life. The disagreement between postmillennialists and premillennialists is *when* this will take place. It is wrong to call premillennialists and dispensationalists pietists and platonic, since we hold to the internal and external rule of God. The difference is how God will carry this out and when he will do it.

66. Saucy, "Presence of the Kingdom," 46.

67. Clough, "Dispensational Premillennialism," 17-18. It is also of interest to note that an article by Clough was published in the first *Journal of Christian Reconstruction*, edited by Gary North, entitled "Biblical Presuppositions and Historical Geology: A Case Study," (Summer 1974):35-48. It is also interesting to note that dispensationalists such as Henry Morris, Duane Gish, and John Whitcomb have been leaders in exposing the darkness of evolution in our day.

68. McClain, *Greatness of the Kingdom*, 531.

Chapter 12

"Rightly Dividing" the Book of Revelation

The validity of the Christian Reconstruction agenda is vitally dependent upon the last book in the Bible, the book of Revelation. Two issues are crucial in correctly interpreting the Apocalypse: the date of its writing and the interpretative approach. We hope to show that Revelation was written after the destruction of Jerusalem and that it will be fulfilled in the future.

THE DATE OF THE BOOK OF REVELATION

The interpretation of no other book in the canon of the Bible is affected by the date in which it was written as much as the Revelation of Jesus Christ. The preterist, postmillennial viewpoint of the Christian Reconstruction movement, as expounded by David Chilton in *The Days of Vengeance*, stands or falls on whether or not the final book of the Bible was written before A.D. 70. Fellow postmillennialist and pre-A.D. 70 preterist Kenneth L. Gentry notes this major weakness when he says, "if it could be demonstrated that Revelation were written 25 years after the Fall of Jerusalem, Chilton's entire labor would go up in smoke."[1] Actually, all one would have to do is to show that Revelation was written any time after the destruction of Jerusalem. If this could be done, then Matthew 24 and Revelation could not be taken in the way Chilton advocates.

Gentry goes on to point out that "Chilton only gives four superficially argued pages in defense of what is perhaps the most crucial matter for consistent preterism: the pre-A.D. 70 date for the composition of Revelation."[2] If the Apocalypse were penned before A.D. 70, this would not by itself rule out the futurist and premillennial view. The futurist view could still be correct since the date does not determine its validity. However, if Revelation were written even one day after the fall of Jerusalem, then it ceases to be a prophecy concerning the destruction of Jerusalem. What are the "superficially argued" points Chilton attempts to make for his position?

External Evidence

First, "St. John's intimate acquaintance with the minute details of Temple worship suggests that the Book of Revelation and the Fourth Gospel must have been written before the Temple services had actually ceased."[3] This argument proves nothing as to whether or not the temple was standing at the time of writing, for at least two reasons.

(1) Revelation is a prophecy from Jesus Christ to John. John recorded the things that Christ and the angel were showing him in the vision, as evidenced by the repeated admonition to write what he saw or heard (Revelation 1:1-2, 11, 19; 4:1; 5:1). John is not the source of these details; therefore, they are not dependent upon whether he was familiar with the temple. John was familiar with the temple, but even if he had never seen it, he still could have written this revelation.

(2) Even if John's familiarity with the temple were needed to write Revelation, it would not require that the temple be standing at the time. People are capable of remembering things from the past in great detail. Also, if John were of the priestly family, as Chilton suggests,[4] then he would certainly have had opportunity to develop familiarity with the temple.

Second, Chilton questions the voice of church tradition concerning the date of Revelation, since it strongly negates his early date viewpoint. This by itself is most interesting, since the Christian Reconstruction movement so often appeals to "the voice of mother church" in support of its views.[5] Chilton often boasts of his view on certain issues as being "the position of the historic, orthodox Church on the question."[6] In fact, Chilton uses a witness from church tradition to suggest that the apostle John "was a priest, and wore the sacerdotal plate." This was a "tradition recorded in Eusebius."[7]

Church tradition should always be listened to on any matter, even though it must sometimes be set aside if it is contradicted by Scripture. Each claim made by church tradition must be weighed to see if it yields insight for the believer. The primary source for early church tradition on the date of Revelation is Irenaeus (A. D. 120-202). Irenaeus wrote his famous polemic, *Against Heresies*, sometime in the last quarter of the second century.

> We will not, however, incur the risk of pronouncing positively as to the name of Antichrist; for if it were necessary that his name should be distinctly revealed in this present time, it would have been announced by him who beheld the apocalyptic vision. For that was seen not very long time since, but almost in our day, towards the end of Domitian's reign.[8]

How does Chilton deal with such a clear statement? He says, "there is considerable room for doubt about his precise meaning (he may have meant that the Apostle John himself 'was seen' by others). The language of St. Irenaeus is somewhat ambiguous."[9] There is not "considerable room for doubt about his precise meaning." The cloudiness is not in the statement by Irenaeus, but in the perception of Chilton.

First, Chilton questions whether "that was seen" refers to "the apocalyptic vision" or to John himself. Since the impersonal pronoun "that" is used we can assume that it refers to John's "apocalyptic vision." Second, since it is called "the apocalyptic vision," which is something John saw, then "was seen" refers to what John saw—"the apocalyptic vision"—rather than someone having seen John. Others who agree with the early date, such as J. A. Hort,[10] say that Irenaeus's statement does refer to the book and not the person.

Last, the progress of the context lends support to "was seen" as a reference to the book of Revelation rather than to seeing John. This is clearly how Eusebius (c. A.D. 265-339) took Irenaeus's statement. In quoting Irenaeus, Eusebius said, "it would have been declared by him who saw the revelation. For it has not been long since it was seen, but almost in our own generation, about the end of Domitian's reign."[11] Eusebius then follows this quotation of Irenaeus with the comment, "These are what he states respecting the Revelation."[12] Clearly Eusebius and the other early witnesses to the Domitian date understood what Irenaeus meant or the tradition would never have developed.

The great church historian Philip Schaff (1819-1893), who holds to the early date of Revelation, does not doubt the clear testimony of Irenaeus and the early church: "The traditional date of composition at the end of Domitian's reign (95 or 96) rests on the clear and weighty testimony of Irenaeus, is confirmed by Eusebius and Jerome, and has still its learned defenders."[13]

By and large, those who hold to an early date do not try to plant doubts about the accuracy of church tradition. They just attempt to argue on other grounds.

Another factor which should not be ignored is that Irenaeus was from Asia. The apostle John was also from Ephesus in Asia. Irenaeus was discipled in the faith by men who were discipled by the apostle John. Therefore, with only one generation between Irenaeus and John, this is the strongest evidence possible. Irenaeus was in a position to receive the best possible witness on the date of Revelation.

Chilton's approach is nothing more than a debater's technique. When you do not have strong reasons against something then you try to cast doubt upon the reliability of the source.

But no reason exists to doubt the veracity of the source. Otherwise, Chilton would have given some specific reasons rather than resorting to the use of the word "may."

Some might want to question the reliability of Irenaeus. Actually Irenaeus is one of the most reliable of all the early church fathers:

> Until the mid-1940s archaeological discovery of some second century Gnostic writings, all of the information known about the movement was revealed in the writings of Irenaeus. He would first carefully state what the Gnostics believed, then refute them. When secular scholars analyzed the ancient documents and compared them with those of Irenaeus, they were greatly impressed with his careful scholarship, objectivity and accuracy. In the light of his fair and scholarly treatment of the Gnostic doctrines which he believed to be heresy, it is ludicrous to reason that Irenaeus would be less careful and accurate with facts about the Book of Revelation which he held to be the Word of God.[14]

The overwhelming voice of the early church believed that Revelation was written after the fall of Jerusalem. Chilton tries to minimize this by noting the heavy reliance on Irenaeus for support of this tradition. Yet in addition to Irenaeus there is Clement of Alexandria, Origen (no friend of Premillennialism), Victorinus, and Eusebius, to name just a few. But even if these are all traced back to Irenaeus, they believed the testimony and had no witnesses to the contrary. Since they were much closer to Irenaeus, they may have been privy to contrary evidence that we no longer have today. Even if this is not the case, Irenaeus's testimony is the best we have.

Chilton concludes his critique of the early church tradition by making a totally unfounded, unsupported, and speculative statement: "Certainly, there are other early writers whose statements indicate that St. John wrote the Revelation much earlier, under Nero's persecution."[15] But he does not produce those other early writers. Theodor Zahn sums up the early church tradition and draws the following sane conclusion:

> The correctness of the date [A.D. 96] is also confirmed by all those traditions which refer the exile of John upon Patmos to his extreme old age, or which describe Revelation as the latest, or one of the latest, writings in the N.T. On the other hand, all the differing views as to the date of the composition of Revelation to be found in the literature of the Church are so late and so manifestly confused, that they do not deserve the name of tradition.[16]

The strength of external evidence in favor of the later date is so strong that even opponents of the late date are forced to admit it:

> The testimony of this external evidence is so strong that even Hort, an advocate for a Neronian date, concluded, "If external evidence alone could decide, there would be a clear preponderance for Domitian." On the principle that a strong tradition must be allowed to stand unless internal evidence makes it impossible, which is certainly not true in this case, the Domitianic dating must have the decision in its favor.[17]

Donald Guthrie adds this observation: "It would be strange, if the book really was produced at the end of Nero's reign, that so strong a tradition arose associating it with Domitian's."[18] If there were some validity to the early date, some trace of this competing tradition should have surfaced. However, it has not!

Chilton retorts that: "A good deal of the modern presumption in favor of a Domitianic date is based on the belief that a great, sustained period of persecution and slaughter of Christians was carried on under his rule."[19] He goes on to say that this belief "does not seem to be based on any hard evidence at all."[20] A little later, Chilton says concerning Domitian, "It is true that he did temporarily banish some Christians; but these were eventually recalled."[21] This evidence, however, does not argue for Chilton's position. Domitian's practice of banning Christians is exactly the reason John was on the island of Patmos.

> It is a well-known fact that banishment for the sake of the Christian faith was a form of imperial violent justice, of whose exercise under Nero nothing is known; it is employed, however, by Domitian in company with other regular measures.[22]

A stronger case can be made for more severe persecution under Domitian than Chilton admits.

One of the main points in the Revelation is that even though persecution was occurring at the time of writing, the major portion was yet to come. Since Nero's persecutions "appear to be local [Rome] and brief though fierce,"[23] the question is raised as to why the Revelation, if penned during the early date, was not addressed to Jerusalem? Instead it went to the seven churches in Asia. The later date "also accords with the fact that the persecution under Domitian, unlike that under Nero, was due to the refusal of the Christians to worship the emperor."[24] There is no hard evidence of persecution under Nero in Asia during any part of his reign.

> All that we can say from the evidence of persecution is that it accords with all that we know of Domitian that there should have been such persecution, and that there is no other period in the first century which fits nearly as well.[25]

In addition, Revelation 2:13 says that a believer named Antipas had been "killed among you." Once again, this text is not referring to what happened in Rome, but in Asia. Furthermore, the church at Smyrna (2:10) is told of future persecutions that will last for ten days. Guthrie says,

> In certain passages regarding the great harlot (i.e. Rome) there are statements about her being drunk

with the blood of the saints (xvii.6, xviii.24, xix.2; cf. also xvi. 6, xx.4), which suggests a period of widespread persecution. . . . The next question which arises is whether this persecution situation fits best into the Domitianic period. The majority of scholars would answer in the affirmative.[26]

External evidence from two other Christian fathers, Eusebius and Sulpicius Severus, also included references to persecution under Domitian.[27]

What other external evidence supports a Domitian date for the book of Revelation? One major argument is that the earlier date would not correspond well with some of the conditions describing the seven churches of Revelation 2-3. First, according to Polycarp (c. A.D. 70-155), a bishop of Smyrna and disciple of the apostle John, the church in Smyrna was not founded until after the death of the apostle Paul. Therefore, "from the life of Polycarp we may conclude that it was not until circa 67-70 A.D. that a Church arose in that place, through the efforts of the apostle John & others of the apostolic circle."[28] It is most likely that the church in Smyrna was not yet in existence in A.D. 68 when Chilton says Revelation was written; yet it was one of the seven churches mentioned.

Second, the kind of emperor worship found in Revelation was not in evidence under Nero, but it was enforced under Domitian.[29] The choice portrayed in the Revelation to choose between Christ and Caesar was the case under Domitian, but not under Nero. Nero killed many Christians in Rome because he needed "scapegoats" for his impulsive burning of Rome. "This was in A.D. 64, and there is no proof that his fiendish cruelties to the infant church continued until or during the year A.D. 68."[30] Domitian, however, demanded worship of himself and punished Christians for worshiping Christ instead. Thus the ground of persecution argues for Domitian rather than Nero. Also, keep in mind that the persecution described in Revelation was occurring in Asia. This fits Domitian's empire-wide persecutions, while Nero's persecutions are only said to be in the area of Rome.

Third, in Revelation 1:9 John says, "I, John, your brother and fellow partaker in the tribulation. . . ." If this were written in A.D. 68, then John's partaking of tribulation under Nero would not have been likely, since Nero's persecution was limited to Rome. Domitian's was much more widespread. This text further states that the churches in Asia were also being persecuted. Once again, Nero's persecution, no matter how intense, was not extensive enough to account for Revelation 1:9.

Fourth, the city of Laodicea was destroyed by an earthquake in the early 60s and was rebuilt. The common practice of the day was to receive help from Rome, just as we would from Washington today. However, the inhabitants of this wealthy and self-sufficient city rejected such help and rebuilt the city all on their own.[31] If Revelation were written in A.D. 68, then five years would not be sufficient time to totally rebuild the city, even though they were a wealthy people. Once again, the Domitian date would easily give the needed time for the city to have been totally rebuilt and for the people to have developed the self-sufficient attitude depicted in the Revelation. Fifth, since we know that the apostle Paul was killed between A.D. 64-68, most likely by Nero,[32] and that just before his death he left Timothy in charge of the church in Ephesus (and most likely the rest of Asia), more than two or three years would be needed for the types of heresies to arise that the Revelation deals with. The thrust of Paul's theological rebukes in his epistles was against the legalism of the Judaizers because of the greater influence of Jews in the earlier church. Paul's burden was to uphold the freedom of the gospel. As time passed, these churches began to reflect the more pagan or Gentile error of loose living, the problems dealt with by the Revelation, rather than legalism. This type of change would require more than a few years, but could have easily transpired by the time of Domitian.

When we read the messages to the churches in the Apocalypse, we are in a different atmosphere. Not the narrowness of Judaism, but the wild immorality and worldliness of heathenism, is now striving to gain the upper hand; and the Christian has to overcome, not Judaism but the world in its widest sense.[33]

As far as the ancient records indicate, a fair conclusion is that a date corresponding with the reign of Domitian easily fits the climate required for the writing of the Book of Revelation.

Internal Evidence

After citing no external reasons why Revelation was written under Nero's reign, but trying only to cast doubt upon the clear and historically accepted witness of the early church to a Domitian date, Chilton attempts to cite three internal reasons for his position.

First, "Revelation is primarily a prophecy of the destruction of Jerusalem by the Romans. This fact alone places St. John's authorship somewhere before September of A.D. 70."[34] Chilton says that he will demonstrate this throughout the rest of his commentary. However, this is not a *reason* for the early date of Revelation, since the basis for it being true must rest upon the assumption that it was written to describe the A.D. 70 destruction of Jerusalem. If this were such a clear "fact," then why did none of the early church writings reflect Chilton's views in their interpretation of Revelation? If the A.D. 70 destruction of Jerusalem fulfilled so much of biblical prophecy, then why is this not reflected in the views of the early church? Why is it that all of the early fathers, when referring to Revelation and Matthew 24, see these as future events? They all wrote well after A.D. 70. Did even those who knew the writer of Revelation, the apostle John, not pick up on such an important understanding? If the early date were true, then the early church would have had a twenty-five year head start to establish this view and would have made it more difficult for the later date to have arisen.

Second, Chilton argues that "St. John speaks of Nero Caesar as still on the throne—and Nero died in June 68."[35] If Chilton could show that Nero is the ruler[36] spoken of in Revelation, then he would have a major victory for his view. But he cannot. He plugs Nero into certain passages without demonstrating from those passages that it has to be Nero. Then he turns around and argues that it proves his point.

He concludes his argument by claiming, "more important than any of this, however, we have *a priori* teaching from Scripture itself that all special revelation ended by A.D. 70."[37] Even someone only casually familiar with the Bible should be wondering where he finds this *a priori* teaching from Scripture. The fact is, this statement is based upon *his a priori* theological commitment that the book of Revelation is about the destruction of Jerusalem.

One of the arguments Chilton has used to support his *a priori* belief is his understanding of the seventy weeks of Daniel. In order to interpret Daniel 9:24-27 and have it yield Chilton's conclusion, one has to understand it in a symbolic fashion without a precise meaning. Chilton then concludes from this "give or take 50 years" approach that all of Daniel's seventy weeks have been completed by A.D. 70, therefore the whole of the New Testament had to have been written. Once again, Chilton is asking us to draw hard conclusion from soft support. Much better and more satisfying interpretive options are available.[38] The better view is that the seventy weeks of Daniel have yet to be completed; therefore, Chilton's argument concerning the date of the completion of the New Testament canon does not apply.

Chilton's "internal" arguments come down to whether or not one accepts his later explanation of the book of Revelation. If he is giving the correct interpretation of the Revelation, then that view demands a pre-A.D. 70 date for the book. If not, his attempt is not convincing. Chilton is presupposing his view, then attempting to argue the details in terms of that view, and finally arguing that it proves his assumption. It proves the assumption only if the details can be shown to fit the assumed viewpoint, which we are convinced he does not do.

Conclusion

The sum total of both internal and external evidence most strongly favors the date of A.D. 95-96, rather than the A.D. 68 date proposed by Chilton. The importance of the date, it should be kept in mind, is of ultimate importance to Chilton's view of Revelation and even to his whole system of eschatology, which depends desperately on a pre-A.D. 70 date. As noted at the beginning of this discussion, postmillennialist and preterist Gentry said, "if it could be demonstrated that Revelation were written 25 years after the Fall of Jerusalem, Chilton's entire labor would go up in smoke."[39] However, the premillennial view could be correct no matter when the book was written.

The Futuristic Interpretation of Revelation

An issue that affects Reconstructionists' and Chilton's view of the book of Revelation is whether the book should be interpreted according to a preterist perspective or according to a futuristic approach. Put simply, does Revelation describe events that have already taken place at the time of its writing as the preterists (Latin for past) say, or is it something that primarily has yet to take place as the futurists insist? If the futurist view is correct, then once again Chilton's view "goes up in smoke."

Definitions

Before we begin this investigation, let us get a definition of each view from someone who holds that view. Chilton says that a preterist position means that Revelation "was written to and for Christians who were living at the time it was first delivered. We are wrong to interpret it futuristically."[40] He goes on to elaborate: "the events St. John foretold were 'in the future' to St. John and his readers; but they occurred soon after he wrote of them. . . . For us, the great majority of the Revelation is history: It has already happened."[41] Thus, Chilton is saying that most, if not all, of the Revelation was historically fulfilled in the time of its writing. Therefore, its relevance for today is "as we understand its message and apply its principles to our lives and our culture. Jesus Christ still demands of us what He demanded of the early Church: absolute faithfulness to Him."[42] This means we can look back to it as a model to emulate.

A leading spokesman for the futurist interpretation is John Walvoord, who says that the futuristic approach "regards Revelation as futuristic beginning with chapter 4 and therefore subject of future fulfillment."[43] This view sees the believer looking ahead to what God is going to do, thus giving hope for the future, resulting in faithful and godly living in the present. This is called in Titus 2:13 "the blessed hope."

The Present Value of the Past

As discussed elsewhere in this book, nontheonomists look at Old Testament law as something given to the nation of Israel in the past. We take a preterist approach to Old Testament law. Of course we are chided by Reconstructionists for this position. For example, Bahnsen says, "Ryrie temporally restricts the law of God to a dispensation extending from Sinai to Calvary and contrasts it to the dispensation of grace."[44] Bahnsen's misunderstanding of Ryrie should first be cleared up. Ryrie does not "restrict the law of God," as if he believes that God no longer has a law; rather Ryrie sees "the law of Moses" as a temporal feature relating specifically to the nation of Israel and God's covenant with them. God's character never changes, thus God's moral law never changes. But the outworking of God's one plan is multifaceted. This is why Paul says concerning the current dispensation that it is the product of "the manifold [many sided, multi-dimensional] wisdom of God" (Ephesians 3:9-10).

Currently, God has made a new ⸀covenant with his people—the church—and we live under the "law of Christ" (Galatians 6:2). This does not mean we are totally cut off from a past period of God's work and that if we are not directly under it then it has no current relevance. It does mean that we are not currently living under the economy of Mosaic legislation and the covenant between Yahweh and Israel, but we do look back at the law and "profit" (2 Timothy 3:16) from it and even develop "principles" and "wisdom" from it. Indeed, "the Law is good, if one uses it lawfully" (1 Timothy 1:8).

In principle, this preterist approach to the Mosaic law is similar to Chilton's proposed approach to the Revelation. Remember, he says that even though it happened in the past it still has relevance to us today "as we understand its message and apply its principles to our lives and our culture. Jesus Christ still demands of us what He demanded of the early Church: absolute faithfulness to Him."[45]

Dominion Dispensationalism

Reconstructionists are inconsistent. They allow a contemporary value for Revelation (even though it had historical fulfillment) but do not allow others to assign contemporary value to the Old Testament law (even though it had a historical fulfillment). To follow this logic is to say that most of the New Testament epistles only had relevance to believers in the time in which they were written. The epistles contain statements about the coming of Christ and about apostasy,[46] which Reconstructionists believe happened in A.D. 70. In fact, they believe that the bulk of New Testament prophecy has already been fulfilled. This approach leads to a Reconstructionist form of dispensationalism. The new dispensation is a forty-year period ending in A.D. 70. Many passages most Christians interpret as being fulfilled presently or in the future can only be "applied in principle" today, since they are history.

A great portion of the New Testament deals with subjects "dominion dispensationalists" want to see as past history. In order to salvage any contemporary value, they could only apply much of the New Testament as principles during the current dispensation. According to their own principles, much of the New Testament is not binding upon us today. As one example of how their preterist misinterpretation removes a whole category as having a contemporary impact, let us look at how Reconstructionists deal with the issue of apostasy.

Apostasy: Principle or Actual
Chilton says,

> The 'Great Apostasy' happened in the first century. We therefore have no Biblical warrant to expect increasing apostasy as history progresses; instead, we should expect the increasing Christianization of the world.[47]

Does this mean that apostasy is not occurring today? Assuming the answer to this is no, what passages speak of this danger in the current "millennium"? How do Reconstructionists account for, even by their own admission, so much false doctrine and so little orthodoxy in Christendom today? They often say the church has not made more progress toward the full realization of the millennium because of the unfaithfulness of the majority within the church. In fact, one of these widespread heresies is the belief in the rapture. Why did the early church not seem to recognize that the great apostasy was over? Why did one of the earliest fathers, Irenaeus (A. D. 130-202) write a major work *Against Heresies*?

Motivation for the Present: Past or Future?
Chilton says, "Actually, it is the futurists who have made the Revelation irrelevant—for on the futurist hypothesis the book has been inapplicable from the time it was written until the twentieth century!"[48] Not really. There are many prophetic

passages, especially in the Old Testament, which had a future fulfillment at the time they were given but which also served as a comfort or admonition to those in the present.

Almost all of the prophetic books have a theme similar to the following: A particular issue, problem, or sin is being addressed by the prophet at the time of writing; the prophet warns the people that if they do not repent, God will send judgment; the judgment is described, but with the assurance that the Lord will one day fulfill the promises of blessing to Israel. An example of this is the book of Joel, which concludes with a promise of millennial blessing (3:18-21). Regardless of how one interprets Joel, there are clearly elements that are future to the time in which it was written. So the futurist is taking prophetic literature in a way that is consistent with how believers have always understood it. Futurists are not coming up with a special, new way to deal with the Olivet discourse and the book of Revelation as the preterists have done.

How did such an approach relate to the people in 835 B.C. when much of the book of Joel was not fulfilled—and would not be for several hundred more years? It works in the same way that the futuristic interpretation handles the Revelation and the Olivet discourse. There is a particular current situation about which God's people need his Word. The encouragement for the present is to look to what God will ultimately do in the future. If Chilton says that we can look back to what God has done and have this affect our faithfulness to Jesus Christ in the present, then why, at least in principle, can that not work in the other direction? It can, and does, throughout Scripture.

Lessons from Hall of Famers

Old Testament saints looked forward to the coming of Messiah. Hebrews 11 speaks of many believers who were future-oriented, resulting in a present motivation to godliness and faith. In fact, Hebrews 11:39 says, "And all these, having gained approval through their faith, did not receive what was promised." What is it that was promised? A future reward! But they acted in faith and with motivation in the present because of their future inheritance. Let's look at one of those exhibits from faith's "hall of fame."

Moses had all this world could offer. He had royal standing, education, material wealth, all the things a good Reconstructionist could say should be used to build God's kingdom now. However, like Christ, he took the weak way. "By faith Moses, when he had grown up, refused to be called the son of Pharaoh's daughter; choosing rather to endure ill-treatment with the people of God, than to enjoy the passing pleasures of sin; considering the reproach of Christ greater riches than the treasures of Egypt; for he was looking to the reward" (11:24-26). The future program is what gave him motivation to do what God wanted him to do in the present, not some argument which says you have to have the hope of present success to be really motivated. He could be patient in the present because he looked ahead to the future.

It is amazing that R. J. Rushdoony and Gary North have developed such a detailed and sophisticated case for how future orientation provides motivation for the present. Rushdoony says, "To the degree that future orientation is lacking in a society to that extent it is not only stagnant but also lacks the vitality to correct and to rebuild."[49] In fact Gary North amazingly says,

> The Bible tells us that we are to be slaves to the future. . . . It is this future-orientation that marks the free man's perspective. He makes decisions in terms of the future, has confidence in the future, and can happily sacrifice present income for increased income in the future.[50]

Yet they then say that the premillennialist is without motivation to live a godly life in the present. "The social and intellectual problem for the consistent premillennialist or amillennialist is motivation."[51] All we are motivated to do, they say on the basis of our eschatology, is to sit around "biting our finger nails" waiting for the rapture as the world goes to hell in a handbasket.

> If God is willing to put up with the victory of evil,
> then there is nothing that Christians can do about it
> except try to get out of the way of victorious sinners
> if they possibly can, while handing out gospel tracts
> on street corners and running rescue missions.[52]

Some Reconstructionists have erected a premillennial straw man they love to bash, but this characterization is not reflected in the track record of those who believe in the blessed hope of our Lord's soon return. That track record is one of godly activity. Christian Reconstructionists like to boast that postmillennialism was a great stimulus to American missions. "It was explicitly a postmillennial eschatology which brought about the formation of the American Board of Commissioners for Foreign Missions."[53] If postmillennialism dominated the missions movement one hundred to two hundred years ago, did they also have a great hand in seeing many missions shift from preaching the gospel to changing the culture through the social gospel?

It is often ignored that premillennialism has a tremendous track record in the area of missions as well. George Marsden notes that "Premillennialists . . . had every bit as much enthusiasm for the evangelization of the world as did the most optimistic postmillennialists."[54]

A specific example from the 1800s was Samuel Henry Kellogg (1839-1899). Kellogg was one of the top two graduates, out of a class of one hundred, from Princeton University in 1861. Dr. Kellogg served as a missionary to India for nineteen years, returning for a period upon his wife's death. While in America he was a pastor in Pittsburgh, filled the chair of Systematic Theology in Allegheny (Western) Seminary, and then was the pastor for six years of St. James Square Presbyterian Church, Toronto. He wrote nine books, including *The Book of Leviticus*, *A Handbook of Comparative Religion*, and his most important missions work, *A Grammar of the Hindi Language*. He was the leading translator of the Old Testament into the Hindi language.[55] The translation of the Bible is certainly a future-oriented project. The editor of one of Kellogg's books said:

> Dr. Kellogg elsewhere gives a bit of interesting information about the [Princeton] Seminary class in which he graduated. Among the fifty graduates were just seven Premillennialists. These all volunteered for the foreign field, while none of the others did. Four were permitted to go, and the three who were found physically unfit engaged in home mission work.[56]

Those New Testament passages that speak of the second coming of Christ present it as the strongest of motivations to perseverance, faithfulness, and godly living in the present.[57] It is one of the tests of our faith to purify our trust in him. One who is truly regenerate will serve God and remain faithful to him regardless of the present benefits. Perseverance in the midst of trials is not only a sign of true election, but also a major means of spiritual growth.

The Reconstructionists' claim that dispensationalists cannot motivate anyone in the present is a pragmatic, even worldly, argument which teaches that a person has to have a present benefit in order to be motivated in this life. In fact, Satan challenged God with a similar idea when he asked, "Does Job fear God for nothing?" (1:9). Satan was attacking God's character and plan by saying that God had to pay people off (through blessing) in order to get them to worship and follow him. The book of Job demonstrates this to be false and Satan the unlovely and undesirable person.

The premillennialist can say with Job, "Shall we indeed accept good from God and not accept adversity?" (2:10b). "The LORD gave and the LORD has taken away. Blessed be the name of the LORD" (1:21b). We are called to do the will of God because it is just that—the will of God. Since we are regenerate, we now love to do his will; we love his law (Romans 8:4). That is motivation enough for the true child of God. Love—not present, pragmatic success—is the highest and strongest motivation for serving God. When left with this motive, only true believers will respond to Christ when he says, "If you love Me, you will keep My commandments" (John 14:15).

The most common rationale the Scriptures use is this: "God has ordained a great future, one in which we will reign and rule with Christ in his kingdom. However, often in the present we are called upon to suffer and experience hardships, maybe even death in the process of doing God's will. Our example is Christ, who submitted to suffering and reproach in fulfilling God's plan because he knew that joy lay in the future upon completing God's will." Christ dealt with the suffering of the present by looking to the future (John 16:20-22; Hebrews 12:1-11). This is why we agree with George Ladd, who has said, "the nature of prophecy is to let light shine from the future upon the present."[58] What a motivation—the future upon the present.

Coming or Gone?

An application of this approach is seen in the parables following the Olivet discourse in Matthew 24, which argue for faithfulness in the present, based upon a proper view of the future. In fact, even Reconstructionist James Jordan believes that these parables refer to the second coming, though he takes verses 1-35 to refer to the destruction of Jerusalem. He says, "Now this is not the coming of the Son of Man to the Father, but the final coming at the end of history."[59] Why, on the basis of the hermeneutics Jordan has used to this point in his interpretation of the Olivet discourse, does he suddenly make an arbitrary leap to the second coming of Christ? Using his same interpretive principles, one should say that these parables refer to watching and waiting for the coming in A.D. 70, which is basically how Reconstructionists take the "comings" in verses 1-35.

Jordan and Chilton are aware of where a consistent preterist interpretation leads—to a denial of any second coming at all. Chilton says,

> What about the second Coming of Christ? Since so many prophecies turn out to be references to the destruction of Jerusalem in A.D. 70, how can we be sure that any prophecy refers to a future, literal return of Jesus Christ.[60]

Since most of the references to the second coming have been consigned to A.D. 70, the few passages Reconstructionists use to say the Bible does teach a second coming can just as easily be handled in the same way. In fact, most dominion theology adherents, when challenged to defend the second coming, do not cite Scripture as the basis for their belief;[61] rather they cite the voice of mother church:

> Historic, orthodox Christianity everywhere, with one voice, has always taught that Christ "shall come again, with glory, to judge both the living and the dead" (Nicene Creed). This is a non-negotiable article of the Christian faith.[62]

Notice that the Nicene Creed (produced in A.D. 381) arguably is based upon a futuristic, premillennial interpretation of Scripture. Ironically, then, Chilton has to go to a premillennial source to produce the orthodox and historical creedal statement concerning the second coming.

Warning: Preterist Interpretation
Could Be Spiritually Hazardous!

Chilton issues a warning about his approach to interpreting prophecy. He warns that it can be applied too consistently.

> It has become popular in some otherwise apparently orthodox circles to adopt a heretical form of "preterism" that denies any future bodily Resurrection or Judgment, asserting that all these are fulfilled in

the Resurrection of Christ, the regeneration of the Church, the coming of the New Covenant, & the destruction of Jerusalem in A.D. 70.[63]

It is extremely significant that Chilton uses only a historical argument against what he calls "a heretical form of preterism."[64] If orthodox Christianity has always held these views, which indeed it has, then Christians must have used certain scriptural passages to derive these beliefs. Why did not Chilton use the orthodox church's strongest argument—a scriptural one—since God directs his body through his Word?

We suggest the reason for Chilton's failure to use Scripture is that there is no real difference in the hermeneutics of "heretical preterism" and "orthodox preterism." There is no qualitative difference, only an arbitrary one. In other words, orthodox preterists simply do not want to take their position to its logical conclusion. Orthodox preterists have different theological assumptions than heretical preterists and therefore draw different conclusions from the same texts, but no internal controls exist within the preterist interpretative system.

Double Reference

The better approach to the Olivet discourse and the Revelation is the one taken down through church history, and that is a "double reference" approach. The Hebrew Christian scholar Arnold Fruchtenbaum defines double reference as follows:

> This law observes the fact that often a passage or a block of Scripture is speaking of two different persons or two different events that are separated by a long period of time. But in the passage itself they are blended into one picture, and the time gap between the two persons or two events is not presented by the test itself. . . .
>
> A good example of this law is some of the Old Testament prophecies regarding the first and second comings of Christ. Often two events are blended

into one picture with no indication that there is a gap of time between the first and second coming of Christ.[65]

This approach often blends the preterist event with the future event. Therefore, the single interpretation handles some of the passage as past while other segments are still future. The Olivet discourse did predict the coming destruction of Jerusalem, which is today a past event, but at the same time the bulk of the passage deals with the yet future events of Christ's coming and the end of the age. It is probably true that the disciples thought of the three events (the destruction of the temple, the second coming, and the end of the age) as one event. But as was almost always the case, they were wrong. Ladd has stated the proper relationship between the preterist and future aspects of prophecy and the Olivet discourse:

> The imminent historical judgment is seen as a type of, or a prelude to, the eschatological judgment. The two are often blended together in apparent disregard for chronology, for the same God who acts in the imminent historical judgment will also act in the final eschatological judgment to further his one redemptive purpose. Thus, Daniel viewed the great eschatological enemy of God's people as the historical king of Greece (Antiochus Epiphanes of the Seleucid Kingdom—11:3), who yet took on the coloration of the eschatological Antichrist (Dan. 12:36-39). In the same way, our Lord's Olivet Discourse was concerned with both the historical judgment of Jerusalem at the hands of the Roman armies (Luke 21:20ff.) and the eschatological appearance of Antichrist. (Matt. 24:15ff.). Rome was a historical forerunner of Antichrist.[66]

As noted above, Chilton has said the Revelation had to have a contemporary fulfillment in order for it to be relevant to those to whom it was written. "For us, the great majority of the Revelation is history: It has already happened. . . . His message was contemporary, not futuristic."[67] He then quotes from Russell to bolster that point:

> If this book were really intended to minister faith & comfort to the very persons to whom it was sent, it must unquestionably deal with matters in which they were practically and personally interested. And does not this very obvious consideration suggest the true key to the Apocalypse? Must it not of necessity refer to matters of contemporary history? The only tenable, the only reasonable, hypothesis is that it was intended to be understood by its original readers; but this is as much as to say that it must be occupied with the events and transactions of their own day, and these comprised within a comparatively brief space of time.[68]

If this understanding was to be such a wonderful comfort to the believers at the time of the writing of the New Testament, then why is there absolutely no record of them viewing it in this way? If Chilton and Russell's view is correct, then a majority of the New Testament was not recognized as already fulfilled until recently. It was not until fifteen hundred years later that Chilton's preterist interpretation arose. And this at a time when it could benefit no one, if the preterist criterion of benefit is correct.

History of the Preterist Interpretation
When did the preterist interpretation first arise in the history of the church?

> The promulgation of this view "in anything like completeness" was by a Spanish Jesuit of Antwerp, named Alcasar, in the beginning of the seventeenth century (1614). He was followed throughout that century by some eminent expositors. Later this interpretation was revived in Germany, a large number

of whose outstanding expositors have elaborated it. Nor is this to be wondered at, for the trend of German criticism has been to limit the view of the writers of Scripture to matters within their own horizon.[69]

Tenney further explains:

The Reformers had identified Babylon with the Roman church, and had succeeded in making the Revelation a powerful controversial weapon in their favor. In order to offset this interpretation, Alcasar attempted to show that Revelation had no application to the future, but that its prophecy could be divided into two major sections (chs. 1- 12, 13-19) which dealt respectively with the church's conflict against Judaism & against paganism. Alcasar thus cleverly nullified the attacks upon the Roman church which the Reformers had made so successfully by using the language of Revelation.[70]

This is not just the evaluation of nonpreterists, but of preterists as well. Isbon T. Beckwith wrote a preterist commentary on the book of Revelation in 1919 and said this concerning the origins of his own interpretative viewpoint:

There is in Alcasar no use made of the method spoken of above which finds in the Apocalypse the future history of the Church; that is, he finds in the book no prediction of world-history beyond the time of Constantine, when the millennium began. His work is the first to attempt a complete exposition of the entire premillennial part of the book, as a connected & advancing whole falling within the Apocalyptist's age & the centuries immediately following. It becomes therefore important in the growth of a truly scientific method of exegesis.[71]

The preterist interpretation was rarely used by Protestants until the 1800s. It gained a wide following among German liberals who did not believe the Bible contained predictive prophecy. It was also popular among a number of nineteenth century British Anglican commentators. Therefore, the character of the preterist perspective was conducive to their goals:

> Alcasar's suggestion was followed by some Protestant expositors, but the rise of the modern preterist school came with the prevalence of the technique of historical criticism. Since preterism did not necessitate any element of predictive prophecy or even any conception of inspiration, it could treat the Revelation simply as a purely natural historical document, embodying the eschatological concepts of its own time.[72]

Why Past and Not Future?

Chilton would have us think that the preterist view was a great comfort to the early church when it is clear that they did not even know of such an interpretation. For, as we have seen, this 350-year-old perspective developed as a polemic to help the Roman Catholic church attempt to escape the tag of antichrist that the Reformers were so fond of giving to the institution they had left.

It should be further noted that the result of such a view is to rob believers throughout the entire church age of the true hope that we have—the Blessed Hope. If Chilton is correct, a Christian must have something written specifically and directly to him to have substantive hope. He explains how his interpretation produces relevance for today:

> The primary relevance of the Book of Revelation was for its first-century readers. It still has relevance for us today as we understand its message and apply its principles to our lives and our culture. Jesus Christ still demands of us what He demanded of the early Church: absolute faithfulness to Him.[73]

Since preterists such as Chilton have limited so many aspects of the Bible to past fulfillment but are not comfortable with living with the result of their interpretive approach, they have to come up with devices to make applicable to contemporary life biblical passages that have already been fulfilled.

We propose that Chilton's view is really a blend of the preterist and idealist view, which "is concerned with ideas and principles."[74] The Reconstructionist perspective is not a total idealist approach, but in order to rescue their preterist interpretation from meaninglessness, they have to bring through the back door some of the ideas that were laid to rest in A.D. 70 and that are contrary to the belief of the historic, orthodox church.

Perhaps the real reason Chilton has chosen the preterist approach, since most postmillennialists have not been preterists, is that it is the most antipremillennialist interpretative option on the market. But what he has lost in the process may be more than he bargained for.

Why a Futurist Interpretation

We believe the futurist interpretation is the correct interpretive grid, as the discussion that follows will help show.

The futurist interpretation is the approach used by the earliest church fathers. We do not argue that they had a sophisticated system, but the clear futurist elements were there. This is important, since some of these fathers were discipled by the apostle John.

There are clear links between Revelation, the Olivet discourse, and the book of Daniel. Over eight hundred allusions to Old Testament passages have been identified in the book of Revelation, with Isaiah and Daniel heading the list. The beast of Revelation 13 and 17 and the fourth beast of Daniel 7 are one and the same.[75] This beast is the final Gentile ruler before the fifth kingdom, the kingdom of Christ on earth. The reason this cannot refer to A.D. 70 is that "when the Messianic Kingdom is established it will take the place of 'all the kingdoms under the whole heaven (Dan. 7:27),' and this is simply not the case today."[76] If Reconstructionists continue to insist that we are living in the kingdom period, it certainly does not match up to the realized conditions of blessing and victory so clearly stated. If the establishment of the kingdom is to be gradual, then it is strange that Scripture uses such definitive language.

Both futurists and preterists agree that Revelation is loaded with symbols. The issue is not symbols or no symbols, but rather how they are to be interpreted. While the preterist interprets them as not speaking of actual earthly events (generally speaking), the futurist takes them (generally speaking) as actually taking place in earth history.[77]

The futurist interpreter takes the events of Revelation in the same way he interprets past events. We let Scripture interpret Scripture by seeing how the biblical authors handled prophecy which had already been fulfilled. This gives us help in understanding unfulfilled prophecy. Only the futurist approach is consistent with past standards. Also, there is not just methodological help from comparing Scripture with Scripture, but there is also the discovery of a correspondence of symbols. Gary Cohen has given us a case in point:

> These "last plagues" (Rev. 15:1) of sores, the smiting of the sea, rivers, sun, and the kingdom of the beast with darkness (Rev. 16) cannot be rejected as literal events and allegorized away so easily. This is because the first bowl which inflicts sores upon the men who have the mark of the beast (Rev. 16:1-2) is very similar to the sixth plague of boils which smote the Egyptians (Exod. 9:8-12); the third bowl turning the rivers to blood (Rev. 16:4-7) seems identical to the first Egyptian plague except that the former is on a larger scale (Exod. 7:19-21); the fifth bowl which fills the kingdom of the beast with grievous darkness (Rev. 16:10-11) is the same as the ninth plague of Egypt (Exod. 10:21-23); and the hail of

the seventh bowl (Rev. 16:17-21) is similar to the hail of the seventh Egyptian plague (Exod. 9:22-26). Since the plagues of Egypt literally occurred, is it not reasonable to believe that these similar bowl plagues will in like manner come to pass?[78]

Often in prophetic literature there is an interpreting angel who will explain within the text what the symbols mean (Daniel 12:5-13; Revelation 1:1, 12-20). There are a number of examples of this. And when we observe how the heavenly interpreter handles these symbols, then we see that they yield a literal meaning. Some examples: the seven stars (1:16) are seven angels (1:20); seven candlesticks (1:13) are seven churches (1:20); the incense is the prayers of the saints (5:8); Sodom and Egypt are Jerusalem (11:8); the dragon and the serpent are Satan (12:9); the ten horns are ten (contemporaneous) kings (17:12); and the lake of fire is the second death (20:14).[79]

Preterists believe that Revelation 19 does not refer to a physical return of Christ to earth at the second coming:

> St. John is not describing the Second Coming at the end of the world. He is describing the progress of the Gospel throughout the world, the universal proclamation of the message of salvation, which follows the First Advent of Christ.[80]

If this is so, not a single passage in the book of Revelation speaks about the second coming of Christ. Yet the church throughout the centuries has relied on Revelation for the truth of Christ's literal return. So much for the Reconstructionists' claim to historic orthodoxy. The futurist sees Christ's coming in Revelation 19:11 in the way the angels promised in Acts 1:10-11, "This Jesus, who has been taken up from you into heaven, will come in just the same way as you have watched Him go into heaven." He will return physically to the earth, since he arose physically in his ascension.

Reconstructionists admit that Christ did not come back physically in A.D. 70 in the destruction of Jerusalem.[81] Therefore, it is reasonable to understand that his return will happen in the future as Revelation 19 describes, patterned after Acts 1:10-11. Reconstructionists do not have a biblical passage that corresponds with the Acts passage since they have "preterized" them all away. The futurist view harmonizes the two passages.

> The major problem with the preterist position is that the decisive victory portrayed in the latter chapters of the Apocalypse was never achieved. It is difficult to believe that John envisioned anything less than the complete overthrow of Satan, the final destruction of evil, and the eternal reign of God.[82]

The outline of the book of Revelation is given for us in 1:19: "Write therefore the things which you have seen, and the things which are, and the things which shall take place after these things." This means that there are two divisions within the book of Revelation: "one, the things that fall within the actual lifetime of the seer, the first century [Revelation 1-3], and second, the things which were future to his period [Revelation 4:1-22:5]."[83] An internal textual verification is clearly seen in Revelation 4:1 when it says, "I will show you what must take place after these things."[84] As Tenney concludes, "On this ground the futurist has a good claim for the validity of his method."[85]

The futurist position rests primarily on the issue of interpretation. "The more literal an interpretation that one adopts, the more strongly will he be construed to be a futurist."[86] This will be pursued further in chapter 14, and it is the strongest argument for a futurist position. The futurist approach to Revelation and all prophecy (let us not forget that Revelation is called a "prophecy," 1:1) yields a satisfying capstone to God's Word.

> The preterist viewpoint does not do justice to the predictive element in Revelation. If its premises are accepted, the book is directed only to the day in which it was written, and has no real significance

for the succeeding centuries, except as the principles of truth which were applicable then may still be valid.[87]

If Revelation is not a future prediction then all we have is some abstract, idealistic statements. The futuristic view produces a genuine hope, a blessed hope, because one can see real prophecies as actual future events in which God will bring this present age to a just climax for the righteous. As Genesis provides an explanation of the actual details and events concerning how God began this world, the book of Revelation produces that proper ending. Scroggie rightly declares,

> If the Praeterist view is right, this book no longer bears that relation to all the Scriptures, for assuredly the consummation of the divine purposes was not reached in the fall of pagan Rome. The Bible would be singularly incomplete if it ended there; and the prophetic writings of the Old Testament would become most obscure.[88]

The preterist interpretation leaves one bewildered about the end of all things.

Chapter 12, Notes

1. Kenneth L. Gentry, *"The Days of Vengeance*: A Review Article," *The Counsel of Chalcedon,* June 1987, 11.

2. Ibid., 10.

3. David Chilton, *The Days of Vengeance* (Fort Worth: Dominion Press, 1987), 3.

4. Ibid., 2-3.

5. Ray R. Sutton, "Studies in the Book of Daniel I," cassette tape from series "Eschatology and Dominion," Geneva Tape Library, Tyler, Tex., 1984. In his lecture, Sutton admonishes his listeners to decide biblical matters not just from the text of Scripture alone (our "father"), but to also listen to the voice of our "mother"—church tradition.

6. Chilton, *Days of Vengeance*, 493.

7. Ibid., 2, n. 5.

8. Irenaeus, *Against Heresies*, v.xxx.3.

9. Chilton, *Days of Vengeance*, 3.

10. Henry B. Swete, *Commentary on Revelation* (1911; reprint, Grand Rapids: Kregel Publications, 1977), cvi.

11. *The Ecclesiastical History of Eusebius Pamphilus* , trans. Isaac Boyle (Grand Rapids: Baker Book House, 1977), 188.

12. Ibid.

13. Philip Schaff, *History of the Christian Church*, vol. 1 (Grand Rapids: Wm. B. Eerdmans Publishing Co., 1910), 834.

14. Hal Lindsey, from his forthcoming book *Never Again* in the chapter, "The Great Dominionist Dating Game."

15. Chilton, *Days of Vengeance*, 4.

16. Theodor Zahn, *Introduction of the New Testament* (Minneapolis: Klock & Klock Christian Publishers, 1909), 3:183-84.

17. Donald Guthrie, *New Testament Introduction* (Downers Grove, Ill.: InterVarsity Press, 1970), 957.

18. Ibid., 960.

19. Chilton, *Days of Vengeance*, 4.

20. Ibid.

21. Ibid.

22. J. Peter Lange, *The Revelation of John*, vol. 12 of *Lange's Commentary on the Holy Scriptures* (Grand Rapids: Zondervan Publishing House, 1960), 59.

23. Leon Morris, *Revelation* (Grand Rapids: Wm. B. Eerdmans Publishing Co., 1972), 36.

24. Henry C. Thiessen, *Introduction to the New Testament* (Grand Rapids: Wm. B. Eerdmans Publishing Co., 1943), 323.

25. Morris, *Revelation*, 37.

26. Guthrie, *Introduction*, 952.

27. Ibid., 953.

28. Zahn, *Introduction*, 412-13, 422.

29. Swete, *Revelation*, ci, civ.

30. Charles R. Erdman, *The Revelation of John* (Philadelphia: The Westminster Press, 1936), 20.

31. William Ramsay, *The Letters to the Seven Churches* (1904; reprint, Minneapolis: James Family Publishing Company, 1978), 428.

32. Guthrie, *Introduction*, 664-65.

33. M. J. Brunk, "The Date, Authorship, and Interpretation of the Apocalypse" (Th.D. diss., Dallas Theological Seminary, 1933), 19-20.

34. Chilton, *Days of Vengeance*, 4.

35. Ibid.

36. Ibid., see 329, 344-45, 350-51, 583.

37. Ibid., 4.

38. See for example Harold W. Hoehner, *Chronological Aspects of the Life of Christ* (Grand Rapids: Zondervan Publishing House, 1977); Paul D.

Feinberg, "An Exegetical and Theological Study of Daniel 9:24-27" in *Tradition and Testament: Essays in Honor of Charles Lee Feinberg*, ed. John S. Feinberg and Paul D. Feinberg (Chicago: Moody Press, 1981), 189-220.

39. See n. 1.

40. Chilton, *Days of Vengeance*, 40.

41. Ibid.

42. Ibid., 41.

43. John Walvoord, *The Revelation of Jesus Christ* (Chicago: Moody Press, 1966), 20.

44. Greg Bahnsen, *Theonomy in Christian Ethics* (Nutley, N.J.: The Craig Press, 1977), 21.

45. Chilton, *Days of Vengeance*, 40.

46. Notice the large volume of Scripture in the epistles alone that are devoted to the issue of apostasy: Romans 1:18-32; 10; 16:17-18; 2 Corinthians 11:1-15; 13:5; Galatians 1:6-9; 5:1-12; Philippians 3:2, 18-19; Colossians 2:4-23; 2 Thessalonians 2:1- 12; 1 Timothy 1:3-7; 4:1-3; 6:3-5; 2 Timothy 2:11-26; 3:1-9; 4:15; Titus 1:10-16; Hebrews 2:1-4; 3:7-4:13; 5:12-6:12; 10:26-31; 12:14-17; 1 Peter 3:19-20; 2 Peter 2:1-22; 3:3-10; 1 John 2:18-23; 3:4-12; 4:1-6; 2 John 9; Jude 3-23. Apostasy and its evil effects provide the main message of such books as Galatians, 2 Thessalonians, Hebrews, and Revelation.

47. Chilton, *Paradise Restored: A Biblical Theology of Dominion* (Fort Worth: Dominion Press, 1985), 225.

48. Chilton, *Days of Vengeance*, 41.

49. R. J. Rushdoony, *God's Plan for Victory: The Meaning of Post Millennialism* (Fairfax, Va.: Thoburn Press, 1977), 19.

50. Gary North, *Moses and Pharaoh: Dominion Religion Versus Power Religion* (Tyler, Tex.: Institute for Christian Economics, 1985), 259-60.

51. Gary North, "Christianity and Progress," *Christian Reconstruction*, May-June 1987, 2.

52. Ibid., 3.

53. Greg Bahnsen, "The *Prima Facie* Acceptability of Postmillennialism," *Journal of Christian Reconstruction* 3 (Winter 1976-77):98.

54. George Marsden, *Fundamentalism and American Culture: The Shaping of Twentieth-Century Evangelicalism: 1870-1925* (New York: Oxford University Press, 1980), 97-98.

55. J. J. Lucas, "A Biographical Memoir" in Samuel Henry Kellogg, *Are Premillennialists Right?* (New York: Fleming H. Revell Co., 1923).

56. Ibid., 121.

57. George Peters provides an extensive list of New Testament passages showing how the New Testament uses the second coming to underscore its importance to doctrine, duty, and character. (George N. H. Peters, *The Theocratic Kingdom* [Grand Rapids: Kregel Publications, 1978], 3:323-24.) For Reconstructionists to take most of these passages as relating to the A.D. 70 destruction of Jerusalem is to overrate one event in God's plan to the neglect of a greater event—the second coming. The absence of these passages

for the believer today leaves a huge gap in the New Testament for anyone trying to understand them in harmony with the preterist interpretation. To see them as our yet future hope, these passages offer the present-day believer a wide variety of motivation for the present.

58. George Eldon Ladd, *A Commentary on the Revelation of John* (Grand Rapids: Wm. B. Eerdmans Publishing Co., 1972), 14.

59. James Jordan, "Exposition of Matthew 24:31-51," cassette recording #JJ52, Geneva Media, 708 Hamvasy Lane, Tyler, Tex.

60. Chilton, *Paradise Restored*, 133.

61. Chilton apparently does think that 1 Corinthians 15:51-54 and 1 Thessalonians 4:14-17 are passages teaching the second coming (*Paradise Restored*, 147-8). He says that when it speaks of the resurrection, the second coming is implied (pp. 138-40). However, could not the same approach which they use to dismiss the two resurrections in Revelation 20 (where they make the first resurrection to refer to a spiritual resurrection) apply to these passages? That logic could apply to all the passages if it applies to any.

62. Chilton, *Days of Vengeance*, 264.

63. Ibid., 531.

64. Max R. King, *The Spirit of Prophecy* (Warren, Ohio: Max R. King, 1971) and J. Stuart Russell, *The Parousia: A Study of the New Testament Doctrine of Our Lord's Blessed Coming* (1887; reprint, Grand Rapids: Baker Book House, 1983) are the two works that Chilton is calling heretical preterism.

65. Arnold Fruchtenbaum, *The Footsteps of the Messiah: A Study of the Sequence of Prophetic Events* (San Antonio: Ariel Press, 1982), 4.

66. Ladd, *Revelation of John*, 13.

67. Chilton, *Days of Vengeance*, 40.

68. Russell, *Parousia*, 366.

69. W. Graham Scroggie, *The Great Unveiling: An Analytical Study of Revelation* (1925; reprint, Grand Rapids: Zondervan Publishing House, 1979), 80.

70. Merrill C. Tenney, *Interpreting Revelation* (Grand Rapids: Wm. B. Eerdmans Publishing Co., 1957), 136.

71. Isbon T. Beckwith, *The Apocalypse of John* (Grand Rapids: Baker Book House, 1979), 332.

72. Tenney, *Interpreting Revelation*, 136.

73. Chilton, *Days of Vengeance*, 41.

74. Leon Morris, *Revelation* (Grand Rapids: Wm. B. Eerdmans Publishing Co., 1972), 18.

75. For a discussion of the similarities between the descriptions of this beast in Daniel and Revelation, see Stanley K. Fowler, "A Defense of the Futurist Interpretation of the Apocalypse" (Th.M. thesis, Dallas Theological Seminary, 1972), 23.

76. Ibid., 24.

77. For an example of how futurists interpret the symbols of Revelation see J. B. Smith, *A Revelation of Jesus Christ* (Scottdale, Pa.: Herald Press, 1961), 18-20.

78. Gary G. Cohen, *Understanding Revelation: A Chronology of the Apocalypse* (Collingswood: Christian Beacon Press, 1968), 23.

79. Smith, *Revelation of Jesus Christ*, 18-19.

80. Chilton, *Days of Vengeance*, 481-82.

81. David Chilton, *The Great Tribulation* (Fort Worth: Dominion Press, 1987), 17-25.

82. Robert H. Mounce, *The Book of Revelation* (Wm. B. Eerdmans Publishing Co., 1977), 41-42.

83. Tenney, *Interpreting Revelation*, 140.

84. "After" means "after the present moment; hence, the future." (Ibid., 137.) This is an exact reduplication of the second division in the Greek of 1:19, "the things which shall take place after these things," except for one word difference. Revelation 4:1 replaces "after" in 1:19 with "must." Otherwise the five Greek words are identical. Revelation 4:1 acts as a signpost indicating that in the sequence of things, the futuristic aspect of the prophecy is about to unfold, which we would see as beginning with the tribulation.

85. Ibid., 140.

86. Ibid., 142.

87. Ibid., 146.

88. Scroggie, *Great Unveiling*, 80.

Chapter 13

The Olivet Discourse as the Key to Eschatology

*T*he Olivet discourse is an important passage for the development of anyone's eschatology, but it is especially true in the case of Reconstructionists. There is a uniform agreement among conservative interpreters of the Bible that the book of Revelation is an expansion of our Lord's teaching in Matthew 24-25, Mark 13, and Luke 17 and 21. Since this correlation between the two exists, the "Little Apocalypse" should be examined to determine if the preterist approach, the futurist approach, or a blend of the two should be the proper approach to Christ's sermon and eventually the Revelation.

Reconstructionists believe the Olivet discourse was fulfilled in A.D. 70. The main reason they conclude this may be found in Matthew 24:34, "Truly I say to you, this generation will not pass away until all these things take place." Chilton declares, the "conclusion, therefore—before we even begin to investigate the passage as a whole—is that the events prophesied in Matthew 24 took place within the lifetime of the generation which was then living."[1] Even though the details of the passage do not support this view, his interpretation of "this generation" is used to draw this conclusion, and the rest of the passage is made to fit this position.

If the events described in Matthew 24, through proper exegesis, do end up supporting an A.D. 70 fulfillment, then Chilton is correct. However, if the passage as a whole refers to something eschatological, then Matthew 24:34 should properly be interpreted in light of that time period. If Chilton's view is correct, then all the parts should be in harmony with each other. Said another way, the whole should explain the parts, and the parts should support the whole.

Much of the appeal of Chilton's interpretation is that "the prophecy of the destruction of Jerusalem is a part of this prophetic utterance and is included specifically in Luke's account (Luke 21:20-24)."[2] However, he errs in combining the two accounts, the immediate future and the distant future, into one event. The account in Matthew emphasizes the future aspect of Christ's one prophecy which includes both events. "Although there is some similarity between the destruction of Jerusalem and the ultimate conflict preceding the second coming of Christ, there are many distinguishing particulars."[3]

Chilton is correct when he insists that *generation* means, "the sum total of those living at the same time. . . . [It] always refers to contemporaries."[4] However, he is wrong to assume that it refers to those alive when Christ was on earth. Instead, "this generation" is governed by its connection to verse 34. The qualifying factor is that this generation would "not pass away until all these things take place." Since the phrase "all these things" governs the timing of "this generation" (regardless of how it has been used in other contexts), one has to determine what "all these things" are and when they will be fulfilled. Then we will know whether "this generation" referred to those in Christ's day or to a future generation.

Our position is that this generation "is not the generation to whom Christ is speaking, but the generation to whom the signs will become evident."[5] This is determined by what the preceding text means:

> What we have here is the demonstrative pronoun in
> the predicate position. . . . It points definitely. "This

same group of people who live to see these things (the events of Mt. 24:15 specifically) come to pass are going to live to see the end of the prophecy fulfilled." This interpretation is perfectly logical, since the time span between Mt. 24:15 and the second coming of our Lord is only three and one half years.[6]

Now, let's look at some reasons why the preceding passage in Matthew 24 could not have been fulfilled with the destruction of Jerusalem in A.D. 70.

The Abomination of Desolation

One major reason Matthew 24 could not have been fulfilled in A.D. 70 is that "the abomination of desolation" (24:15) was not accomplished in the destruction of Jerusalem. Matthew adds a parenthetical statement to verse 15: "let the reader understand." What Scriptures can help us to understand? They are Daniel 9:27, 11:31, and 12:11. John Walvoord explains the significance of Daniel 11:31:

> In Daniel 11:31, a prophecy was written by Daniel in the sixth century B.C. about a future Syrian ruler by name of Antiochus Epiphanes who reigned over Syria 175-164 B.C., about 400 years after Daniel. History, of course, has recorded the reign of this man. In verse 31, Daniel prophesied about his activity: ". . . they shall pollute the sanctuary of strength, and shall take away the daily sacrifice, and they shall place the abomination that maketh desolate." This would be very difficult to understand if it were not for the fact that it has already been fulfilled. Anyone can go back to the history of Antiochus Epiphanes and discover what he did as recorded in the apocryphal books of 1 and 2 Maccabees. He was a great persecutor of the children of Israel and did his best to stamp out the Jewish religion and

wanted to place in its stead a worship of Greek pagan gods. . . .

One of the things he did was to stop animal sacrifices in the temple. He offered a sow, an unclean animal, on the altar in a deliberate attempt to desecrate and render it unholy for Jewish worship (cf. 1 Macc. 1:48). First Maccabees 1:54 specifically records that the abomination of desolation was set up, fulfilling Daniel 11:31. In the holy of holies Antiochus set up a statue of a Greek god. . . . In keeping with the prophecy the daily sacrifices were stopped, the sanctuary was polluted, desolated and made an abomination.[7]

This passage sets the pattern and details what the abomination of desolation is. This is further explained by 2 Thessalonians 2:4 and Revelation 13:14-15 in the New Testament. The ruler sets up himself as God in the temple by placing his image in the holy of holies. This will occur three and a half years before the second coming of Christ.

The Daniel 9:27 passage notes that this abomination is to take place in the middle of the seven-year period leading up to the second coming of Christ. The passage says, "in the middle of the week he will put a stop to sacrifice and grain offering; and on the wing of abominations will come one who makes desolate." "In other words, the future prince will do at that time exactly what Antiochus did in the second century B.C."[8]

The final Daniel passage, 12:11, gives "the precise chronology."[9] The text says, "And from the time that the regular sacrifice is abolished, and the abomination of desolation is set up, there will be 1,290 days."

In summary, the abomination of desolation, which the reader is to understand, includes the following elements:

1.   It happens in the Jewish Temple in Jerusalem (Daniel 11:31; 2 Thessalonians 2:4);

2.   It involves a person setting up a statue in place of the regular sacrifice in the holy of holies (Daniel 11:31; 12:11; Revelation 13:14-15);

3.   This results in the cessation of the regular sacrifice (Daniel 9:27; 11:31; 12:11);

4.   There will be a time of about three and a half years between this event and the second coming of Christ (Daniel 9:27; 12:11);

5.   It involves a person setting up a statue or image of himself so that he may be worshiped in place of God (Daniel 11:31; 2 Thessalonians 2:4; Revelation 13:14-15);

6.   The image is made to come to life (Revelation 13:14);

7.   A worship system of this false god is thus inaugurated (2 Thessalonians 2:4; Revelation 13:14-15).

The abomination of desolation "was to be the armed invasion of Jerusalem," according to Chilton.[10] Rather than going to Daniel for an understanding of what Daniel and our Lord wanted the reader to understand, Chilton goes to Luke 21:20-22, with a little help from Josephus, to conclude that it "seems to be the occasion when the Edomites (Idumeans), the age-long enemies of Israel attacked Jerusalem."[11] Let's see if this interpretation measures up to the biblical explanation of the abomination of desolation.

As noted above, the Luke 21:20-24 passage does refer to the A.D. 70 destruction of Jerusalem. Therefore, when verse 20 says, "when you see Jerusalem surrounded by armies, then recognize that her desolation is at hand," it is describing in clear language the destruction of Jerusalem. This is vindicated by the language of the rest of the passage, especially verse 24, "and they will fall by the edge of the sword, and will be led captive into all the nations; and Jerusalem will be trampled under foot." In context, the desolation is the destruction of Jerusalem.

In contrast, the Matthew 24:15 passage has a context of its own which differs from the Luke account. Matthew says, "when you see the abomination of desolation which was spoken of through Daniel the prophet [not Luke], standing in the holy place . . ." Comparison of the description in Matthew and Daniel with the passage in Luke yields differences, which prove that they are two separate events.

In the A.D. 70 destruction of Jerusalem there was no image set up in the holy place, no worship of the image required, and no three-and-a-half year period of time between that event and the second coming of Christ. This is especially true since the destruction of Jerusalem occurred at the end of the siege by Rome. It was over in a matter of days. D. A. Carson notes, "by the time the Romans had actually desecrated the temple in A.D. 70, it was too late for anyone in the city to flee."[12] Finally, no image came to life and beckoned men to worship it.

Josephus tells us that Titus did not want the temple burned, but wanted it spared. However, the Roman solders so hated the Jews that they disobeyed his orders and burned the temple anyway. All Titus was able to do was to go in and look at the holy place shortly before it burned.[13] This does not even come close to the biblical picture of the image set up on the altar in the middle of Daniel's seventieth week, which results in cessation of the regular sacrifice and a rival worship system set up in its place for three and a half years.

Other dissimilarities could be cited, but the point should be clear by now: Chilton cannot make his interpretation of the abomination of desolation fit the text of Scripture. Instead, he ignores the details of the passage he is supposed to be studying and goes to other unrelated passages, importing them into the passage. The better interpretation of the abomination of desolation is that it will occur in the future, and it will be fulfilled in accordance with the descriptions laid out by Holy Writ. Neither the text nor the facts of history are able to make it fit into an A.D. 70 fulfillment.

Another major dissimilarity between Chilton and Matthew 24 is that in Matthew's account "neither the city nor the temple are destroyed, and thus the two situations stand in sharp contrast."[14] (The Luke 21 passage does record the "days of vengeance" which befell Jerusalem.) Let us look at some other details related to the fact that the future fulfillment of Matthew 24 is one in which Christ delivers the Jews rather than destroying them as in A.D. 70.

Deliverance, Not Destruction

First, as Luke shifts from the A.D. 70 destruction of Jerusalem in 21:20-24 to the second coming of Christ in 21:25-28, he says to "straighten up and lift up your heads, because your redemption is drawing near" (v. 28). This is the language of deliverance, not destruction. This language of deliverance is reflected in Zechariah 12-14. These three chapters include three important factors: (1) Jerusalem is surrounded by the nations who are seeking to destroy it (12:2-9; 14:2-7); (2) the Lord will fight for Israel and Jerusalem and defeat the nations who have come up to lay siege against the city (14:1-8); and (3) at this same time the Lord will also save Israel from her sins and she will be converted to Messiah (12:9-14).

Factor one fits very well into the language of Matthew 24—the nations have surrounded Jerusalem. It does not fit the A.D. 70 destruction of Jerusalem, since that was accomplished by one nation—Rome. Zechariah 14:2 says, "I will gather all the nations against Jerusalem to battle. . . ." It would also be difficult to see how a single nation would fit this passage even if hyperbole were used.

Factor two also fits Matthew 24, but not Chilton's view. Zechariah 14:3 says, "Then the LORD will go forth and fight against those nations, as when He fights on a day of battle." Matthew 24:22 speaks of God's intervention into the affairs at that time when it says, "unless those days had been cut short no life would have been saved; but for the sake of the elect those days shall be cut short." Luke 21:28 says to look up for the redemption that is near. This interventionist language parallels the Zechariah account, but not the A.D. 70 destruction of Jerusalem.

The third factor speaks of the conversion of Israel. This certainly did not happen in A.D. 70, since the destruction of Jerusalem at that time was due to the nation's rejection. As already cited above, the picture in the Gospels is one of conversion: they are to look up for their redemption, and the elect are to be gathered from the four winds of the earth (Matthew 24:31). Furthermore, Zechariah 14:5 describes the Lord as coming with all his holy ones. The next verse speaks of how "in that day there will be no light; the luminaries will dwindle." This is language similar to Matthew 24:29-31, which pictures the Lord coming in the clouds and the darkening of light and luminaries.

Chilton finds himself in a dilemma as he tries to handle the Zechariah passages within his system. In an effort to deal with Zechariah 12:10, which includes the phrase, "so that they will look on Me whom they have pierced," Chilton understands that it is the basis for Matthew 24:30. He says that in the Matthew passage "their mourning would not be that of repentance, but sheer agony and terror."[15] He says Matthew uses the Zechariah passage totally out of context.

The problem for him arises in his interpretation of Matthew 24:30 as having an A.D. 70 fulfillment. However, the Zechariah passage relates the mourning to the realization that Jesus has been the Messiah all along, and that it is a mourning of repentance, caused by God's pouring out upon them "the Spirit of grace and of supplication," resulting in their repentance and conversion to Jesus the Messiah. Since Matthew quotes from a passage which speaks of the future conversion of Israel in a context that, according to Chilton, is one of judgment upon Israel for rejection of Messiah, he needs to solve the contradiction. However, there is no support from the text or the context of either passage to support his view. Problems do not exist for the futurist view of Matthew 24 since this is something that will be fulfilled at the second coming.

Reconstructionists believe that Israel will be converted to Christ in the future.[16] Their problem is that Matthew cites a passage (Zechariah 12:10) which speaks of this future conversion in a context Reconstructionists say refers to the destruction of Jerusalem. Reconstructionists are correct when they say that in Matthew 23:36 Jesus is clearly telling "of an imminent judgment on Israel for rejecting the Word of God, and for the final apostasy of rejecting God's Son."[17] Futurists agree that this was fulfilled upon the Christ-rejecting generation of Jesus' day by the A.D. 70 destruction of Jerusalem. This is noted in Luke 21:20-24.

Israel's Future Conversion

Chilton is also correct when he says, "Jesus' statement in Matthew 23 sets the stage for His teaching in Matthew 24. Jesus clearly told of an imminent judgment on Israel for rejecting the Word of God."[18] However, Chilton needs to take into account all the factors which make up the disciples' three-part question recorded in Matthew 24:3—"Tell us, when will these things be, and what will be the sign of Your coming, and of the end of the age?" The neglected factor concerns the second coming of Christ in 23:39. This forms the contextual basis for the second question in 24:3. Chilton only wants the judgment aspect of Matthew 23 to form the basis for the questions of 24:3, but 23:39 clearly shows that Christ's coming was on their mind as well.

Three Questions

The three questions in Matthew 24:3 are:

- When will the temple be destroyed?
- What will be the sign of Christ's coming?
- What will be the sign of the end of the age?

The first question is answered in Luke 21:20-24, since Luke is the one who specializes in the A.D. 70 aspects. Luke records Jesus' warning about the soon-to-come destruction of Jerusalem—the days of vengeance. The second and third questions are answered in Matthew 24. What is the specific sign? The sign is the great tribulation, which will precede the end of the age and the coming of Christ. "It is an unmistakable sign. There will be no question about it for anybody who experiences its horrors. It will be a clear sign preceding the second coming of Jesus Christ."[19]

Since Reconstructionists believe the conversion of Israel is still in the future, as noted above, and Matthew 23:39 links the coming of Christ with their conversion, it would disrupt their preterist interpretation to admit that "coming" in Matthew 24 is tied to the conversion of the Jews and is yet future. It is clear that Israel was not both cursed and blessed in the A.D. 70 destruction.

Messiah told the disciples that they would not see him until the Jews say, "Blessed is He who comes in the name of the Lord!" (Matthew 23:39). This is a Messianic greeting and did not happen in A.D. 70. Just as Zechariah 12:10 records, Israel will one day in the future confess her national sin and call for Messiah to return immediately before his second coming.

Therefore, Matthew 23:39 informs the context of Matthew 24:1-3 and tells us that "coming" in 24:3 is a question about what we call the second coming. These points show that the preterist interpretation does not handle the text properly, while the futurist view does.

Contrasts between the A.D. 70 Destruction of Jerusalem and Matthew 24

Does the destruction of Jerusalem really fulfill the statement of Matthew 24:21, "for then there will be a great tribulation, such as has not occurred since the beginning of the world until now, nor ever shall"? Verse 22 says, "unless those days had been cut short; no life would have been saved." The days of the siege of Jerusalem were not cut short; rather the Romans persisted until they accomplished their goal of capturing the city. There was no cutting short of anything. On the other hand,

Messiah's intervention at the second coming to save Israel makes perfect sense of the text. He comes back to save his people.

If there was a siege around the city which prohibited people from exiting the city, as there was in the A.D. 70 event, then what meaning would 24:26 have when it warns about chasing after false Messiahs? "If therefore they say to you, 'Behold, He is in the wilderness,' do not go forth." How could someone go to the wilderness with the Roman army surrounding them, without being captured or killed? But this is not a problem if Matthew 24 is describing a future event.

The language of the coming of Christ is sudden and interventionist. Matthew 24:27 says, "just as the lightning comes from the east, and flashes even to the west, so shall the coming of the Son of Man be." It does not matter how swift an army is, it could never come with that kind of speed. The Roman destruction of Jerusalem in the past was a slow process of years. The coming of Christ in the future occurs in a moment. The language of Matthew 24 fits better with the future coming of Christ.

Verses 24-27 note that Christ's coming will be of such magnitude and manifested so clearly as to be self-evident. A believer is not to listen to claims that Christ has come back, and they missed it. "His appearance will be of such a supernatural character that no one will doubt Who it is that has come."[20] Many will not like the reality of the event, but all will know that it is Christ who is returning. Chilton's notion does not fit with this depiction of Christ's coming as something the whole world will see in a moment of time and something that is obvious to all. However, the language of this passage comports easily with the futuristic understanding of the text.

The language of verses 27-31 speaks of a worldwide picture rather than the limited location of Jerusalem. Along the same line, verse 9 says that "you will be hated by all nations on account of My name." How does this relate to the localized destruction of Jerusalem in A.D. 70? Since the nations of the world will be involved in surrounding Jerusalem in a future siege, this worldwide scope fits the future second-coming perspective best. So then, the futurist interpretation of Matthew 24 makes better sense than does a Reconstructionist view that the passage concerns the destruction of Jerusalem in A.D. 70.

Internal Inconsistency of a Preterist View of Matthew 24

Another problem with the Reconstructionists' preterist interpretation is its internal inconsistency. Reconstructionists interpret some words and phrases symbolically, while interpreting like phrases literally. Certainly we all may be guilty of inconsistency at times, but Reconstructionists lack a hermeneutic that helps them decide between symbolic and nonsymbolic terms. Their view would be more convincing, at least consistent with its principles, if it were even in handling the text and followed some consistent system of interpretation.

Chilton interprets the famines and earthquakes of Matthew 24:7 as actual, literal events which took place at a time around A.D. 70. He cites the Jewish historian Josephus, who recorded the destruction of Jerusalem, to document that these things happened around that time.[21] By doing this he is taking these events to have happened literally and not symbolically. However, when he comes to other descriptive phrases which are no different in how they are used in the text, he decrees them to be symbolic. Were these phrases taken literally they would disallow Chilton's viewpoint.

According to Chilton it must be stressed concerning the physical phenomena of Matthew 24:29—the sun darkening, the moon not giving light, and the stars falling—"that none of these events literally took place. God did not intend anyone to place a literalist construction on these statements."[22] He does say, "Poetically, however, all these things did happen: as far as these wicked nations were concerned, 'the lights went out.' This is simply figurative language. . . . "[23] How does the quality of the language in 24:29 differ from that of 24:7? It does not differ. Chilton, therefore, should interpret the famines and earthquakes poetically and figuratively as the nations starving from the lack of God's Word or the earthquakes as the nations being shaken by God's Word. But he should not interpret them as literal events if he is going to take similar language differently.

To take similar phrases in different ways, there must be specific reasons in the context which require such a departure from the literal meaning. Chilton does not cite reasons for taking one literally and the other poetically. This kind of approach suggests to us that Reconstructionists read passages in a normal manner until it does not fit their theology. They then declare it to be figurative or poetical and plug in their interpretation, without giving due exegetical justification from the text for their departures. This interpretative schizophrenia is a tip-off that they are not properly handling the Word of God. If they were, there should be greater continuity in their hermeneutic and their application of it.

Parabolic Concurrence with a Futurist Interpretation of the Olivet Discourse

All of the parables following the discourse of 24:1-31 focus on the coming of Christ, not on the destruction of Jerusalem. Take for example the parable in verses 40-41: "Then there shall be two men in the field; one will be taken, and one will be left. Two women will be grinding at the mill; one will be taken, and the other will be left." This does not come close to fitting the picture of the siege and destruction of Jerusalem where everyone was either killed or taken into slavery. No one was left. This is the language of a surgical removal in a future event.

Verse 36, which appears in the "days of Noah" historical illustration, says, "but of that day and hour no one knows. . . ." If, as Reconstructionist James Jordan says, verses 36 and following refer to the second coming,[24] then "that day" would have to refer to verses 1-31 of the preceding context. Therefore, since it refers to the second coming in verse 36, the preceding verses could not refer to the past destruction of Jerusalem.

Jordan is advocating greater discontinuity in the text than the grammar allows.

How can Jordan, after taking the references to "coming" in verses 1-35 as referring to Christ's coming in judgment in A.D. 70, turn around and say that starting at verse 36 through the end of the chapter, it refers to the second coming? Either he is wrong about the first 35 verses, and they do refer to the second coming, or he should take verse 36 and following as a reference to the A.D. 70 destruction. If he were to take the whole of the Olivet discourse as already fulfilled, as Chilton does the whole book of Revelation, then he is left with the problem of where does the Bible actually teach the second coming? What he should do is become consistent and take the whole passage to refer to a future event—the second coming of Christ. The Reconstructionist, preterist interpretation of the Olivet discourse only needs one example of a future event for its interpretation to fail. Many futurist events have been cited. With this kind of twisting of Scripture, no wonder fellow Reconstructionist and postmillennialist Greg Bahnsen described Chilton's approach as "error laid upon error to reach this height of imagination."[25]

Evangelization of the Whole World

Even though Chilton believes that Matthew 24:14—"And this gospel of the kingdom shall be preached in the whole world for a witness to all the nations, and then the end shall come"—was fulfilled before A.D. 70, we believe it was not. Chilton asks, "Could the Gospel have been preached to the whole world within a generation of these words (24:14)? . . . Not only could it have happened, but it actually did."[26]

If we look closely at Matthew 24:14 we notice that there are two phrases which modify "shall be preached"—"in the whole world" and "to all the nations." In the first phrase, the adjective "whole" indicates that it is the world in its totality that is in view. So are the Reconstructionists saying that the gospel was preached before A.D. 70 in the Western hemisphere? Were the American Indians evangelized? What about Central and South America? However, if this is a reference to the future second coming, which we believe it is, then literally the whole world will be evangelized and then the end shall come.

The second phrase, "to all the nations," is especially interesting in light of what Reconstructionists have said about this phrase. Gary North under a heading called "International Theocracy" says:

> I am calling for international theocracy . . . for this international theocracy is exactly what the Bible requires. . . . Every nation is as much under God's sovereign rule as every individual is. The goal of the gospel is to subdue every soul, every institution, and every nation under God. . . . Just as every redeemed individual is told by God to conform himself to the image of Christ, as perfect humanity . . . so is every human institution, including every nation . . . especially since Christ commanded the disciples to *disciple* the nations—not simply hearts, minds, souls, families, and local churches, but *nations* (Matthew 28:18-20) . . . to exercise covenantal control of every civil government.[27]

North believes that the phrase "all the nations" in the Great Commission refers to literally every nation on the globe. If this is true for Matthew 24:14 as well, all the nations could not have been preached to before the A.D. 70 destruction of Jerusalem. It is convenient, but not hermeneutically sound, for the Reconstructionists to interpret this phrase in two different ways. If their logic is followed, it would have required the total fulfillment of the Great Commission in A.D. 70. However, if this passage refers to a future fulfillment just before the second coming, then there is no such problem. Once again, the specifics of the text do not fit into a Reconstructionist interpretation of the Olivet discourse, but they do within a futurist perspective.

Stanley Toussaint makes an observation which helps in understanding the passage:

The key to understanding the discourse is found in this first sentence. The disciples thought that the destruction of Jerusalem with its great temple would usher in the end of the age. The Lord separates the two ideas and warns the disciples against being deceived by the destruction of Jerusalem and other such catastrophes. The razing of the temple and the presence of wars and rumors of wars do not necessarily signify the nearness of the end. Therefore the disciples are warned against the things which could lead them astray.[28]

Reconstructionists would do well to heed the true warning of Messiah. They should not make the same mistake in their understanding that the disciples apparently were making, before being instructed by Christ in the Olivet discourse. There is a separation between the destruction of the temple and the end of the age and the coming of Messiah. It is error to combine them.

Future, Not Past

Chilton started his discussion of the Olivet discourse by saying that the "conclusion, therefore—before we even begin to investigate the passage as a whole—is that the events prophesied in Matthew 24 took place within the lifetime of the generation which was then living."[29] We noted that the phrase "this generation" is dependent upon the meaning of the preceding context to establish its chronological significance. We have then shown many reasons why Matthew 24 could not have been fulfilled in A.D. 70, as Chilton declares, but rather awaits a future fulfillment shortly before Christ's second coming.

Since Chilton came to the conclusion, before he studied the passage as a whole, that the Matthew 24 events took place within the lifetime of the generation which was then living, it is easy to see why he has gone astray in explaining this important section of Scripture. He imposed his wrong conclusion of 24:34 upon the details of the rest of the discourse. In contrast, the proper approach should have included studying the passage as a whole and then drawing overall conclusions. If this is done, it will lead to a futurist interpretation.

If the Olivet discourse is future, then so is the book of Revelation, since all agree that they are speaking of the same events. And so is the great tribulation, the antichrist, the apostasy, and other "end time" events, which Reconstructionists all put in the past. If these are all in the future, then the whole Reconstructionist agenda goes up in smoke, since prophecy is not about the church conquering evil in this age, but about Jesus Christ returning, judging the world, and setting up his glorious kingdom.

If Reconstructionist eschatology is wrong, then their whole movement is misdirected about the present and their agenda should be redirected. Their view of prophecy determines the direction a believer should be going in the present age. This is evident from a recent meeting of some one hundred leaders of the Reconstruction movement. These leaders produced a list of ten points of belief "which all saw as the fundamentals of the Christian Reconstruction Movement."[30] Point seven insisted on a postmillennial view of the kingdom of God and this present age. They affirmed the belief that one's view of the future is important to what we do in the present, and they are right. Unfortunately, since the predictions of the Olivet discourse were not fulfilled in the past but are yet to happen, the Reconstructionist agenda for the present is, for the most part, wrong.

Chapter 13, Notes
_____

1. David Chilton, *The Great Tribulation* (Fort Worth: Dominion Press, 1987), 4.

2. John F. Walvoord, "Christ's Olivet Discourse on the Time of the End: Signs of the End of the Age," *Bibliotheca Sacra* 128 (October-December 1971):316.

3. Ibid., 316-17.

4. Chilton, *Great Tribulation*, 3.

5. John F. Walvoord, "Christ's Olivet Discourse on the Time of the End: How Near Is the Lord's Return?" *Bibliotheca Sacra* 129 (January-March 1972):24.

6. Randolph O. Yeager, *The Renaissance New Testament* (Bowling Green: Renaissance Press, 1978), 3:322.

7. Walvoord, "End of the Age," 318-19.

8. Ibid., 319.

9. Ibid.

10. Chilton, *Great Tribulation*, 12.

11. Ibid.

12. D. A. Carson, "Matthew," in *The Expositor's Bible Commentary*, ed. Frank E. Gaebelein (Grand Rapids: Zondervan Publishing House, 1984), 8:500.

13. See David Chilton, *Paradise Restored: A Biblical Theology of Dominion* (Fort Worth: Dominion Press, 1985), 274-76.

14. Walvoord, "End of the Age," 317.

15. David Chilton, *The Days of Vengeance: An Exposition of the Book of Revelation* (Fort Worth: Dominion Press, 1987), 66.

16. Chilton, *Paradise Restored*, 126-31.

17. Chilton, *Great Tribulation*, 4.

18. Ibid.

19. Walvoord, "End of the Age," 322.

20. Stanley D. Toussaint, *Behold the King: A Study of Matthew* (Portland, Ore.: Multnomah Press, 1980), 278.

21. Chilton, *Paradise Restored*, earthquakes, 92; famines, 263- 64.

22. Chilton, *Great Tribulation*, 20.

23. Ibid.

24. James Jordan, "Exposition of Matthew 24:31-51," cassette recording #JJ52, side two, from Geneva Media, Tyler, Tex., 1983.

25. Greg L. Bahnsen, "Another Look at Chilton's *Days of Vengeance*," cited by the editor in *The Counsel of Chalcedon*, July 1988, 3.

26. Chilton, *Great Tribulation*, 10.

27. Gary North, *Healer of the Nations: Biblical Principles for International Relations* (Fort Worth: Dominion Press, 1987), 56-57.

28. Toussaint, *Behold the King*, 270.

29. Chilton, *Great Tribulation*, 4.

30. Joseph C. Morecraft, III, "The Christian Reconstruction Dialogue," *The Counsel of Chalcedon*, December 1987, 7.

Chapter 14

Interpreting Prophecy

"*F*or a long time now I have been praying for Greg Bahnsen to write a critique of 'the Tyler hermeneutic.' I agree with Doug Wilson that that hermeneutic 'will prove destructive in any serious attempt to restore a biblical foundation for our society.' In his insightful, concise and irrefutable way, Greg Bahnsen puts the blowtorch to 'the Tyler hermeneutic,' for which I praise Almighty God."[1]

> Joseph C. Morecraft, III
> Reconstructionist pastor

Hermeneutics is "the science of interpretation."[2] It has also been called both a science and an art.[3] Ramm adds that the primary purpose of hermeneutics is "to ascertain what God has said in Sacred Scripture; to determine the meaning of the Word of God."[4] He correctly warns that "every one of those places where our interpretation is at fault, we have made substitution of the voice of man for the voice of God."[5] All sincere Christians certainly want the voice of God instead of the voice of man when we attempt to understand the Scriptures.

An often-asked question by believers is, "How is it that different Bible students studying the same text can come up with often opposite interpretations of a passage?" Both are genuine believers, equally well trained in biblical languages, church history, and theology and equally sincere in their devotion to Christ. The answer lies not in the text but with how we interpret Scripture. This is why the question of hermeneutics is key to understanding areas of difference in biblical interpretation.

The importance of hermeneutics has been observed in the debate surrounding the recent rise of postmillennialism within the Christian Reconstruction movement. Since how one goes about interpreting the Bible is a product, at least to some extent, of one's theology, then we need to look at the hermeneutics of Reconstructionists.

> The fatal weakness of the new postmillennialism is that its Scriptural support is derived precisely from those very passages which also form the backbone of the other views of what can be expected to happen before Christ returns.
>
> When opposing views use precisely the same text for support against each other, it isn't the text which has produced the contrast; it probably was something else— "newspaper exegesis," if you will, or theological presuppositions.[6]

When it comes to interpreting prophecy those in the postmillennial Reconstructionist camp take a different approach than do premillennialists. The hermeneutical approach of neo-postmillennialism is rightly said to be a blend of the literal and nonliteral approaches.[7] The differences revolve around how to interpret symbolic language. Chilton describes symbols "as a set of patterns and associations. By this I mean that Biblical symbolism is not a code. It is, instead, a way of seeing, a perspective."[8] He goes on to illustrate this principle by noting how the word *water* is used in the Bible:

When the Bible tells us a story about water, it is not "really" telling us about something else; it is telling us about water. But at the same time we are expected to see the water, and to think of the Biblical associations with regard to water. The system of interpretation offered here is neither "literalistic" nor "symbolic"; it takes the "water" seriously and literally, but it also takes seriously what God's Word associates with water throughout the history of Biblical revelation. . . . Water is supposed to be something like a "buzzword," a term that calls up many associations and connotations.[9]

Of course, the fact that water "calls up many associations and connotations" is the problem. How do you know if your associations and connotations are warranted by the particular text?

Chilton cites some basic rules for the study of biblical imagery:

1. Read visually; try to picture what the Bible is saying.
2. Read Biblically; don't speculate or become abstract, but pay close attention to what the Bible itself says about its own symbols.
3. Read the Story; try to think about how each element in the Bible contributes to its message of salvation as a whole.

In addition to these rules, Chilton attempts to give objective guidelines to help in determining the proper handling of a symbol:

First, all creation is primarily symbolic. . . . The central value of anything is that it is a symbol of God. All other values and relationships are secondary. . . .

Second, symbolism is analogical, not realistic. . . . The symbolism is analogical, not metaphysical.[10]

The problem with the above two standards is that they are still subjective at heart. Also, Chilton uses this to deny the literalness of something which forms the basis or foundation for a symbol. All symbols are based upon real, actual, literal things. The movement is from literal to symbolic. Because Chilton places the primacy on symbolism over literalness, he is in danger of abstracting the actual out of existence and making it into pure idealism.

An example of this can be seen from a Bible class Tommy had in college. The theologically liberal instructor argued that Jonah was not really swallowed by a great fish (it was just an exaggerated fish story), since Jonah's prayer in chapter 2 is in poetic structure and full of symbolism. He would say, "it doesn't matter whether or not this really happened, what matters is the meaning."

But it does matter if something literally happened or not. There is no meaning if there are no real events in history. This is why one who interprets the Bible should take seriously the actual event and the meaning as well. Both are important and reinforce each other.

Two more rules Chilton proposes to help objectify his hermeneutic are:

> First, [the interpreter] must be faithful to the system of doctrine taught in the Bible. . . . Second, the interpreter must keep in mind that the symbols in the Bible are not isolated; rather, they are part of a system of symbolism given in the Bible, an architecture of images in which all the parts fit together. If we honestly and carefully read the Bible theologically and with respect to the Bible's own literary structure, we will not go very far astray.[11]

Again, a significant problem with these two rules is that they are both subjective. The supposed check on this hermeneutic is comparable to telling a child to quit eating ice cream when he thinks he's had enough. Children never think they have had enough, unless they have been trained. They need rules or "laws" that say, "You have had enough when you finish one scoop." Proper hermeneutics requires that interpretation be checked by exegesis (the data from the text). This is not an objection to symbolism, but rather a demand to hear neopost-millennialists verify that their symbolism is biblical, that is, put together and used in the same way that the Bible uses it.

The problem with many Reconstructionists is that they are long on interpretation and theological presuppositions, and short on specific exegesis and "crux" passages to support their theology. Reconstructionists are good at telling you what their theology is and even at exhorting you to put it into practice, but they cannot give specific verses to back it up.

Interpretive Maximalism

Another example of the subjective foundation upon which many Reconstructionists have built their hermeneutics is found in James Jordan's "Interpretive Maximalism." Jordan explains,

> Some events are clearly and pointedly symbolic and typological, while some are only vaguely and generally so.

> We have to explain this in order to distance ourselves from the "interpretive minimalism" that has come to characterize evangelical commentaries on Scripture in recent years. We do not need some specific New Testament verse to "prove" that a given Old Testament story has symbolic dimensions. Rather, such symbolic dimensions are presupposed in the very fact that man is the image of God. Thus, we ought not to be afraid to hazard a guess at the wider prophetic meanings of Scripture narratives, as we consider how they image the ways of God.

> Such a "maximalist" approach as this puts us more in line with the kind of interpretation used by the Church Fathers. It seems dangerous, because it is

not readily evident what kinds of checks and balances are to be employed in such an approach.[12]

This kind of "interpretive maximalism" is also being discussed within evangelical circles in general. One evangelical has asked,

> Should the meaning of Scripture be restricted to the results of a rigid grammatical-historical exegesis? Or is there a deeper meaning that goes beyond the results of grammatical-historical analysis? If a deeper meaning exists, how does one ascertain what precisely it is?[13]

Jordan suggests "that the check and balance on interpretation is the whole rest of Scripture and of theology."[14] The first standard is the proper check and balance since Paul instructed the Corinthians not to exceed "what is written, in order that no one of you might become arrogant in behalf of one against the other" (1 Corinthians 4:6). However, the addition of theology as a check produces division, not only within evangelicalism, but also within Reconstructionism. Jordan should learn that the full meaning of Scripture comes from a full study of the whole of Scripture.[15]

By implying that Scripture is not enough—we need guesses that flow from our theology—Jordan is calling into question the sufficiency of Scripture alone as our guide. Fellow Reconstructionist Doug Wilson gives this warning about Jordan's hermeneutic:

> If our theology is allowed, in any measure, to regulate how the Scriptures are handled, then humanistic dross is inserted into the pure Word of God. Do we want some sort of Protestant magisterium? God forbid! Theology must never regulate Scripture. Scripture must regulate theology.[16]

This is our charge: Because subjective factors, such as theological bias, have been introduced into the interpretative process, Reconstructionists are able to manipulate the text to get it to mean what their theology desires. Jordan and Chilton, the two major users of "interpretive maximalism," still have not established a biblical foundation for their attempts at exegesis. The reader should now have a better understanding as to why Chilton and others so often have to spend so much of their time "developing" their theology from other scriptural "themes" so that they can then explain the passage at hand. In reality, it is by these excursions that they are stating their theology so that they may use this "imaginative theology" to twist the texts of Scripture. If the Bible teaches something, it should be able to be seen from specific texts, as well as from the theology of the whole of Scripture.

Reconstructionist Greg Bahnsen considers "interpretive maximalism" to be the first of three fatal flaws in Chilton's commentary on Revelation, *Days of Vengeance*. Bahnsen's evaluations include:

> David's commitment to the imaginative guesswork of interpretive maximalism renders his commentary on Revelation unsound. . . . Error is laid upon error to reach this height of imagination. . . . These kinds of flaws and misreadings make the commentary unreliable for the reader. . . . We must all realize that, while creativity is a virtue in an original author, it is a crime in an interpreter.[17]

A SYSTEM OF EXEGESIS

John F. Walvoord's criticism of classical postmillennialism's system of exegesis applies equally to this new brand of postmillennialism expressed by Chilton and other Reconstructionists:

> Postmillennialism is based on the figurative interpretation of prophecy which permits wide freedom in finding the meaning of difficult passages. . . . As

a system of theology based upon a subjective spiritualizing of Scripture, postmillennialism lacks the central principles necessary for coherence. Each postmillennialist is left more or less to his own ingenuity in solving the problem of what to do with prophecies of a millennium on earth. . . . The result is that postmillennialism has no unified front to protect itself from the inroads of other interpretations. At best postmillennialism is superimposed upon systems of theology which were developed without its aid.[18]

Figurative Figures

The basic hermeneutical issue that divides the preterist interpretation from the futurist is just how literally a person should take the symbols and how he should go about deciding their meaning. The futurist usually takes symbols more literally than does the preterist. How do we determine which approach is the right one?

Chilton says, "Scripture interprets Scripture."[19] This means that you use as a control mechanism examples of predictive, symbolic language that have already been fulfilled and recorded in the Bible. Reconstructionist Greg Bahnsen notes that in order to shed light on the controversy, just talking about hermeneutic theory will not do: "the opponents must get down to hand-to-hand exegetical combat on particular passages and phrases."[20] This establishes the first criterion from which we can state principles of interpretation. Let's get down to exegetical combat by looking at some examples.

If the preterist view of the Olivet discourse (Matthew 24:3-26:2) is advocated, Matthew 24:29-31 must be explained:

But immediately after the tribulation of those days the sun will be darkened, and the moon will not give its light, and the stars will fall from the sky, and the powers of the heavens will be shaken, and then the sign of the Son of Man will appear in the sky, and then all the tribes of the earth will mourn, and they will see the Son of Man coming on the clouds of the sky with power and great glory. And He will send forth His angels with a great trumpet and they will gather together His elect from the four winds, from one end of the sky to the other.

How does Chilton explain this language which futurists say refers to physical phenomena surrounding the second coming of Christ? Let's look at his handling of "the clouds of heaven" in verse 30:

"and then all the tribes of the land will mourn, and they will see the Son of Man coming on the clouds of heaven with power and great glory." The word *tribes* here has primary reference to the tribes of the land of Israel; and the "mourning" is probably meant in two senses. First, they would mourn in sorrow over their suffering and the loss of their land; second, they would ultimately mourn in repentance for their sins, when they are converted from their apostasy (see Romans 11).[21]

Chilton may be correct to say that *tribes* refers to Israel. If that is the case, then he would want to be consistent with the context and see the next verse as also referring to Israel. Instead he sees verse 31 as a reference to evangelism by people in this present age:

The word *angels* simply means *messengers* (cf. James 2:25), regardless of whether their origin is heavenly or earthly; it is the context which determines these are heavenly creatures being spoken of. The word often means preachers of the Gospel (see Matthew 11:10; Luke 7:24; 9:52; Revelation 1-3). In context, there is every reason to assume that Jesus is speaking of the worldwide evangelism and conversion of the nations which will follow upon the destruction of Israel.[22]

While it is true that James 2:25 uses the Greek word *angelos* to refer to human messengers, such is not the case in Matthew. Chilton should follow his own advice and allow the context to determine the meaning of *angelos*. But he does not list specific factors which argue for taking *angelos* in the way he understands.

Chilton simply states his view without validation. In not one of the four passages he cites is anyone obviously preaching the gospel. Matthew 11:10 quotes Malachi 3:1 concerning the ministry of John the Baptist. But John did not preach the gospel. Luke 7:24 is a reference to the messengers sent from the imprisoned John the Baptist to ask Christ if he was the Messiah. They ask Christ a question; they don't proclaim the gospel. Luke 9:52 tells of Christ sending messengers ahead of him so that they could make arrangements for Christ to be received in a Samaritan village. A far cry from preaching the gospel.

The final reference to the seven angels of Revelation 1-3 is the most absurd of them all, since there is no conclusive proof that the *angelos* are men instead of angels. Perhaps they are related to this inspection of the churches by the Head in a way similar to the angelic witness to the agreement of the Mosaic law between God and Israel (Deuteronomy 30:19, cf. Acts 7:53; Galatians 3:19). But not one of those passages refers to the preaching of the gospel.

Chilton compounds his error by stating that *angelos* is *often* used to mean "preacher of the Gospel." But of the nearly two hundred times that *angelos* is used in the New Testament, only six times does it refer to an earthly messenger. Certainly the basic meaning of the word, messenger, is central regardless of whether it refers to an angelic messenger or a human messenger. There is no way that Chilton's use of the adjective "often" can even remotely be supported. In fact, it is never used of the preaching of the gospel. Chilton's tactic of simply stating his viewpoint as a reason for a word or passage to be taken in a certain way is common throughout his writings.

Perhaps this is justified in his eyes as part of "interpretive maximalism." It is necessary to explain one's understanding of a passage when trying to show the feasibility of an interpretation. But it is misuse if it is substituted as a textual reason in support of an interpretation.

Why should *angelos* be understood to mean an angelic messenger and not a human messenger? First, since the word refers to an angelic messenger about 97 percent of the time, the burden of proof is on someone who wishes to take it the other way. This proof must flow from clear evidence taken from both the immediate and surrounding context.

Second, verse 31 is a reference to Deuteronomy 30:4, as Chilton points out.[23] However, he takes it to refer to the church and not Israel. But Moses is speaking to Israel, not the church, for this verse is an historic prediction of God regathering Israel in a future time. Matthew 24:31 is a corroborating prediction of the fulfillment of the Deuteronomy passage. This fits well with premillennialism, but not with the postmillennialism of Chilton.

Next Chilton tries to deal with the allusion to mourning from Zechariah 12:10.

> and the "mourning" is probably meant in two senses. First, they would mourn in sorrow over their suffering and the loss of their land; second, they would ultimately mourn in repentance for their sins, when they are converted from their apostasy (see Romans 11).[24]

Once again, we are amazed at the explanation Chilton gives. Not because we do not know biblical symbolism. Quite the contrary, as we look at Zechariah 12:10 we are at a loss to know where Chilton gets the first sense of mourning mentioned above. Look at what the text of Zechariah 12:9-10 says:

> [9]"And it will come about in that day that I will set about to destroy all the nations that come against Jerusalem.

> [10]And I will pour out on the house of David and on
> the inhabitants of Jerusalem, the Spirit of grace and
> of supplication, so that they will look on Me whom
> they have pierced; and they will mourn for Him, as
> one mourns for an only son, and they will weep
> bitterly over Him, like the bitter weeping over a
> first-born."

There is nothing in the context concerning anything relating to their weeping because they have lost their land. Neither is there a reference to this in Matthew 24. Rather, they are weeping because they looked upon the One they pierced. They looked upon Jesus during the end of the future tribulation period and realized that he is the Messiah their forefathers crucified. The reason for this is that their unbelief has been removed by God: "I will pour out on the house of David and on the inhabitants of Jerusalem, the Spirit of grace and supplication, so that . . . " God's grace leads Israel to repent of their rejection of Messiah.

Chilton categorically disagrees with this: "Israel had gone beyond the point of no return; their mourning would not be that of repentance, but sheer agony and terror."[25] But God's efficacious "Spirit of grace" does not produce a futile repentance of only agony and terror. Zechariah 13:1 says, "In that day [the day of mourning] a fountain will be opened for the house of David and for the inhabitants of Jerusalem, for sin and for impurity." Could the Bible be any clearer that this is a mourning of repentance? Further, Zechariah 12:9 describes God destroying the nations that have come up against Jerusalem. This did not happen in A.D. 70. In A.D. 70 it was the other way around—the nations destroyed Jerusalem.

Chilton's second reason—"they would ultimately mourn in repentance for their sins, when they are converted from their apostasy (see Romans 11)"—is correct as demonstrated above. However, if his first reason is true, and he believes it is, then his second reason cannot also be correct, since the two conflict with each other. If the first reason is related to A.D. 70, as in

Chilton's scheme, then the second reason is still future. There-fore the passage has to refer to either reason one or reason two if Chilton's preterist view is correct, but not to both.

This is not a problem for the futurist understanding of the Matthew 24 passage or the Zechariah 12 passage, since it would reject reason one and see both passages referring to the same future event. The premillennial futurist view makes the best sense of the text.

Chilton continues with his explanation of the passage:

> But how is it that they would see Christ coming on the clouds? This is an important symbol of God's power and glory, used throughout the Bible. For example, think of the "pillar of fire and cloud" through which God saved the Israelites and de-stroyed their enemies in the deliverance from Egypt (see Exodus 13:21-22; 14:19-31; 19:16-19). In fact, all through the Old Testament God was coming "on clouds," in salvation of His people and destruction of His enemies: "He makes the clouds His chariot; He walks upon the wings of the wind" (Psalms 104:3). When Isaiah prophesied of God's judgment on Egypt, he wrote: "Behold, the Lord is riding on a swift cloud, and is about to come to Egypt; the idols of Egypt will tremble at His presence" (Isaiah 19:1). The prophet Nahum spoke similarly of God's destruction of Nineveh: "In whirlwind and storm is His way, and clouds are the dust beneath His feet" (Nahum 1:3). God's "coming on the clouds of heaven" is an almost commonplace Scriptural sym-bol for His presence, judgment, and salvation.[26]

We do not disagree with Chilton's contention that "God's 'coming on the clouds of heaven' is an almost commonplace Scriptural symbol for His presence, judgment, and salvation." The meaning of the symbol is not the point of difference. The main point of difference is whether it happens in a physical, visible, or literal way, and when it happens. According to Chilton:

> The destruction of Jerusalem was the sign that the Son of Man, the Second Adam, was in heaven, ruling over the world and disposing it for His own purposes. At His ascension, He had come on the clouds of heaven to receive the Kingdom from His Father; the destruction of Jerusalem was the revelation of this fact. In Matthew 24, therefore, Jesus was not prophesying that He would literally come on the clouds in A.D. 70 (although it was figuratively true). His literal "coming on the clouds," in fulfillment of Daniel 7, took place in A.D. 30, at the beginning of the "terminal generation." But in A.D. 70 the tribes of Israel would see the destruction of the nation as the result of His having ascended to the throne of heaven, to receive His Kingdom.[27]

Chilton's theology tells him that if it was a literal fulfillment, then it could not have happened in A.D. 70. A literal fulfillment requires a future event. Chilton's first series of references are to the pillar of fire and cloud in Exodus. In 13:21-22 the Lord was literally leading Israel with a cloud by day and a pillar of fire by night. The pillar/cloud was physically there, not merely representative of something that was going on in heaven that the people could not see. It stood for God's presence and guidance. Chilton's view does not allow this kind of direct correspondence between the physical phenomena and the people's observation of it. There would only be a secondary correspondence: the destruction of Jerusalem was the visible witness that Christ was ruling in heaven.

Exodus 14:19-31 is further support for a literal understanding of *clouds* in Matthew 24. This passage speaks of the pillar/cloud blocking the Egyptians from getting at Israel and its role in defeating Egypt. The glory cloud was not just symbolic of some other means God used to defeat the Egyptians.

Rather, there was a physical display coming from the glory cloud itself, resulting in the defeat of Egypt. This use corresponds with the premillennial understanding in Matthew 24, but not of Chilton's view. Again, the thunder and lightning flashes of Exodus 19:16-19 are literal phenomena, not just symbols of God's power. Dispensationalist Robert Dean observes:

> If Chilton's highly symbolic interpretation is followed through consistently in the verses he cites, one major effect is that the plagues of Egypt, which are clearly delineated as physical, become sociopolitical descriptions.[28]

Reconstructionist James Jordan agrees that it is wrong to go for an either/or relationship on figurative language. This is our position: "in the economy of Biblical interpretation, we ought to avoid pitting the literal or physical meaning of a text against its symbolic or typological dimensions."[29] He made this statement in reference to interpreting Genesis, which means that the creation is both physical or actual, as well as symbolic. The Matthew 24 symbols are literal as well.

What Chilton has done is to take away the literal dimension of language in these instances, leaving no objective control on the meaning. Once that control is removed in the name of biblical symbolism, he can give it any meaning he desires.

Chilton's position is based upon inference. If you assume that the Bible teaches certain things, then texts can be interpreted in a way that does not negate the postmillennial view. This is why Chilton cannot develop his theology from within specific texts but must go to outside passages, wrongly developing themes from other texts that he then plugs into the desired text. There should not be a conflict between one's theology and the text, resulting in a fancy reworking of the text to fit the proposed theology. A view should be able to be developed within a passage as well as from the totality of Scripture.

In a biblical approach, you start with specifics and move to generalities. This can be seen by what Van Til has said concerning the way God has revealed himself to man. We start with a specific God (not some abstract idea about god) who has revealed himself in specifics from which we draw theology. Contrary to this, the Greeks started with a general idea and tried to cram the specifics into it—idealism. It is amazing that Reconstructionists, when pushed on their eschatology, always resort to top-down or theological arguments. If their position was what the Bible really taught, you should be able to argue both ways, from theology or exegesis. If a theological concept is taught in the Bible, it should be able to be found in specific biblical passages.

The proper interpretation of "the Son of Man coming on the clouds of the sky with power and great glory" (Matthew 24:30) requires language that is not at all different from that used in the Exodus passages. In the exodus the Son of Man was present in the glory cloud in a literal, physical way. So he will be again.

Matthew 24:29 says "the sun will be darkened." Chilton says in reference to the darkening of the sun "that none of these events literally took place . . . as far as these wicked nations were concerned, the lights went out. This is simply figurative language."[30] The question must be raised: Did the sun literally not shine over the land of Egypt and at the same time shine in the land of Goshen during the ninth plague (Exodus 10:21-29)? Of course. Once again, the physical event was the sign of God's sovereignty. How does Chilton propose that the wicked nations understand that "the lights went out"?

Similarly, during the crucifixion of our Lord, did darkness really fall over the whole land of Israel about the sixth hour until the ninth hour (Luke 23:44-45)? Sure it did. It was a pattern of the final darkness that will accompany the final judgment at the end of the world. "When He died, the sun refused to shine (Lk. 23:45). When He comes again it will not shine (Mt. 24:29)."[31] The both/and model we are presenting here does greater justice to the text than does Chilton's inadequate approach.

The point is clear: If these events are to happen literally, in a manner corresponding to the Exodus events, then the whole preterist view is wrong and the theology of the Christian Reconstruction movement is also wrong, because it cannot be supported from the text of Scripture.

Invisible Signs

Another example of hermeneutical differences comes from Gary North. North contends that a literal interpretation of Matthew 24:29-30 is impossible since its fulfillment would be unrealistic:

> At least one of these verses obviously cannot be taken literally: ". . . the stars shall fall from heaven." If the stars literally fall from heaven, they have to fall down to somewhere. Down? What meaning does "down" have for the stars? Only one: down to the earth. Does anyone today believe that whole galaxies will visibly fall down from the sky "to" somewhere?[32]

In spite of North's arguments this passage describes a literal event for the following reasons. First, stars literally do fall from heaven. They are called "falling stars," "shooting stars," "comets," or "meteors." The Greek word for star can be used in this way.[33] "Stars" that fall to the earth often disintegrate and burn up as they enter the earth's atmosphere. Robert Gundry has said, "The falling of the stars refers to a shower of meteorites, and the shaking of the heavenly powers of God's displacing 'the spiritual forces of wickedness in the heavenly places' (Eph 6:12)."[34] This is what causes the people of the earth to try to hide in caves (Revelation 6:12-17). Perhaps this is similar to the Lord's raining fire and brimstone upon Sodom and Gomorrah (Genesis 19:23-26)?

Second, it makes sense that the heavens and earth are physically affected by man's sin at the end of history, just as it was when man fell at the beginning of history. With the literal view, Genesis and Revelation recount the beginning and ending of history. Revelation notes the magnitude of the shaking of the heavens and the earth in judgment. Noah's flood had physical effects, and so too will the judgment of the tribulation prior to Christ's coming.

Since God put the stars in the heavens to be "signs" (Genesis 1:14), wouldn't their being displaced during God's greatest judgment be the ultimate fulfillment of their original purpose? Matthew 24:30 speaks of "the sign of the Son of Man in heaven." Perhaps this refers to such a shaking of the heavens. Because it is such a great, unique, and unrepeatable physical phenomenon, Chicken Little will not be mistaken when the sky actually does fall.

There is no such thing as a signless sign. This is what Reconstructionists would be saying if their view is correct. Robert Dean says,

> Gen. 1:14 states that one of the purposes for the sun, moon, and stars is to serve as "signs" in the heavens. Are these references to sun, moon, and stars to be taken merely as symbols with no physical referent? This would be absurd.[35]

The Dominionist interpretation yields an invisible sign. A sign that cannot be seen is no sign. North would rather not have a sign than have one that does not say what he wants to see. The sun, moon, and stars are signs that can be observed in the heavens. An interruption of their arrangement will constitute a sign to be seen by all.

Elliot E. Johnson has stated a good principle for interpreting symbols in prophetic language:

> Though the language is expressive, it does not exclude specific reference; and though the genre includes symbolism, it does not negate actual and

historical reference through the symbol. This may be defended by two lines of reasoning.

(1) The concept of "prophetic revelation" necessarily includes the use of language that implies factual information (a reference to history) as well as expressions of attitude and feeling. . . .

(2) The concept of "literal interpretation" affirms that the meaning of a symbol is determined by textual and contextual considerations. It may appear that such a method would exclude figures and symbols altogether. Properly understood, however, literal interpretation does not claim that the interpretive approach or technique determines textual meaning; it is the literary genre that does that.[36]

HOW SCRIPTURE INTERPRETS SCRIPTURE

To understand how Scripture interprets Scripture, let's look at some passages that contain a future prediction and have a recorded fulfillment.

When we look at prophecies of Christ's first coming, we see that they were fulfilled in a literal manner, rather than figuratively. One good example is the precision of the 483 years predicted until the coming of Messiah in the seventy weeks of Daniel (9:24-27). It is not possible to go into detail here,[37] but the point is that Daniel predicted precisely the year in which Messiah would be cut off. "The *terminus ad quem* of the sixty-ninth week was on the day of Christ's triumphal entry on March 30, A.D. 33."[38] This kind of precise accuracy requires a literal fulfillment.

Other examples include the following Old Testament predictions and their New Testament fulfillment:

1. Christ would be born of a virgin—Isaiah 7:14 (Matthew 1:20-25);

2. Christ would be a descendant of Abraham—Genesis 22:18 (Matthew 1:1);
3. Christ would be of the tribe of Judah—Genesis 49:10 (Matthew 1:2);
4. Christ would be of the house of David—Jeremiah 23:5 (Luke 3:23, 31);
5. Christ would be a prophet—Deuteronomy 18:18 (Matthew 21:11);
6. Christ would be preceded by a messenger—Isaiah 40:3 (Matthew 3:1-2);
7. Christ would begin his ministry in Galilee—Isaiah 9:1 (Matthew 4:12-13);
8. Christ would suddenly enter the temple—Malachi 3:1 (Matthew 21:12);
9. Christ would enter Jerusalem on a donkey—Zechariah 9:9 (Luke 19:35-37);
10. Christ would be a stone of stumbling to Jews—Psalm 118:22 (1 Peter 2:7);
11. Christ would be a light to the Gentiles—Isaiah 60:3 (Acts 13:47-48);
12. Christ would rise from the dead—Psalm 16:10 (Acts 2:31);
13. Christ would be betrayed by a friend—Psalm 41:9 (Matthew 10:4);
14. Christ would be sold for thirty pieces of silver—Zechariah 11:12 (Matthew 26:15);
15. This payment would be thrown in God's house—Zechariah 11:13 (Matthew 27:5);
16. The money would be used to buy the potter's field— Zechariah 11:13b (Matthew 27:7);
17. Christ would be accused by false witnesses—Psalm 35:11 (Matthew 26:59-61);
18. Christ would remain silent before accusers—Isaiah 53:7 (Matthew 27:12-19);
19. Christ would be wounded and bruised—Isaiah 53:5 (Matthew 27:26);

20. Christ would be smitten and spat upon—Isaiah 50:6 (Matthew 26:67);
21. Christ would be mocked—Psalm 22:7-8 (Matthew 27:31);
22. Christ would fall under the weight of the cross—Psalm 109:24-25 (John 19:17);
23. Christ would have his hands and feet pierced—Psalm 22:16 (Luke 23:33);
24. Christ would be crucified with thieves—Isaiah 53:12 (Matthew 27:38);
25. Christ would have his garments parted and lots cast for them—Psalm 22:18 (John 19:23);
26. Christ would suffer thirst—Psalm 69:21 (John 19:28);
27. Christ would be offered gall and vinegar—Psalm 69:21 (Matthew 27:34);
28. Christ's bones would not be broken—Psalm 34:20 (John 19:33);
29. Christ would have his side pierced—Zechariah 12:10 (John 19:34);
30. Christ would be buried in a rich man's tomb—Isaiah 53:9 (Matthew 27:57-60);
31. Darkness would come over the land—Amos 8:9 (Matthew 27:45).[39]

None of these fulfillments were taken in a figurative way by the New Testament writers. In example 31, darkness literally occurred. It may have also symbolized the darkness of sin, but it got physically dark as well. And Christ will actually come back on a cloud in the future. Christ really fell under the weight of the cross; it was not just figurative of the weight of sin. Christ was betrayed for thirty, not twenty-nine or thirty-one pieces of silver, not gold or platinum. These things literally took place.

The literal interpretation of prophecy is consistent with Old Testament usage and is demonstrated to be the way the

New Testament understood the Old. The literal hermeneutic is a consistent approach to interpreting the Bible, from Genesis to Revelation. There is no need for a special approach to prophecy. The literal interpretation of the Bible takes into account the following:

First, words are used denotatively and connotatively. It is true that connotative speech is richer and carries with it many implications. Someone can say "Joe died last night" (denotative), or he can say "Joe kicked the bucket" (connotative). Since both expressions could be taken in a denotative way, the context would indicate whether a description is to be taken plainly or figuratively. However, whether one speaks directly or in a figure, either way, the event of Joe's death really happened.

> Symbols, figures of speech and types are all interpreted plainly in this method and they are in no way contrary to literal interpretation. After all, the very existence of any meaning for a figure of speech depends on the reality of the literal meaning of the terms involved. Figures often make the meaning plainer, but it is the literal, normal, or plain meaning that they convey to the reader.[40]

Reconstructionists often use figures of speech to manipulate the text to say that certain events are not going to happen in the way the church has historically understood them. This is called spiritualization.

Second, different literary genre must be taken into account when trying to understand the meaning of the text. For instance the Bible contains history (narrative), biography, epistles, poetry, wisdom, parables, allegories, dialogue, tragedy, and satire. Let's consider a brief example of one of these genre.

> "For every beast of the forest is Mine, The cattle on a thousand hills." (Psalm 50:10)

The student of Hebrew literature knows by the poetic genre that the second line, like the first, is speaking of God's ownership of all of his creation. His ownership is not limited to a thousand hills. This is a figure of speech within a poetic genre, set in parallelism so that the reader can compare and contrast the two lines and discover the meaning.

But it is another thing entirely to arbitrarily say as Chilton says that the figure of a thousand years, set within a prose context, means simply "'a large, rounded-off number' . . . standing 'for manyness.'"[41] All agree that it is used symbolically in Psalm 50, but the phrase "a thousand years" occurs six times within the narrative of Revelation 20. This genre is not poetic; it is prose nonfiction. Revelation 20:4-5 contains a vision and 20:6 its interpretation. In both vision and interpretation a thousand years is mentioned. The vision is in the aorist tense, but the interpretation is in the future tense.[42] This means that 20:6 is an interpretation of 20:4-5, and one does not use a symbol to explain a symbol. The explanation in verse 6 would make no sense if it were not literal.

Numbers Don't Count

Nathaniel West said that the tendency to spiritualize the numbers in Scripture results in "numbers that don't count."[43] This is the effect of the Reconstructionists' approach—symbolic numbers don't count. Chilton and his followers would have us believe that the major use of numbers in the Bible goes contrary to the very purpose of numbers—counting. For them numbers don't count and signs cannot be seen. It appears, once again, that if the numbers of prophecy were taken in the way the Bible uses numbers in the other sections of Scripture, then it would disprove the Reconstructionists' whole theology. They do not want to take numbers literally because it would not support postmillennialism.

Reconstructionists keep insisting that numbers used in prophetic passages are used symbolically, which may or may not be true depending on the particular context.

> Plainly, nothing is gained, either for Post-millennialism,
> or No-millennialism, by hoisting the flag "Symbol-

ical numbers don't count!" To regard a number as symbolic does not require us to deny its chronological value. To affirm its chronological value is not to deny its symbolic character. The 70 weeks are both. So are the 1000 years.[44]

This is the only sane position to take: Numbers do count and they also have a symbolic character. To always require a symbolic interpretation for numbers used in the prophetic literature is to do violence to God's word.

A Symbolic Example of Reconstructionist Hermeneutics

James Jordan gives us further insight into how Reconstructionists handle the prophetic literature:

> The prophets often see the "sun, moon, and stars" falling to the earth. One of the most frequently encountered mistakes in Bible prophecy today is the notion that this always refers to the end of the world at the second coming of Jesus Christ. Actually, though, this expression usually refers to the collapse of some particular nation.[45]

Jordan now defines and illustrates what he calls "the language of heavenly collapse," which is his framework and device for doing away with passages that would otherwise be taken to refer to the second coming:

> Suppose we wrote a prophetic poem about the destruction of America, and included in the poem these lines:
>
> > The sun was darkened, the moon eclipsed;
> > The stars fell, they fell to the ground;
> > Fifty in ranks, trampled under foot;
> > Her rulers imprisoned, caged in darkness.
>
> Let's analyze this section of our "poem." It has an ABBA structure, which Bible scholars call a

"chiasm." The first line, about the darkening of sun and moon, is explained by the last line about the imprisonment of our rulers. The second and third lines clearly refer to the defeat of the fifty states. This would be obvious to us would it not? Anyone who has had a high school class in literature could figure it out.

But, when we come to the Bible, all this common sense gets thrown out the window. Prophecy teachers assume that the language of heavenly collapse must always refer to the end of the world in some literal sense. Not so, however. Right in Genesis One we are told that the sun, moon, and stars were designed as symbols, symbols of rulers, symbols of the times in which they rule.[46]

Let's look at Jordan's hermeneutic. First, his illustration is clearly a poem. It used poetic features such as parallelism, as Jordan noted when he observed the ABBA arrangement. But not all prophetic literature is poetic. Therefore, some of his points are invalid.

Second, in his poem there is a clear syntactical relation-ship between figures of speech and their meaning. This is clear because of the poetic genre. The connotative use of "sun" in the first line is explained by its denotative parallel in the fourth line as a "ruler." The same thing occurs with "stars" in line two, which is explained by its referent "fifty" in line three.

Third, in this example there are clear factors within the context itself which yield the figurative understanding of sun, moon, and stars. Even though the context is limited, only four lines, the meaning is apparent and specific reasons in the passage can be cited for taking it the way Jordan advocates. But such specific indicators are absent from the passages Chilton and Jordan want to interpret in their unique way.

Fourth, in their effort to explain the Olivet discourse and Revelation with their "heavenly collapse" language, they are not able to establish this approach from passages that clearly use the figures in that way. They go to passages that have references to the sun, moon, and stars and simply state that this is "heavenly collapse" language, not Science 101. Thinking they have established this category, they go to the Olivet discourse or Revelation and explain it the same way. It is true that sun, moon, and stars are used figuratively, but not in the way Jordan is suggesting. Even if there were such an approach, it would still have to be demonstrated in each specific instance that any given passage should be explained in that way. This they have not done.

Fifth, even in Jordan's example, "fifty" was used to represent something specific and not general. Each of these states were geographical realities. You could walk in one, live in each one. They really existed. It would not mean just a bunch of states, but the complete United States. If 49 were used, it would mean a partial destruction. If the thousand years of Revelation 20 were used in a similar way, it would be a literal reference. Numbers may have symbolic meanings, but there are limits and specificity to their usage.

Sixth, Jordan says, "Right in Genesis One we are told that the sun, moon, and stars were designed as symbols, symbols of rulers, symbols of the times in which they rule." Genesis 1 does not say this. It does say that the sun, moon, and stars are signs, but the text never uses the word "symbol." Aren't signs and symbols the same? No! Signs are indicators, while a symbol represents or stands for something else. The sun, moon, and stars represent themselves; they are not symbolic of some hidden rulers. When the sun stood still in Joshua's long day, it was a sign that God was on Israel's side. The sun is not used here symbolically but actually. At the end of the world, the sun, moon, and stars cease ruling as a physical sign that God is getting ready to alter the physical features of his creation to reflect his judgment of the earth. To argue otherwise is the kind of hermeneutical slight-of-hand Reconstructionists resort to in their attempt to project credibility for their interpretation.

Jordan's illustration accomplishes just the opposite of his intention. Rather than establishing his speculative hermeneutic, it demonstrates how figures of speech and genre both work together to give a control to language which can be checked by indicators in the text itself. The preterist approach is just another example of spiritualization.

Our Triune God has stated things both literally and symbolically in the Bible. The proper approach is to admit both and image God in this matter. Literal interpretation takes into account symbolism as well as actual historical events. Reconstructionists tend to want to idealize the events to fit their theology.

Reconstructionist Inconsistencies

Reconstructionists argue strongly for the literalness of time indicators such as days and years in Genesis. North declares, "The words of Genesis 1 inform us of the fact that God created all things in six days."[47] Rushdoony takes the years in the early part of Genesis to be literal, as indicated by his understanding that Adam lived 930 years.[48] In addition, Chilton believes that Revelation is the fulfillment of themes begun in Genesis, so that a certain relationship exists between the two.[49] Given this kind of thinking, it is strange that Reconstructionists declare days and years in Genesis to be literal and then say that days and years in Revelation are figurative. Creation accounts are taken literally, while eschatology is symbolic. Dispensationalist George Zeller calls our attention to this schizophrenia:

> If Dr. North were to follow the same literal approach that he uses in Genesis 1-2 and apply that to Revelation chapter 20, then he would be a premillennial dispensationalist and he would be forced to abandon his postmillennialism. But instead he abandons his literal hermeneutic. He takes Genesis 1-2 very literally. Days mean days. Morning and evening means

morning and evening. Fifth day means fifth day.
But when he comes to Revelation, suddenly everything changes. Everything is not symbolic. A
thousand years (mentioned 6 times in Rev. 20) does
not mean a thousand years. The thousand years represents "a vast, undefined period of time."[50]

The literal hermeneutic is consistent with the usage and
patterns set up in Genesis, while at the same time setting up
a certain symmetry of fulfillment, which displays God's satisfactory completion of history in spite of the challenge of evil.
It also takes into account God's rich variety in literary style,
while not changing hermeneutics according to subject matter.
The preterist approach is designed to make their theology work,
when a proper interpretation would otherwise demonstrate it
to be invalid. Charles Ryrie has explained the literal hermeneutic in the following way:

> Dispensationalists claim that their principle of her-
> meneutics is that of literal interpretation. This means
> interpretation which gives to every word the same
> meaning it would have in normal usage, whether
> employed in writing, speaking or thinking. This is
> sometimes called the principle of grammatical-
> historical interpretation since the meaning of each
> word is determined by grammatical and historical
> considerations. The principle might also be called
> normal interpretation since the literal meaning of
> words is the normal approach to their understanding
> in all languages.[51]

The best method for interpreting prophecy is simply the
consistent application of the grammatical-historical interpretation, upon which orthodox Christianity is built. Why the need
to change horses in the middle of the race, if it is not because
theology is improperly controlling interpretation? E. R. Craven
makes the following observations about the two systems:

Normal is used instead of *literal* (the term generally employed in this connection) as more expressive of the correct idea. No terms could have been chosen more unfit to designate the two great schools of prophetical exegetes than *literal* and *spiritual*. These terms are not antithetical, nor are they in any proper sense significant of the peculiarities of the respective systems they are employed to characterize. They are positively misleading and confusing. *Literal* is opposed not to *spiritual* but to *figurative*; *spiritual* is in antithesis on the one hand to *material*, on the other to *carnal* (in a bad sense). The *Literalist* (so called) is not one who denies that *figurative* language, that *symbols*, are used in prophecy, nor does he deny that great *spiritual* truths are set forth therein; his position is simply, that the prophecies are to be *normally* interpreted (i.e. according to the received laws of language) as any other utterances are interpreted—that which is manifestly literal being regarded as literal, that which is manifestly figurative being so regarded. The position of the Spiritualist (so called) is not that which is properly indicated by the term. He is one who holds that whilst certain portions of the prophecies are to be *normally* interpreted, other portions are to be regarded as having a *mystical* (i.e. involving some secret meaning) sense. Thus, for instance, Spiritualists (so called) do not deny that when the Messiah is spoken of as "a man of sorrow and acquainted with grief," the prophecy is to be *normally* interpreted; they affirm, however, that when He is spoken of as coming "in the clouds of heaven" the language is to be "spiritually" (mystically) interpreted. The terms properly expressive of the schools are *normal* and *mystical*.[52]

It must be added that the criterion for determining normal interpretation is not some abstract idealism, but rather the cultural, historical, and grammatical context of the Bible itself. This is why the application of a literal hermeneutic, which yields a futurist understanding of prophecy, reveals the intended meaning God has for us in the prophetic literature.

Any interpretation of a given text should be supported both from the details within the text as well from how the interpretation harmonizes with the teachings of the rest of Scripture. Chilton's hermeneutical approach is more in line with a secret-key-to-understanding-the-text approach than a valid dimension of the grammatical-historical-contextual method long recognized by the church as the proper approach to Scripture. The proper interpretation of the prophetic text is a futuristic one. It is this future, this "Blessed Hope," true believers long for. "And though you have not seen Him, you love Him" (1 Peter 1:8a).

Chapter 14, Notes

1. Joseph C. Morecraft, III, "Editorial," *The Counsel of Chalcedon*, July 1988, 3.

2. Milton S. Terry, *Biblical Hermeneutics: A Treatise on the Interpretation of the Old and New Testaments* (Grand Rapids: Zondervan Publishing House, n.d.), 17.

3. Bernard Ramm, *Protestant Biblical Interpretation: A Textbook of Hermeneutics* (Grand Rapids: Baker Book House, 1970), 1.

4. Ibid., 2.

5. Ibid.

6. Aiken G. Taylor, "Postmillennialism Revisited," *The Presbyterian Journal*, 6 September 1978, 10.

7. Meredith G. Kline, "Comments on an Old-New Error," *Westminster Theological Journal* 41 (Winter 1981):182-83.

8. David Chilton, *Paradise Restored: An Eschatology of Victory* (Tyler, Tex.: Reconstruction Press, 1985), 18.

9. Ibid., 19-20.

10. David Chilton, *Days of Vengeance* (Fort Worth: Dominion Press, 1987), 32-33.

11. Ibid., 38-39.

12. James Jordan, *Judges: God's War Against Humanism* (Tyler, Tex.: Geneva Ministries, 1985), xii.

13. Douglas A. Oss, "Canon as Context: The Function of *Sensus Plenior* in Evangelical Hermeneutics," *Grace Theological Journal* 9 (Spring 1988):105.

14. Jordan, *Judges*, xiii.

15. This is what Oss concludes, "Canon as Context," 107.

16. Doug Wilson, *Law and Love: Constructive Criticism for Reconstructionists* (Moscow, Idaho: Ransom Press, 1988), 11.

17. Greg L. Bahnsen, cited by Joseph C. Morecraft, III, in his editorial in *The Counsel of Chalcedon*, July 1988, 3.

18. John F. Walvoord, *The Millennial Kingdom* (Grand Rapids: Zondervan Publishing House, 1959), 33-34.

19. David Chilton, *The Great Tribulation* (Fort Worth: Dominion Press, 1987), 3.

20. Greg Bahnsen, "The *Prima Facie* Acceptability of Postmillennialism," *Journal of Christian Reconstruction* 3 (Winter 1976-77):57.

21. Chilton, *Great Tribulation*, 22-23.

22. Ibid., 25-26.

23. Ibid., 26.

24. Ibid., 23.

25. Chilton, *Days of Vengeance*, 66.

26. Chilton, *Great Tribulation*, 23.

27. Ibid., 25.

28. Robert L. Dean, "Essentials of Dispensational Theology," *Biblical Perspectives*, January-February 1988, 6, n. 13.

29. James B. Jordan, "The Separated Waters: Studies in Genesis One," *The Geneva Review*, March 1987, 5.

30. Chilton, *Great Tribulation*, 20.

31. Randolph O. Yeager, *The Renaissance New Testament* (Bowling Green: Renaissance Press, 1978), 3:312.

32. Gary North, "1988: Dispensationalism's Year of Crisis," *Dispensationalism in Transition*, January 1988, 1.

33. Henry George Liddell and Robert Scott, s.v. "aster," *A Greek-English Lexicon* (Oxford: Oxford University Press, 1968), 261.

34. Robert H. Gundry, *Matthew: A Commentary on His Literary and Theological Art* (Grand Rapids: Wm. B. Eerdmans Publishing Co., 1982) 487.

35. Dean, "Dispensational Theology," 4.

36. Elliot E. Johnson, "Apocalyptic Genre in Literal Interpretation," *Essays in Honor of J. Dwight Pentecost*, ed. Stanley D. Toussaint and Charles H. Dyer (Chicago: Moody Press, 1986), 204-5.

37. For a detailed explanation of the factors involved in arriving at the above conclusion see Harold W. Hoehner, *Chronological Aspects of the Life of Christ* (Grand Rapids: Zondervan Publishing House, 1977).

38. Ibid., 139.

39. These examples are taken from Josh McDowell, *Evidence That Demands a Verdict* (San Bernardino, Calif.: Here's Life Publishers, 1972), 147-83.

40. Charles C. Ryrie, *Dispensationalism Today* (Chicago: Moody Press, 1973), 87.

41. Chilton, *Days of Vengeance*, 506.

42. This argument was made by S. Lewis Johnson (Unpublished classnotes, Revelation 228, Dallas Theological Seminary, 1976).

43. Nathaniel West, *The Thousand Years in Both Testaments* (New York: Fleming H. Revell, 1880), 327.

44. Ibid., 330.

45. James B. Jordan, "Abraham's Astral Prophecy: Studies in Genesis One," *The Geneva Review*, January 1988, 5.

46. Ibid.

47. Gary North, *The Dominion Covenant: Genesis* (Tyler, Tex.: The Institute for Christian Economics, 1982), 428.

48. R. J. Rushdoony, *The Institutes of Biblical Law* (Phillipsburg, N.J.: Presbyterian & Reformed Publishing Co., 1973), 359.

49. See Chilton, *Paradise Restored*, 15-63.

50. George Zeller, "The Inconsistencies of the Postmillennial Reconstructionists" (Unpublished paper, 1988), 1.

51. Ryrie, *Dispensationalism Today*, 86-87.

52. E. R. Craven, editor of J. P. Lange, *Commentary on the Holy Scriptures: Revelation* (Grand Rapids: Zondervan Publishing House, n.d.), 98.

Chapter 15

The Dangers of Christian Reconstructionism

While in college in 1974, Tommy spent an evening in the home of a professor who was hosting Gary North. The conversation for the evening ranged from a Christian view of economics to the dangers of Charles Finney. Toward the end of the evening, Tommy, who was quite interested in how post-millennialism could be developed from the Bible, asked North what passages of Scripture he appealed to for his eschatology. Tommy recounts North's reaction: "I will never forget his response. He just looked down at the floor and stared, not answering. I prompted him, but he continued to stare at the floor."

This incident serves as a microcosm of our first criticism, not just of postmillennialism, but of many features of the entire Christian Reconstruction movement. Though many of its leaders are brilliant, though its worldview is intriguing, and though its goals are noble, it is just not taught in the Bible. A proper exegesis of God's Word will not produce their most basic ideas.

A second major objection to Reconstructionism is that it just does not work. It never has worked in the past, will not work in the present, and will only lead the church astray in the future. If Christian Reconstruction is taught in the Bible, why do we not have communities of the kingdom around the world? There should be examples of institutional millenniums which could serve as models of the millennium to come. But there are none. In fact, the church has not been able even to come close to the conditions Reconstructionists say will exist over the face of the globe before Christ returns. But far more worrisome than these two criticisms are the potential dangers posed by the movement's current resurgence.

Cultural Backlash

A study of the history of the western church since the Reformation will show that postmillennialism grows and flourishes during periods when the church and often secular society stresses the confidence and abilities of man. While postmillennial theologians say that it is God to whom they are looking for victory, nevertheless the track record demonstrates that their view does gain popular support at times when the secular society is optimistic about human accomplishments. After a period of growth in the "can do" spirit, disillusion usually sets in and Christians are driven to the Scriptures to gain direction for the future. This is a pattern which can be seen within the last century of Christian history.

Over one hundred years ago there lived in Holland a Calvinist pastor by the name of Abraham Kuyper (1837-1920). It would not be overstating things to say that Kuyper was one of the most remarkable men in the history of the church. What Kuyper did from 1870-1920 was to spearhead a movement that was "nationwide in intent and comprehensive in scope, addressing every facet of national life with a coherent ideology and specific program."[1] To a large degree, Kuyper and the Dutch Church achieved many of the goals for Holland that Reconstructionists in our day aim for in the United States. One Reconstructionist has said, "reconstructionists still look to Kuyper as one of their key intellectual forefathers."[2]

What did this movement accomplish? Under the leadership and direction of Kuyper, Christians controlled the largest newspaper in the nation, founded the Free University in Amsterdam to educate in terms of their perspective, established a national Christian day school movement, founded a new Christian denomination, founded a political party which controlled the legislature for over a decade, founded a Christian labor union, and elected Kuyper to the office of prime minister of the Netherlands for four years.[3] This movement is credited with the "development of modern European civilization and its finest fruits: progressive science and emancipated art; constitutional, republican government and civil liberties; thriving agriculture, commerce, and industry; and a purified family life."[4]

These great accomplishments were not the product of optimistic Reconstructionists who wanted to see the millennium fully established. On the contrary, they would be labeled by Reconstructionists as pessimists.[5] These Dutch Christians were reacting to the humanism spawned by the French Revolution and were attempting to protect the church, their families, and other institutions from its poison.

But what happened to the great progress the Dutch made during those fifty years? Why is contemporary Holland 180 degrees from the Holland of Kuyper's time? Very likely Reconstructionists would say the problem was that Kuyper and his following were amillennialists, with a few premillennialists mixed in. In short, they did not have the optimistic view of the future needed to sustain such a movement.

But this critique does not adequately account for their ability to begin and sustain such a movement. The rapid decline was due, at least in part, to modern Dutch culture's conscious reaction to most facets of Christianity. The depravity of the human heart must never be underestimated. Only the sovereign grace of God is able to tame it. Even though Reconstructionists are Calvinists, they do not consistently apply to their eschatology the Calvinistic recognition of man's depravity. History needs the cataclysmic intervention of Christ for societal salvation, just as each sinner needs a similar event for personal salvation.

If postmillennialism were true, the progress made by Kuyper should have had some continuity because of the grace of God; it produced instead a backlash. This is just the kind of ebb and flow we see throughout history. Sometimes the church has such a great influence on a society that it changes the world around it. Most of the time, however, it is the other way around. This was also true of Israel's history. At times there was revival, and the people obeyed God's Word. But all too often the opposite was true. It is important to notice that this ebb and flow within the church's history is what we would expect if the premillennial, or even the amillennial, view—that the world is being prepared for worldwide judgment before Christ's coming—is true. The wheat and the tares are growing up together.

The potential danger which lies ahead is that the non-Christian world will so react to this attempt at a Christian takeover that certain aspects of Reconstructionism could draw out a more severe reaction to Christianity than would have normally occurred.

One of the aspects of Reconstructionism which often needlessly provokes a backlash is Rushdoony's view that

> the death penalty is required by Scripture for a number of offenses. These are for
>
> 1. murder, but not for accidental killings (Ex. 21:12-14);
> 2. striking or cursing a parent (Ex. 21:15; Lev. 20:9; Prov. 20:20; Matt. 15:4; Mark 7:10). It should be noted that Christ condemned the scribes and Pharisees for setting aside this law;
> 3. kidnaping (Ex. 21:16; Deut. 24:7);
> 4. adultery (Lev. 20:10-21);
> 5. incest (Lev. 20:11-12, 14);
> 6. bestiality (Ex. 22:19; Lev. 20:15-16);
> 7. sodomy or homosexuality (Lev. 20:13);
> 8. unchastity (Deut. 22:20-21);

9. rape of a betrothed virgin (Deut. 22:23-27);
10. witchcraft (Ex. 22:18);
11. offering human sacrifice (Lev. 20:2);
12. incorrigible delinquency or habitual criminality (Deut. 21:18-21);
13. blasphemy (Lev. 24:11-14, 16, 23);
14. sabbath desecration (Ex. 35:2; Num. 15:32-36); now superseded;
15. propagation of false doctrines (Deut. 13:1-10);
16. sacrificing to false gods (Ex. 22:20);
17. refusing to abide by the court decision and thus denying the law (Deut. 17:8-13);
18. failing to restore the pledge or bailment (Ezek. 18:12, 13), because such an act destroyed the possibility of community trust and association.[6]

It is true that "those who practice such things are worthy of death" (Romans 1:32), but to advocate the implementation of the full list of capital offenses prescribed for Israel during the church age goes beyond what God expects the magistrate to enforce during this age (Romans 13:1-3). The magistrate is directly under the stipulations of the Noahic Covenant, not the Mosaic law.

This is not an argument against the death penalty administered by the magistrate during the church age, since the Noahic Covenant prescribes that, but a disagreement over the extent to which it should be applied. To carry it over to religious areas, as Rushdoony advocates, would require the state to be wrongly intermingled with the church. Paul would not have argued for the death penalty in Romans 13 if it did not apply to at least the civil realm.

Synthesis of the Sacred and Profane

At the same time that Dutch Christianity was producing the Kuyper revolution with its pessimistic eschatology, American Christianity was producing the Social Gospel movement. This was at a time (1870-1920) when the optimism of American postmillennialism was at an apex. The problem was that the long term effect of an overall climate of optimism within American Christianity and within the culture at large was one of the major ingredients which had a hand in producing the man-centered theology of liberalism in America. But it was certainly an optimistic time in American history.

Postmillennialism believes that Christianity is to take over institutions before Christ returns. "Postmillennialists believe that God can and will transform social institutions for the better in the future. They believe that God will use Christians to achieve this improvement."[7]

This resulted in a synthesis of Christianity with increasingly fewer Christian values under the guise of Christianizing the culture. This synthesis became worse and worse, until these so-called "Christianized" institutions eventually have become anti-Christian. God has not decreed that Christians take over institutions during the church age. This will happen in the millennium. God has not given the church a proper dose of grace to Christianize the world. It is not that God's grace is not powerful enough; rather he has not directed his grace to that end during this age.

The ironic facts of history indicate that when the church is most concerned about remaining pure in doctrine and faithfully living for Christ, the result is often a high level of Christian influence in society. As the church separates and protects itself from false teachings and stresses sound doctrine, a strong Christianity emerges to the benefit of society. However, to attempt to establish a long-term change of institutions before Christ returns will only result in the leaven of humanism permeating orthodox Christianity.

The above point draws our attention to an incompatible marriage within the Reconstructionist theological system. We believe that Cornelius Van Til's (1895-1987) apologetics are at odds with the postmillennial spirit. Since Van Til's epistemology stresses the absolute sufficiency of Scripture resulting in no need to intermingle with non-Christian systems, this leads to a separation from the pollution of non-Christian thought. The believer is to be a light shining in the darkness, not a light mixed with darkness. On the other hand, postmillennialism leads to a penetration of institutions, resulting in a spirit of compromise so that the institution may function. We expect to see increasing tension between these two factors in the days ahead as Reconstructionists will be tempted to yield veracity for the sake of pragmatism.

The last ten to fifteen years have witnessed the revival of a new man-centered optimism called "new age" thought. Within the church there has been a similar growth in "positive" Christianity. It is not surprising that Reconstructionists and Christian positivists are increasingly merging (see appendix A).

Often Reconstructionists say that it was the retreat of Christians influenced by a premillennial philosophy which led to the erosion of the great Judeo-Christian heritage. The truth is that sinners, not Christians, are the ones responsible for an immoral society. One example of the many castigations made against dispensationalism is given by Greg Bahnsen: The "dispensational approach to Scripture and its parenthesis view of the church was tied to a withdrawal into individualistic, reactionary moral rules which produced, in overall cash value, sociopolitical impotence."[8]

However, it can also be argued that postmillennialism, with its view of taking over society, had as much if not more to do with the squandering of our biblical heritage. This is because postmillennialism, in effect, intermingles its Christianity with non-Christian thinking and thus is taken over by the world. It unwittingly mixes the holy with the common. In this way, postmillennialism contributed to the wrong intermingling of Christianity with the world's system. But if Bahnsen is complaining that when people converted from postmillennialism to premillennialism they quit trying to establish the kingdom, he is correct.

Meredith Kline has observed that Reconstructionists have a problem keeping the holy and the common separate in a way that reflects the biblical pattern because of their view that what God promised to Israel is now extended to all the nations.

> To accept the Chalcedon theory, one would have to read the biblical record as though it were not the history of the particular kingdom of Israel but an historicized myth about Everynation.

> We have treated the equation made in theonomic politics between the ordinary civil institutions of the world with the Israelite theocratic kingdom as tantamount to a denial of the holy status of the Israelite kingdom. We might have put it the other way around. Instead of saying that the Chalcedon mistake is that of sacralizing the other nations. What it amounts to either way is that Chalcedon divests the concept of holy of any genuinely biblical meaning. And inevitably Chalcedon does the same to the concept of the non-holy, or common. It renders pointless and meaningless the biblical distinction between the holy and the common.[9]

Since God has not decreed victory during the church age, Reconstructionists will always end up becoming wrongly related to this world's system in their effort to take over the world for Christ. The net result is that they will participate in the apostasy of the church to a greater or lesser degree at any given time. Some examples have already been noted.

The biblical approach is to expose evil with the light (Ephesians 5:13) and to call men to escape the wrath to come by trusting in Jesus Christ as their Savior and having their names recorded among those who will participate in the coming of the future kingdom of God. The premillennial view of separating from evil while calling men to the light does not lead to improper synthesis with the world; our calling is not to Christianize the world, but to evangelize the world. As we shall see, it is more consistent with a Van Tilian approach. In the process, this will involve a certain degree of involvement in this world's system, yet with the knowledge that we will never be able to redeem society. The church is the model to the world of how things should be. It is a light upon a hill during the darkness of this current age, but during the Millennium it will be a light so bright that the knowledge of the Lord will fill the earth as the water does the sea.

Romans 1 teaches that society goes downhill because men are sinners, and they manifest their rebellion against God by producing an ungodly culture and society. It is not because believers did not become active in politics. This is the approach Cornelius Van Til advocates. Van Til's strictly biblical epistemology is said to be a basis for the Christian Reconstruction Movement. But it is also recognized by North to be a basis for the destruction of the Reconstructionist's position:

> Rushdoony had recognized that Van Til had utterly destroyed the philosophical foundation of natural law theory and all other common-ground intellectual constructs to link intellectually the believer and the unbeliever. In principle, he had thereby also destroyed the cultural and civilizational links, but he never discussed this inescapable implication of his work. . . .
>
> Van Til never adopted biblical law as his proposed alternative. He never proposed any alternative. Van Til was like a demolition expert; he spent his life blowing up bridges between covenant-breakers and covenant-keepers. But he offered no solutions. Thus, he gained few followers, and he offered no earthly hope. His amillennial pessimism was fully consistent with his cultural pessimism. He never trusted theonomic postmillennialism, which is why we search in vain for any public acknowledgment on his part of the existence of Rushdoony or me, or any favorable printed words for either of us. He regarded the Christian Reconstruction movement as a fringe movement, not the cutting edge.[10]

North is incorrect when he says that Van Til offered no solutions. Van Til faithfully preached the gospel of Jesus Christ as the solution to flee the wrath to come. North is right in saying Van Til did not aspire to build a Christian society since God's calling is for us to "expose by the light" the evil of this age, not to take over the darkness.

However, North has uncovered a key point: Van Til believed that orthodox Christians are to separate from the evil of this world, including the world systems, institutions, and, to some extent, society itself. The drift toward synthesis with the world cannot be avoided by postmillennialists, since their theology tells them there is a progressive development of God's kingdom during the present age. This conclusion cannot be avoided, for they believe that, at some point, these institutions will become Christianized. They do not want to be the ones standing in the way of progress, for this may be tantamount to standing in the way of God. Therefore, there is a tendency for Reconstructionists to prematurely trust that they have captured an institution for God. This unwittingly allows them to bring into the church destructive non-Christian thought and influence, regardless of how much they believe their Van Tilian epistemology will deliver them from.

In a recent television interview, Reconstructionist David Chilton said that "some Reconstructionists haven't been able to decide yet whether they want to be Christians or whether they want to be members of a right-wing political cult."[11] This kind of talk from within the Reconstructionist movement itself demonstrates that even some of their own wonder about the extent of intermingling with the world's system.

The Raising of False Hopes

Reconstructionist Peter Leithart has called our attention to a potential danger which seems to be a real possibility as this decade comes to a close. This danger is that the false hopes the Dominionists have engendered in many Christians have only resulted in cosmetic reform, if even that.

In the face of widespread failure, many conservative activists have lost heart. They have concluded that fundamental reform is impossible. . . . Their idealism has been shattered and they have become cynical, because they have learned "how the world really works." As a result they have become less activist.[12]

Some within the movement display a naive perspective of church history. One Reconstructionist pastor, when challenged about the feasibility of the church realizing the Reconstructionist vision, retorted that

leadership is now shifting to the hundreds of local pastors and laymen in small local churches across the nation that are starting to grow, both numerically and theologically. Their people are being trained in the Reconstruction army. And at least in Presbyterian circles, we have one advantage on Dispensationalists: covenant children. We're baptizing and catechizing a whole generation of Gary Norths, R. J. Rushdoonys, and David Chiltons.[13]

While it is certainly the calling of Christian parents to train up children in the fear of the Lord, this does not mean that these children will fulfill their parents' aspirations. There are too many examples in church history of the failure of a godly group of believers to pass their passion and vision on to the next generation. God does not have grandchildren, only children.

Reconstructionists often say that the full manifestation of the kingdom has not yet dawned because we are only now getting our theology properly arranged. When the failures of past Christians in attempting to bring in the kingdom of God are pointed out to them, such as the Puritans, they often say that they have taken their strengths and corrected their weaknesses and now have the tools for true victory. Gary North called it "the 'new, improved' Christian Reconstruction movement."[14]

In a recent interview Rushdoony was asked, "Are you suggesting that we return to the early American ideas about these concepts . . . regarding such things as voting and equality?" Rushdoony replied,

> I'm not interested in going back, I'm interested in going forward—rethinking every area of American life and thought in terms of Scripture and applying the Word of God across the board. We can't return to the past. We can make a better future.[15]

North cites some specific developments which, when combined, will make a powerful force for the Christianization of America:

> A new Puritanism is developing—a Puritanism which offers men the hope of God honoring social transformation. . . . We are now in a position to fuse together in a working activist movement the three major legs of the Reconstructionist movement: the Presbyterian-oriented educators, the Baptist school headmasters and pastors, and the charismatic tele-communications system. When this takes place, the whole shape of American religious life will be transformed.[16]

In an essay, North and Chilton outline their goal for the Christian Reconstruction movement as one in which "Christians must strive to conquer the whole world for Jesus Christ."[17] In order to accomplish this they say that Christians need a certain theology, and it must be put together in a certain way.

> We believe that there are four fundamental aspects of Christian belief that too often have been missing, as a unit, from the days of the early church fathers until the 1960s. Because we are convinced that this four-part doctrinal position is now recognized by a tiny minority of Christians, its influence will again begin to spread.[18]

It was only about four years later that North revealed yet another "breakthrough" ingredient that must make up the central core of Reconstructionist theology if the church is going to be successful. The breakthrough was the covenant, which when added to the essential doctrinal position will surely result in the Christianization of the world.[19] In fact, North says that Sutton's view of the covenant is an "even more fundamental doctrine"[20] than the other four points for Christian Reconstruction.

Haunted by the past failures of previous generations of postmillennialists to Christianize the world, Reconstructionists continue to seek the missing link, almost as if the agenda of Scripture is insufficiently clear. These breakthroughs, or proper alignment of theological factors, are admissions that their post-millennial forefathers did not have it together. The church has had to wait for the biblical law breakthrough of Rushdoony, or the eschatology breakthrough of Chilton, or the covenant breakthrough of Sutton in order finally to enable it to conquer. Their brilliant insights almost assume the role of a new revelation, which former generations did not have.

Even if these are revolutionary breakthroughs, one should be more humble about them. One Reconstructionist, Doug Wilson, has rightly complained about North's boastings:

> This type of boasting, and the selfish ambition that fuels it, is not a sin that is content to remain alone. . . . This means that, unless there is repentance, the worthy emphasis on ethics found in the Reconstructionist movement is doomed in the long run. And why doomed? Because the law of God cannot be kept by people who think that arrogant boasting is a virtue.[21]

Besides, even fellow Reconstructionists debate whether or not many of these breakthroughs are supported by Scripture. Greg Bahnsen gives the following critique of Sutton's five-point covenantal structure:

The monumental error is [Chilton's] artificially im-
posing the covenantal structure advocated by Ray
Sutton upon the text of Revelation like a Procrustean
bed. . . . You see, Sutton's five point outline does
not arise inductively from a study of the text of
Scripture itself . . . you can be sure somebody before Sutton would have noticed anything that clear.[22]

Gary North even used the analogy of the church fiddling
with a lock on a door, trying to get it open. If we continue
playing with that lock, eventually it will open and we will be
able to go through the door.[23] This paints the picture that the
church will eventually, either through its brilliant understanding
of Scripture or merely through a lucky break, like a fumble in
football, hit on the right formula, and the kingdom will break
upon the land in all of its glory. This is the traditional postmillennial panacea, or maybe we should more strongly say, illu-
sion.

Reconstructionists say the full flower of the kingdom has
yet to arrive because the church has not yet matured properly[24]
(this is similar to the Manifest Sons of God doctrine and the
teaching of Earl Paulk, discussed in appendix A). Or more
frequently they say that the church is just not faithful, as if
God does things for the church based upon her faithfulness
rather than the faithfulness of Christ. If the church would just
believe God's marching orders, then the enemy would be conquered.

This kind of thinking is characteristic of the explanations
used by postmillennialists when things do not work out the
way they preached. There has always been some excuse. Some
used to say, if only we can get rid of the antichrist pope, then
surely the morning rays of the kingdom are on their way. If
we could just get away from the spiritual pollution of Europe
and have one nation which could be that model nation, that
city on a hill to light the way for the other nations, then surely
the times of refreshing will fall. If we can only cast off that
evil blight of slavery, from this city upon a hill, then his truth

will come marching in. The Puritans failed because they did not have the benefit of a consistently Reformed epistemology, as Van Til has now given us. Surely this is the key. It is just a matter of time until all falls into place and then the church will start acting like the church. North boasts, "Time is on the Reconstructionists' side, not the side of our many critics. I believe that Christians have plenty of time to work toward the transformation of this world."[25]

Unfortunately, the only thing the Christian Reconstruction movement will likely produce will be a contribution toward the development of moralism instead of biblical Christianity.

Moralism

Moralism is fostered when a culture or society believes that being a good Christian means measuring up to a public consciousness of right and wrong. Christians so defined can even have a biblical morality, but it falls short of the spirituality God requires and which only he can give as a sovereign, gracious gift. Especially since we believe that it does not appear to be God's will to convert a majority of people during this age, we also believe that attempts to impose biblical morality upon a society will always result in moralism. What makes this tragic is that a Reconstructionist such as Gary North has recognized that moralism is "essentially humanistic."[26] Yet his beliefs could very well lead to the progress of that form of humanism.

Jacques Ellul notes that "In the minds of most of our contemporaries, Christianity primarily means morality. The spiritual aspect is forgotten except among a few."[27] Ellul explains the rise of moralism in the early church:

> From the end of the second century the church . . . could not avoid multiplying moral rules in antithesis to the gospel. As a result, conduct conforming to a certain moral code became the criterion of the Christian life; piety and prayer, etc., were transformed into moral rules; Christianity took on the appearance

of a moral system to those outside it; and theology underwent profound modification with the according of a new prominence to works. As everyone knows, the Lutheran Reformation brought a break with this. But the downward slope is so steep that immediately after the first generation of Reformers had rediscovered Christian freedom, there was a return to moral rigidity, especially with Calvin, and morality again achieved domination over "life in Christ."[28]

To the extent that the Christian Reconstruction movement has an influence on the church and society, many will think of themselves as Christian if they hold to a certain economic theory or a particular view on foreign policy and vote for the right candidates. A case in point is the unbiblical Reconstructionist notion that there is such a thing as a "Christian nation," in which is held a common view of God, a common system of courts, common biblical law, judgment by citizens, and continuity.[29] To implement such a system would require many who are not believers to submit to this so-called framework.

Certainly all men are currently under God's rule, even in their rebellion. Also, all men will one day acknowledge Jesus Christ as Lord. But true Christianity requires a person to be regenerated by God. Then Christ's righteousness is imputed to their account, and they desire to obey God because of what he has done. They have a new attitude because they have a new nature. They now love the law of God and will grow in maturity toward obeying God. However, the unbeliever may keep the morality of the Bible, to a greater or lesser degree, but still be dead spiritually. Something cannot be Christian without the dynamics of spiritual regeneration. The rise of Reconstructionism will only result in moralism and not the true progress of Christianity.

Deemphasizing Man's Depravity

Reconstructionists claim to be Calvinists, and this they are when it comes to personal salvation. They believe fallen man lacks the innate ability to do anything which pleases God. They believe man does not have a free will when it comes to the things of God. Therefore, for someone to be saved, God has to give the ability to believe before they can come to Christ. However, when it comes to applying the depravity of man to the social arena, they tend to become Arminian in their view of man. They stress what the unregenerate man can do, rather than his limitations.

Reconstructionists often say that premillennialists do not take seriously the power of God when it comes to salvation, since they believe that Christ must intervene in history before his rule is established. However, just as it would go against Scripture to say that an unbeliever can do works to make himself pleasing to God, so it would go against Scripture to say that we can bring in the kingdom before the return of Christ. For the kingdom to be established, the earth, as well as the individual, must be regenerated. This is what Messiah meant when he said that "*in the regeneration* when the Son of Man will sit on His glorious throne, you also shall sit upon twelve thrones, judging the twelve tribes of Israel" (Matthew 19:28). The victory of the kingdom awaits the roll back of the curse when society will be transformed. However, the curse of death must await the final judgment after the thousand year reign of Christ (1 Corinthians 15:26).

We should learn from history that every time Christians have tried to establish the kingdom on earth, it has led to disastrous results. We believe the reason for this lack of success is that God has not given the church the necessary tools and graces to establish an earthly kingdom. In addition, Christians are still sinful and have an extremely poor track record when it comes to getting along with each other, let alone running the world in a millennial fashion. This fact is evidenced within the Reconstructionist movement itself. Reconstructionists have a reputation for splintering and demonstrate an inability to get along with each other.[30]

The question needs to be raised: If we are to bring in the kingdom through the present resources God has given the church, and yet the leaders of this movement cannot get along among themselves, how are the rank and file supposed to progress beyond the example of their leadership? Is unity something that will just happen when the fullness of the kingdom nears? This is not to say that Reconstructionists need to agree on every point. There are always differences between people within any framework. But they should be able to get along with each other and at least be on speaking terms with one another, even though they disagree. After all, they are writing books and articles on international relations and church renewal. It is not unreasonable to expect that those who advocate a position which requires a high degree of unity among Christians should be able to get along with each other.

Subtle Infiltration of
Non-Reconstructionist Organizations

Christian Reconstructionists proclaim themselves the only ones with biblical answers to the problems presently facing the world:

> Christian Reconstruction in general is winning by default. . . . When the long-awaited Christian revival hits, our views will sweep the field, both academically and politically, simply because nobody else will be on the field.[31]

They note the influence that they are having in conservative political circles because no one else has developed blueprints for changing the world. North views himself as a man and a movement with the answers, working toward building an army to implement their plans. He once said, "We were shepherds without sheep. No longer."[32] North sees himself becoming the leader and defender of the charismatics and evangelicals within the Dominion Theology movement.

An example of this is the Reconstructionist domination of the Coalition on Revival (C.O.R.). Dr. Jay Grimstead is the founder and director of the organization. Grimstead was formerly director of the International Council on Biblical Iner-

rancy and has apparently used this relationship to recruit many
to be on the steering committee of C.O.R. From reading the
list of those on that committee, it is likely that a good number
are not aware that C.O.R. has such a strong Reconstructionist
agenda and orientation.

This Reconstructionist orientation is seen in the number
of their camp on the steering committee: Bob Mumford, Dennis
Peacocke, Bob Weiner, Gary DeMar, R. E. McMaster, Jr.,
Gary North, and R. J. Rushdoony. But the main problem is
that much of the language and agenda appears to have come
from Reconstructionist influence. In a recent C.O.R. publication, the following statement is listed as one of the sins which
are to be confessed: "We have concerned ourselves more with
Heaven, the future, and escaping this world at Christ's Second
Coming, than with preparing His Bride to be spotless, beautiful,
glorious, and pleasing to Him when He comes."[33]

C.O.R. has adopted postmillennial and theonomic language on several issues:

> We affirm that to be salt and light to the world means
> to influence it for good and to show it the way to
> live and conduct its affairs. In short, it means getting
> God's will to "be done on earth as it is in heaven"
> and to "make disciples of all nations, teaching them
> to obey whatsoever I have commanded you." Christ
> instituted the Church as the world's teacher. The
> world will not know how to live or which direction
> to go without the Church's biblical influence on its
> theories, laws, actions, and institutions. To be salt
> and light, the Church cannot exist in a Christian
> "ghetto" or have a dichotomous view that falsely
> divides life into the spiritual versus the physical-
> historical-measurable.[34]

This heavenization of the earth is Reconstructionist language for bringing in the kingdom before the return of Christ.
Notice that the references to the Lord's Prayer, the Great Commission, and the "salt and light" passages all are used in a

Reconstructionist way. Where does the Bible teach that "Christ instituted the Church as the world's teacher?" Is this a poorly drawn conclusion from the Great Commission?

In another statement Jay Grimstead repeats the language of making the earth into heaven: "in each sphere of life we can 'get God's will done on earth as it is in heaven.'"[35] In the same letter he says the goal of C.O.R. is to "re-establish our country on the Biblical law base on which it once stood." This is also a clear and distinct Reconstructionist goal.

Grimstead was one of those who attended and spoke at The Christian Reconstruction Dialogue in Dallas in the fall of 1987. His topic was "The Role of Eschatology in Christian Reconstruction." Morecraft says that a two-fold consensus was reached because of Grimstead's presentation:

> (1). one's interpretation of Revelation 20 is not essential to the movement; and (2). there must be a general, personal, cultural, and historical victory-orientation to Christian Reconstruction, if it is to last. Without a victory- orientation, Christian Reconstruction has no vision.[36]

The significance of the "victory-orientation" statement by Grimstead, who claims to be a premillennialist,[37] is that one has to be at least an "operational postmillennialist" to agree with it. "Victory-orientation" means that there will be a Christian take-over of the world before Christ returns. This could in no way refer to the premillennial view of victory at the second coming and the subsequent rule of Christ in the future thousand-year kingdom.

Grimstead has admitted that "a lot of us [premillennialists] are reading their books and getting a lot of help about how to change society based on the Bible. On the other hand, we're not accepting their full postmillennialism, and we're not accepting their eschatology in general."[38] A statement like this makes us wonder if Grimstead understands the significance and outworkings of the various eschatologies. The fact that premillennialists are not formally accepting postmillennialism does not bother Reconstructionists at this stage of the ballgame. They are content to have premillennialists act like postmillennialists. In fact in a debate between Reconstructionists and non-Reconstructionists, Tommy pointed out that the reason Reconstructionists were stressing ethics over eschatology at the debate was because they were more interested in getting people to act like postmillennialists than they were in having them hold to the formal system. Gary North agreed with that assessment.

North is correct when he points out that a person cannot be involved in Christian Reconstruction (whose goal is to bring in the kingdom in this present age) and remain a premillennialist over the long haul. "It first turns people into psychological postmillennialists. They yearn for victory, so that they can see Old Testament law producing the promised fruits (Deut. 28:1-14). Then they become openly postmillennial."[39] North does not mind when Christians "are talking theological premillennialism and psychological postmillennialism."[40] This was the same point North made in reference to Jerry Falwell's political involvement in the early 1980s.

> By identifying himself as a point man, Jerry Falwell has been forced, institutionally and financially, to abandon the language of premillennial dispensationalism, whether he still believes it or not. He has adopted the language of victory.
>
> Christians are rallying to support Falwell and others like him who stand up and fight. In doing so, they are steadily abandoning premillennialism, psychologically if not officially.[41]

The theology of the Bible is supposed to predetermine how a Christian is to act. One's view of the future impacts what we do in the present, because it gives direction to present activity. Our eschatology tells us where we are headed, which influences the steps we take in the present to get there. Therefore, if someone is convinced that the Bible teaches a premillennial future, he will work toward certain goals in the present because of the future. Since the Bible tells us clearly what the future holds and what our calling is during the present age, then in order to be faithful to God and his Word we should be presently involved in this world according to that mandate. If the Bible teaches premillennialism, then we should be involved in this present world in a different way than someone who is postmillennial.

Making the Preaching of the Gospel Secondary

Another danger the Reconstructionist movement inclines toward is the blunting and lessening of efforts to evangelize the world as believers are distracted by misguided political and social involvements. Reconstructionists truly believe in evangelism and practice it, but often the practical effect is that Christians become more interested in developing blueprints for taking over the world than in our true calling to evangelize it.

Premillennialists believe that our primary calling is to preach the gospel. Evangelization should characterize our involvement in society. Of course we are to help people, but we mustn't think that our help will ultimately result in the establishment of the kingdom. Rather our actions demonstrate to our fellow man the love and concern God has shown us in redemption.

We are to pray for our civil governmental leaders, not so that we can take over, but so that God will be pleased to restrain evil. Under conditions of freedom, we will be able to "lead a tranquil and quiet life in all godliness and dignity" (1 Timothy 2:2), and thus be able to lead men to Christ (1 Timothy 2:1-6). This understanding should affect our involvement in the present.

This current world is headed toward judgment. After that judgment, Christ will take over control of the world and rule it. But until that happens, the message and activities for believers should be, "Flee the wrath to come by finding safety in Jesus Christ."

How have others behaved in Scripture who believed in impending judgment? Noah and Enoch before the flood did not try to rebuild society. Rather Noah built an ark and called upon his fellow man to escape the judgment by entering the ark with him. "By faith Noah, being warned by God about things not yet seen, in reverence prepared an ark for the salvation of his household, by which he condemned the world, and became an heir of the righteousness which is according to faith" (Hebrews 11:7). Enoch is said to have been a preacher of righteousness (Jude 14-15), not one who was attempting to change society. These men acted in a manner consistent with their view of the future. They did not try to create a synthesis between a position which said that judgment is near and the other which taught that we could, with God's help, restore a godly society.

Jeremiah was a pessimist. God sent him to the people of Israel to tell them that they were under his judgment. They could have repented, but God said through Jeremiah's prophecy that they would not, and therefore they would be destroyed. "'For I have set My face against this city for harm and not for good,' declares the LORD. 'It will be given into the hand of the king of Babylon, and he will burn it with fire'" (Jeremiah 21:10). What would have been the prudent course of action in light of God's plan? It certainly would not have been to start a Reconstructionist movement to return the nation to its roots. That had already been tried by the prophets. The godly response would be to act in accordance with God's message.

But Jeremiah 23 tells us there were optimists in the land who tried to get the people to follow their false direction. Notice in this extensive quote what their positive message says:

> Thus says the LORD of hosts,
> "Do not listen to the words of the prophets who are
>   prophesying to you.
> They are leading you into futility;
> They speak a vision of their own imagination,
> Not from the mouth of the LORD.
> They keep saying to those who despise Me,
> 'The LORD has said, "You will have peace"';

And as for everyone who walks in the stubbornness
     of his own heart,
They say, 'Calamity will not come upon you.'
But who has stood in the council of the LORD,
That he should see and hear His word?
Who has given heed to His word and listened?
Behold, the storm of the LORD has gone forth in
     wrath,
Even a whirling tempest;
It will swirl down on the head of the wicked.
The anger of the LORD will not turn back
Until He has performed and carried out the purposes
     of His heart;
In the last days you will clearly understand it.
I did not send these prophets,
But they ran.
I did not speak to them,
But they prophesied.
But if they had stood in My council,
Then they would have announced My words to My
     people,
And would have turned them back from their evil
     way
And from the evil of their deeds."
                                   (Jeremiah 23:16-22)

The Word of the Lord goes even further and tells Jeremiah
that the source of their false optimism is their own dreams.
This false positivism was the product of their own hopes and
ambitions about the future, not of God. The Lord speaks a
stern word concerning those who tried to pass off their own
views as the Word of the Lord (Jeremiah 23:32).

The question is not whether believers should be involved
in this world, but how and in what ways. Too many unthinking
evangelicals have seen in the Reconstruction movement a convenient philosophy of Christian involvement in society and
politics. Therefore many, though not all, have adopted the

Reconstructionist agenda without examining the postmillennial root that has produced the fruit. Many may examine the root and like what they see. If this is the case, then fine, at least they are aware. But for those who have not previously examined the basis for Reconstructionism, we hope that our analysis of the movement has caused them to see what Scripture really says.

It might be argued that even if Reconstructionist theonomy and postmillennialism is not correct, at least their worldview is attractive. Certainly all can benefit from some of the insights Reconstructionists have given the church. In fact, their own worldview includes many factors gleaned from non-Reconstructionists.[42] However, they themselves see these insights as a product of their distinctive way of thinking. Therefore, we must be aware if we are buying into their total system when we take a bit of information to use within our own theology.

Attitudes

Part of the fruit of the Reconstructionist movement that no Christian, regardless of his eschatology, should want to adopt are certain attitudes which seem to be characteristic of its members. Not all display this sometimes arrogant and boastful attitude, but many of the movement's leaders have made it one of the traits that outsiders recognize when they come into contact with Reconstructionists. We can only hope this boasting does not flow from what Jeremiah identified in his day as the product of false dreams (23:32).

Reconstructionist pastor Doug Wilson wrote the booklet *Law and Love: Constructive Criticism for Reconstructionists* in which he notes three criticisms of the movement. Two of the three were directed at Gary North and had to do with attitudes:

> 1. Mr. Gary North (along with some others) exhibits in his writing a churlish disposition that is not in keeping with our high calling as Christians. In addition, many Reconstructionist authors who do not

exhibit this attitude do not distance themselves from those who do.

2. Mr. Gary North exhibits in his writing an utter lack of humility in evaluating how God will use the publications with which he is associated. Again, other Reconstructionists allow this attitude to continue unchecked.[43]

Many examples of this elitist attitude of boasting and churlish disposition could be cited here. But just one will be given which combines both elements:

> I am throwing down the gauntlet to the opponents of the Christian Reconstruction movement. I am challenging all comers, and I am doing it the smart way: "Let's you and Chilton fight." Furthermore, "Let's you and Bahnsen fight." If anyone wants to fight me, I will switch on my word processor and give him my best shot, but I am such a sweet and inoffensive fellow that I don't expect that anyone will waste his time trying to beat me up. But someone in each of the rival pessimillennial camps had better start producing answers to what Christian Reconstructionists have already written. Specifically, someone had better be prepared to write a better commentary on Revelation than *The Days of Vengeance*. I am confident that nobody can.[44]

With assaults like this, it is not surprising that Professor John Frame of Westminster Seminary, who is as sympathetic to Reconstructionists as one could be while not being a Reconstructionist himself, has said that the movement has a noticeable absence of Christian love toward their Christian brothers. He notes that Scripture says we are to love our enemies, yet Reconstructions often do not even do the lesser and love their brethren.[45]

Bad attitudes among Reconstructionists have even been documented by one of their own ministries. This is found in a reader survey distributed by Geneva Ministries of Tyler, Texas. Editor Michael Gilstrap says,

> Without question the # 1 criticism was that some of our writing, etc. betrayed a spirit of arrogance—a "know it all" attitude. We are too sarcastic and too caustic in our treatment of those we disagree with. Over and over again, these and similar comments surfaced. . . .
>
> In answering the survey question, What would you add to Geneva Ministries?, one reader succinctly commented "Humility of mind consistent with Philippians 2:3,4,5." In answer to the next question asking for constructive criticism, the same reader offered, "Knowledge puffs up— love edifies—your caustic humor and criticism in my opinion communicates a 'gnostic puffery' attitude not consistent with Ephesians 4:3-6 or Ephesians 4:29-32!" And these are but samples! I have 40 to 50 similar comments![46]

These rebukes should produce an improvement among Reconstructionists in the days ahead.

This issue of attitude brings up another characteristic of some within the movement. North, for example, is so sure that his position is correct that it is often hard to engage in a discussion on Reconstructionism without having to endure a propaganda assault even the most zealous Marxist would be proud of. This is probably one of the reasons he often calls for debate. Yet the interaction too often ends up as a proclamatory sermon, rather than an interchange. As one becomes familiar with North, you soon realize that he is constantly scheming and calculating how he can further the cause, seemingly at the expense of finding truth.

Benefits of the Movement

Although he is critical of the attitudes of leading Reconstructionists, John Frame also believes that the Christian Reconstruction movement is one of the most important movements of our day. "Rushdoony is one of the most important Christian social critics alive today."[47] Reconstructionists cannot be ignored and should not be ignored by those who do not agree with them. They do have something worth saying, even though we believe that many of their emphases are wrong and even dangerous.

Christians should have a distinct worldview, and many have not attempted to develop one in the past. Christians should be involved in combating evil in our day, and the Old Testament law should not be ignored by the church. After all Paul says, "all Scripture is profitable" (2 Timothy 3:16). Reconstructionists have forced many to examine how their theology relates to the totality of life and Scripture. They have taken the consistently biblical epistemology of Van Til and applied it to many different areas. They have made a great contribution to the development of the Christian school movement and have emphasized the important place of the family in society. They have contributed greatly to such movements as the prolife cause and the new Christian right in politics, and have helped formulate a philosophy and practice for Christian businesses and economics.

Reconstructionists have shown that you can be both intellectual and practical by the way they have written and built their organizations. They have exerted a great influence in a short period of time. They have made contributions to the study of biblical theology and philosophy, have caused a renewed interest in eschatology, and have issued a challenge, especially to dispensationalism, to clarify our position in terms of their contributions. This challenge should be met in the days ahead as we are driven back to Scripture to see if these things are true. This book is one of the first efforts, though an introductory and survey attempt, to interact with their position.

Assuming that the Christian Reconstructionists are wrong, as we have advocated, they will at least have helped the church of Jesus Christ to see the truth a little more clearly as we work through their challenges. (This would be in addition to the true and genuine contributions they have and will continue to make to the church.) May we always respond to challenges to what we believe to be the truth as the noble-minded Bereans did when they "examined the Scriptures daily, to see whether these things were so" (Acts 17:11).

Chapter 15, Notes

1. James D. Bratt, *Dutch Calvinism in Modern America: A History of a Conservative Subculture* (Grand Rapids: Wm. B. Eerdmans Publishing Co., 1984), 14.

2. Gary DeMar and Peter Leithart, *The Reduction of Christianity: Dave Hunt's Theology of Cultural Surrender* (Fort Worth: Dominion Press, 1988), 36.

3. Ibid., 14-15.

4. Ibid., 16.

5. Gary North, *Dominion and Common Grace: The Biblical Basis of Progress* (Tyler, Tex.: Institute for Christian Economics, 1987), 269.

6. R. J. Rushdoony, *The Institutes of Biblical Law* (Phillipsburg, N.J.: Presbyterian & Reformed Publishing Co., 1973), 235.

7. Gary North, *Is the World Running Down? Crisis in the Christian Worldview* (Fort Worth: Dominion Press, 1988), 280.

8. Greg Bahnsen, *Theonomy in Christian Ethics* (Nutley, N.J.: The Craig Press, 1977), 11.

9. Meredith G. Kline, "Comments on an Old-New Error: A Review Article," *Westminster Theological Journal* 41 (Winter 1981):178.

10. Gary North, "Cutting Edge or Lunatic Fringe?" *Christian Reconstruction,* January-February 1987, 2.

11. David Chilton, from television interview with Bill Moyers, "God and Politics," part 3 on *Moyers.*

12. Peter J. Leithart, "Cynicism and Cosmetic Reform," *Chalcedon Report*, February 1988, 3.

13. Personal letter from John A. Gilley to Thomas D. Ice, 9 November 1987.

14. Gary North, "Stones and Cornerstones in Christian Reconstruction," *Christian Reconstruction,* March-April 1988, 2.

15. Loren Mitchell, "An Interview With R. J. Rushdoony," *The Counsel of Chalcedon*, February 1988, 14.

16. Gary North, "The Three Legs of Christian Reconstruction's Stool," in *Backward Christian Soldiers?* (Tyler, Tex.: Institute for Christian Economics, 1984), 146, 150.

17. Gary North and David Chilton, "Apologetics and Strategy," *Christianity and Civilization: Tactics of Christian Resistance*, ed. Gary North, Summer 1983, 107.

18. Ibid.

19. North spoke highly of Sutton's views of the covenant, saying such things as: "You are about to read the most remarkable single exercise in theology that you have ever read, or are likely ever to read" (p. xi). "The author has found the key above all other keys to interpreting the Bible" (p. xi). "We have waited over three millennia for someone to say plainly: 'This is what the Bible is really all about'" (p. xi). "Sutton's book will be regarded in retrospect as a turning point in Christian theology" (p. xiii). "Publisher's Preface" in Ray Sutton, *That You May Prosper: Dominion by Covenant* (Tyler, Tex.: Institute for Christian Economics, 1987).

20. Gary North, "Chilton, Sutton, and Dominion Theology," essay published by Institute for Christian Economics, n.d., 3.

21. Doug Wilson, *Law and Love: Constructive Criticism for Reconstructionists* (Moscow, Idaho: Ransom Press, 1988), 10.

22. Greg L. Bahnsen, "Another Look At Chilton's *Days of Vengeance*," *Journey Magazine*, March-April 1988, 13.

23. Gary North, lecture given at the National Affairs Briefing, Dallas, Tex., August 1980.

24. See for example, Gary North's "Sanctification and Perfection," *Christian Reconstruction*, March-April 1987. North says, "Will the church as a collective, covenantal organization mature unto perfection? Paul says that it will" (p. 2). Paul nowhere says that in the way North means it.

25. Gary North, "Eschatology and Personal Motivation," *Christian Reconstruction*, September-October 1987, 2.

26. Gary North, "In Defense of Biblical Bribery," in R. J. Rushdoony, *The Institutes of Biblical Law* (Phillipsburg, N.J.: Presbyterian & Reformed Publishing Co., 1973), 837.

27. Jacques Ellul, *The Subversion of Christianity* (Grand Rapids: Wm. B. Eerdmans Publishing Co., 1986), 69.

28. Ibid., 73.

29. Gary North, *Healer of the Nations: Biblical Principles for International Relations* (Fort Worth: Dominion Press, 1987), 34-36.

30. Examples are the splits between Rushdoony and North, and between North and Chilton. In addition, the Tyler, Texas, branch is beginning to move away from Bahnsen's theonomy (Gary North, "Stones and Cornerstones," 2.) Even though North is Rushdoony's son-in-law, they are not on speaking terms. North says the essence of the rift is "Tyler's disagreement with Mr. Rushdoony about the requirement of local church attendance and taking the Lord's Supper" (Gary North, "Honest Reporting as Heresy: My Response to *Christianity Today*," essay distributed by Institute for Christian Economics, 1987, 7). North contends that Rushdoony will not speak to him, even when their schedules bring them into the same room together (ibid.). Chilton's complaint is that North, his former employer, has a major character flaw: "Gary North is brilliant. He's taught me a lot. He knows a heck-of-a-lot about economics, but he also has this streak of anger and I can't explain where it comes from or why it is, but it's there. And it comes out in his theology and it's very destructive" (Chilton, *Moyers*).

31. North, "Personal Motivation," 2.

32. Personal letter from Gary North to Peter Lalonde, 30 April 1987.

33. "An Act of Contrition and Repentance," *A Manifesto for the Christian Church*, Coalition on Revival, 4 July 1986.

34. Coalition on Revival, "A Statement of Essential Truths and a Call to Action," no. 18.

35. Letter from Jay Grimstead for C.O.R., July 1987, 3.

36. Joseph C. Morecraft, III, "The Christian Reconstruction Dialogue," *The Counsel of Chalcedon*, December 1987, 6.

37. Jay Grimstead, tape recorded message given at a C.O.R. meeting at American Baptist Church of the Savior, Denver, Colo., 8 April 1987. "Most of us associated with the Coalition on Revival are premillennialists. We believe there is going to be a one thousand year reign."

38. Ibid.

39. Personal letter from Gary North to Thomas Ice, 23 June 1986.

40. Gary North, *Is the World Running Down? Crisis in the Christian Worldview* (Tyler, Tex.: Institute for Christian Economics, 1988), 295.

41. Gary North, "The Stalemate Mentality," in *Backward Christian Soldiers?*, 107.

42. Geneva Ministries has in the past used Henry Van Til's *The Calvinist Concept of Culture* as their main textbook. Van Til was not a Reconstructionist and was not a postmillennialist.

43. Wilson, *Law and Love*, 3.

44. Gary North, "Publisher's Preface" to David Chilton, *The Days of Vengeance* (Fort Worth: Dominion Press, 1987), xxxii.

45. John Frame, *"The Institutes of Biblical Law*: A Review Article," *Westminster Theological Journal* 38 (Winter 1976):195-217. See especially pp. 215-16 for Frame's comments on Reconstructionists' lack of Christian love.

46. Michael R. Gilstrap, "We're Listening! Interaction with Reader Comments," *The Geneva Review*, Special Edition, May 1988, 1.

47. Frame, "Review Article," 195.

Appendix A

Heat and Light: The Charismatic Connection

O ne of the most interesting developments within the last decade has been the surprising relationship between the Christian Reconstruction movement and the charismatic movement. Most who were following the writings of Reconstructionists before 1982 never would have thought that such a relationship would be possible.

SHIFTING ATTITUDES TOWARD CHARISMATICS

Historically, Calvinism and charisma have not mixed. Nevertheless, many within the two movements have much in common and if current trends continue will be deeply intertwined by the 1990s.

Earlier Anticharismatic Stance

Judging from a few comments by Reconstructionists, one gets the impression that, next to dispensationalists, Pentecostals are one of the last groups they would want to be around. Rushdoony has said,

If the law is denied as the means of sanctification, then, logically, the only alternative is Pentecostalism, with its antinomian and unbiblical doctrine of the Spirit. Pentecostalism does, however, represent a very logical outgrowth of antinomian theology.[1]

In Arminian churches, and especially the so-called "holiness" churches (Pentecostal and others), sanctification is associated with various emotional binges which are far closer to the methods of ancient Baal worship, which, in its extreme, went into cutting and even castrating oneself. . . . Because of its radical antinomianism, modernism is often congenial to various aspects of Pentecostalism, speaking in tongues in particular. In all these manifestations, man's way is paramount.[2]

James Jordan echoes a similar sentiment:

Pentecostalism also all too often has little use for Scripture. The emphasis in the movement as a whole is upon direct, mystical experiences with God (roughly defined). The stimulation of glands has priority over the reformation of life. This is most pronounced in the various healing cults and "name it and claim it" sects, which are all over the airwaves today. This is nothing more than medicine man religion, and scarcely Christian at all. It has little more relation to Christianity than do the "cargo cults" of Polynesia. Not all charismatics are this bad, of course, but the tendency is there in all too many of them. The effect is that the Word of God is rendered null and void.[3]

The Thawing-Out Process Begins
Developments in the last few years have witnessed a cooling off—or perhaps we should say a warming up—by

Reconstructionists toward charismatics and Pentecostals.[4] Certain charismatics (the positive confession/manifest sons/restoration wing) are merging with certain Calvinists (the Reconstructionists) because at heart their theology is the same. It has just taken a while for them to realize the affinities. North rightly notes that his Reformed brethren are skeptical about the merger:

> This growing alliance between charismatics and Reconstructionists has disturbed Reformed Presbyterians almost as much as it has disturbed premillennial dispensationalists. It has led to accusations of heresy against both groups from all sides. . . . This represents one of the most fundamental realignments in U.S. Protestant church history.[5]

One indicator of the thaw between the two groups was a meeting in Dallas in October 1987 billed as "The Christian Reconstruction Dialogue." The meeting was attended by about a hundred people from throughout the United States and six foreign countries.[6] The gathering was held so that the leaders of "the various streams of the Christian Reconstruction Movement could come together and get to know each other." One attendee, Joe Morecraft, further explains,

> It was a "dialogue" in that we spent most of our time talking to each other, openly and honestly, about the ingredients of the Christian Reconstruction Movement we all had in common, and the places where we disagreed. Even in these areas, we found that we were moving toward a consensus. I would imagine that this meeting was much like an embryonic ecumenical council, similar to those of the early church.[7]

Roughly two-thirds of those present were charismatics and one-third noncharismatic Calvinists, among them Morecraft, Jay Grimstead of the Coalition on Revival (C.O.R.), Gary North, and Rousas J. Rushdoony. Some of the charismatics present were Dennis Peacocke, Bob Mumford of the shepherding movement, John Mears, and Earl Paulk.

Morecraft believes this coming together and blending of the strengths of each group will produce a greater corporate effect. He excitedly says that "God is blending Presbyterian theology with Charismatic zeal into a force that cannot be stopped."[8] This statement portrays a naive assumption that charismatics do not have a theology which accounts for their zeal or that they can adopt Presbyterian theology and maintain their zeal.

Morecraft then lists those beliefs held in common by both Calvinists and charismatics and viewed by both groups as the fundamentals of the Christian Reconstruction movement:

First, Christ is Lord of every area of life and society.

Second, the Bible applies to every area of life and society.

Third, Christians are accountable to the Great Commission of Matthew 28 and the Dominion Mandate of Genesis 1:28.

Fourth, biblical law, of both O.T. and N.T., is still applicable today.

Fifth, there must be a personal, cultural, and historical victory-orientation to the Christian Reconstruction Movement.

Sixth, the church is God's instrument of revival-reformation-reconstruction in the world.

Seventh, the Kingdom of Christ was inaugurated with the life, death and resurrection of Christ and is advancing progressively through history to triumphant consummation at Christ's physical return to earth.

Eighth, knowledge of church history is essential to Christian Reconstruction.

Ninth, the work of Christian Reconstruction is the work of the Holy Spirit. It can be done only in his power and under his leading.

Tenth, the starting point and goal of Christian Reconstruction is the true worship of the triune God in spirit and in truth.[9]

No wonder Morecraft was so excited about the meeting. The Reconstructionists have every major plank in their system spelled out in this ten point affirmation. (There may be some among the hundred attendees who consider themselves to be premillennialists, but that position is inconsistent with point seven.)

In a surprising statement for one who is supposed to be not only a Reformed Calvinist but a follower of Van Til, Morecraft enthusiastically declares,

God is mixing the LIGHT of the Reformed Faith with the HEAT of the Charismatic Movement. A person can be in the light, and freeze to death. He can also be warm but be in total darkness. It is the mixture of light and heat that brings forth life and growth.[10]

The Difficulty of the Mixture

Why is Morecraft's perspective on the synthesis of Reformed theology and the charismatic movement anti-Van Til? To put it as simply as we know how, the synthesis between two conflicting perspectives is wrong. If the Reformed faith is the outworking of a proper understanding of God's Word while charismatic doctrines are not, which Calvinists advocate, then to try to blend truth and error is a compromise of the truth.

If Van Til's approach of starting with God and his inerrant Word and developing the biblical system from within Scripture itself is true,[11] then Morecraft has in effect abandoned a tenet of his Reformed faith in order to try to effect a greater good—the bringing in of the kingdom.

Rather than using the analogy of heat and light, a better example would be a favorite one of Van Til—light and darkness. If the Reformed faith is true, then you cannot mix it with charismatic practice, which is the product of charismatic theology. Since Calvinism and charismatic theology are at odds on many points, Morecraft, along with other Reconstructionists who think along the same lines, should lay aside their Reformed faith and embrace the charismatic approach. Or they should get in step with their Reformed faith and drive out the leaven of the wrong theology and practice of charismatics.

Writing within a Van Tilian framework, Gary North has said that since one cannot over a long period of time act contrary to one's beliefs, either the new right would have to change its theology and become more Calvinistic and postmillennial or eventually they would withdraw from political involvement.[12] Whether this is true is not the point here. But if it is intellectual schizophrenia for one group to believe one thing and act contrary to that belief, then that charge also applies to Reconstructionists who act similarly.

Those who say that Calvinists and charismatics can meaningfully get together should follow the advice North gave to the new Christian right. If the Reconstructionist view of things is correct, they should be faithful to their own theology and trust that God will bring in the kingdom in his own time, rather than give in to what appears to us to be the hope of some visible success and expansion of their numbers and influence by merging with other less orthodox trends. If their theology is correct, then they should wait until the charismatics become more orthodox and Reformed before they intermingle. After all, a good Calvinist should say, "Is anything too hard for the Lord!"

A Synthetic Worship

A specific example of this synthesis is seen in Morecraft's desire that charismatic and Calvinist worship influence each other. "I particularly pray that Calvinists and charismatics will influence each other in their doctrines of worship."[13] Notice that Morecraft says "*doctrines* of worship."

Apparently his prayer is being answered, at least within the Calvinist camp. Peter Leithart discusses in a recent article the value of the fact that many within the Reformed faith are being influenced by charismatics. After noting some of the strengths of charismatic worship Leithart says:

> At its best, Charismatic worship focuses on the Lord, not on the preacher or even the experience of the worshiper. The Charismatic movement has, in short, challenged evangelicalism in general and the Reformed community in particular to rethink traditional forms of worship.[14]

Leithart does not draw any hard and fast conclusions in his article, and he thinks the Reformed faith should in most ways stay the course in their worship tradition. But he clearly thinks it is a good idea for Reformed worshipers to be open to learning from their charismatic, Reconstructionist brothers.

What is amazing about Leithart's openness to considering some degree of synthesis between charismatic and Reformed worship is that he has argued elsewhere that subjectivism (which is similar to, and even more developed in, today's charismatic movement) was one of the main causes for the decline of Puritan Christianity, which he thinks so highly of.[15] He sees the Reconstructionist movement as a restoration of Puritanism.

> Reconstructionist Christianity is far more than a resurrection of Puritanism. It is a refined Puritanism, tried in the furnace of opposition (Ps. 66:10f.), and hence more consistent to the basic premises of Calvinism than seventeenth-century Puritanism.[16]

Is charismatic worship more consistent with the basic premises of Calvinism? We do not think so, and most Reformed Christians would agree this surfaces one of the historic problems with which postmillennialism has been plagued.

THE HISTORIC PROBLEM OF AMALGAMATION

The postmillennialists' optimistic approach to Christianity and the world often has them working with unbelievers and believers who are less than orthodox. The result is often a movement that goes beyond what a biblical Christian could support. One of those situations was the postmillennial involvement in the rise and development of the Social Gospel of the last century. Gary Scott Smith has shown recently that a large segment of the Social Gospel movement actually was given its direction and impetus by evangelicals, not liberals:

> During the one hundred years prior to the development of [the Social Gospel] in the 1870s and 1880s, however, many evangelicals labored vigorously to improve social conditions. . . . Evangelical Christians provided the example, inspiration, and principles for much of the Social Gospel . . . [but] the evangelical ideology of the millennium merged without a break into what came to be called the Social Gospel in the years after 1870.[17]

This is not to say that evangelical postmillennialists wanted the movement to end up in the secular humanism of today, but their social action did contribute to and often merged into the Social Gospel. They held similar views with liberal postmillennialists and thus joined forces to try to influence society in a common direction.[18] As is often the case, many today would be horrified at what has grown out of the seeds of good intent. Much of liberalism's New Deal and the Great Society during the last sixty years have had the corrupted goal of bringing in a man-made messianic kingdom.

This postmillennial impetus within liberal humanism is one of the main points Rushdoony notes in his work, *The Messianic Character of American Education*.[19] He points out mistakes the early Puritans made in establishing public education, how it was later corrupted and then used by the unitarians (and now the progressives) to bring in the messianic socialist state.

Postmillennialism has had other troublesome associations in its past. David Chilton is forced to acknowledge some of the less desirable members within the postmillennial family tree: "Examples of the Postmillenarian heresy would be easy to name as well: the Munster Revolt of 1534, Nazism, and Marxism (whether "Christian" or otherwise)."[20]

Why will Chilton own up to these "heresies" but not the postmillennial link with the Social Gospel movement?[21] Perhaps the latter association strikes too close to home. The wedding of certain charismatic theologies with the Reconstruction movement may be too similar to what occurred over a hundred years ago when Puritan postmillennialism degenerated into the Social Gospel. If this is indeed happening, then we can expect to see the spread of optimistic eschatology at the expense of historic orthodoxy. The bad theology of some of the charismatics will, if they continue to intermingle, overpower and conquer the orthodoxy of the well-intentioned Reconstructionists. And once again, the tendency of postmillennialism to raise false hope will have occurred. This pessimistic result could very well contribute to the apostasy the Bible warns the church against.

Will today's new improved version of postmillennialism be able to avoid this traditional pitfall? Not likely, since a synthesis between many of the "positive confession" charismatics and Reconstructionists is already taking place.

THE BURGEONING ALLIANCE WITH CHARISMATICS

The Positive Confession Link

Perhaps *optimism* can account for the attraction the Reconstructionists have for certain charismatics, especially those in "positive confession" circles. Gary North notes the spread of postmillennial optimism into this branch of the charismatic movement as he critiques Dave Hunt's *The Seduction of Christianity*:

> [Hunt] implicitly associates New Age optimism with an optimistic eschatology. He recognizes (as few of the "positive confession" leaders have recognized) that they have become operational postmillennialists. . . . He sees clearly that a new eschatology is involved in "positive confession," a dominion eschatology.[22]

North later boasts of an inroad of Reconstructionist views into the ministry of positive confession minister Robert Tilton:

> Mr. Hunt understands far better than most observers what is really taking place. Indeed, it has already begun: bringing together the postmillennial Christian reconstructionists and the "positive confession" charismatics. . . . It began when Robert Tilton's wife read Gary DeMar's *God and Government* in late 1983, and then persuaded her husband to invite a group of reconstructionists to speak before 1,000 "positive confession" pastors and their wives at a January 1984 rally sponsored by Rev. Tilton's church. The all-day panel was very well received. . . .
>
> Mr. Hunt sees that if this fusion of theological interests takes place, then the day of unchallenged dominance by the old-timed dispensational eschatology is about to come to an end. A new fundamentalism is appearing.[23]

In a later essay, North admits to some potential problems with misdirected optimism:

> If all a person gains from the Christian Reconstruction movement in general is its optimistic eschatology, then he is skating on thin ice. Optimism is not enough. In fact, optimism alone is highly dangerous.

The Communists have a doctrine of inevitable victory; so do radical Muslims. So did a group of revolutionary communist murderers and polygamists, the Anabaptists who captured the German city of Munster from 1525-35, before they were defeated militarily by Christian forces. Optimism in the wrong hands is a dangerous weapon.[24]

The reason these two movements are coming together is simple. They both believe that if a theology is positive, then it must be right. Charismatics have optimism which is applied to their personal life, while Reconstructionists have stressed social optimism. North explains why they have joined hands:

> Some Pentecostals weren't satisfied. They had seen God at work. . . . They recognized that God moves in history to heal the sick and dying. Always in the back of any Pentecostal's mind is this nagging question: "If God can heal a sick person, why can't He heal a sick society?" . . . Then, in the late 1970s, a handful of Pentecostal-charismatics discovered Christian Reconstruction. They finally got the answer they had been waiting for: God can heal a sick society. Better yet: God will heal a sick world through a great movement of the Holy Spirit. These men dropped dispensationalism, and adopted a world-and-life view that is consistent with the victories that charismatics have seen first-hand."[25]

In this case it was not a matter of a positive and a negative attracting, but two positives joining together.

This misguided optimism is, however, a major error within the Reconstructionist movement. As we've already seen, it was postmillennialism that provided the optimistic climate in which the Social Gospel grew.

In spite of his warning about misdirected optimism, North claims his efforts have caused the spread of the optimistic eschatology within charismatic circles: "I am probably the per-

son most responsible for devising a strategy for speeding up
this drift toward postmillennialism, which I think Mr. Hunt is
aware of."[26]

It appears that many Reconstructionists feel they can work
with various groups, even those with opposing beliefs in important areas of theology,[27] because they believe God has destined
the course of this age to be one of a gradual Christianization
of the world, rather than the apostasy that will lead up to the
great tribulation and Christ's second coming.

The Kingdom Theology Link

Bishop Earl Paulk is probably the most visible and well-
known leader within the broader movement often called
"Dominion Theology," "Kingdom Theology," or "Kingdom
Now." He is pastor of the twelve thousand member Chapel
Hill Harvester Church in Atlanta, and he has a nationwide
weekly television program on the Trinity Broadcasting Network
(TBN). Gary North has spoken at a conference on dominion
theology at Paulk's church and advises them in the area of
Christian Reconstruction.

Bishop Paulk gives the following definition of kingdom
theology:

> Scripture teaches that the Kingdom of God is always
> now. The Kingdom of God is the rule of God in the
> universe; it is at hand in any generation who reaches
> out to understand that the rule of God is within us.
> The Kingdom of God within believers takes on the
> characteristics of salt and light in impacting the sys-
> tems of this world. . . .
>
> The exciting challenge of demonstrating responsible
> Christianity is waking up a generation of young
> people to confront the oppressive ideologies of Marx-
> ism. God is calling forth the best that is within
> us—talents, intellect, skills—to confront the king-
> doms of this world with alternatives which come

from the Lord. In every area of life, God is giving solutions to the perplexities of this age to people of faith and prayer.[28]

Paulk, like Reconstructionists, does not believe that Israel and the church are distinct entities within God's single plan: "I believe that references to Israel in Scripture refer both to natural Israel as well as to the Church."[29] Bishop Paulk's brother and fellow minister, Don Paulk, adds: "The Church today is Spiritual Israel. When we speak of blessing Israel, that refers to blessing the cause of God."[30] Therefore, they adopt much of the biblical teaching about Israel's place in the future kingdom and apply it to the church today (thus the designation "kingdom now"). This is another similarity between Reconstructionists and charismatics.

The rapture is called by Paulk, "The Great Escape Theory."[31] He believes this doctrine hinders the church from its job of establishing the kingdom of God on earth before Christ returns. Paulk believes further that the establishment of the kingdom is being prevented by disunity in the church. It is instructive to note who he considers legitimate members of the church:

> What would a meeting be like which brought together liberal evangelicals, such as we are, conservative theologians, represented by Holiness groups and Southern Baptists, and Catholics, Seventh-Day Adventists, and members of the Church of Jesus Christ of Latter-Day Saints? Many of these groups have become so different that we almost regard them as enemies, rather than as brothers and sisters in the faith. How can we step over these walls that have been built so high?
>
> It is my honest opinion that bridging these walls is what Paul is talking about when he says that the Kingdom of God cannot come to pass until "we all come in the unity of the faith." He specifically does

not say anything about doctrine, because he is not concerned about doctrinal points. . . . [32]

As long as the world of religion continues to act as it is acting now, there will never be a Kingdom of God in reality. For so long as we have said, "Why don't the Seventh-Day Adventists change? Why don't the Mormons change?" Perhaps we should be the ones to change.[33]

Paulk wants to know how to "step over these walls that have been built so high." It is clear that he believes the wall between Christianity and Mormonism is to be torn down by eliminating the doctrinal differences that separate us. Does he not realize that for us to change and become like the Mormons would require us to deny Jesus Christ? Someone willing to deny the faith for the sake of "unity" would be willing to believe many other false doctrines as well. Is this the kind of person Reconstructionists, who are doctrinally oriented people, want to team up with?

We have searched the Bible in vain for the passage where the apostle Paul lays down the unity of the faith as a condition for the coming in of the kingdom. Paulk seems to have in mind Ephesians 4:13, yet the kingdom of God is not even found in that context. The maturing of the church, the body of Christ, is what Paul is talking about.

Moreover, how can Paulk assert that Paul is not talking about doctrine. "The unity of *the faith*" is a synonym for doctrine or teaching, the content of what we believe. In fact, Paul contrasts "the faith" in verse 13 with "every wind of doctrine" in verse 14. So Paul's appeal to unity does have something to do with doctrine after all.

The unity to be achieved is a unity of the faith which will protect the church from being tossed around by false doctrine, such as Mormonism. Apparently Paulk has not attained this unity of the faith himself or he would not be interested in merging with Mormons.

Paulk then explains how the kingdom will be brought in by the church, an explanation that has been called a "Manifest Sons of God" doctrine[34]:

> Until we come into the unity of the faith and exhibit perfection, Christ-likeness, and maturity, there is no way that Jesus Christ can come again. The apostles, prophets, evangelist, pastors, and teachers were given for the perfecting of the saints, and unless that perfection is reached, the Kingdom of God cannot be established. The whole world groans, waiting for someone to demonstrate the principles of the Kingdom, waiting until "we all come in the unity of the faith, and of the knowledge of the Son of God, unto a perfect man, unto the measure of the stature of the fullness of Christ." This is the most important and critical issue in the world today. There is absolutely no way that the Kingdom of God can come to pass until the walls of division are broken down and we comprehend what is meant by "unity of the faith."[35]

Paulk and fellow kingdom theology advocates teach that the "five fold ministries"—the ministries of apostles, prophets, evangelists, pastors, and teachers mentioned in Ephesians 4:11 for the building up of the saints—must first be restored before believers can be properly matured. (This assumes, of course, that at some point God withdrew all of these ministries, which is not true.) Then God will manifest who the true sons of God are, paving the way for Christ's second coming.[36] Once perfection is reached on earth in Christ's church, they argue, Christ will be able to return to earth:

> Some of the strongest fundamental churches still preach that Christ will return to gather national Israel unto Himself, and I say that is deception and will keep the Kingdom of God from coming to pass! Likewise, those who are waiting for Christ to catch

a few people away so God can judge the world are waiting in vain!

Jesus Christ has now done all He can do, and He waits at the right hand of His Father, until you and I as sons of God, become manifest and make this world His footstool. He is waiting for us to say, "Jesus, we have made the kingdoms of this world the Kingdom of our God, and we are ruling and reigning in Your world. Even so, come, Lord Jesus."[37]

It would be wrong even to imply that Reconstructionists believe fully in the Manifest Sons of God doctrine, but both Reconstructionists and Manifest Sons of God advocates are working toward bringing in the kingdom before Christ can return to the earth again. The Manifest Sons of God position believes the church must accomplish certain things and reach a certain level of performance, unity, and perfection before Christ can return. The church must establish the kingdom of God on this earth. To this Reconstructionists should say a hearty Amen.

Other Key Charismatic Links

Who are some of the other key charismatic players within the camp of dominion theology?

Bob Mumford of the shepherding movement has a sixteen lesson video series, "Kingdom Philosophy of Life," in which he advocates a Reconstructionist agenda. According to Mumford, a kingdom view of life needs the foundation of a doctrine of ultimate truth (permanence), a doctrine of providence (confidence), optimism toward the future (motivation), and binding comprehensive law (reconstruction).

Gary North cites five fundamental points upon which the Reconstructionist movement rests: The sovereignty of God, biblical law, Cornelius van Til's biblical presuppositionalism, biblical optimism, and the covenant.[38] Mumford has four of the five in his system.

Bob Weiner of Maranatha Campus Ministries was one of the first to start sending his college students to Reconstructionist conferences. North notes that "the leadership of Maranatha is devotedly postmillennial."[39]

Many have wondered whether Pat Robertson is a Reconstructionist. The official answer appears to be no. However, since he has had Rushdoony and North as guests on the "700 Club" a number of times over the years and has faculty at his university who either are Reconstructionists or sympathetic to their causes, it is probable that he has been greatly influenced by the movement. Joe Kickasola, a professor at CBN University, has taught a course called "Law and Society: A Basic Course in Theonomy" in the graduate school.[40] Guest lecturers during the semester included Rushdoony and Greg Bahnsen. Harvard Law School graduate Herbert Titus, dean of the Schools of Law and Public Policy, contributed an essay to Rushdoony's *Law and Society*.[41]

Gary North often talks of those who, like Pat Robertson, consider themselves premillennialists but operate like postmillennialists.[42] In fact North points out that,

> Pat Robertson was so concerned (with good reason) that his evangelist peers might think that he had switched to Chilton's version of postmillennialism that he wrote a personal letter to many of them (including one to me) in the summer of 1986 that stated that he had not adopted Chilton's theology.[43]

What kind of language is Pat Robertson using that would cause some to think he has become a postmillennialist? One major example was the keynote address he gave at Dallas '84, a convention for Maranatha Campus Ministries. After making a reference to Beatle John Lennon's song, "Imagine," Robertson first called for his listeners to imagine a world free of godlessness, evil, and degradation, a world where righteousness prevails and God's Word and those who teach it are welcomed and honored. Then he said:

> Now you say, "That sounds like the Millennium."
> Well maybe some of it does, but some of it we're
> going to see. These things can take place now in
> this time . . . and they are going to because I am
> persuaded that we are standing on the brink of the
> greatest spiritual revival the world has ever known!
> . . . Hundreds of millions of people are coming into
> the kingdom . . . in the next several years.[44]

Regardless of what one thinks about theological labels, Pat
Robertson may be one of the most postmillennial premillennialists ever to have walked the earth. It is evident he has been
deeply influenced by the Reconstructionists.

There are a number of other charismatics who have been
influenced to some degree by Reconstructionism. By no means
a complete list, we could include charismatics such as Larry
Lea, Dennis Peacocke, and Richard Hogue. In addition, many
lesser-known pastors are now proclaiming a dominion message.

DOMINION PARALLELS BETWEEN RECONSTRUCTIONISTS AND CHARISMATICS

We believe the reason Reconstructionists and certain
charismatics are finding a common basis for cooperation is
theological. Many of their beliefs are similar in their conclusions. Though they often arrive at these conclusions by different
means, the deeper one looks at what both believe and teach,
the greater the similarities.

Before we make the comparisons, let it be clearly understood that Reconstructionists are well within the stream of
historic, Christian orthodoxy. They believe in the Trinity, the
inerrancy of Scripture, the deity and humanity of Jesus, total
depravity, salvation by grace through faith, and godliness in
the Christian walk. They are orthodox, Reformed Calvinists in
most areas of theology. Therefore, we are not saying they
believe that men can become "gods," as most of the Manifest
Sons of God (MSOG) or Latter Rain charismatics teach.

We also are not saying that all of the categories dealt with below are wrong, just that the two traditions have parallel beliefs. However, it is interesting that, independent of each other and based upon different approaches, these two diverse groups have arrived at remarkably similar teachings. This affinity is now being developed as the two groups are reading each other's materials, working together on many projects, and attempting a synthesis between the two traditions. Gary North sees the Reconstructionists as the brains of the movement and the charismatics as the feet.[45]

1. Adam's Lost Dominion.

MSOG: "Some believe that when Adam and Eve committed 'grand treason' and lost dominion over the earth. . . ."[46]
Reconstructionist: "Why doesn't God seem to own [the earth] now? Why are some areas of life seemingly under the exclusive control of Satan, the evil one? Because Adam sold his birthright to Satan."[47]

2. Dominion over the Earth.

MSOG: "God's people are going to start to exercise rule, and they're going to take dominion over the power of Satan."[48] "We are rulers of this planet—it's time we take over!"[49]
Reconstructionists: "But it is dominion that we are after. Not just a voice. It is dominion we are after. Not just influence. It is dominion we are after. Not just equal time. It is dominion we are after. World conquest."[50]

3. Kingdom Now.

MSOG: "Scripture teaches that the Kingdom of God is always now."[51]
Reconstructionists: "Christians rule with Christ in His Kingdom now, in this age."[52]

4. Bringing in or Establishing the Kingdom.

MSOG: "The kingdoms of this world must become the Kingdoms of our God. And we are the ones to do it! . . . I want to . . . see the Kingdom of God established NOW! We will learn how to literally take over a city."[53]

Reconstructionist: "As Christ-followers we are to establish dominion, we are to establish Christ's Kingdom, which is to consume all other kingdoms."[54]

5. **Israel**.

MSOG: "There is no more old covenant with Israel, and there never will be."[55]

Reconstructionist: "Ethnic Israel was excommunicated for its apostasy and will never again be God's Kingdom. . . . The Bible does not tell of any future plan for Israel as a special nation."[56]

6. **Restoration**.

MSOG: "We do not live in the time of the great falling away. We are leaving that day and entering a new day, a new age, a new beginning of life and restoration."[57]

Reconstructionists: "The kingdom of God becomes truly worldwide in scope. This involves the beginning of the restoration of the cursed world. The curse will then be lifted progressively by God."[58]

7. **The Rapture**.

MSOG: "Some are also anti-rapture—rather than go to heaven. God's Army of Overcomers will establish the Kingdom of God on earth."[59]

Reconstructionists: "The modern doctrine of the 'Rapture' is too often a doctrine of flight from the world, in which Christians are taught to long for escape from the world and its problems, rather than for what God's Word promises us: Dominion. . . . A good deal of modern Rapturism should be recognized for what it really is: a dangerous error that is teaching God's people to expect defeat instead of victory."[60]

8. **Breakthroughs/New Revelation**.[61]

MSOG: "The offices of apostle and prophet have the anointing to perceive and proclaim new revelation truth. The apostle and prophet have the ministry to establish and lay the foundation for new truth in the Church. . . . Once an apostle or prophet receives by the Spirit a new restorational truth and establishes it as a valid ministry then the teacher teaches it in detail."[62]

Reconstructionists: These remarkable, path-breaking discoveries can be found in his book, *That You May Prosper*. . . . Sutton's thoroughgoing development of the covenant structure has to be regarded as the most important single theological breakthrough in the Christian Reconstruction movement since the publication of R. J. Rushdoony's *Institutes of Biblical Law*.[63]

9. The Second Coming.

MSOG: "Jesus Christ has now done all He can do, and He waits at the right hand of His Father, until you and I as sons of God, become manifest and make this world His footstool. He is waiting for us to say, 'Jesus, we have made the kingdoms of this world the Kingdom of our God, and we are ruling and reigning in Your world.'"[64]

Reconstructionists: "The Bible teaches that the Second Coming of Christ . . . will take place at the end of the Millennium. . . . Until then, Christ and His people are marching forth from strength to strength, from victory to victory. We shall overcome."[65]

10. The Manifest Sons of God.

MSOG: "Jesus Christ has now done all He can do, and He waits at the right hand of His Father, until you and I as sons of God, become manifest and make this world His footstool."[66]

"The true Body of Christ, which is the True Church, will eventually become mature and be manifested as God's great family of Sons."[67]

Reconstructionists: The whole creation awaits the godly dominion of the New Creation saints of God (Rom. 8:19-23). . . . The whole of creation groans and travails in pain earnestly awaiting the manifestation of the sons of God (Rom. 8:22, 19).[68]

11. **The Curse Removed**.

MSOG: "When the church becomes so conformed to His image that those who die do not pass through the grave, but become instead gloriously changed in the twinkling of an eye, it will be that church which will bring the Kingdom of God to pass on the earth (Rom. 8:18, 22-23; Eph. 1:13-14). . . . Death will not be conquered by Jesus returning to the earth. It will be conquered when the church stands up boldly and says, "We have dominion over the earth!"[69]

Reconstructionists: "Victory in history is not going to be a discontinuous, unexpected event for God's people. Each Christian's victory over spiritual death at the day of resurrection is to be preceded by a partial, imperfect spiritual victory, in time and on earth, through personal self-discipline in terms of God's law. Similarly, victory over physical death also will not be a discontinuous event: we are told by God that we shall expect health, long life, and an end to miscarriages."[70]

"The kingdom of God becomes truly worldwide in scope. This involves the beginning of the restoration of the cursed world. The curse will then be lifted progressively by God."[71]

"Preaching the gospel should be so comprehensive as to affect every individual, group, institution, and nation. The curse of sin and death is removed as more and more people come under the preaching of the gospel (Rom. 8:18- 25)."[72]

11. **Coming Revival**.

MSOG: "Whole nations will turn to God. The Church will become glorious and victorious and cause the glory of the Lord to fill the earth as the waters cover the sea."[73]

Reconstructionists: "A coming revival, possibly before the twentieth century is over, a revival greater than any other in man's history."[74]

12. **The Church as Spiritual/New Israel**.

MSOG: "The Church today is Spiritual Israel."[75]

Reconstructionists: "The Church is spiritual Israel."[76]

13. **Unity of the Church**.

    MSOG: "When we reach the place where our total beings are devoted to this truth, and we are all hearing the same voice of God, we will be able to demonstrate to the world that we have transcended our doctrinal differences and are witnesses to the unity of the faith, that will bring about the establishment of the Kingdom of God. This is what God has called us to do."[77]

    Reconstructionists: "The quest for spiritual unity among all redeemed men is not only legitimate; it is required by God. . . . Christians are to work toward the creation of a one-world Christian order."[78]

14. **Covenant Theology**.[79]

    MSOG: "In almost any Christian bookstore, about 99% of the books will say that 'God's timeclock is Israel' and that 'God's covenant is still with Israel.' There is no comprehension that, according to God's Word, the old covenant is dead and gone and the new covenant is with the people who accept Jesus Christ as Lord and Saviour. Whatever has been written concerning the law and prophecies about Israel as a nation is now transferred to spiritual Israel, which is the people of God."[80]

    Reconstructionists: "So, the historical difference is that God's first bride was Israel of the Old Covenant. As a people, she was divorced and excommunicated. Since God could never do this to His own Son on a permanent basis— even when Christ died and was cut off, God raised Him from the dead—the New Covenant Bride will never be cast aside.[81]

The two major wings of dominion theology, the Manifest Sons of God and the Reconstructionists, have much in common theologically. Their common beliefs in many areas (although they are not in agreement in many other areas and often arrive at similar positions by different ways) should prove a fertile ground for a close relationship in coming days.

CONCLUSION

If postmillennialism is wrong, which we believe it is, then the church age will end in apostasy, not revival. If premillennialism is correct, and we believe that it is, then those who believe that the church is to bring in the kingdom before the return of Jesus Christ have made a major error in their understanding of the Bible. It is impossible to wrongly interpret such vast amounts of Scripture without harmful results. One harmful result is that the Reconstructionists will influence a large segment of the church to set its mind on the things that are on earth and not on things above (Colossians 3:2). This wrong perspective will lead to a wrong merger with the things and systems of this world, rather than calling this world to flee from the wrath to come by seeking refuge in Jesus Christ.

Appendix A, Notes

1. Rousas J. Rushdoony, *The Institutes of Biblical Law* (Phillipsburg, N.J.: Presbyterian & Reformed Publishing Co., 1973), 307.

2. Ibid., 552-53.

3. James B. Jordan, *The Sociology of the Church* (Tyler, Tex.: Geneva Ministries, 1986), 8.

4. This fact has been acknowledged by Gary North in an article entitled "Reconstructionist Renewal and Charismatic Renewal" in the May-June 1988 issue of *Christian Reconstruction*. In fact the essay was sparked by North's being informed about the contents of this appendix in advance of publication.

5. Gary North, "Reconstructionist Renewal and Charismatic Renewal," *Christian Reconstruction*, May-June 1988, 2.

6. Joseph C. Morecraft, III, "The Christian Reconstruction Dialogue," *The Council of Chalcedon*, December 1987, 6.

7. Ibid.

8. Ibid., 7.

9. Ibid.

10. Ibid.

11. This means that the biblical approach to life and issues is self-contained within the Scriptures and does not need help from other approaches from without, or a synthesis of two systems to produce a third greater or stronger approach.

12. Gary North, "The Intellectual Schizophrenia of the New Christian Right," *Christianity & Civilization: The Failure of the American Baptist Culture*, ed. James B. Jordan (Spring 1982):1-40.

13. Morecraft, "Dialogue," 7.

14. Peter Leithart, "Liturgy or Chaos?" *The Geneva Review*, January 1988, 4.

15. Peter J. Leithart, "Revivalism and American Protestantism," *Christianity & Civilization: The Reconstruction of the Church*, ed. James B. Jordan (1985):46-84.

16. Ibid., 81.

17. Gary Scott Smith, "The Men and Religion Forward Movement of 1911-12," *Westminster Theological Journal* 49 (Spring 1987):92-93.

18. Among the Social Gospel advocates who claimed to be postmillennial was Shirley Jackson Case. Case, professor of early church history and New Testament interpretation at the University of Chicago, wrote *The Millennial Hope: A Phase of War-Time Thinking* (1918) as a polemic against the rising tide of premillennialism during the First World War. He identified himself as a postmillennialist:

"The [postmillennialists] do not look for early relief through the sudden coming of Christ. On the contrary, they expect a gradual and increasing success of Christianity in the present world until ideal conditions are finally realized. Then will follow the millennium. At its close a brief period of apostasy will set in. . . . After the brief period of final tribulation is past, Christ will come in glory, a general resurrection will occur, judgment will be enacted, the old world will be destroyed by fire, the wicked will be consigned to torment, and the righteous will enter upon an eternal life of bliss." (Shirley Jackson Case, *The Millennial Hope: A Phase of War-Time Thinking* [Chicago: University of Chicago Press, 1918], 209.)

19. R. J. Rushdoony, *The Messianic Character of American Education: Studies in the History of the Philosophy of Education* (Nutley, N.J.: The Craig Press, 1963).

20. David Chilton, "Orthodox Christianity and the Millenarian Heresy," *The Geneva Review*, June 1985, 3.

21. Chilton writes, "The dominion outlook is equated with the liberal "Social Gospel" movement in the early 1900s. Such an identification is utterly absurd, devoid of any foundation whatsoever. The leaders of the Social Gospel movement were evolutionary humanists and socialists, and were openly hostile toward Biblical Christianity. It is true that they borrowed certain terms and concepts from Christianity, in order to pervert them for their own uses. Thus they talked about the "Kingdom of God," but what they meant was far removed from the traditional Christian faith" (David Chilton, *Paradise Restored: A Biblical Theology of Dominion* [Fort Worth: Dominion Press, 1985], 228). Why would someone like Shirley Jackson Case, "a Social Gospeler," write a whole book defending what he called postmillennialism against the pessimistic premillennialism of his day, if he did not view himself as an optimistic postmillennialist? (Case, *Millennial Hope*, 209.)

22. Gary North, *Unholy Spirits: Occultism and New Age Humanism* (Fort Worth: Dominion Press, 1986), 388-89.

23. Ibid., 392-93. The 17 March 1987 issue of the *Austin American-Statesman*, page A-11, ran an article entitled "Born-again Christians, 'kingdom theology' vs. communists." The story centered around Bishop Earl

Paulk of the ten-thousand-member congregation at Chapel Hill Harvester Church in Decatur, Georgia. It tells of Paulk's conversion to "kingdom theology" about six years ago, and that Gary North was a keynote speaker at a recent conference at their church, as well as the fact that North serves as an adviser to one of the church's ministries. Paulk, in his book *Held in the Heavens Until* . . . (Atlanta: Kingdom Dimension Publishers, 1985), argues that Christ cannot come back to the earth until a certain amount of dominion (maturity) is achieved by the church. This appears to be a blend of postmillennialism with the old Pentecostal error often called the "Manifest Sons of God" teaching.

24. Gary North, "Chilton, Sutton, and Dominion Theology," Undated essay published by Institute for Christian Economics, p. 4. Rushdoony acknowledges growth of their views among the charismatics also: "So, years ago I came to the post-mil faith. *Now it's growing like wildfire all over the country.* It is spreading into Baptist circles, as is theonomy. A very large section of the charismatic movement is becoming Reformed, theonomic, and postmillennial, also" (Michael D. Philbeck, "An Interview with R. J. Rushdoony," *The Council of Chalcedon*, October 1983, 14.) It could be questioned as to just how Reformed the charismatic movement is becoming.

25. North, "Reconstructionist Renewal," 2.

26. North, *Unholy Spirits*, 391.

27. North admits in *Unholy Spirits* that people such as Robert Tilton have some real theological problems:

"Mr. Hunt points out that the language used by other 'positive confession' ministers is similar to the man-deifying language of the New Age 'positive thinking' theology. There is no doubt that this accusation can be documented, and that some of these leaders need to get clear the crucial distinction between the imputed human perfection of Jesus Christ and the non-communicable divinity of Jesus Christ. This Creator-creature distinction is the most important doctrine separating the New Agers and orthodox Christianity." (p. 388)

"Mr. Hunt implies that the poor wording of the 'positive confession' charismatics' Christology reflects their eschatology. It doesn't. It simply reflects their sloppy wording and their lack of systematic study of theology and its implications, at least at this relatively early point in the development of the 'positive confession' movement's history." (p. 392)

28. Earl Paulk, "Paulk Answers," *Thy Kingdom Come*, November 1987, 2-3.

29. Ibid., 3.

30. Don Paulk, "Editorial Comment," *Thy Kingdom Come*, November 1987, 1.

31. Earl Paulk, *The Great Escape Theory* (Decatur, Ga.: Chapel Hill Harvester Church, n.d.).

32. Earl Paulk, *Unity of Faith* (Decatur, Ga.: Chapel Hill Harvester Church, n.d.), 4.

33. Ibid., 8.

34. This idea of manifesting the sons of God comes from Romans 8:18-23. However, this passage says the sons of God will be revealed at the redemption of the body, or the resurrection, not during the present time. For further

understanding on the Manifest Sons of God teachings see Albert James Dager, "Kingdom Theology," part 3, *Media Spotlight*, 1987, 14-21; Pauline Griego MacPherson, *Can the Elect Be Deceived?* (Denver: Bold Truth Press, 1986), especially ch. 4; Richard M. Riss, *Latter Rain* (Etobicoke, Ont.: Honeycomb Visual Productions, 1987); and Judith A. Matta, *The Born Again Jesus of the Word-Faith Teaching* (Fullerton, Calif.: Spirit of Truth Ministry, 1987).

35. Paulk, *Unity of Faith*, 12-13.

36. Manifest Sons of God prophet Bill Hamon summarizes the doctrine in the following way:

The Company of Prophets will prepare the way for the restoration of the office of the apostle which will take place in the 1990s.

The restoration of the apostle to full recognition and authority will bring the Church to maturity, unity, and proper church structure. Signs and wonders will be wrought which will cause the world to look to the Church for answers and miracles needed. Whole nations will turn to God. The Church will become glorious and victorious and cause the glory of the Lord to fill the earth as the waters cover the sea. When all five-fold ministries are fully restored, all the saints are moving in their membership ministry, and the Church is unified and perfected, then Jesus can return and set up His Kingdom and establish His eternal reign with His Bride/Church. Planet Earth will be purified to become the headquarters for Jesus and His Church to rule and reign over His vast domain forever and ever and even forevermore. Amen! (Bill Hamon, "God's Wave of Restoration for the 1980s," *Thy Kingdom Come*, August 1987, 11.)

37. Earl Paulk, *The Handwriting on the Wall* (Decatur: Ga.: Chapel Hill Harvester Church, n.d.), 20.

38. Gary North, "Chilton, Sutton, and Dominion Theology," 3.

39. Gary North, "Competence, Common Grace, and Dominion," *Biblical Economics Today*, June-July 1985, 4.

40. Joe Kickasola, "Law and Society: A Basic Course in Theonomy," cassette recordings from the Mt. Olive Tape Library, Mt. Olive, Miss.

41. Rousas Rushdoony, *Law and Society: Institutes of Biblical Law*, vol. 2 (Vallecito, Calif.: Ross House Books, 1982), 710-26.

42. For example, see North's comments on page 1 of "Chilton, Sutton, and Dominion Theology."

43. Ibid.

44. Tape recording of a speech given by Pat Robertson at "Dallas '84," Maranatha Campus Ministries convention, cited by Albert James Dager, "Kingdom Theology," *Media Spotlight*, part 3, 1987, 12-13.

45. Personal letter from Gary North to Peter Lalonde, 30 April 1987.

46. MacPherson, *Can the Elect Be Deceived?*, 46.

47. Gary North, *Liberating Planet Earth* (Fort Worth: Dominion Press, 1987), 22.

48. Ern Baxter, cited by MacPherson, *Can the Elect Be Deceived?*, 52.

49. Sam Fife, cited by MacPherson, *Can the Elect Be Deceived?*, 45.

50. George Grant, *The Changing of the Guard: Biblical Principles for Political Action* (Ft. Worth: Dominion Press, 1987), 50-51.

51. Paulk, "Paulk Answers," 2.

52. David Chilton, *Days of Vengeance* (Fort Worth: Dominion Press, 1987), 587.

53. Earl Paulk, cited by MacPherson, *Can the Elect Be Deceived?*, 143.

54. Tom Rose, "Christ's Kingdom: How Shall We Build?" *Journal of Christian Reconstruction* 8 (Summer 1981):52.

55. Paulk, *Great Escape Theory*, 13.

56. Chilton, *Paradise Restored*, 224.

57. David Hulse, cited by MacPherson, *Can the Elect Be Deceived?*, 159.

58. Gary North, *Unconditional Surrender: God's Program for Victory* (Tyler, Tex.: Geneva Press, 1981), 199.

59. MacPherson, *Can the Elect Be Deceived?*, 46.

60. Chilton, *Paradise Restored*, 53.

61. Much of the "new doctrine" taught by MSOG or Kingdom Now advocates is based upon their direct revelations. As far as we know, Reconstructionists have never received new revelations. However, their brilliant theological "breakthroughs" often function in a similar way. These breakthroughs are often perceived as the basis for furthering the advance of the kingdom. This would be a similar purpose for which the new revelations function for the MSOG. Whether it is through the mysticism of MSOG or the rationalism of Reconstructionists, the result is they believe they have a divine authority to add new ideas to further the progress of the kingdom.

62. Hamon, "God's Wave of Restoration," 10.

63. Gary North, "Publisher's Preface," Chilton, *Days of Vengeance*, xviii.

64. Paulk, *Handwriting on the Wall*, 20.

65. Chilton, *Paradise Restored*, 148.

66. Paulk, *Handwriting on the Wall*, 20.

67. George R. Hawtin, cited by MacPherson, *Can the Elect Be Deceived?*, 56.

68. Kenneth J. Gentry, Jr., "The Greatness of the Great Commission," *Journal of Christian Reconstruction* 7 (Winter 1981):39, 47.

69. Earl Paulk, cited by Dager, "Kingdom Theology," 20.

70. Gary North, *Is the World Running Down? Crisis in the Christian Worldview* (Tyler, Tex.: Institute for Christian Economics, 1988), 111.

71. North, *Unconditional Surrender*, 199.

72. Gary DeMar, *Ruler of the Nations: Biblical Principles for Government* (Fort Worth: Dominion Press, 1987), 171.

73. Hamon, "God's Wave of Restoration," 11.

74. North, *Is the World Running Down?*, 291.

75. Don Paulk, "Editorial Comment," 1.

76. Kenneth L. Gentry, Jr. "Searching Scripture," *The Counsel of Chalcedon*, March 1982, 15.

77. Paulk, *Unity of Faith*, 16.

78. Gary North, *Healer of the Nations: Biblical Principles for International Relations* (Fort Worth: Dominion Press, 1987), 45-46.

79. Here we are stressing that aspect of Covenant theology which believes that the New Covenant replaced Israel's promises with the church. This is sometimes called "Replacement Theology." We believe that both covenants are equally valid and will be fully fulfilled.

80. Earl Paulk, *Handwriting on the Wall*, 17.

81. Ray Sutton, *That You May Prosper* (Tyler, Tex.: Institute for Christian Economics, 1987), 273.

Appendix B

Is Christian Reconstructionism Anti-Semitic?

Reconstructionist theology is having an impact upon evangelical support for the nation of Israel. In *Dispatch from Jerusalem*, a newsletter of the pro-Israel organization, Bridges for Peace, editor Clarence Wagner notes "signs of diminishing support for Israel among charismatics. The change in attitude is due to the influence of 'Kingdom Now' or Reconstructionist theology.[1] Wagner adds that this theology "sees no significance in national Israel today, and denies that Israel has a place in God's plan or His covenants. According to this view, the Old Testament covenants are for the church, the true Israel, and the curses are for Israel.[2]

We believe there is the potential for anti-Semitism within the Reconstructionist movement.[3] Let us hasten to add that they have not said anything explicitly anti-Semitic to date. The danger lies in their misunderstanding of God's plan concerning the future of the nation of Israel. Reconstructionists advocate the replacement of Old Testament Israel with the church, often called the "New Israel." They believe that Israel does not have a future different from any other nation. "Although Israel will someday be restored to the true faith, the Bible does not tell of any future plan for Israel as a special nation."[4]

Reconstructionists must be commended for their proper understanding from Romans 11 and other passages that a large number of Jews will be saved in the future. This is an advance over amillennialism, which often does not take this prophecy seriously. However, since they reject the Bible's teaching that Israel as God's covenant nation has a destiny, they sometimes make statements about Israel that are very harsh. For example Gary North has boasted that he has a book already in his computer for when "Israel gets pushed into the sea, or converted to Christ."[5] One Reconstructionist pastor, in criticizing the approach to Scripture which sees a future for national Israel, reeled off the following pronouncement against Israel, calling it "a sinful, apostate, Christ-rejecting, blasphemous, Middle Eastern nation as 'God's Chosen People.' "[6] Restorationist Rick Godwin expressed a similar attitude in a message detailing how the church is the new Israel:

> But didn't he say if you bless them? So we've got to bless the Jew. We've got to bless Israel. Yes, and you hear Jerry Falwell and everybody else say the reason America's great is because America's blessed Israel. They sure have. Which Israel? The Israel—the Church. . . . That was the Israel of God. Not that garlic one over on the Mediterranean Sea. You've got nothing but wasted money over there. And we've got the Arabs hating us because they think Jesus is racial now. And Jesus isn't racial. There's neither Jew nor Gentile in Christ Jesus. He is not a respector of nations and He is not a respector of persons. He is a respector of one Israel and Jew and it's you: Jew and Gentile in Christ.[7]

Earlier in the message, Godwin taught the Reconstructionist view that the Olivet discourse was fulfilled in A.D. 70, when Israel was cursed, divorced, and excommunicated as God's elect nation. Godwin encouraged his listeners to get copies of David Chilton's books to further educate themselves about this viewpoint. This kind of attitude has more often than not led to an anti-Semitic practice.[8]

Reconstructionists have argued that lack of support for modern Israel does not make one anti-Semitic. Steve Schlissel, a Reconstructionist pastor of Jewish descent, has written:

> Dispensationalists believe that the Jewish people have a title to the land that transcends virtually any other consideration, including unbelief, rebellion and hatred toward Christ and His church. Consequently, anti-zionism is equated with antisemitism.
>
> The reconstructionist, on the other hand, makes a distinction. He believes that the Jewish people may exercise the title only when they comply with the condition of repentance and faith. He has nothing against Jews living in "eretz yisrael" *per se*, but he recognizes that the far more significant question is Israel's *faith*.[9]

Schlissel make a good point: Anti-Zionism is not the same as anti-Semitism. This is clearly true since some Jews are also anti-Zionists. They believe that only the personal appearance of Messiah will fulfill the land promises to Israel. Schlissel is unique among Reconstructionists in that he believes Israel has a future as a special nation. He does not believe that the church has replaced Israel, thus becoming the New Israel. Therefore, Schlissel's view is similar to that of dispensationalists.

Since it is the replacement feature of covenant theology that bears the potential for anti-Semitism, Schlissel's defense cannot speak for the mainstream of Reconstructionists. In fact, he is proving our point by removing the replacement feature of mainstream Reconstructionism's potential for anti-Semitism.

Premillennialists believe that Jews must come to faith in Christ in order to be saved. They are lost, as are all outside of Christ, until they receive forgiveness for their sins. However, we believe this will happen in the future, resulting in fulfillment of all the promises made by God to Abraham and Israel. This is why many of us believe that the current nation of Israel is a forerunner to the fulfillment of this future hope for Israel. We know they are in unbelief, but the fact that God is gathering them together gives us hope that he will soon convert them and bring blessing to the world.

If Romans 11 teaches that national Israel has been cut off from present blessing, and Reconstructionists believe this as well as premillennialists, then it also teaches that national Israel will one day be restored to the place of blessing. The symmetry in the passage demands both halves of the equation. Anything short of what the Bible teaches leaves the door open for the future development of anti-Semitism. This point should be watched in the days ahead to see if Reconstructionists do develop anti-Semitic tendencies and if their replacement theology encourages others to adopt this attitude.

ISRAEL'S FUTURE

Those passages that depict Israel's temporary rejection of Jesus as Messiah also teach her future restoration. Arthur W. Kac has said, "the impressive number of these Bible citations merely proves that the restoration of Israel is not a stray teaching."[10] If those passages concerning Israel's setting aside are to be taken literally, then why should those of restoration not be taken in a similar manner? They should! But Dominionists often ignore the scores of biblical texts which speak of the yet coming conversion of Israel and God's corresponding fulfillment of her promises. Please take note of the following passages which speak of a yet future plan for national Israel:

Deuteronomy 4:27-31

> "And the LORD will scatter you among the peoples, and you shall be left few in number among the nations, where the LORD shall drive you. And there you will serve gods, the work of man's hands, wood

and stone, which neither see nor hear nor eat nor smell. But from there you will seek the LORD your God, and you will find Him if you search for Him with all your heart and all your soul. When you are in distress and all these things have come upon you, in the latter days, you will return to the LORD your God and listen to His voice. For the LORD your God is a compassionate God; He will not fail you nor destroy you nor forget the covenant with your fathers which He swore to them."

Isaiah 2:2-3

> Now it will come about that in the last days,
> The mountain of the house of the LORD
> Will be established as the chief of the mountains,
> And will be raised above the hills;
> And all the nations will stream to it.
> And many peoples will come and say,
> "Come, let us go up to the mountain of the LORD,
> To the house of the God of Jacob;
> That He may teach us concerning His ways,
> And that we may walk in His paths."
> For the law will go forth from Zion,
> And the word of the LORD from Jerusalem.

Isaiah 14:1-3

> When the LORD will have compassion on Jacob, and again choose Israel, and settle them in their own land, then strangers will join them and attach themselves to the house of Jacob. And the peoples will take them along and bring them to their place, and the house of Israel will possess them as an inheritance in the land of the LORD as male servants and female servants; and they will take their captors captive, and will rule over their oppressors.

Jeremiah 23:5-6

> "Behold, the days are coming," declares the LORD,
> "When I shall raise up for David a righteous Branch;
> And He will reign as king and act wisely
> And do justice and righteousness in the land.
> In His days Judah will be saved,
> And Israel will dwell securely;
> And this is His name by which He will be called,
> 'The LORD our righteousness.'"

Jeremiah 32:37-42

> "Behold, I will gather them out of all the lands to which I have driven them in My anger, in My wrath, and in great indignation; and I will bring them back to this place and make them dwell in safety. And they shall be My people, and I will be their God; and I will give them one heart and one way, that they may fear Me always, for their own good, and for the good of their children after them. And I will make an everlasting covenant with them that I will not turn away from them, to do them good; and I will put the fear of Me in their hearts so that they will not turn away from Me. And I will rejoice over them to do them good, and I will faithfully plant them in this land with all My heart and with all My soul. For thus says the LORD, 'Just as I brought all this great disaster on this people, so I am going to bring on them all the good that I am promising them.'"

Ezekiel 36:22-32

> "Therefore, say to the house of Israel, 'Thus says the Lord GOD, "It is not for your sake, O house of Israel, that I am about to act, but for My holy name, which you have profaned among the nations where you went. And I will vindicate the holiness of My

great name which has been profaned among the nations, which you have profaned in their midst. Then the nations will know that I am the LORD," declares the Lord GOD, "when I prove Myself holy among you in their sight. For I will take you from the nations, gather you from all the lands, and bring you into your own land. Then I will sprinkle clean water on you, and you will be clean; I will cleanse you from all your filthiness and from all your idols.

Moreover, I will give you a new heart and put a new spirit within you; and I will remove the heart of stone from your flesh and give you a heart of flesh. And I will put My Spirit within you and cause you to walk in My statutes, and you will be careful to observe My ordinances. And you will live in the land that I gave to your forefathers; so you will be My people, and I will be your God. Moreover, I will save you from all your uncleanness; and I will call for the grain and multiply it, and I will not bring a famine on you. And I will multiply the fruit of the tree and the produce of the field, that you may not receive again the disgrace of famine among the nations. Then you will remember your evil ways and your deeds that were not good, and you will loathe yourselves in your own sight for your iniquities and your abominations. I am not doing this for your sake," declares the Lord GOD, "let it be known to you. Be ashamed and confounded for your ways, O house of Israel!" ' "

Ezekiel 39:25-29

Therefore thus says the Lord GOD, "Now I shall restore the fortunes of Jacob, and have mercy on the whole house of Israel; and I shall be jealous for My holy name. And they shall forget their disgrace and all their treachery which they perpetrated against

Me, when they live securely on their own land with no one to make them afraid. When I bring them back from the peoples and gather them from the lands of their enemies, then I shall be sanctified through them in the sight of the many nations."

Amos 9:11-15

"In that day I will raise up the fallen booth of David,
And wall up its breaches;
I will also raise up its ruins,
And rebuild it as in the days of old;
That they may possess the remnant of Edom
And all the nations who are called by My name,"
Declares the LORD who does this.

"Behold, days are coming," declares the LORD,
"When the plowman will overtake the reaper
And the treader of grapes him who sows seed;
When the mountains will drip sweet wine,
And all the hills will be dissolved.
Also I will restore the captivity of My people Israel,
And they will rebuild the ruined cities and live in
    them,
They will also plant vineyards and drink their wine,
And make gardens and eat their fruit.
I will also plant them on their land,
And they will not again be rooted out from their land
Which I have given them,"
Says the LORD your God.

Zephaniah 3:14-15

Shout for joy, O daughter of Zion!
Shout in triumph, O Israel!
Rejoice and exult with all your heart,
O daughter of Jerusalem!
The LORD has taken away His judgments against
    you,
He has cleared away your enemies.

The King of Israel, the L ORD, is in your midst;
You will fear disaster no more.

Zechariah 8:7-8

> "Thus says the L ORD of hosts, 'Behold, I am going to save My people from the land of the east and from the land of the west; and I will bring them back, and they will live in the midst of Jerusalem, and they will be My people and I will be their God in truth and righteousness.'"

Zechariah 8:13-15

> "'And it will come about that just as you were a curse among the nations, O house of Judah and house of Israel, so I will save you that you may become a blessing. Do not fear; let your hands be strong.'

> For thus says the L ORD of hosts, 'Just as I purposed to do harm to you when your fathers provoked Me to wrath,' says the L ORD of hosts, 'and I have not relented, so I have again purposed in these days to do good to Jerusalem and to the house of Judah. Do not fear!'"

Romans 11:15, 25-27

> For if their rejection be the reconciliation of the world, what will their acceptance be but life from the dead? . . .

> For I do not want you, brethren, to be uninformed of this mystery, lest you be wise in your own estimation, that a partial hardening has happened to Israel until the fulness of the Gentiles has come in; and thus all Israel will be saved; just as it is written,

> > "The Deliverer will come from Zion,
> > He will remove ungodliness from Jacob.
> > And this is My covenant with them,
> > When I take away their sins."

406   Appendix B

Appendix B, Notes

1. Cited in "Charismatics and Israel," *Countdown*, March 1988, 15.

2. Ibid.

3. Two essays on this subject are Gary North, "Some Problems with 'Messianic' Judaism," *Biblical Economics Today*, April-May 1984; and James B. Jordan, "Christian Zionism and Messianic Judaism," Appendix B in David Chilton, *The Days of Vengeance* (Fort Worth: Dominion Press, 1987), 612-21.

4. David Chilton, *Paradise Restored* (Tyler, Tex.: Reconstruction Press, 1985), 224.

5. Personal letter from Gary North to Peter Lalonde, 30 April 1987.

6. Personal letter from John A. Gilley, Grace Reformed Presbyterian Church of Oklahoma City, to Thomas Ice, 9 November 1987.

7. Rick Godwin, tape recorded message delivered at Metro Church, Edmond, Okla., 11 April 1988.

8. For more on how anti-Semitism has grown out of covenant theology see Hal Lindsey's forthcoming book, *Never Again*.

9. Steve M. Schlissel, "To Those Who Wonder If Reconstructionism Is Anti-Semitic," *The Counsel of Chalcedon*, July 1988, 13.

10. Arthur W. Kac, *The Rebirth of the State of Israel* (Chicago: Moody Press, 1958), 28.

Appendix C

Bringing in the Kingdom

Reconstructionists often say they do not believe that they are to bring in the kingdom. While it is true that they believe the kingdom was established by Christ at his first coming, they clearly believe that some phase of the kingdom is to be mediated by Christ through the agency of the church during the present age. As a result, Dominionists often use "take over," "bringing in," or "establishing" the kingdom language. Reconstructionist leader David Chilton admitted on national television, "The trouble is there are some Reconstructionists who speak in terms of a take-over. That scares me to death. I used to do it."[1]

In order to demonstrate that Dominionists do use "take-over" language, we provide the following collection of quotes from Reconstructionists saying that the church is to Christianize the world or to establish the kingdom. All emphases in the quotes are original.

R. J. Rushdoony

God's Plan for Victory:
The Meaning of Postmillennialism

I believe that the world will see the progressive triumph of Christ's people until the whole world is Christian and a glorious material and spiritual era unfolds. (p. 2)

The impact of the church as it confronted Rome, as it confronted the barbarians, and, again, at the Reformation, was to conquer, to subdue kingdoms to the Christ of Scripture and to His infallible law-word. . . . Reformation means to proclaim the saving power of Christ, and to apply the whole word of God to every area of life. *Anything short of that is not the Gospel.* (p. 15)

People who expect the world to end very soon, and are planning on being raptured out of it, are not likely to be concerned about dominion over the earth, nor the application of God's law to the whole of life. (p. 47)

God has a plan for the conquest of all things by His covenant people. That plan is His law. (p. 57)

The Institutes of Biblical Law

God's purpose is not the dominion of sin but the dominion of redeemed man over the earth under God. According to St. Paul, the very creation around us groans and travails, waiting for the godly dominion of the children of God (Rom 8:19-23). (p. 451-2)

Law and Society

The land law is basic because it is the earth which must be subdued and made into God's Kingdom, and it is on earth that God's will must be done. The Lord's Prayer sets forth: "Thy kingdom come. Thy will be done in earth, as it is in heaven" (Matt 6:10). (pp. 322-23)

David Chilton

Days of Vengeance

> Christianity is destined to take over all the kingdoms of the earth. God has given His people a "covenant grant" to take possession and exercise dominion over His creation. . . . The Church is to take the initiative in fighting against the forces of evil—she must attack, and not merely defend—and she will be successful. She must pray for, expect, and rejoice in her enemies' defeat. God will give His Church enough time to accomplish her assignment. (p. 587)

Paradise Restored:
An Eschatology of Dominion

> [Matthew 5:13-16] is nothing less than a mandate for the complete social transformation of the entire world. And what Jesus condemns is ineffectiveness, failing to change the society around us. . . . We *must* change the world; and what is more, we *shall* change the world. (p. 12)

> He has predestined His people to victorious conquest and dominion over all things in His Name. (p. 167)

> Our goal is world dominion under Christ's lordship, a "world takeover" if you will. (p. 214)

Gary North

Is the World Running Down?
Crisis in the Christian Worldview

> Hardly anyone preaches judgment for restoration's sake . . . as a way to restore them to faith in Him and to enable His people to engage once again in the task of Christian reconstruction: building the kingdom of God on earth, by means of His law. (p. 249)

Healer of the Nations:
Biblical Principles for International Relations

> The goal of establishing Christ's international kingdom can be presented to citizens of any nation. (p. 167)

"Editor's Introduction" in George Grant, *The Changing of the Guard: Biblical Principles for Political Action*

> Whenever a speaker begins to argue that Christians have a responsibility to work to build God's Kingdom on earth, unless he is talking only about personal evangelism or missions, someone will object. . . . Each Christian serves as a worker in God's Kingdom. (p. xi)

> Christians are required by God to become active in building God's visible Kingdom. (p. xxxi)

Liberating Planet Earth

> How can we disciple the earth if we are not involved in running it? (p. 25)

> If the Christian church fails to build the visible kingdom by means of Biblical law and the power of the gospel, despite the resurrection of Christ and the presence of the Holy Spirit, then what kind of religion are we preaching? (p. 138)

Unconditional Surrender

> It is strange that Christians today cannot envision the program for conquest God has established for His people. (p. 201)

Dominion and Common Grace:
The Biblical Basis of Progress

> The parable (Matt 13:24-30, 36-43) refers to the building of the kingdom of God, not simply to the institutional church. (p. 71)

If the Christian church fails to build the visible kingdom by means of biblical law and the power of the
gospel, despite the resurrection of Christ and the
presence of the Holy Spirit, then what kind of religion are we preaching? (p. 143)

Gary DeMar and Peter Leithart

The Reduction of Christianity:
Dave Hunt's Theology of Cultural Surrender

The reign of Christ—His Messianic kingdom—is
meant to subdue every enemy of righteousness, as
Paradise is regained for fallen men by the Savior.
(p. 335)

Gary DeMar

Ruler of the Nations:
Biblical Principles for Government

God has not called us to forsake the earth, but *to
impress heaven's pattern on earth.* (p. 123)

Christians must be obedient to the mandate God has
given to extend His Kingdom to every sphere of
life, to every corner of the globe (Gen 1:26-28; Matt
28:18-20). (p. 184)

Peter Leithart

"Politics: An Image of the Kingdom,"
Chalcedon Report, July, 1988

Thus, the mission of the Church . . . is not to retreat
from culture, but to transform the world into a God-
honoring place, into an image of heaven, and part
of this task is political. (p. 7)

George Grant

The Changing of the Guard:
Biblical Principles for Political Action

Christians have an obligation, a mandate, a commission, a holy responsibility to reclaim the land for Jesus Christ—to have dominion in civil structures, just as in every other aspect of life and godliness.

But it is dominion that we are after. Not just a voice.

It is dominion we are after. Not just influence.

It is dominion we are after. Not just equal time.

It is dominion we are after.

World conquest. That's what Christ has commissioned us to accomplish. We must win the world with the power of the Gospel. And we must never settle for anything less. . . . Thus, Christian politics has as its primary intent the conquest of the land—of men, families, institutions, bureaucracies, courts, and governments for the Kingdom of Christ. (pp. 50-51)

Christ's disciples were to be world-changers. . . . They *were* to work for the coming of the Kingdom. They *were* to see that God's will was done on earth. (p. 90)

In short, we must take authority over the nations with the applied rule of Christ Jesus. (p. 115)

Bringing in the Sheaves

The army of God is to conquer the earth, to subdue it, to rule over it, to exercise dominion. Christians are called to war. And it is a war we are expected to win. (p. 98)

Ray Sutton

That You May Prosper

> Everything belongs to Christ and should be governed by His Word. The State is no exception. . . . Unless there is a *Christocracy*, society ends up in some kind of bondage. . . . Beginning with this presupposition, so basic to the Christian faith, let us turn our attention to the final sphere of society, and examine how to take dominion. (p. 177)

> Yes, Acts parallels the Book of Joshua. Joshua is the account of the conquest of the land; Acts is the story of the conquest of the world. (p. 202)

> The Bible specifies a special kind of *lawsuit* that can be filed with God against the wicked called a *covenantal lawsuit*. This Biblical concept is consistently used by the prophets, many of their books being structured according to the Deuteronomic covenant. With a covenantal lawsuit, however, the five points of covenantalism are all turned toward accusations against lawless covenant-breakers and enemies of the Church, calling down God's sanctions on them. Yes, a covenant lawsuit asks God to kill the wicked. God destroys the wicked one of two ways: by conversion or destruction. So, a covenantal lawsuit is not "unloving." *But it is the Biblical method for taking dominion when opposition is met!* (p. 204)

Joseph C. Morecraft, III

"Christ's Dominion over the Nations"
The Counsel of Chalcedon, January 1987.

> How can *you* establish and advance the crown rights of Christ the King in the United States? . . . Be

satisfied with nothing less than the total Christianization of the U.S.A. Do your part in it and keep at
it until you see the victory banners of Christ unfurled
over every heart, home, business, church, school,
courtroom, legislative hall, science lab, doctor's
office and recreational center in our nation. (p. 15)

Raymond P. Joseph

We have given up the belief that we are *supposed*
to work for victory on this earth . . . to expect the
eventual "takeovers" of cultural institutions . . . for
the bringing of every "high thing" into obedience
to Christ, the King. Oh, we believe that these "victory" Scriptures are true, all right, but we
"spiritualize" them, and relegate their main fulfillment to some future age, after Christ comes back.
And so we take the heart belief right out of God's
people, the belief that they are called to take dominion of the land, as Joshua was called of God to
conquest Canaan for Christ, and replace it with one
of a kind of "holding action," winning as many
people as possible, and building as many local
churches as possible, and all the while waiting for
some future time till Christ comes back so that we
can really see the Kingdom built! (pp. 22-23)

Tom Rose

"Christ's Kingdom: How Shall We Build?"
Journal of Christian Reconstruction, Summer 1981

As Christ-followers we are to establish dominion,
we are to establish Christ's Kingdom, which is to
consume all other kingdoms (Dan. 2:44; 7:18-27).
(p. 52)

Recently, a Reformed pastor in Tulsa told me of an instance which shows modern-day Christians' lack of understanding concerning Christ's mandate to build his Kingdom. . . . What kind of Kingdom-building vision do they have? What kind of Kingdom-building vision do Christians have? (p. 54)

Appendix C, Notes

1. David Chilton, from television interview with Bill Moyers, "God and Politics," part 3 on *Moyers*.

Glossary

AMILLENNIALISM. The belief that the millennium is an internal, spiritual rule of Christ during the present church age. A newer form holds that the millennium will be the future state of believers in heaven. This view differs from premillennialism and postmillennialism in that it does not believe in an earthly millennium. Amillennialists believe that this current age will see many come to Christ through the preaching of the gospel, but that a majority will reject Christ's offer. In addition, the age will end in apostasy, thus requiring God's personal and intervening judgment. This view surfaced in the fourth century.

CALVINISM. A systematic understanding of what the Bible teaches centered around the sovereignty of God. Named for the Reformer, John Calvin, it sees people believing the gospel as a response to God's predestination, election, and calling of sinners to Christ. Calvinism is also a label for certain views of society, economics, and government. It is the foundation for Western civilization which Reconstructionists desire to restore. Puritans were Calvinist.

CHRISTIAN RECONSTRUCTION. The recently articulated belief that it is the moral obligation of Christians to recapture every institution for Jesus Christ, both individual and social. Since God is sovereign he has willed it. The Bible and God's law give the church its needed direction. One's relationship with God is a covenantal relationship made possible through the gospel. Because there is no common ground between biblical and non-Christian thought, the Christian is to use the Bible and the Bible alone to govern his thinking. Then God will bless the church's effort to Christianize the earth. Since God's kingdom was established at Christ's first coming, godly dominion will be mediated through the church before the return of Christ. The victory of God's kingdom on earth will be during and continuous with this present era.

CULTURAL MANDATE or DOMINION MANDATE. This mandate is God's command to Adam to fill and subdue the earth (Genesis 1:28). The notion also involves the responsibility of all mankind to develop and rule every aspect of God's creation according to his Word. Dominionists believe that this, along with the Great Commission, is their "marching orders" for Christianizing the world.

DISPENSATIONALISM. A system of theology based upon the biblical word *dispensation*. It is an effort to try to understand God's plan for history. Dispensationalist Charles Ryrie says, "The world is seen as a household administered by God in connection with several stages of revelation that mark off the different economies in the outworking of his total program. These economies are the dispensations in dispensationalism. . . . Thus a dispensation may be defined as 'a distinguishable economy in the outworking of God's program.'" Dispensationalists believe they come closer to properly handling Scripture with their consistent application of the grammatical-historical interpretation, often called literal or normal interpretation. The theological result is a consistent distinction between the Bible's use of Israel and the church. "Applying this hermeneutical principle," Ryrie concludes, "leads dispensationalism to distinguish God's program for Israel from his program for the church. Thus the church did not begin in the OT but on the day of Pentecost, and the church is not presently fulfilling promises made to Israel in the OT that have not yet been fulfilled." As with most systems of theology, there is a spectrum of different types of dispensationalism.

DOMINION THEOLOGY. The belief that the church is to exercise rule over every area of society, people as well as institutions, before Christ returns.

ESCHATOLOGY. The study or doctrine of "last things." It is commonly called prophecy. The three schools of eschatology are: amillennialism, premillennialism, and postmillennialism.

GREAT COMMISSION. Christ's command to his disciples and all believers to make disciples of all the nations (Matthew 28:18-20). Dominionists believe this includes the Christianization of the world, while non-Dominionists see it referring to evangelism and discipleship, with Christianization awaiting the return of Christ.

KINGDOM NOW. The belief that this current age is the kingdom of God spoken of in the Bible. Therefore Christians are currently responsible, by God's power, to see that it is developed to maturity.

OLIVET DISCOURSE. Christ's response to the disciples' questions about the future (Matthew 24, Mark 13, Luke 17 and 21). Reconstructionists believe these passages refer to the destruction of Jerusalem in A.D. 70 and not the second coming of Christ as premillennialists advocate.

POSTMILLENNIALISM. The belief that Christ will return after the millennium. All postmillennialists believe the current age is the kingdom, while some believe the millennial phase of the kingdom is present and others hold it is yet future when the world has been Christianized. Postmillennialists also believe the church is the agent through which this return to Eden will be mediated by Christ the King from heaven. Most postmillennialists stress the preaching of the gospel, resulting in a conversion of most of mankind, as the means for Christianization. However, the more recent Reconstructionist version adds to evangelism, obedience and faithfulness to the Bible (law) as a condition for victory. Some postmillennialists believe the conversion of the world will be a slow, gradual process taking perhaps thousands of years. Others believe that conversion could happen within a short period of time (about ten years) as the result of a great revival. Postmillennialism was the last of the major eschatologies to develop. It was first taught within the church in the seventeenth century.

PREMILLENNIALISM. The belief that Christ will return at the end of this current age (the church age) before the millennium. Upon his return, Christ will judge the world, bind Satan, and rule from Jerusalem for a thousand years. This current age will see many come to Christ through the worldwide preaching of the gospel, but the majority will reject the message. This will bring down God's personal and intervening presence to judge an apostate church and world. Some premillennialists believe that Christ's coming is imminent and that he could come suddenly, at any moment, for the church before the seven-year tribulation period (pretribulational rapture). Others believe the church will be preserved through the tribulation and will be taken out at the end (posttribulational rapture). Premillennialism is the oldest eschatological system. It can be found in some form in the earliest writings of the church fathers.

PURITANISM. A loosely organized reform movement in the English-speaking world during the sixteenth and seventeenth centuries. The name comes from their desire to "purify" the Church of England from all Catholic traditions which they felt to be unbiblical. This later developed into beliefs concerning purity of the self and society.

Puritans were a highly educated and intense people whose ideas were the leading influence in the founding of America. Reconstructionists see themselves leading a revival of the Puritan spirit.

RAPTURE is a word used by the Latin Bible to translate the English phrase "caught up" in 1 Thessalonians 4: 17. In that sense it is a biblical term. While most Christians claim to believe in the rapture, the term was popularized by those holding to a pretribulational (Christ removing the church before the seven-year tribulation) timing for that event. Since postmillennialists and amillennialists have not really distinguished between the Second Coming and the Rapture, it has not been an issue within their schools of thought, except as they have spoken out against the pretribulational school. The debate within premillennialism has been the timing of the Rapture in relation to the tribulation. Basically the two views are pretribulationalism and posttribulationalism (Christ removes the church at the end of the tribulation). Premillennialists within the early church did not deal with the timing of the Rapture, even though some spoke of the Lord's return as an imminent event, as do modern pretribulationalists. Others saw the church going through the tribulation similar to modern posttribulationalists. With the rise of Augustine's view of amillennialism in the fifth century, premillennialism totally disappeared for almost twelve hundred years until the early 1600s. This silence explains the lack of development within premillennialism for over a millennium. Since no one even thought in terms of premillennialism the system had great potential for development as it began to gain ground during the seventeenth and eighteenth centuries. By the early 1800s the more literal, futurist interpretation of prophecy was beginning to be revived. It was within this climate that scholars began looking at prophecies relating to Israel and their fulfillment while contrasting them with God's program for the church. By the 1830s J.N. Darby began teaching that the timing of the Rapture would be pretribulational. Actually the modern posttribulational teaching of the Rapture was the result of a reaction to the pretribulational timing of the Rapture by some a few years after Darby. Virtually all dispensationalists believe in a pretribulational Rapture. The debate over the timing of the Rapture has become the major disagreement within premillennialism.

REFORMED. A word that denotes the Calvinistic wing of the Reformation. The Reformers, who wanted to implement certain reforms within the Catholic church, were excommunicated from Rome. Their resulting expression of Christianity became known as the Reformed tradition. Reconstructionists are within this tradition; Lutherans and Anabaptists are not.

REVELATION, Interpretive Approaches to the Book of. The most common interpretive approaches to the book of Revelation are the preterist, historicist, futurist, and idealist views. They could be viewed as past, present, future, and timeless. The *preterist* (Latin for "past") view is the one advocated by Reconstructionists. Preterists understand the book of Revelation, the Olivet discourse, and virtually all prophecy as having been fulfilled in God's judgment upon apostate Jews for their rejection of Jesus as Messiah in the A.D. 70 destruction of Jerusalem. Postmillennialists and amillennialists can use this approach, but not premillennialists. *Historicists* equate the current church age as fulfilling the book of Revelation. This has often led to date setting as students of this view attempt to coordinate contemporary events with passages in Revelation. All three eschatological views have adopted this approach. While all three eschatological schools can hold the *futurist* approach, it is the main system of premillennialists. It sees most of Revelation, the Olivet discourse, and other prophetic portions as yet future. The *idealist* does not believe that timing is important. The real issue is the ideals or principles for life that one should glean from Revelation.

THEONOMY. A term coined by Greg Bahnsen to denote the Reconstructionists' view of "biblical law." The term is a compound of two Greek words: *theos* (God) and *nomos* (law); thus, "God's law." Reconstructionists believe that God's law applies to every area of life and all men, believers and unbelievers, should obey it. Theonomy is described by Bahnsen as follows: "The Christian is obligated to keep the whole law of God as a pattern for sanctification and this law is to be enforced by the civil magistrate where and how the stipulations of God so designate." Modern theonomy contends that all Old Testament law is still in force, and all men are obligated to obey it unless it has been specifically negated in the New Testament. Theonomy goes beyond simply using Old Testament law as a principle or wisdom and insists that we have an obligation to obey it.

TRIBULATION, The Great. For Premillennialists the great tribulation is the future seven-year period of miraculous judgment poured out by God upon the world. This is the period in which personalities such as the beast or antichrist rise to temporary world prominence. Reconstructionists believe the great tribulation has already taken place in the fall of Israel.

WESTMINISTER CONFESSION OF FAITH (1647). This Confession was one of the last statements of faith to come out of the Reformation. It serves as a standard of orthodoxy for many Reformed traditions. Since many Reconstructionists come from churches governed by the Westminster Confession, there is now a debate as to whether theonomy is in line with the Confession.

An Annotated Bibliography of Dominion Theology

PRO

Books

GREG BAHNSEN

Theonomy in Christian Ethics. Phillipsburg, N.J.: Presbyterian & Reformed Publishing Co., 1977, 1984. This is the major attempt to defend the Reconstructionist view of the use of OT law today. He believes that OT law carries over into the church age unless specifically abrogated, i.e. ceremonial law which Christ fulfilled in his death and resurrection. Also, that the new covenant should govern how OT law is applied today. It also stresses that regeneration of the NT believer now empowers the believer to implement the OT law in conjunction with NT law.

Homosexuality: A Biblical View. Grand Rapids: Baker Book House, 1978. Here Bahnsen applies theonomy to an area of law and life. He still believes in the death penalty for those engaged in homosexual acts. The book is pre-AIDS, but gives a comprehensive treatment of Scripture and extrabiblical data.

By This Standard: The Authority of God's Law Today. Tyler, Tex.: Institute for Christian Economics, 1985. This is a popular presentation of theonomy, although it has toned down some of the more controversial aspects. It takes an approach along the lines of "Don't you think all of the Bible applies today?" Most Christians would, of course, say *yes*. Therefore, many will think they are theonomists.

DAVID CHILTON

Productive Christians in an Age of Guilt Manipulators. 3d ed. Tyler, Tex.: Institute for Christian Economics, 1985. Chilton attempts to give a blow-by-blow answer to Ron Sider's Christian socialism. Argues for a free market approach. North hired him to produce this book for a debate with Sider.

Paradise Restored: An Eschatology of Dominion. Tyler, Tex.: Reconstruction Press, 1985. According to Gary North, "This is the greatest book in the history of the Church on eschatology." This is the standard work on the theonomic neopostmillennialism of the the Christian Reconstruction movement. Chilton argues for an A.D. 70 fulfillment of the Olivet discourse and the book of Revelation. He presents and defends the preterist position, while attacking the futurist view of eschatology. We are now in the mediatorial kingdom.

The Days of Vengeance: An Exposition of the Book of Revelation. Fort Worth: Dominion Press, 1987. As would be expected from Chilton, according to North, this is the greatest commentary in the history of the church on the book of Revelation. Chilton says, "Revelation is primarily a prophecy of the destruction of Jerusalem" (p. 4). "The Book of Revelation is not about the Second Coming of Christ" (p. 43). He calls premillennialism a heresy invented in the first century by Cerinthus, and postmillennialism the historic orthodox position of the church (p. 494). Chilton's fertile, allegorical interpretative mind yields such interpretive breakthroughs from seeing the signs of the zodiac in Revelation to a traditional preterist notion that Nero fulfills the 666 of the mark of the beast.

The Great Tribulation. Fort Worth: Dominion Press, 1987. A paperback effort attempting to deal with some loose ends concerning the tribulation—which ended in A.D. 70. This book appears to be a "cut and paste" job from Chilton's *Vengeance* and *Paradise* works on the tribulation along with a few added comments. It is supposed to be a more popular work on eschatology from his preterist, postmillennial viewpoint.

Power in the Blood: A Christian Response to AIDS. Brentwood, Tenn.: Wolgemuth & Hyatt Publishers, 1988. This is Chilton's book on AIDS. He does understand AIDS to be a curse from God, as he sees all sickness. Repentance is the solution. The book contains a lot of helpful information on the subject. It is also interesting to discover that his view of healing seems to be sympathetic with that of the Wimber movement.

GARY DEMAR

God and Government. 3 vols. Atlanta: American Vision Press, 1982-86. This workbook format is designed to go along with the seminar DeMar teaches on the subject from the theonomic, postmillennial viewpoint.

Ruler of the Nations: Biblical Blueprints for Government. Biblical Blueprints Series, vol. 2. Fort Worth: Dominion Press, 1987. This explains what a Christian Republic is and how to go about making one.

and PETER LEITHART. *The Reduction of Christianity: Dave Hunt's Theology of Cultural Surrender*. Fort Worth: Dominion Press, 1988. This is a take-off on Hunt's controversial book *The Seduction of Christianity*, in which Hunt mentioned some potential dangers with Reconstructionism. Gary North contracted DeMar and Leithart to critique Hunt's dispensational eschatology. They attempt to answer those who say the Reconstructionist view of the kingdom makes their movement open to New Age influence. They say that Hunt's view is one of retreat from the church's responsibility to transform the world through Christian dominion.

428   **Bibliography**

KENNETH L. GENTRY

The Christian and Alcoholic Beverages: A Biblical Perspective.
Grand Rapids: Baker Book House, 1986. Argues for moderation
in alcoholic use, against prohibitionist and abstentionist viewpoints.

GEORGE GRANT

*Bringing in the Sheaves: Transforming Poverty into Productiv-
ity.* Atlanta: American Vision Press, 1985; Brentwood, Tenn.:
Wolgemuth & Hyatt Publishers, 1988. Grant has been a pastor
for the last ten years of Believers Fellowship in Humble (Houston), Texas. Here he applies many OT laws to the modern
context to show how poverty can be transformed into produc-
tivity. This book grew out of Grant's involvement with the poor
and homeless in the Houston area.

The Dispossessed: Homelessness in America. Westchester, Ill.:
Crossway Books, 1986. In this work, Grant tries to zero in on
the problem of the homeless in America with the help of biblical
law.

*In the Shadow of Plenty: Biblical Principles of Welfare and
Poverty.* Biblical Blueprints Series, vol. 4. Fort Worth: Dominion Press; Nashville: Thomas Nelson Publishers, 1986. The
title is self-explanatory. An example would be how we could
apply the gleaning principle to today, instead of our current
welfare system.

*The Changing of the Guard: Biblical Blueprints for Political
Action.* Biblical Blueprints Series, vol. 8. Fort Worth: Dominion
Press, 1987. The back cover says, "If this is what it's like to
win, how bad must it be when we lose?" Grant argues that
Christian impact in the political arena would improve if we
would follow the biblical principles of political engagement
outlined in this book.

JAMES JORDAN

The Law of the Covenant: An Exposition of Exodus 21-23.
Tyler, Tex.: Institute for Christian Economics, 1984. An effort
to justify theonomy by detailing a view of the Mosaic law.
While one of the more exegetical works within the movement,
it still has the theologizing/philosophizing, which is a trademark
of the movement.

Judges: God's War against Humanism. Tyler, Tex.: Geneva
Ministries, 1985. This commentary on Judges includes in the
introduction a philosophy of hermeneutics which Jordan tries
to follow. He attempts what he calls a "maximalist" approach
to interpretation. We might call it fancy allegory.

The Sociology of the Church: Essays in Reconstruction. Tyler,
Tex.: Geneva Ministries, 1986. Even though the Tyler branch
thinks the church must be reconstructed prior to the world's
reconstruction (this differs from Rushdoony, who thinks the
family goes first), this is their first book on the subject, except
for a Journal Symposium. It includes an essay entitled "Christian Zionism and Messianic Judaism." Jordan accuses the Dallas Seminary dispensationalists of in effect being Christian
Zionists. While Jordan tries to avoid it, are he and the dominion
theology movement heading toward an anti-Semitic position?

GARY NORTH

An Introduction to Christian Economics. Nutley, N.J.: Craig
Press, 1973. A collection of essays on economic themes from
his Christian perspective. Includes an essay on inflation in
Isaiah 1.

None Dare Call It Witchcraft. New Rochelle, N.Y.: Arlington
House Publishers, 1976. An excellent philosophical/theologi-
cal/historical argument that western rationalism has collapsed
into mysticism and magic. This is certainly the standard view

today by most historians. He believes we are at the end of the line of this phase of our culture.

Editor, *Foundations of Christian Scholarship: Essays in the Van Til Perspective*. Vallecito, Calif.: Ross House Books, 1976. Not all the contributors to this volume are Reconstructionists, but the work tries to set forth a biblical perspective in the areas of philosophy, theology, mathematics, history, economics, psychology, education, political science, sociology, and apologetics. John Frame's essay on theology and Greg Bahnsen's on apologetics are especially recommended.

How You Can Profit from the Coming Price Controls. New Rochelle, N.Y.: Arlington House Publishers, 1977. Since these price controls have not come quite as fast as North predicted, this book is long out of print.

Unconditional Surrender: God's Program for Victory. Rev. ed. Tyler, Tex.: Institute for Christian Economics, 1981, 1987. Here we have a popular treatment in a systematic form of the whole Christian Reconstruction/dominion theology approach. North wrote it in a couple of weeks as a simple statement of their movement. Still a good overview.

Successful Investing in an Age of Envy. Fort Worth: Steadman Press, 1981, 1982, 1983. An investment strategy to try to help people retain their wealth in a changing economic climate. Gives specific strategies.

The Dominion Covenant: Genesis. 2d ed. Tyler, Tex.: The Institute for Christian Economics, 1982, 1987. This is the first in a series by North who is attempting to write what he calls "an economic commentary on the Bible." It is questioned by many why the word commentary is used to describe this collection of essays about Genesis and economic themes.

Government by Emergency. Fort Worth: American Bureau of Economic Research, 1983. Argues that the government increasingly will use emergencies, such as the energy crisis, to usurp due process of law in this country in order to control our lives.

The Last Train Out. Fort Worth: American Bureau of Economic Research, 1983. A negative critique of Reaganomics, why it failed, what it will give rise to in the future, and what types of investments should be made to protect oneself.

Wealth and Poverty. Edited by Robert G. Clouse. Downers Grove, Ill.: InterVarsity Press, 1974. North is one of four contributors. He presents the free market approach to economics, while the other three are on a spectrum to the left of North.

Backward, Christian Soldiers? An Action Manual for Christian Reconstruction. Tyler, Tex.: Institute for Christian Economics, 1984. A collection of essays taken from his newsletters arguing for proper motives and rationale for Christian Reconstruction. The title stems from an essay he wrote early in his career.

75 Bible Questions Your Instructors Pray You Won't Ask. Rev. ed. Fort Worth: Dominion Press, 1984, 1988. A question/answer format in which North defends predestination, postmillennialism, and kingdom now eschatology. The book seems to be especially aimed at those who have a relationship to Dallas Seminary. The introductory material includes an account of North's conversion to Christ through a dispensationalist pastor who was a Dallas graduate, and an endorsement from North's current pastor, Ray Sutton, a Dallas graduate and a Reconstructionist. Except for predestination, he argues against the Dallas position.

Moses and Pharaoh: Dominion Religion Versus Power Religion. Tyler, Tex.: Institute for Christian Economics, 1985. This is volume 1 of the 3 volumes of his economic commentary on Exodus.

Coined Freedom. Fort Worth: American Bureau of Economic Research, 1985. An argument for gold and how it can be used in an economy to protect from governmental influences.

12 Deadly Nega-Trends. Fort Worth: American Bureau of Economic Research, 1985. North's tongue-in-cheek response to New Age futurists. He lists these "trends" in order of importance as: the federal deficit, inflation, Social Security, third world debt, bank failures, taxes, unemployment, illegal immigration, government by emergency, where you live in the U. S., terrorism, Soviet blackmail. Judging from his tone in his newsletters, he would probably include AIDS in that list today.

Unholy Spirits: Occultism and New Age Humanism. Fort Worth: Dominion Press, 1986. Wanting to get in on the popular interest of the New Age movement within evangelicalism, North reissued this revised edition of *None Dare Call It Witchcraft.* He attacks Dave Hunt and his dispensational eschatology as part of the problem and defends the likes of Robert Tilton who is helping, according to North, bring in the kingdom. Premillennialists wonder whose kingdom they are bringing in.

The Sinai Strategy: Economics and the Ten Commandments. Tyler, Tex.: Institute for Christian Economics, 1986. This is volume 2 on Exodus with one more volume to come.

and ARTHUR ROBINSON. *Fighting Chance: Ten Feet to Survival.* Cave Junction, Ore.: Oregon Institute of Science and Medicine, 1986. They argue for the true threat of nuclear war and how it can be survived.

Conspiracy: A Biblical View. Fort Worth: Dominion Press, 1986. North believes in attempts at conspiracy, but argues that God is sovereign, thus we should get on with his kingdom building and not let the David Rockefellers of this world bother us.

Honest Money: Biblical Principles of Money and Banking. Biblical Blueprints Series, vol. 5. Fort Worth: Dominion Press; Nashville: Thomas Nelson Publishers, 1986. The title is self-explanatory. This series, edited by North, is an attempt to lay out the Reconstructionist agenda and worldview. They are putting forth a blueprint for changing the world and bringing in the kingdom. These books are written only by those who are postmillennial and strongly reflect that perspective.

Dominion and Common Grace: The Biblical Basis of Progress. Tyler, Tex.: Institute for Christian Economics, 1987. An attempt to show that common grace is how God restrains evil, while special grace converts sinners. As special grace converts more and more to Christ (special grace is the conduit of common grace) resulting in an increasing common grace, Christianization of the world becomes possible. An ingenious but wrong explanation of how things are really getting better even though they are getting worse.

Inherit the Earth: Biblical Principals for Economics. Biblical Blueprints Series, vol. 7. Fort Worth: Dominion Press, 1987. North lays out seven principles of economics.

Liberating Planet Earth: An Introduction to Biblical Blueprints. Biblical Blueprints Series, vol. 1. Fort Worth: Dominion Press, 1987. North gives an introductory overview of the whole Biblical Blueprints Series and includes a rousing pep talk on how we can do it. "Step by step, person by person, nation by nation, Christians are to disciple the nations" (p.9).

Healer of the Nations. Biblical Blueprints Series, vol. 9. Fort Worth: Dominion Press, 1987. This is North's attempt at developing a theory for international relations. It is built upon the concept that there is such a thing as a Christian nation. A nation becomes a Christian nation when the leaders accept the call from ambassador/missionaries to submit to biblical law and covenant. His Christian nation view is modeled upon Israel from the Old Testament, blended with North's modifications which fit contemporary times. He says Christians in each nation form the link on which to develop international relations.

Is the World Running Down? Crisis in the Christian Worldview. Fort Worth: Dominion Press, 1988. North attempts to put forward a philosophy of change. This is done by interacting with Jeremy Rifkin's view of change and entropy. North is critical of Henry Morris and the creationist movement's use of the "Second Law" in arguing against evolution. He argues that

Christ's resurrection is the basis for upward change. This book also includes some of his strongest attacks against dispensationalism. A sample includes: "Pessimism, thy name is Dallas Theological Seminary! Maybe Dallas Seminary did not invent fundamentalist pessimism, but it surely is the U.S. wholesale distributor" (p. 265).

ROUSAS JOHN RUSHDOONY

By What Standard? An Analysis of the Philosophy of Cornelius Van Til. Phillipsburg, N.J.: Presbyterian & Reformed Publishing Co., 1958. Rushdoony's first book. A favorable analysis of the apologetics and philosophy of Van Til. Van Til is not a Reconstructionist. In fact, Gary North has on more than one occasion bemoaned the fact that Van Til never made it into their camp, saying that Van Til only tore down systems but could not construct them.

Van Til. Phillipsburg, N.J.: Presbyterian & Reformed Publishing Co., 1960. An explanation of Van Til from the "Modern Thinkers" series, for which Rushdoony was the editor.

Intellectual Schizophrenia: Culture, Crisis & Education. Phillipsburg, N.J.: Presbyterian & Reformed Publishing Co., 1961. Shows the drift in modern education toward socialism, a direction inconsistent with our nation's founding.

The Messianic Character of American Education: Studies in the History of the Philosophy of Education. Nutley, N. J.: Craig Press, 1963. A historical survey of American liberal education by studying the major personalities, such as Horace Mann and John Dewey.

This Independent Republic: Studies in the Nature and Meaning of American History. Tyler, Tex.: Thoburn Press, 1964. A defense of the American Christian Republic.

The Nature of the American System. Tyler, Tex.: Thoburn Press, 1965. Another historical/political study of the foundations of this country.

Freud. International Library of Philosophy and Theology: Modern Thinkers Series. Phillipsburg, N.J.: Presbyterian & Reformed Publishing Co., 1965. There are not many Christian critiques of people like Freud that do not mix the philosophy being critiqued with Christianity. Rushdoony on Freud is one of the few who does not mix. Quite good.

The Religion of Revolution. Victoria, Tex.: Trinity Episcopal Church, 1965. A little known and circulated book, which is typical of Rushdoony. He rightly calls revolution what it really is—religion.

The Mythology of Science. University Series: Historical Studies. Nutley, N.J.: Craig Press, 1967. This is an insightful critique of the philosophy of evolution.

The Foundations of Social Order: Studies in the Creeds and Councils of the Early Church. Phillipsburg, N.J.: Presbyterian & Reformed Publishing Co., 1968. Rushdoony attempts to show that when the church has had a strong creedal Christology, then maximum freedom, progress, and blessing is experienced by its citizens.

The Biblical Philosophy of History. Phillipsburg, N.J.: Presbyterian & Reformed Publishing Co., 1969. As the title indicates, this is Rushdoony's philosophy of history.

The Myth of Over-Population. University Series: Historical Studies. Nutley, N.J.: Craig Press, 1969. Argues that the problem is not too many people but under-production due to our failure to obey God's law. Of course, this is an issue a postmillennialist needs to handle.

Bread upon the Water: Columns from the California Farmer. Nutley, N.J.: Craig Press, 1969. An attempt to develop a Christian view of agriculture.

Politics of Guilt and Pity. Tyler, Tex.: Thoburn Press, 1970. Rushdoony argues that since modern man has violated God's law of civil government, then he attempts to self-atone for his sins by irrational do-good-ism.

Thy Kingdom Come: Studies in Daniel and Revelation. Phillipsburg, N.J.: Presbyterian & Reformed Publishing Co., 1970. An attempt to put forth his postmillennialism. Like all of Rushdoony's works, it is theological and philosophical in its rationale and argumentation, rather than exegetical.

Law and Liberty. Tyler, Tex.: Thoburn Press, 1971. A series of radio programs which defend the theonomic use of law by answering common objections such as, "Can we legislate morality?"

The One and the Many: Studies in the Philosophy of Order and Ultimacy. Tyler, Tex.: Thoburn Press, 1971. Rushdoony is at his best as a philosopher/theologian and especially when he is developing the thought of Van Til, and this is one of his best and most original works. Rushdoony shows how Van Til's "trinitarian epistemology" solves the classic problem of the one and the many. He applies it to various disciplines to illustrate.

"The Doctrine of Man" and "The Doctrine of Marriage" in *Toward a Christian Marriage.* Edited by E. Fellerson. Phillipsburg, N.J.: Presbyterian & Reformed Publishing Co., 1972. Rushdoony believes that the family is the foundational institution in society, thus the most important area of Reconstruction.

The Institutes of Biblical Law. Phillipsburg, N.J.: Presbyterian & Reformed Publishing Co., 1973. Easily Rushdoony's most important work. An exposition of the Ten Commandments as the law structure for all areas of society today.

The Flight from Humanity: A Study of the Effect of Neoplatonism on Christianity. Tyler, Tex.: Thoburn Press, 1973. Argues that modern escapism is the product of a platonic dialectic which seeks salvation from the physical through the spiritual.

The Politics of Pornography. New Rochelle, N. Y.: Arlington House Publishers, 1974. Argues that pornography is destructive to the central institution—the family— resulting in the destruction of society.

"Implications for Psychology" in *Foundations of Christian Scholarship: Essays in the Van Til Perspective*. Edited by Gary North. Vallecito, Calif.: Ross House Books, 1976. A critique of some of the humanistic themes in modern psychology.

Revolt Against Maturity: A Biblical Psychology of Man. Tyler, Tex.: Thoburn Press, 1977. Rush presents the thesis that our society revolts against maturity because of the evolutionary premise underlying it. Since in evolution you grow old and die, this produces a quest for youth. On the other hand, the Bible, he says, prizes old age and faithfulness to God.

God's Plan for Victory: The Meaning of Postmillennialism. Tyler, Tex.: Thoburn Press, 1977. A short book with rational arguments for postmillennialism.

The Necessity for Systematic Theology. Vallecito, Calif.: Ross House Books, 1979. It is not a question of whether or not to have a systematic theology; it is Which one?

and ED POWELL. *Tithing and Dominion*. Vallecito, Calif.: Ross House Books, 1979. Says that tithing is the key to our social and political problems. As we start to tithe we lay the groundwork for dominion.

The Philosophy of the Christian Curriculum. Vallecito, Calif.: Ross House Books, 1981. Here Rushdoony lays out the contents of a Christian educational curriculum. He deals with the content of what should be and what should not be in the curriculum from a Christian view. He tries to summarize a Christian curriculum in various areas such as history, grammar, mathematics, science, language, and so on.

Law and Society: Volume II of the Institutes of Biblical Law. Vallecito, Calif.: Ross House Books, 1982. These are three- to five-page essays on various issues within the Rushdoony tradition.

The Roots of Inflation. Vallecito, Calif.: Ross House Books, 1982. Shows that inflation is really a spiritual problem.

Salvation and Godly Rule. Vallecito, Calif.: Ross House Books, 1983. More essays similar to *Law and Society.*

Christianity and the State. Vallecito, Calif.: Ross House Books, 1986. Rushdoony puts forth his view of what a Christian civil government should be.

HERBERT SCHLOSSBERG

Idols for Destruction: Christian Faith and Its Confrontation with American Society. Nashville: Thomas Nelson Publishers, 1983. Schlossberg calls American humanistic society an idolatrous culture, ripe for God's judgment. He cites six major idols of modern society and calls for repentance and reconstruction. He has said at a conference in Tyler in 1985 that he has been most influenced in his thinking by Rushdoony. He appears to also be a postmillennialist.

and MARVIN OLASKY. *Turning Point: A Christian Worldview Declaration.* Westchester, Ill.: Crossway Books, 1987. Like *Idols for Destruction* this work is not a militant Reconstructionist work. In fact it is passively so. But worldview is so important to the movement that they are constantly coming out with work after work on the subject. Look for many more.

RAY SUTTON

Who Owns the Family? God or the State? Biblical Blueprints Series, vol. 3. Fort Worth: Dominion Press; Nashville: Thomas Nelson Publishers, 1986. This 1976 Dallas Seminary graduate specializes in home and family matters. Argues that God owns the family and has covenantly delegated it to family members, not the government.

That You May Prosper: Dominion by Covenant. Tyler, Tex.: Institute for Christian Economics, 1987. North says that Sutton has made a major breakthrough in understanding the covenant. Sutton has reworked Kline's five points of an ancient near eastern treaty and has come up with the following: (1) Transcendence, (2) hierarchy, (3) ethics, (4) sanctions, and (5) continuity. Reconstructionists are now seeing this as *the* framework for much of the Bible. This is viewed as another mechanism which the church has not had in the past and that will bring in the long-awaited kingdom.

ROBERT L. THOBURN

The Christian and Politics. Tyler, Tex.: Thoburn Press, 1984. A popular presentation of the Reconstructionist view of government, with suggestions on how to get involved in the 1984 election. Thoburn served one term in the Virginia House of Delegates.

The Children Trap: The Biblical Blueprint for Education. Biblical Blueprints Series, vol. 6. Fort Worth: Dominion Press; Nashville: Thomas Nelson Publishers, 1986. This founder of the successful Fairfax Christian Schools lays down the Reconstructionist view of education.

OTHERS

Child, John Graham. *Biblical Law in the Theology of R. J. Rushdoony: A Systematic Theological Analysis and Appreciation*. Th.M. thesis submitted to the University of South Africa, June 1985. Child is so enthused about Rushdoony, his excitement cannot be hid. This shows the worldwide impact this movement is having.

Crenshaw, Curtis I. and Grover E. Gunn. *Dispensationalism Today, Yesterday, and Tomorrow*. Memphis: Footstool Publications, 1985. This is a "letter" to dispensationalists from two former dispensationalists, both having attended Dallas Theological Seminary. This is one of those "anti" books which attacks dispensationalism as a deviant approach to Scripture. It does not offer a replacement, except for a comment here and there. You cannot necessarily tell they are postmillennialists from the book, but other sources indicate that they are.

Elniff, Terrill Irwin. *The Guise of Every Graceless Heart: Human Autonomy in Puritan Thought and Experience*. Vallecito, Calif.: Ross House Books, 1981. This master's thesis argues that the great society of the Puritans broke down because of their rationalistic epistemology. From a Reconstructionist perspective, this implies that with Van Til's epistemology, Puritanism can now fulfill its calling, having been purged of this major failure.

Metcalf, Robert and Tom Rose. *The Coming Victory*. Memphis: Christian Studies Center, 1981. A Reconstructionist polemic.

Journals and Periodicals

Chalcedon Report. Chalcedon, P. O. Box 158, Vallecito, CA 95251. The oldest Reconstructionist newsletter. Edited by Garry J. Moes. A monthly publication.

Christianity and Civilization. Geneva Ministries, P. O. Box 131300, Tyler, TX 75713. Edited by James Jordan and Gary North. Also uses the Symposium format.

The Journal of Christian Reconstruction. The Chalcedon Foundation, P. O. Box 158, Vallecito, CA 95251. Edited by Gary North 1974-81 and Douglas Kelly 1982-present. The format of each issue is centered around a symposium on a subject.

Newsletters

The Biblical Worldview, P. O. Box 720515, Atlanta, GA 30328. Gary DeMar's ministry, American Vision, produces this monthly publication.

The Counsel of Chalcedon, 3032 Hacienda Court, Marietta, GA 30066. Produced by Chalcedon Presbyterian Church, Pastor Joe Morecraft, who once made an unsuccessful bid for election to Congress.

Geneva Ministries, P. O. Box 131300, Tyler, TX 75713. This publication includes the writings of Ray Sutton, George Grant, James Jordan, and Mike Gilstrap. Monthly.

Institute for Christian Economics, P. O. Box 8000, Tyler, TX 75711. Produced by Gary North. Monthly.

Note: The above does not include the rapidly multiplying material coming out of the Charismatic branch of Dominion Theology.

Non-Reconstructionist Postmillennial Books Still in Print

Boettner, Loraine. *The Millennium*. Phillipsburg, N.J.: Presbyterian & Reformed Publishing Co., 1957. Boettner represents the older, more traditional postmillennialism. This was for years the only visible postmillennial work in print. It is not really in line with the more "positive amillennial" approach of theonomic neopostmillennialism. Much of Boettner's argument is like this: "This is what old Princeton believed. How could such great Calvinist scholars such as the Hodge and B. B. Warfield be wrong?"

Brown, David. *Christ's Second Coming: Will It Be Premillennial?* 1876. Reprint. Grand Rapids: Baker Book House, 1983. Another classic postmillennial work.

Campbell, Roderick. *Israel and the New Covenant*. Phillipsburg, N.J.: Presbyterian & Reformed Publishing Co., 1954. A postmillennial work by a Canadian layman.

Clouse, Robert, ed. *The Meaning of the Millennium: Four Views*. Downers Grove, Ill.: InterVarsity Press, 1977. Boettner presents and defends his postmillennial views.

Davis, John Jefferson. *Christ's Victorious Kingdom: Postmillennialism Reconsidered*. Grand Rapids: Baker Book House, 1986. Davis is not necessarily a Reconstructionist and has written a work more in line with classical postmillennialism than with neopostmillennialism. He certainly does not have the arrogant attitude characteristic of the Reconstructionists.

De Jong, J. A. *As the Waters Cover the Sea: Millennial Expectations in the Rise of Anglo-American Missions, 1640-1810.* J.H. Kok N.V. Kampen, 1970. Out of print and hard to get. De Jong is impressed by how many Puritans and Reformed Christians were postmillennialists.

Kik, J. Marcellus. *An Eschatology of Victory.* Phillipsburg, N.J.: Presbyterian & Reformed Publishing Co., 1971. This is an exposition of Matthew 24 and Revelation 20 from a postmillennial perspective. He seeks to establish and defend the second coming as having occurred in A.D. 70 in the destruction of Jerusalem. According to a personal letter to Tommy Ice, David Chilton says that it is the definitive exegesis on these two passages. He further says that no premillennialist has answered this work.

Murray, Iain. *The Puritan Hope.* Carlisle, Penn.: The Banner of Truth Trust, 1971. This is a historical theology work which argues that postmillennialism was the major thrust for world missions. It attempts to summarize Puritan eschatology. David Chilton says this was the book that, along with other events, persuaded him to become a postmillennialist. Many neopostmillennialists use this as a source for their historical arguments.

Russell, J. Stuart. *The Parousia: A Study of the New Testament Doctrine of Our Lord's Second Coming.* 1887. Reprint. Grand Rapids: Baker Book House, 1983. The back cover provides this summary of the book: "The author of this important but neglected nineteenth-century study establishes Christ's parousia (second coming) as 'the nucleus and centre of a cluster of great events,' including the close of the Jewish economy, the judgment of Israel, the destruction of Jerusalem, and the resurrection of the dead. He concludes that the parousia, 'with its connected and concomitant events,' took place, as Christ predicted, during the period when Jerusalem was destroyed."

CON

Chismar, Douglas E. and David A. Rausch. "Regarding Theonomy: An Essay of Concern." *Journal of the Evangelical Theological Society* 27 (September 1984):315-23.

Clapp, Rodney. "Democracy as Heresy." *Christianity Today*, 20 February 1987, 17-23.

Fowler, Paul B. "God's Law Free from Legalism: Critique of Theonomy in Christian Ethics." Unpublished paper. Dr. Fowler was formerly of Reformed Seminary in Jackson, Mississippi, when Greg Bahnsen was dismissed from the faculty because of the propagation of his theonomy views.

Frame, John. *"The Institutes of Biblical Law*: A Review," *Westminster Theological Journal* 38 (Winter 1976):195-217.

Geisler, Norman L. "A Premillennial View of Law and Government," *Bibliotheca Sacra* 142 (July-September 1985):250-66.

Harris, R. Laird. "Theonomy and Christian Ethics. A Review." *Covenant Seminary Review* 5 (Spring 1979):1-15.

Hollingsworth, Ted L. "Rousas John Rushdoony's Intellectual Influence on the Christian Day School Movement." D.R.E. thesis, Temple Baptist Theological Seminary, 1980.

Ice, Thomas D. "An Evaluation of Theonomic Neopostmillennialism." *Bibliotheca Sacra* 145 (July-September 1988):281-300.

Karlberg, Mark W. "Reformation Politics: The Relevance of OT Ethics in Calvinist Political Theory." *Journal of the Evangelical Theological Society* 29 (June 1986):179-91.

Kline, Meredith G. "Comments on an Old-New Error." *Westminster Theological Journal* 41 (Fall 1978):172-89.

Lightner, Robert P. "Theonomy and Dispensationalism." *Bibliotheca Sacra* 143 (January-March 1986):26-36.

_____ . "Nondispensational Responses to Theonomy." *Bibliotheca Sacra* 143 (April-June 1986):134-45.

_____ . "A Dispensational Response to Theonomy." *Bibliotheca Sacra* 143 (July-September 1986):228-45.

Long, Gary D. *Biblical Law and Ethics: Absolute and Covenantal, An Exegetical and Theological Study of Matthew 5:17-20.* Rochester, N.Y.: Backus Book Publishers, 1981. Long, a Dallas Seminary graduate, argues against Bahnsen's interpretation of Matthew 5:17 from a Reformed Baptist perspective.

"Postmillennialism's Resurgency." *Journey.* March-April 1988. This issue is devoted to the revival of postmillennialism. The editor of this conservative Presbyterian publication, R. E. Knodel, Jr., admits that he is a recent convert to postmillennialism.

Taylor, Aiken G. "Postmillennialism Revisited." *Presbyterian Journal*, 6 September 1978, 11.

_____ . "Theonomy and Christian Behavior." *Presbyterian Journal*, 13 September 1978, 9-10, 18-19.

_____ . "Theonomy Revisited." *Presbyterian Journal*, 6 December 1978, 12-13, 22.

_____ . "Theonomy and Christian Ethics. A Review." *Presbyterian Journal*, 31 August 1977, 18.

"Theonomy: Boon or Bust?" *Journey.* November-December 1986. Complete issue devoted to the subject. Contains both pro and con.

Tucker, William B. "Theonomic Application for a Sociology of Justification by Faith: Weakness in the Social Criticisms of Rousas John Rushdoony as Revealed in the Doctrine of Sanctification by Law." Master's thesis, Gordon-Conwell Theological Seminary, 1984.

Scripture Index

Subject Index

Questions or comments concerning the subject matter of this book should be addressed to:

Thomas Ice
Biblical Perspectives Ministries
4904 Summerset Trail
Austin, Texas 78745

Biblical Perspectives is published six times a year. The cost of a yearly subscription is $10. A sample copy will be sent to all who enclose a self-addressed stamped envelope. Information concerning audio and video tapes, as well as other materials relating to Dominion Theology and other issues are available to those sending a self-addressed stamped envelope.